T0214539

Lecture Notes in Computer Science 11047

Commenced Publication in 1973
Founding and Former Series Editors:
Gerhard Goos, Juris Hartmanis, and Jan van Leeuwen

Editorial Board

More information about this series at http://www.springer.com/series/7412

Yanio Hernández Heredia · Vladimir Milián Núñez
José Ruiz Shulcloper (Eds.)

Progress in Artificial Intelligence and Pattern Recognition

6th International Workshop, IWAIPR 2018
Havana, Cuba, September 24–26, 2018
Proceedings

Springer

III Conferencia Científica
Internacional
Universidad de las Ciencias Informáticas

Editors
Yanio Hernández Heredia
Universidad de las Ciencias Informáticas
Havana
Cuba

José Ruiz Shulcloper
Universidad de las Ciencias Informáticas
Havana
Cuba

Vladimir Milián Núñez
Universidad de las Ciencias Informáticas
Havana
Cuba

ISSN 0302-9743   ISSN 1611-3349   (electronic)
Lecture Notes in Computer Science
ISBN 978-3-030-01131-4   ISBN 978-3-030-01132-1   (eBook)
https://doi.org/10.1007/978-3-030-01132-1

Library of Congress Control Number: 2018955423

LNCS Sublibrary: SL6 – Image Processing, Computer Vision, Pattern Recognition, and Graphics

This Springer imprint is published by the registered company Springer Nature Switzerland AG
The registered company address is: Gewerbestrasse 11, 6330 Cham, Switzerland

Preface

The 6th International Workshop on Artificial Intelligence and Pattern Recognition (IWAIPR 2018) was the biennial event of a series of pioneer conferences on artificial intelligence and pattern recognition in the scientific community active in these fields in Cuba and other countries.

As has been the case for previous editions of the conference, IWAIPR 2018 hosted worldwide participants with the aim of promoting and disseminating ongoing research on mathematical methods and computing techniques for artificial intelligence and pattern recognition, in particular in bioinformatics, cognitive and humanoid vision, computer vision, image analysis and intelligent data analysis, as well as their application in a number of diverse areas such as industry, health, robotics, data mining, opinion mining and sentiment analysis, telecommunications, document analysis, and natural language processing and recognition. Moreover, IWAIPR 2018 was a forum for the scientific community to exchange research experience, to share new knowledge, and to increase the cooperation among research groups working in artificial intelligence, pattern recognition, and related areas.

IWAIPR 2018 received 101 contributions from 12 countries. After a rigorous blind reviewing process, where three highly qualified reviewers reviewed each submission, 42 papers authored by 138 authors from seven countries were accepted. The scientific quality of the accepted papers was above the overall mean rating.

Like the most recent editions of the conference, IWAIPR 2018 was a single-track conference in which all papers where presented in oral sessions. IWAIPR 2018 presentations were grouped into six sessions: Artificial Intelligence and Applications; Biometrics, Image, and Video Analysis; Data Mining and Applications; Machine Learning Theory and Applications; Pattern Recognition and Applications; Signals Analysis and Processing.

We like to point out that the reputation of the IWAIPR conferences is growing and therefore the proceedings are published in the series *Lecture Notes in Computer Science* by Springer.

Besides the 42 accepted submissions, the scientific program of IWAIPR 2018 also included the contribution of an outstanding invited speaker, namely, Edwin Diday (Paris-Dauphine University, CEREMADE, France). The paper of this keynote appears in these proceedings.

IWAIPR 2018 was organized by Universidad de las Ciencias Informáticas, Cuba (UCI) and the Cuban Association for Pattern Recognition (ACRP) with the sponsorship of the Cuban Society for Mathematics and Computer Sciences (SCMC). We acknowledge and appreciate their valuable contribution to the success of IWAIPR 2018.

We gratefully acknowledge the help of all members of the Organizing Committee and of the Program Committee for their support and for the rigorous work in the reviewing process.

We also wish to thank the members of the local committee for their unflagging work in the organization of IWAIPR 2018 that has helped create an excellent conference and proceedings.

We are especially grateful to Alfred Hofmann (Vice President Publishing, Computer Science, Springer), Anna Kramer (Assistant Editor, Computer Science Editorial, Springer), and Volha Shaparava (Springer Nature OCS Support) for their support and advice during the preparation of this LNCS volume.

Special thanks are due to all authors who submitted to IWAIPR 2018, including those of papers that could not be accepted.

Finally, we invite the artificial intelligence and pattern recognition communities to attend IWAIPR 2020 in Havana, Cuba.

September 2018

Yanio Hernández Heredia
Vladimir Milián Núñez
José Ruiz Shulcloper

Organization

IWAIPR 2018 was organized by Universidad de las Ciencias Informáticas, endorsed by the Cuban Association for Pattern Recognition and Cuban Society for Mathematics and Computer Science and sponsored by Universidad de las Ciencias Informáticas, Cuba.

Program Chairs

Yanio Hernández Heredia	Universidad de Las Ciencias Informáticas, Cuba
Vladimir Milián Núñez	Universidad de Las Ciencias Informáticas, Cuba
José Ruiz Shulcloper	Universidad de Las Ciencias Informáticas, Cuba

Local Committee

Miriam Nicado García	Universidad de las Ciencias Informáticas, Cuba
Beatriz Aragón Fernández	Universidad de las Ciencias Informáticas, Cuba
Raydel Montesino Perurena	Universidad de las Ciencias Informáticas, Cuba
Nadiela Milan Cristo	Universidad de las Ciencias Informáticas, Cuba
Natalia Martínez Sánchez	Universidad de las Ciencias Informáticas, Cuba
Hector Raúl González Diez	Universidad de las Ciencias Informáticas, Cuba
Yadian Guillermo Pérez Betancourt	Universidad de las Ciencias Informáticas, Cuba
Yunia Reyes González	Universidad de las Ciencias Informáticas, Cuba
José Manuel de León Cano	Universidad de las Ciencias Informáticas, Cuba
Maidelis Milanés Luque	Universidad de las Ciencias Informáticas, Cuba
Rigoberto David García Mauri	Universidad de las Ciencias Informáticas, Cuba
Madelis Pérez Gil	Universidad de las Ciencias Informáticas, Cuba
Alexander Dicson Reyes	Universidad de las Ciencias Informáticas, Cuba

Program Committee

Sergey Ablameyko	Belarusian State University, Belarus
Daniel Acevedo	Universidad de Buenos Aires, Argentina
Niusvel Acosta	Advanced Technologies Applications Center, Cuba
Leticia Arco	Univiversidad Central Marta Abreu de Las Villas, Cuba
Ali Ismail Awad	Al Azhar University, Egypt
Rafael Bello	Universidad Central Marta Abreu de Las Villas, Cuba
Rafael Berlanga-Llavori	Universitat Jaime I Castelló, Spain
Nadia Brancati	Institute of High-Performance Computing and Networking, Italy
María Elena Buemi	University of Buenos Aires, Argentina

José Ramón Calvo de Lara	Advanced Technologies Applications Center, Cuba
Sergio Cano	Universidad de Oriente, Cuba
Jesús Ariel Carrasco-Ochoa	Instituto Nacional Astrofísica, Óptica y Electrónica, México
Gérard Chollet	French National Centre for Scientific Research, France
Eduardo Concepción	Universidad de Cienfuegos, Cuba
Alfonso Estudillo-Romero	Universidad Nacional Autónoma de México, México
Jacques Facon	Pontificia Universidade Católica do Paraná, Brazil
Gustavo Fernandez	Austrian Institute of Technology, Austria
Carlos Ferrer	Universidad Central Marta Abreu de Las Villas, Cuba
Francesc J. Ferri	Universidad de Valencia, Spain
Yaima Filiberto	Universidad de Camagüey, Cuba
Andrés Gago-Alonso	Advanced Technologies Applications Center, Cuba
Edel García-Reyes	Advanced Technologies Applications Center, Cuba
María Matilde García	Universidad Central Marta Abreu de Las Villas, Cuba
Eduardo Garea-Llano	Advanced Technologies Applications Center, Cuba
Lev Goldfarb	University of New Brunswick, Fredericton, Canada
Luis Gomez	Universidad de Las Palmas de Gran Canarias, Spain
Antoni Grau	Universitat Politecnica de Catalunya, Spain
Raudel Hernández	Advanced Technologies Applications Center, Cuba
Laurent Heutte	Université de Rouen, France
Xiaoyi Jiang	Universitat Münster, Germany
Martin Kampel	Vienna University of Technology, Austria
Vitaly Kober	CICESE, México
Manuel S. Lazo-Cortés	Instituto Nacional Astrofísica, Óptica y Electrónica, México
Aurelio López-López	Instituto Nacional Astrofísica, Óptica y Electrónica, México
Daniela López	Universidad de Buenos Aires, Argentina
Juan Valentín Lorenzo-Ginori	Universidad Central Marta Abreu de Las Villas, Cuba
Francesco Marra	Università degli Studi di Salerno, Italy
José Francisco Martínez Trinidad	Instituto Nacional Astrofísica, Óptica y Electrónica, México
Nelson Mascarenhas	Federal University of Sao Carlos, Brazil
José E. Medina Pagola	Universidad de las Ciencias Informáticas, Cuba
Heydi Mendez	Advanced Technologies Applications Center, Cuba
Ana Maria Mendonça	Universidade do Porto, Portugal
Marcelo Mendoza	Universidad Técnica Federico Santa María, Chile
Manuel Montes y-Gómez	Instituto Nacional Astrofísica, Óptica y Electrónica, México
Annette Morales González	Advanced Technologies Applications Center, Cuba
Carlos Morell	Universidad Central Marta Abreu de Las Villas, Cuba
Vadim V. Mottl	Russian Academy of Sciences, Russia
Alexandra Moutinho	Universidade de Lisboa, Portugal
Alberto Muñoz	Carlos III University, Spain

Alfredo Muñoz	Advanced Technologies Applications Center, Cuba
Pablo Muse	Universidad de la República, Uruguay
Lawrence O'Gorman	Bell Laboratories, USA
Kalman Palagyi	University of Szeged, Hungary
Talita Perciano	Lawrence Berkeley National Laboratory, USA
Airel Pérez	Advanced Technologies Applications Center, Cuba
Hemerson Pistori	Catholic University, Campo Grande, Brazil
Osvaldo Andrés Pérez	Advanced Technologies Applications Center, Cuba
José Felipe Ramírez	Universidad de las Ciencias Informáticas, Cuba
Pedro Real	University of Seville, Spain
Carlos A. Reyes-García	Instituto Nacional Astrofísica, Óptica y Electrónica, México
Cesar San Martin	Universidad de La Frontera, Chile
Ramón Santana Fernández	Universidad de las Ciencias Informáticas, Cuba
Juan Humberto Sossa Azuela	Instituto Politécnico Nacional, México
Concetto Spampinato	University of Catania, Italy
Enrique Sucar	Instituto Nacional Astrofísica, Óptica y Electrónica, México
Alberto Taboada-Crispi	Universidad Central Marta Abreu de Las Villas, Cuba
Eanes Torres Pereira	Universidade Federal de Campina Grande, Brazil
Rafael Trujillo-Rasúa	Universidad de las Ciencias Informáticas, Cuba
Vera Yashina	Russian Academy of Sciences, Russia

Additional Reviewers

Cristian Martinez	UNSa, Argentina
Delia Irazu Hernandez Farias	Instituto Nacional Astrofísica, Óptica y Electrónica, México
Roberto Lopez	UACh, Mexico
Andrés Rosso	Universidad Nacional de Colombia, Colombia
Michael MacNeil	Lawrence Berkeley National Lab
Juan Javier Sánchez Junquera	Instituto Nacional Astrofísica, Óptica y Electrónica, México, Mexico
Yanet Fors Isalguez	Universidad Autónoma del Estado de Morelos, Mexico

Sponsoring Institutions

Universidad de las Ciencias Informáticas, Cuba (UCI)

Cuban Association for Pattern Recognition (ACRP)

Cuban Society for Mathematics and Computer Science (SCMC)

Contents

Biometrics, Image and Video Analysis

Data Mining and Applications

Machine Learning Theory and Applications

Pattern Recognition and Applications

Signals Analysis and Processing

Keynote Lecture

Improving Explanatory Power of Machine Learning in the Symbolic Data Analysis Framework

E. Diday[(⊠)]

CEREMADE, Paris-Dauphine University, Paris, France
diday@ceremade.dauphine.fr

Abstract. Many nice machine learning methods are black box producing very efficient rules but hard to be understandable by the users. The aim of this paper is to help user by tools allowing a better comprehension of these rules. These tools are based on characteristic properties of the original variables in order to remain in the natural language of the user. They are based on three principles, first on local models fitting at best clusters to be found, second on a symbolic description of these clusters and their Symbolic Data Analysis, third on characteristic criterion increasing the explanatory power of the rules by an adaptive process filtering explanatory sub populations.

Keywords: Symbolic data analysis · Machine learning · Symbolic clustering

1 Introduction

In Data Science the aim is to extract new knowledge from Standard, Big and complex data. Another characteristic of Data Science is that its methods and tools are not developed in order to be applied for only a specific domain but for any domain providing data. Often industrial data are unstructured with variables defined on different units. They can also be multi sources (as mixture of numerical and textual data, with images and networks). In order to reduce the size, the complexity and the efficiency of the models associated to such data, a key solution is to use classes, of row statistical units, which are considered as new statistical units. "Classes" are as usual, subsets of any statistical set of units as for example: teams of football players, Region of inhabitant, Level of consumption in health insurance. There are at least three advantages of considering classes instead of standard units. First, classes can be the units that interest the most the users. For example, "regions" instead of their "inhabitants" or "species" instead of "specimen", "teams" instead their players or "documents" instead of their "words". Second, classes induce local models often (but not always!) more efficient than global ones. Third, classes give a concise and structured view on the data as they can be organized by a partition, a hierarchical clustering, a pyramid (for overlapping clusters) or a Galois lattice. In clustering classes (called "clusters") are not known and can be obtained by a clustering process called "Dynamical Clustering Method" (i.e. DCM) (see [11]) or for fuzzy classes by EM (see [18]), improving iteratively the fit between each obtained cluster and its local

© Springer Nature Switzerland AG 2018
Y. Hernández Heredia et al. (Eds.): IWAIPR 2018, LNCS 11047, pp. 3–14, 2018.
https://doi.org/10.1007/978-3-030-01132-1_1

associated model. In the case of unsupervised data, clusters can be modeled for example, by means (as in the "k-means" method), distributions (as in mixture decomposition) or factorial axis (which leads to local factorial analysis). In case of supervised data, clusters can be modeled by regressions (or more generally by canonical analysis), neural networks, SVM, etc. In both cases the obtained classes can be described in order to express their within-class variability by vectors of intervals, probability distributions, weighted sequences, functions, and the like, called "symbolic data". Hence, we obtain a symbolic data table that we can study in order to obtain explanatory information on the given classes or obtained clusters. We can also use these symbolic data in order to measure the explanatory power of each class or cluster. More generally a "symbolic data table" is a table where classes of individuals are described by at least one symbolic variable. Standard variables can also describe classes by considering the set of classes as a new set of units of higher level.

The Fig. 1 is an example of symbolic data table. The statistical units of the ground population are players of French cup teams and classes of players are teams called Paris, Lyon, Marseille and Bordeaux. The variability of the players inside each team is expressed by the following symbolic variables: "Weight" which value is the interval of [min, max] weight of the players of the associated team, "National Country" which value is the list of their nationality, "Age bar chart" is the frequency of the age players being in the intervals: [less than 20], [20, 25], [25, 30], [more than 30], respectively, denoted: (0), (1), (2), (3) in Fig. 1. The symbolic variable "age" is called "bar chart variable" as the interval of age on which it is defined are the same for all the classes and can therefore be considered as categories. The last variable is numerical as its values for a team is the frequency of the French players in this team among all the French players of all the teams. Hence, this variable produces a vertical bar chart in comparison with the symbolic variable "age" of horizontal bar charts value in Fig. 1. By adding to the French the same kinds of columns associated with the other nationalities, we can obtain a new symbolic variable whose values are a list of numbers, where each number is the frequency of having players in a team of a nationality among all the players having this nationality among all the teams. A team can also be described by standard numerical or categorical variables as for example, its expenses or the number of goals in a season.

French Cup teams	Weight	National Country	Age	Frequency of French among all French
Paris	[73, 85]	{France, Argentina, Senegal}	{(0) 30%, (1) 70%}	30%
Lyon	[68, 90]	{France, Brazil, Italia}	{(0) 30%, (1) 65%, (2) 5%}	25%
Marseille	[77, 85]	{France, Brazil, Algeria}	{(1) 40%, (2) 52%, (3)8%}	28%
Bordeaux	[80, 90]	{France, Argentina}	{(0) 40%, (1) 60%}	17%

Fig. 1. An example of symbolic data table where teams of the French Cup are described by three symbolic variables of interval, sequence of categories, "horizontal" bar charts and a numerical variable inducing a "vertical" bar chart.

More generally, the first characteristic of the so-called "symbolic variable" is that they are defined on classes. Their second characteristic, is that their values take the variability between the individuals inside these classes into account by "symbols" representing more than only one category or number. Hence, the standard operators of numbers cannot be applied to the values of these kinds of variables, so these values are not numerical: that is why they are called "symbolic" and represented by "symbols" as intervals, bar chart and the like.

The first aim of the so called "Symbolic Data Analysis" (SDA) is to describe classes by vectors of symbolic data in an explanatory way. Its second aim is to extend Data Mining and Statistics to new kinds of complex data coming from the industrial domain. We cannot say that SDA give better results than standard data analysis we can just say that SDA can give good complementary results when we need to work on units which have a higher level of generality. For example, if we wish to know what makes a good player, for sure the data concerns individuals units, but if we wish to know what makes a good team, in this case the units are the teams and so, there are classes of individuals.

Complex data constitute an important source of symbolic data. We consider "complex data" as data set which cannot be considered as a "standard statistical units x standard variables" data table. This is the case when data are defined by several data tables with different statistical units and different variables coming from multi sources sometimes at multi levels. In this case one of the advantage of "symbolic data" is that unstructured data with unpaired samples at the level of row units, become structured and paired at the classes' level. By definition, a "class of complex data" is a vector of standard classes defined on different statistical space of units. For example, in Official Statistics a Region can be considered as a class of complex data denoted CR = (Ch, Cs, Ci) where Ch is the class hospitals, Cs the class of schools, Ci the class of inhabitants, of this region.

Example of complex data, classes and symbolic variables in Official Statistics:

National Statistical Institutes (NSI) organize census in their regions on different kinds of populations: hospitals, schools, inhabitants etc. Each of these populations are associated to their own characteristic variables. For hospitals: number of beds, doctors, patients, etc.; for schools: number of pupils, teachers, etc.; for inhabitants: gender, age, socio professional category, etc. The regions are the classes of units described by the variable available for all these populations of different sizes. If we have n regions and N populations (of hospitals, schools, etc.), then we get after aggregation, a symbolic data table with n rows and p1 + ... + pN columns associated to the N sets of symbolic value variables characteristic of each of the N populations. For sure other variables (standard or symbolic) can be added in order to describe other aspects of the regions.

Symbolic Data Analysis (SDA) is an extension of standard data analysis and data mining to symbolic data. SDA has several advantages. As the number of classes is lower than the number of individuals, SDA facilitates interpretation of results in decision trees, factorial analysis etc. SDA reduces simple or Complex and/or Big Data. It also reduces missing data and solves confidentiality (when individuals are confidential but classes are not confidential). It allows adding new variables at the right level of generality.

The theory and practice of SDA have been developed in several books [2, 3, 15], many papers (see overviews in [1, 9]), and several international workshops Special issue related to SDA has been published, for example in the RNTI journal, edited by, Guan et al. [20] on 'Advances in Theory and Applications of High Dimensional and Symbolic Data Analysis'; in the ADAC journal on SDA, edited by Brito et al. [4]; in IEEE Trans Cybern [25]. We indicate among many others, four examples of application in nuclear power point [6], epidemiology [21], in cancerology [23], and in face recognition [24].

The paper present three sections after the introduction. The first is devoted to the building of symbolic data from given classes or obtained clusters. The next section shows that the explanatory power of the symbolic data describing a class can be measured by different criteria which provide a measure of the explanatory power of this class. In the next section we show that any tool of machine learning can be transformed by a clustering process in local tools, often more adapted than global ones. Then, based on the explanatory criteria characterizing individuals, classes and variables we show how to improve the explanatory power of any machine learning tool by filtering explanatory sub populations.

2   Building Symbolic Data from Given Classes or Clusters

The aim is to study the symbolic data table provided by the description of given classes (as in supervised learning) or given clusters (obtained from a clustering process), in order to get complementary knowledge enhancing the usual standard interpretation (by means, variance, etc.). For example, in mixture decomposition clustering the description of each class is just given by the analytical expression of the joint probability density f_i associated to each class. Hence in case of Gaussian model, the joint is described by a big correlation matrix heavy to interpret when there are numerous variables. Building a symbolic data table where the units are the given classes or the obtained clusters can be done in three ways: directly if the obtained clusters define a partition, from the marginal induced by the joint distribution associated to each cluster provided by EM or DCM, or from the membership weight of the individuals if we have fuzzy clusters as in EM mixture decomposition.

If L_k, is the representative of the class P_k, then the weight $t_k(u)$ of an individual u in class P_k, which takes the value x_i^j for the variable j and the individual I, is given by: $t_k(u) = d(u, L_k)$ where d is the dissimilarity used by the clustering method which has produced the classes. In case of fuzzy clusters (like in EM), $t_k(u)$ is the fuzzy weight of u in the kth class. Then, the histogram for the kth class and the jth variable is given by:

$$H_{kj} = \left(\frac{\sum_{i=1}^{N} t_k(x_i)_{I_1}\left(x_i^j\right)}{\sum_{v=1}^{V} \sum_{i=1}^{N} t_k(x_i)_{I_v}\left(x_i^j\right)}, \ldots, \frac{\sum_{i=1}^{N} t_k(x_i)_{I_V}\left(x_i^j\right)}{\sum_{r=1}^{P} \sum_{i=1}^{N} t_k(x_i)\left(x_i^j\right)} \right) \tag{1}$$

where $\delta_{I_v}\left(x_i^j\right)$ is a vector of Dirac mass defined on V intervals $(I_1, \ldots, I_V)$ partitioning the domain D_j of the numerical variable X_j such that: $\delta\left(x_i^j\right) = (\delta_{I_1}\left(x_i^j\right), \ldots, \delta_{I_V}\left(x_i^j\right))$ where $\delta_{I_v}\left(x_i^j\right)$ takes the value 1 if $x_i^j \in \gamma I_v$ and 0 elsewhere. When the I_v are categorical values instead of intervals, we obtain a bar chart and $\delta\left(x_i^j\right)$ takes the value 1 if x_i^j is the category I_v and the value 0 elsewhere.

When instead of a fuzzy partition $(P_1, \ldots, P_K)$ as the one given by EM we have an exact partition denoted $\left(P_1', \ldots, P_K'\right)$ as the one induced by $P_K' = \{x_i/f(x_i, a_k) \geq f(x_n, a_k)\}$ or directly by DC, we can build in the same way an histogram or a bar chart by setting: $t_k(x_i) = 1$, for any $k = (1, \ldots, K)$ and $i = (1, \ldots, N)$.

In SDA, in order to increase the explanatory power of the obtained symbolic data table, first the chosen number of intervals I_v is preferably chosen not numerous (about 5, but it can be increased if needed), second the size and position of these intervals can be obtained in an optimal way in order to maximize the distance between the symbolic description of the classes (see [16]). After an EM mixture decomposition, the joints f_i associated to each class C_i are described by their marginal f_{ij}. These marginal are then described by several kinds of symbolic data as histograms or interquartile intervals or any kind of property, mean, mean square, percentiles, correlation between some characteristic variables and the like. More generally, from any clustering method we obtain a symbolic data table on which SDA can be applied.

3 Explanatory Power of Classes or Clusters from Their Associated Symbolic Data Table

Our aim in SDA is to get a meaningful symbolic data table maximizing the discrimination power of the symbolic data associated to each variable for each class. A discrimination degree can be calculated by a normalized sum (to be maximized) of the dissimilarity two by two between the symbolic descriptions. Such kind of dissimilarities can be found in [3, 7, 8, 15]. In case of histogram value variables an example of discriminating tool is given in [DID 2013] by optimizing the lenght of the histograms intervals. There are at least three ways: distances between rows in each column, to be maximized, entropy in each cell to be minimized, correlations between columns to be maximized. More details are given in [9].

Other kinds of explanatory power of a symbolic data table can be defined. First, we can define a theoretical framework for SDA in the case of categorical variables (see [17, 19]. Let be three random variables C, X, S defined on the ground population Ω in the following way: C a class variable: $\Omega \rightarrow P$ such that C(w) = c where c is a class of a given partition P. X a categorical variable: $\Omega \rightarrow M$ such that X(w) = x is a category among the set of categories M of this variable. From C and X, we can build a third random variable defined as follows: S: $\Omega \rightarrow [0, 1]$ such that S(w) = s(X(w), C(w)) = s (x, c) the proportion of the category x inside the class c. In other words s(x, c) can be considered as the probability of the category x knowing the class c: s(x, c) = Pr (X = x/C = c). If we denote $f_c(x)$ the value of the bar chart induced by the class c and the category x, we have $f_c(x) = s(x, c)$.

Characterization of a class by an event: We say basically that a category is "characteristic" of a class if it is frequent in the class and rare in the other classes. In order to insight what we develop in this section, we start with a simple example.

Example: Suppose $f_c(z)$ is higher than 0.9 (i.e. $f_c(x)$ belongs to the event $E(z, c)$) = [0.9, 1]) and $f_{c'}(x)$ for most of the classes class $c' \in P$ different of c, belongs to the event $E(z, c')) = [0, 0.9[$. In this case, we can say that the category x is characteristic of the class c versus the other classes of the partition P for the event [0.9, 1] as its frequency takes a value in this event for the class c which is rare for the other classes of the partition P.

A characterization criterion W, varying between 0 and 1, of a category z and a class c can be measured by:

$W(z, c, E) = f_c(z)/(1+g_{z, E(z, c)}(c))$, where $E(z, c)$ is an event defined by an interval included in [0, 1]containing $f_c(z)$ and $Pr(S_x \in E(z, c)) = |\{w \in \Omega/z = X(w),$ $S_z(w) = s(z, C(w)) \in E(z, c))|/|\Omega|$, defines g:

$g_{z, E(z, c)}(c) = Pr(S_z \in E(z, c))$. Hence, $g_{z, E(z, c)}$ associates to a class c and a category z, the frequency of individuals of Ω satisfying the event $E(z, c)$ with $z = X(w)$ and $c = C(w)$. If the ground population is infinite, we suppose that Ω is a sample. Hence, given an event E, the criterion W express, how much a category z is characteristic of a class c versus the other classes c' of the given partition P. This criterion means that a category z is even more characteristic of a given class c and for an event E, its frequency in the class c is large and the proportion of individuals w taking the z category in any class c' (including c) and satisfying to the event $E(z, c)$ is low in the ground population Ω. Giving z and c, several choices of E can be interesting.

Four examples of events E:

For a characterization of x and c in the neighborhood of $s(z, c)$:

$E_1(z, c) = [s(z, c) - \varepsilon, s(z, c) + \varepsilon]$ for $\varepsilon > 0$ and $s(z, c) \in [\varepsilon, 1- \varepsilon]$ where ε can be a percentile.

For a characterization of the higher values than $s(z, c)$: $E_2(z, c) = [s(z, c), 1]$.

For a characterization of the lower values than $s(z, c)$: $E_3(z, c) = [0, s(z, c)]$.

In order to characterize the existence of the category z in any: $E_4(z, c) =]0, 1]$.

Hence, a category z is characteristic of a class c when it is frequent in the class c and rare in a neighborhood of $s(z, c)$ if $E = E_1$, rare above (resp. under $s(z, c)$ if $E = E_2$ or $E = E_3$, rare to appear outside of c in the other classes c' if $E = E_4$.

In fact there are four cases to consider depending on the fact that in a class c a category z is frequent or not and among the set of classes it is frequent or not in $E(z, c)$. Hence, we have four cases called FF, FR, RF, RR, the cases FF and RR cannot give any specific value to $W(z, c, E)$, but the case FR (resp. RF) where the category is frequent (resp. rare) in c and rare (resp. frequent) in the other classes' leads to a value of $W(z, c, E)$ which is high (resp. low). Therefore, we can say that z is a specific category of c iff $W(z, c, E)LogW(z, c, E)$ is close to 0. Other kinds of characterization criterion can be used. The popular 'test value,' developed in [22], may also be used to measure a characterization of a category in a bar chart contained in a cell. The p-value is the level of marginal significance within a statistical hypothesis test representing the probability of the occurrence of a given event. A simple way can be the ratio between the frequency of a category in a class and the mean of the frequencies of the same category in all the classes of the given partition.

Characterization of classes and symbolic bar chart variables

Asymbolic data table of bar chart variables can be transformed in a data table where each column is associated to a category, by summing on the characterization of all the cells of each row (resp. column) we obtain a characterization of each class (resp. variable). In the same way, in summing on the characterization of all the cells, we can obtain a characterization of the symbolic data table. In the same way we can find the most typical or atypical class or bar chart variables or symbolic data table. In the following, we focus on characterization but for sure in the same way we could consider the singular or specific case.

It can be shown that the standard Tf-Idf (very popular in text mining) is a case of the W criterion and a parametric version of this criterion can be defined (see [17]).

4   Improving Explanatory Power of Machine Learning by Using a Filter

We show in three steps that any learning machine process can be improved in the efficiency and the explanatory power of its provided rules: in the first step by a dynamical clustering process optimizing at each step a first objective function we obtain local learning models, defined by couples of clusters and local associated predictive models (regression, neural network, SVM, Bayesian, decision tree, etc.) in case of supervised data or couple of cluster and mean, distribution or factorial axis in case unsupervised learning; in the second step the obtained clusters are described by symbolic data (induced by only the explanatory variables in case of supervised data or by all the variables in case of unsupervised data), which leads to the explanatory power of each cluster, measured by a second objective function of characterization; in the third step we provide an allocation rule to any new unit (only known by its explanatory values, i.e. without knowing its predictive values, in case of supervised data) if it improves simultaneously the first and the second objective function (i.e. at least improving one without degrading the other). Several kinds of allocation rules are proposed including Latent Dirichlet models (see Diday [19]).

Hence, in the first step, we use **The "Dynamical Clustering Method" (DCM):** Starting from a given partition $P = (P_1, ..., P_k)$ of a population, this method is based on an alternative use of a representation function g which associates a representation L to a class C and an allocation function f which associate a class C to a point x of the population: $f(x) = C$ in order to improve a given criterion at each step until convergence.

Proof. starting from a partition $P = (P_1, ..., P_K)$ of the initial population, the representation function applied to the classes P_i produces a vector of representation $L = (L_1, ..., L_K)$ among a given set of possible representations, where $g(C_i) = L_i$. A quality criterion can be defined in the following way: $W(P, L) = \sum_{i=1}^{k} f(P_i, L_i)$ where w measures the fit between each class P_i and its representation L_i it decreases when this fit increases.

Starting from a partition $P^{(n)}$, the value of the sequence $u_n = W(P^{(n)}, L^{(n)})$ decreases at each step n of the algorithm. Indeed, during a the allocation step an individual x belonging to a class $P_i^{(n)}$ is affected to a new class $P_j^{(n+1)}$ iff $W(P^{(n+1)}, L^{(n)}) \leq W(P^{(n)}, L^{(n)}) = u_n$. Then, starting from the new partition $P_j^{(n+1)}$, we can always define a new representation vector $L^{(n+1)} = \left(L_1^{(n+1)}, \ldots, L_K^{(n+1)}\right)$ where for any i = 1 to K, $L_i^{(n+1)} = g\left(P_i^{(n+1)}\right)$ fit best to $P_i^{(n+1)}$ than $L_i^{(n)}$ or remains unchanged (i.e. $L^{(n+1)} = L^{(n)}$. This means: $f\left(P_i^{(n+1)}, L_i^{(n+1)}\right) \leq f\left(P_i^{(n+1)}, L_i^{(n)}\right)$ for i = 1 to K.

Hence, at this step, we have $u_{n+1} = W(P^{(n+1)}, L^{(n+1)}) \leq W(P^{(n+1)}, L^{(n)}) \leq W(P^{(n)}, L^{(n)}) = u_n$. As this inequality is true for any n, this positive sequence decreases and converges.

Moreover, notice that in the case where $W(P_i, L_i) = \sum_{w \in P_i} f(w, L_i)$, the allocation step consists to change w from one class to another when $f(w, L_j) < f(w, L_i)$. Notice also that a simple condition of convergence is that for any C_i taken among all the possible subsets of the given population and L_i taken among the given set of possible representations: $f(C_i, g(C_i)) \leq f(C_i, L_i)$.

In case of unsupervised data, the classical k-means method is the case where L_i is the mean of the class C_i. When L_k are probability densities, we have a mixture decomposition method which improves the fit (in term of likelihood) between each class (of the partition) and its associated density function. More precisely, in this case each individual is associated by the allocation function to the density function of highest value for this individual. There are many other possibilities such as when representation of any class can be a distance, a functional curve, points of the population, a factorial axis etc. For an overview see [12, 13].

In case of supervised data we can settle for example: $W(P_i, L_i) = \sum_{w \in P_i} f(w, L_i)$ and $f(w, L_i) = \|Y(w) - M_i(w)\|$ where Y(w) is the predictive value given by the supervised data sample and $M_i(w)$ is the value given by the model M_i applied to the class P_i. The convergence of the method is then obtained if for any C_i and L_i taken among a given family of models, $f(C_i, g(C_i)) \leq f(C_i, L_i)$ where $g(C_i) = M_i$ is the best fitting model to the class C_i among a given family of models.

For example in the representation by a regression, each individual is allocated to the class C'_i if this individual fit the best the regression L_i among all the possible regressions, (see [5]), more generally in case of representation by canonical axis see [14]. Notice that this method contains in case of unsupervised data: local PCA (Principal Component Analysis) (See Fig. 2) and local correspondence analysis. In case of supervised data it contains local regression (see Fig. 2) and local discriminant analysis (See Fig. 2).

Notice that we can extend this fuzzy partitioning method in order to get fuzzy local models by considering the $f_i(x, a_i)$ to be the fit between x and a model M_i with parameters a_i.

In the second step we enhance the explanatory power of the clustering by a characterization measure. The characterization measure of an individual w for the jth

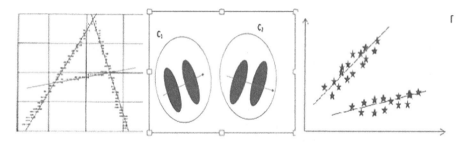

Fig. 2. Local PCA: find simultaneously classes and first axes of local PCA which fit the best Local Discriminant Analysis: find simultaneously classes and first axes of local factorial discriminant analysis which fit the best. Local Regression: find simultaneously classes and local Regressions which fit the best.

variable, the kth class and the event E with: $x = (x_1,\ldots, x_p)$, $x_j = (x_{j1},\ldots, x_{jp})$, X_j $(w) = x_{jm}$, $C(w) = c_k$ is defined by: $\mathbf{W}(x_{jm}, c_k, E) = f_c(x_j)/g_{x, E(xjm, ck)} (c_k)$ Therefore, we can define a characterization measure of an individual $CI(w) = \sum_{j = 1, p} W(x_{jm}, c, E)$.

We can define a characterization measure of a symbolic variable X_j by: $CV(X_j) = \sum_{k = 1, K} \text{Max}_{m = 1, mj} W(x_{jm}, c_k, E)$. We can also define a characterization measure of a class c by:

$CC(c) = \sum_{j = 1, p} \text{Max}_{m = 1, mj} W(x_{jm}, c, E)$.

We can then place in order from the less to the more characteristic the individuals w, the symbolic variables X_j and the class c_i by using respectively the CI, CV or the CL characteristic measure. All these criteria can then enhance the explanatory power of the local machine learning tool used. These orders are respectively denoted O_{CI}, O_{CV}, O_{CL}.

In the third step we suppose that we have already obtained a clustering from a basic sample where the predictive values are given in case of supervised data. Then, the aim is to allocate new individuals to their best cluster. We have to consider two cases depending on the fact that the data are supervised or not.

In case of unsupervised data we have to allocate new individuals to the best fitting representative associated to each cluster. For example, in the case of the k-means, we associate any new individual to the cluster of closest mean. If the representative is a distribution like in Mixture decomposition any new individual is allocated to the cluster which associate density function maximizes the likelihood of this individual. For any individual and in any case we can obtain an order of preference of the clusters from the best fitting representative to this individual to the less representative. Hence, by this way, an individual can place the clusters in an order denoted O_1.

In case of supervised data the aim is first to allocate a new individual (which predictive value is not given) to the best cluster and then to obtain its predicted value from the local model associated to this cluster. For example, if we allocate a new individual to a cluster modeled by a local regression, we can then obtain its predictive value by using this regression. The same can be done if instead of having a local regression, we have a local decision tree, a local SVM, a local neural network etc. In order to find the best new individual allocation we can only use the given data without the predicted value variable as for the new individuals for sure this value is not given. Coming back to the basic sample where now the predicted value variable associate to each individual is its cluster. We can then use, on these data, a supervised machine learning tool for which any individual can have an order of preference to the clusters from the best allocation to the worse. Hence, by this way, an individual can place the clusters in an order denoted O_2.

We can also associate to any new individual its fit to the symbolic description associated to any obtained cluster. For example, in the numeral case, if the symbolic descriptions are density functions f_j, we can use the likelihood product of the $f_j(x_j)$ for $j = 1$, p where x_j is the value taken by this individual for the jth initial variable. We can then place in order the clusters from their best to the lower fit to this individual. We can also replace $f_j(x_j)$ by $W(xj, c, E)$ in the categorical case. Hence, by this way, an individual can place the clusters in an order denoted O_E. Finally given a new unit, we can place in order the obtained clusters by two ways: O_E or O_i (i = 1 or 2) where O_E is an explanatory order. Several strategy are then possible. Having chosen one of them we can continue the machine learning process: we allocate the new individual to a cluster and then adding it to this cluster, then finding a best fit representative and so on until the convergence of DCM until a new partition and its local models.

Machine learning filtering strategies:

The idea is to add (i.e.to filter) a new individual to the cluster and to a symbolic description if it improves simultaneously at best the fit between the cluster and its representative (i.e. its associated model in case of supervised learning) and the explanatory power of its associated symbolic description.

The first kind of filtering strategy is to continue the learning process only with only the individuals which have at best position the same cluster in the order O_E and O_i. Another kind of strategy is to continue the learning machine process with only the individuals whose clusters at best position are not more fare then a given rank k. Then the individual is allocated to the cluster of best rank following O_E or O_i alternatively or depending if you wish more explanatory power or better decision. Other strategies are also possible by adding O_{CI}, and (or) O_{CL} to O_E and O_i. It is also possible to reduce the number of variables by choosing the first ones in the O_{CV} order. In any filtering strategy, the learning process progress with individuals which improve the explanatory power of the machine learning as much as possible without degrading at all or not much the efficiency of the obtained rules. When a sub-population is obtained, the process can continue with the remaining population and lead to other subpopulations.

5   Conclusion

We have first introduced Symbolic Data Analysis which can give useful complementary knowledge to any standard data analysis. We have recalled local data analysis obtained by Dynamic Clustering which can give more accurate results to any kind of data analysis. We have defined several kinds of characterization criteria which allow to place in order individuals, clusters and variables following their explanatory power. We finally gave several strategies for filtering individuals which give the best explanatory of the machine learning process by alternatively improve rules and explanatory power.

Much remains to be done in order to compare and improve the different criteria and strategies and to test the results with different black box machine learning methods (Neural network, SVM, Deep machine learning, etc.) on different kinds of data.

References

1. Billard, L., Diday, E.: From the statistics of data to the statistic of knowledge: symbolic data analysis. JASA J. Am. Stat. Assoc. **98**(462), 470–487 (2003)
2. Billard, L., Diday, E.: Symbolic Data Analysis: Conceptual Statistics and Data Mining. Wiley Series in Computational Statistics, p. 321. Wiley, Chichester (2006). ISBN: 0-470-09016-2
3. Bock, H., Diday, E.: Analysis of Symbolic Data: Exploratory Methods for Extracting Statistical Information from Complex Data, p. 425. Springer, Heidelberg (2000). https://doi.org/10.1007/978-3-642-57155-8. ISBN: 3-540-66619-2
4. Brito, P., Noirhomme-Fraiture, M., Arroyo, J.: Special issue on symbolic data analysis. Adv. Data Anal. Classif. **9**, 1–4 (2015)
5. Charles, C.: Régression typologique et reconnaissance des formes. Thèse de 3ème cycle, Juin 1977, Université Paris IX-Dauphine and INRIA Rocquencourt 78150 (France) (1977)
6. Courtois, A., Genest, Y., Afonso, A., Diday, E., Orcesi, A.: In service inspection of reinforced concrete cooling towers – EDF's feedback, IALCEE 2012 Vienne. Autriche (2012)
7. De Carvalho, F.A.T.: Extension based proximity coefficients between constrained Boolean symbolic objects. In: Hayashi, C., et al. (eds.) Data Science, Classification, and Related Methods. Studies in Classification, Data Analysis, and Knowledge Organization, pp. 370–378. Springer, Berlin (1998). https://doi.org/10.1007/978-4-431-65950-1_41
8. De Carvalho, F., Souza, R., Chavent, M., Lechevallier, Y.: Adaptive Hausdorff distances and dynamic clustering of symbolic interval data. Pattern Recogn. Lett. **27**, 167–179 (2006)
9. Diday, E.: Thinking by classes in data science: symbolic data analysis. In: WIREs Computational Statistics Symbolic Data Analysis, vol. 8, p. 191, September/October 2016 © 2016 Wiley Periodicals, Inc. (2016)
10. Diday, E.: The Dynamic clusters method in non-hierarchical clustering. Int. J. Comput. Inf. Sci. **2**(1), (1973). https://doi.org/10.1007/bf00987153
11. Diday, E., Schroeder, A.: A new approach in mixed distributions detection. RAIRO **10**(6), 75–106 (1975)
12. Diday, E., Simon, J.C.: Clustering analysis. In: Fu, K.S. (ed.) Communication and Cybernetics Digital Pattern Recognition, vol. 10, pp. 47–94. Springer, Berlin (1979). https://doi.org/10.1007/978-3-642-67740-3_3
13. Diday, E., et al.: Optimisation en classification automatique, INRIA publisher (2 books 887 pages). INRIA, 78150 Rocquencourt, France (1980). ISBN 2-7261-0219-0
14. Diday, E: Canonical analysis from the automatic classification point of view. Control Cybern. **15**(2) (1986)
15. Diday, E., Noirhomme-Fraiture, M. (eds.): Symbolic Data Analysis and the SODAS software. Wiley, Chichester (2008). ISBN 978-0-470-01883-5
16. Diday, E., Afonso, F., Haddad, R.: The symbolic data analysis paradigm, discriminate discretization and financial application. In: Advances in Theory and Applications of High Dimensional and Symbolic Data Analysis, HDSDA 2013. Revue des Nouvelles Technologies de l'Information vol. RNTI-E-25, pp. 1–14 (2013)

17. Diday, E.: Explanatory power of clusters based on their symbolic description. In: Saporta, G., Wang, H., Diday, E., Guan, R. (eds.) Advances in Data Sciences. ISTE-Wiley (2019)
18. Dempster, A., Laird, N., Rubin, D.: Maximum likelihood from incomplete data with the EM algorithm. J. R. Stat. Soc. Ser. B Stat. Methodol. **39**, 1–38 (1977)
19. Emilion, R., Diday, E.: Symbolic data analysis basic theory. In: Saporta, G., Wang, H., Diday, E., Guan, R. (eds.) Advances in Data Sciences. ISTE-Wiley (2019)
20. Guan, R., Lechevallier, Y., Saporta, G., Wang, H.: Advances in Theory and applications of High Dimensional and Symbolic Data Analysis, vol. E25. Hermann, MO: RNTI (2013)
21. Guinot, C., Malvy, D., Schemann, J.-F., Afonso, F., Haddad, R., Diday, E.: Strategies evaluation in environmental conditions by symbolic data analysis: application in medicine and epidemiology to trachoma. ADAC (Adv. Data Anal. Classif.) **9**(1), 107–119 (2015)
22. Lebart, L., Morineau, A., Km, W.: Multivariate Descriptive Statistical Analysis. Wiley, New York (1984)
23. Nuemi, G., et al.: Classification of hospital pathways in the management of cancer: application to lung cancer in the region of burgundy. Cancer Epidemiol. J. **37**, 688–696 (2013)
24. Ochs, M., Diday, E., Afonso, F.: From the symbolic analysis of virtual faces to a smiles machine. IEEE Trans. Cybern. **46**(2), 401–409 (2016). https://doi.org/10.1109/tcyb.2015.2411432
25. Su, S.-F., Pedrycz, W., Hong, T.-P., De Carvalho, F.A.T.: Special issue on granular/symbolic data processing. IEEE Trans. Cybern. 344–401 (2016)

Artificial Intelligence and Applications

Classification of Neuron Sets from Non-disease States Using Time Series Obtained Through Nonlinear Analysis of the 3D Dendritic Structures

Leonardo Agustín Hernández-Pérez[1,2](✉) ⓘ,
José Daniel López-Cabrera[2] ⓘ, Rubén Orozco-Morales[3] ⓘ,
and Juan Valentín Lorenzo-Ginori[2] ⓘ

[1] Empresa de Telecomunicaciones de Cuba S.A, Santa Clara, Villa Clara, Cuba
leonardo.hernandez@etecsa.cu
[2] Informatics Research Center, Universidad Central
"Marta Abreu" de Las Villas, 54830 Santa Clara, Villa Clara, Cuba
[3] Department of Automatics and Computational Systems,
Universidad Central "Marta Abreu" de Las Villas,
54830 Santa Clara, Villa Clara, Cuba

Abstract. The nonlinear dynamic analysis of time series is a powerful tool which has extended its application to many branches of scientific research. Topological equivalence is one of the main concepts that sustain theoretically the nonlinear dynamics procedures that have been implemented to characterize the discrete time series. Based on this concept, in this work a novel way to analyze dendritic trees with high complexity is reported, using features obtained through splitting the 3D structure of the dendritic trees of traced neurons into time series. Digitally reconstructed neurons were separated into control and pathological sets, which are related to two categories of alterations caused by the reduced activity of the adult born neurons (ABNs) in the mouse olfactory bulb. In the first category, a viral vector encoding a small interfering RNA (siRNA) to knock-down sodium channel expression and a second category a naris occlusion (NO) method is applied to reduce the activity of ABNs that migrate to the olfactory bulb. Using the method proposed in this study the mean result of the correct classification was improved in 4.8 and 2.76% for the NO and siRNA sets respectively, while the maximum correct classification rates were improved in 9.53 and 2.5% respectively, when compared to methods based in the use of morphological features.

Keywords: Neuron trees · Time series · Neuron classification

1 Introduction

Most studies where neuron sets are compared use currently classification methods [1] which by means of using morphological features determine how different the neurons are from each set. The classification of neurons into types has been much debated since the inception of modern neuroscience [1]. The most widely used tool is the Sholl

Y. Hernández Heredia et al. (Eds.): IWAIPR 2018, LNCS 11047, pp. 17–25, 2018.
https://doi.org/10.1007/978-3-030-01132-1_2

analysis [2], because it allows obtaining information about the complexity of dendritic branches on the neuronal trees. An example is the morphological analysis of the dendritic structure of pyramidal neurons from the cerebral cortex of the chimpanzee and its contrast to the cortex of the human brain [3]. Another example of Sholl analysis application is found in [5]. In this article we study how is affected the morphology of adult neurons by means of using two mechanisms of neuronal activity reduction. Firstly, this is done by means of the use of a viral vector which codes a small-interference RNA (siRNA) to suppress the sodium channel communication. Another mechanism known as naris occlusion (NO) to reduce the level in one of the nasal circuits. NO consists in cauterizing one of the nares. In the previously cited reference the Sholl analysis [3] is used to determine if there exist significant differences in the dendritic structure between the sets: (control – siRNA) and (control – NO). For the case in which siRNA was used, changes in the dendritic structure can be appreciated in certain regions of the dendritic tree while when NO was used as reduction mechanism of the neuronal activity, the changes were not located in a specific region but they could be appreciated along all the dendritic tree.

Recently published studies assert that the complexity of the brain, its hierarchical structure, as well as the sophisticated topological structure in which it organizes the neurons, are unexplainable in the neurosciences neither through the Euclidean geometry, nor using linear dynamics [4, 5]. Using the nonlinear dynamic analysis of time series is possible to investigate some important characteristics of an event using only the information contained in its associated time series. In particular, a dynamic multidimensional system can be described using the information obtained by measuring sequentially only one of its representative variables [6].

In this study the databases published in [5] were used to compare the method based in obtaining morphological features with that based in obtaining features by means of the decomposition of the 3D neuronal structure into numerical series (which will be called time series in this article). In the following this method will be called "time-series based method."

Using the method proposed in this study, the mean values of the correct classification rate were improved for the sets NO and siRNA in 4.8 and 2.76% respectively, when compared to methods based in the use of morphological features.

2 Methods

2.1 Data Bases

In order to test the method based in the dendrites' trees decomposition into time series two databases of traced neurons were used which were published in [7] The first database comprises two sets of neurons (control and siRNA). A total of 40 cells (20 for each set) were included. Five cells per hemisphere were extracted from each animal. The other database was also comprised by two groups (control and NO) having 42 cells (21 for each group). A more detailed description on the protocol employed to inject the lentivirus, naris cauterization, the immunohistochemical procedure, the digital image processing and neuron tracing procedures can be found in [5].

2.2   Time Series Representation of Neurons Trees

A dynamic multidimensional system can be described using the information obtained by measuring sequentially only one of its representative variables [6]. Based on this concept, in this work we evaluated one-dimensional (1D) time series drawn from the three-dimensional (3D) neuronal structures using the procedure applying in [8]. The 3D structure of the reconstructed neuronal tree can be decomposed into time series from the coordinate system values of each point in the morphological structure of the tree. Figure 1 shows the projection in the XY plane of a 3D reconstructed neuron.

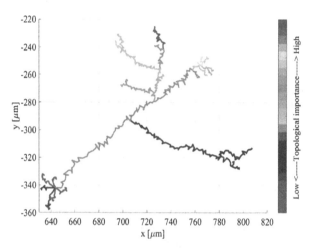

Fig. 1. XY plane projection of the traced neuron, Control A512R cell 4, the color bar uses 24 levels to show each one of the dendrites which compose this neuron. This color bar represents the topological importance of each neuron's dendrite, where those close to red are the most important. (Color figure online)

The time series were obtained from the coordinates of the neuronal tree elements, properly arranged and transformed as series of intervals which are termed as: coordinates' series with jumps (CS-WJ) and without jumps (CS-WOJ) see Fig. 2. The other time series were obtained using the L2-norm to obtain the Euclidian distance between adjacent nodes in the traced neuron and these are termed spatial series with jumps (SS-WJ) and without jumps (SS-WOJ). To determine which dataset of features showed the best performance, we built two new datasets taking the best 15 ranked features from each dataset: the first one, with the features obtained from each dataset of series (CS-WJ, CS-WOJ, SS-WJ, and SS-WOJ) totaling 60 features and termed U-SERIES dataset, and the second one adding to the first group the 15 best morphological features obtained from L-measure termed U-MORPHO. And finally the morphological dataset obtained through L-measure [9] which contains 81 features (MORPHO). Seven datasets were obtained in total for each neurons' set.

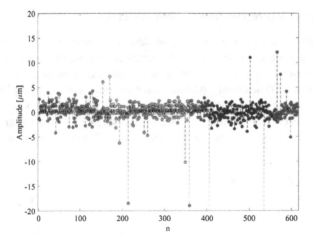

Fig. 2. Illustrating the series corresponding to the neuron shown in Fig. 1. This contains the topological information pertaining the neuron, the first samples correspond to the dendrites having the largest relevance while the dendrites with the least topological relevance are located rightmost. In this case, the apical dendrites possess more topological relevance than the basal dendrites.

2.3 Nonlinear Dynamic Test

Topological equivalence (homomorphism) is one of the primary concepts that lie beneath as theoretical support in all the procedures that were implemented on the basis of nonlinear dynamics theory, to characterize the discrete time series. To apply the Takens' embedding theorem [6] it is necessary to apply two fundamental tests: 1. showing that the series obtained are chaotic and 2. Reconstructing the attractor from the information obtained from one of its time series.

This chaos test was applied to each one of the time series used in this study and the result was that all the series are highly chaotic. Most of the tools that are used to determine chaos in a time series are based in calculating the Lyapunov's exponent [10]. We used here the most referenced tool of this kind, Chaos Data Analyzer (CDA), [11, 12]. The CDA tool was used in this research to test the presence of chaos in the time series that were analyzed. CDA tool are based in calculating the Lyapunov's exponent [10].

2.4 Obtaining Features from Time Series

Using the MATS tool [13], a dataset of metrics was extracted from each one of the four previously obtained series. Three kinds of metrics are originated by MATS: linear, nonlinear, and others. Nonlinear metrics contain a group of correlation, dimension and complexity metrics, as well as modeling metrics. In this work we investigated a total of 175 metrics. A complete relation is shown in Appendix 1 (Online Resource 2) in [8].

To compare the aforementioned metrics, we made use of the morphometric features obtainable by the L-measure software [14]. This tool allows obtaining a total of 220 metrics. For some features, these parameters are obtained with repeated values or are without interest for the morphological analysis of the neuronal trees. We select 81 as those having significance for this study, see Appendix 2 (Online Resource 3) in [8].

2.5 Classification Process

The classification process was made with the purpose of comparing the behavior of the features obtained from the time series in relation with the morphological features. The classification was made using the Weka tool [15]. We used 52 different classifiers. A recursive attribute selection process was performed using all the default *Weka* values (10-fold cross-validation and random seed). All the evaluators used a ranker type searching algorithm. We excluded the classifiers based on artificial neural nets because of their high computational cost. For more details see "Feature selection and classification" in [8]. Due to the large amount of features that were used, 175 for the time series and 81 for Euclidian metrics, the classification process was preceded by a feature selection that guaranteed a 10:1 instances to features ratio [15].

Given the large number of features extracted from the sets of neurons, and according to [15], a recursive procedure [16] was implemented to eliminate approximately one half of them in every iteration, in order to have approximately one feature for every ten instances having in mind to have at least 10 instances per feature.

3   Results

3.1   Recursive Classification Process

Table 1 shows useful rankings that meet the 10:1 ratio of TNI (total number of instances)/FEAT (number of features), including rankings with four or fewer features The first column contains the number of features (FEAT), the second column exhibits the percentage of correctly classified instances (CCI), the third column shows the total number of instances (TNI), the fourth column the number of correctly classified instances (NCCI), the fifth column the number of incorrectly classified instances (NICI), the sixth column the area under the receiver operating characteristic (ROC) curve, and the last column the F-Measure defined in Weka [16].

Table 1. Example of the recursive procedure, a dataset with 42 instances and 81 features needs seven recursive cycles to obtain 41, 21, 11, 6, 4, 3, 2 and 1 features. Only the classification results with 4, 3, 2 and 1 features are taken into account to keep an acceptable instance-to-feature ratio.

FEAT	CCI	TNI	NCCI	NICI	ROC	F-measure
4	78.57	42	33	9	0.83	0.79
3	85.71	42	36	6	0.87	0.86
2	85.71	42	36	6	0.85	0.86
1	78.57	42	33	9	0.75	0.78

3.2   Chaos Test

To make appropriate tests to verify whether the time series exhibit chaotic behavior or not the computational tools CDA [12] was used, see Table 2.

Table 2. Results of Chaos test. Estimated of Lyapunov exponent using CDA. These results correspond to the Nares occlusion set. Two spatial series were obtained from each neuron (SS-WJ and SS-WOJ) as well as six series of coordinates (CS-WJ$_x$ CS-WJ$_y$ CS-WJ$_z$ CS-WOJ$_x$ CS-WOJ$_y$ and CS-WOJ$_z$). For more information about the time series and the Chaos test see [8].

Neuron name	SS-WJ	SS-WOJ	CS-WJ$_x$	CS-WJ$_y$	CS-WJ$_z$	CS-WOJ$_x$	CS-WOJ$_y$	CS-WOJ$_z$
A398R_Cell_1	0.63	0.60	0.13	0.34	0.13	0.55	0.57	0.55
A398R_Cell_2	0.62	0.54	0.14	0.48	0.14	0.61	0.63	0.61
A398L_Cell_1	0.74	0.61	0.12	0.09	0.12	0.56	0.55	0.56
A398L_Cell_2	0.57	0.55	0.15	0.21	0.15	0.57	0.50	0.57

3.3   Nares Occlusion Set

Table 3 shows the summarized results for each dataset with min, mean, max and standard deviation. Notice that the mean value of all classifications using CS-WJ is about 72.02%, and using U-SERIES is less than 72%. However, the U-MORPHO and U-SERIES features dataset improved the classification reaching 95.24% of correct classification with a mean of 73.16 for the U-MORPHO dataset. On the other hand, MORPHO alone reached 85.71% of correct classification with a 67.22% mean.

Table 3. Comparison of all classification results (1316) for each dataset of features from the Naris Occlusion set. The best outcomes are highlighted in bold.

Dataset	Min	Mean	Max	SD
MORPHO	47.62	67.22	85.71	8.60
SS-WOJ	40.48	61.51	78.57	7.79
SS-WJ	45.24	64.81	85.71	8.10
CS-WOJ	47.62	67.73	88.10	9.54
CS-WJ	45.24	72.02	92.86	9.15
U-SERIES	47.62	71.83	**95.24**	9.92
U-MORPHO	47.62	**73.16**	**95.24**	10.68

3.4   siRNA-KD Set Results

To analyze the siRNA set we conducted the same trials previously described, having obtained the best classification (75.37% correct) with U-SERIES, see Table 4. The U-MORPHO showed a maximum of 92.5% and a mean value of 75.01%, which is higher than the mean value 72.61% obtained with the morphological features (MORPHO). Table 4 shows the summarized results for each dataset with min, mean, max and standard deviation. The latter shows that the results exhibit a wide variability around the mean, reaching values higher than 10 in five out of the seven datasets.

Table 4. Comparison of all classification results (1316) for each dataset of features from the siRNA-KD set. The best outcomes are highlighted in bold

DATASET	Min	Mean	Max	SD
MORPHO	47.50	72.61	92.50	10.25
SS-WOJ	47.50	72.58	87.50	9.52
SS-WJ	47.50	69.50	90.00	8.52
CS-WOJ	42.50	72.78	87.50	10.15
CS-WJ	45.00	73.50	92.50	10.30
U-SERIES	47.50	**75.37**	**95.00**	10.26
U-MORPHO	47.50	75.01	92.50	10.46

The comparative analysis among the various datasets used in this work revealed that the best dataset was the union of series (U-SERIES) with a significant statistical difference in comparison to the other datasets.

4 Discussion

We performed in this research two neuron classification tasks corresponding respectively to two available databases: (control – siRNA) and (control – NO). We consider that the results of these experiments were similar to those obtained in [8]. There are several facts that demonstrate this, these are: (1) the series of coordinates show in general better results than the spatial series. We considered at the beginning that integrating the coordinate series in a spatial one would lead to at least similar results while it would also reduce the dimensionality of the data set. However, the results revealed that obtaining the spatial series from the information of each coordinate implies a significant loss of information. We observed that using together all the diversity of features in each of the interval series corresponding to the coordinates allows a better characterization of the neuron's 3D structure. We consider that information loss in the spatial series is due to the fact that integrating the coordinates through the L2 norm suppresses information on the true extension of the neurons' morphology. (2) We obtained improvements in the results by means of the series union, mostly in experiment 1 (siRNA KD vs Control.) (3) The union of morphological and series-derived features also favored an improvement of the classification, with better results in (Nares occlus vs Control) experiment. (4) In both cases and without considering the U-SERIES and U-MORPHO series, the CS-WJ datasets had the best results in classification. (5) In the two experiments, the MORPHO dataset showed a better performance than datasets SS-WJ and SS-WOJ. All the previously mentioned issues have been shown in a regular way in the results obtained for each one of the studied sets.

4.1   Morphological Features Vs. Time Series Features

The results suggest that the intuitive morphology features used usually in studies like this are an incomplete description of relevant differences in morphology; here it is worth to notice that it is common in nonlinear systems to find even counter-intuitive behavior of systems. We considered in this research that the neuron structure can be described by a time series having nonlinear properties and we hypothesized that this could reveal some characteristics that are not appreciated from the intuitive morphological features. The main purpose of this work has been using also these characteristics for improving the results of neuron classification.

4.2   Sholl Analysis, Morphological and Time Series Metrics

The features constructed in this work are also of spatial nature but in this case they are derived from a study based in the time series theory, which makes them conceptually different to those obtained using the L-Measure software or the Sholl analysis.

The analysis of Sholl has the advantage of allowing the evaluation of dendritic complexity along the entire three-dimensional structure of the neuron tree, identifying the places where the complexity is greater or lesser, as shown in [17]. However as these measures are reported as a function of a sphere radius having discrete size, the result can be misleading if we do not take properly these radii. On the other hand the automation of Sholl analysis is relatively complex when working with sets of neurons.

Using time series measures we explored the variability of the main branches and branch segments associated to them along their path from the root until the terminations, by means of the features obtained from time series. Time series analysis allows obtaining a great variety of features in a unique structure which describes the high neuronal tree complexity. On the other hand, it includes the nonlinear analysis which has demonstrated to be a powerful tool to quantify the complexity of spatial structures with irregular forms [5].

5   Conclusion

This paper addresses a new approach to the task of neuron classification in the analysis of neuron trees using the tools of non-linear dynamic analysis. The three-dimensional structure of neurons is split in time series to obtain four different feature datasets. Using the Weka tool we compared these new datasets with traditional morphological metrics datasets obtained using L-measure. Our method improved the classification results for the NO set (4.8% of CCI) as well as for siRNA set (2.76% of CCI) when compared to classification using conventional morphological features.

References

1. Armañanzas, R., Ascoli, G.A.: Towards automatic classification of neurons. Trends Neurosci. **38**, 307–318 (2015). https://doi.org/10.1016/j.tins.2015.02.004
2. Sholl, D.A.: Dendritic organization in the neurons of the visual and motor cortices of the cat. J. Anat. **87**, 387–406 (1953)
3. Bianchi, S., Stimpson, C.D., Bauernfeind, A.L., Schapiro, S.J., Baze, W.B., McArthur, M.J., et al.: Dendritic morphology of pyramidal neurons in the chimpanzee neocortex: regional specializations and comparison to humans. Cereb. Cortex **23**(10), 2429–2436 (2013). https://doi.org/10.1093/cercor/bhs239
4. Di Ieva, A., Grizzi, F., Jelinek, H., Pellionisz, A.J., Losa, G.A.: Fractals in the neurosciences, part I: general principles and basic neurosciences. Neurosci. Rev. J. Bringing Neurobiol. Neurol. Psychiatry **20**, 403–417 (2013). https://doi.org/10.1177/1073858413513927
5. Di Ieva, A., Esteban, F.J., Grizzi, F., Klonowski, W., Martín-Landrove, M.: Fractals in the neurosciences, part II: clinical applications and future perspectives. Neurosci. Rev. J. Bring. Neurobiol. Neurol Psychiatry **21**, 30–43 (2015). https://doi.org/10.1177/1073858413513928
6. Rand, D., Young, L.-S. (eds.): Dynamical Systems and Turbulence, Warwick 1980. LNM, vol. 898. Springer, Heidelberg (1981). https://doi.org/10.1007/BFb0091903
7. NeuroMorpho_Linkout. http://neuromorpho.org/NeuroMorpho_Linkout.jsp?PMID=12902394
8. Hernández-Pérez, L.A., Delgado-Castillo, D., Martín-Pérez, R., Orozco-Morales, R., Lorenzo-Ginori, J.V.: New features for neuron classification. Neuroinformatics 1–21 (2018). https://doi.org/10.1007/s12021-018-9374-0
9. Scorcioni, R., Polavaram, S., Ascoli, G.A.: L-Measure: a web-accessible tool for the analysis, comparison and search of digital reconstructions of neuronal morphologies. Nat. Protoc. **3**, 866–876 (2008). https://doi.org/10.1038/nprot.2008.51
10. Rosenstein, M.T., Collins, J.J., Luca, C.J.D.: A practical method for calculating largest Lyapunov exponents from small data sets. Phys. D **65**, 117–134 (1993)
11. Sprott, J.C.: Chaos and Time-Series Analysis. Oxford University Press, Oxford (2003)
12. Hamilton, P., West, B.: Software review chaos data analyzer, professional version. Nonlinear Dyn. Psychol. Life Sci. **4**, 195–199 (2000). https://doi.org/10.1023/A:1009580513427
13. Kugiumtzis, D., Tsimpiris, A.: Measures of analysis of time series (MATS): a MATLAB toolkit for computation of multiple measures on time series data bases. ArXiv10021940 Stat. (2010)
14. Scorcioni, R., Lazarewicz, M.T., Ascoli, G.A.: Quantitative morphometry of hippocampal pyramidal cells: differences between anatomical classes and reconstructing laboratories. J. Comp. Neurol. **473**, 177–193 (2004). https://doi.org/10.1002/cne.20067
15. Foster, K.R., Koprowski, R., Skufca, J.D.: Machine learning, medical diagnosis, and biomedical engineering research—commentary. Biomed. Eng. OnLine **13**, 94 (2014). https://doi.org/10.1186/1475-925X-13-94
16. Bouckaert, R., et al.:: WEKA Manual for Version 3-6-13. CreateSpace Independent Publishing Platform (2015)
17. Dahlen, J.E., Jimenez, D.A., Gerkin, R.C., Urban, N.N.: Morphological analysis of activity-reduced adult-born neurons in the mouse olfactory bulb. Front. Neurosci. **5** (2011). https://doi.org/10.3389/fnins.2011.00066

Evaluating the Max-Min Hill-Climbing Estimation of Distribution Algorithm on B-Functions

Julio Madera[1(✉)] and Alberto Ochoa[2]

[1] Department of Computer Science, University of Camagüey, Camagüey, Cuba
julio.madera@reduc.edu.cu
[2] Instituto de Cibernética, Matemática Y Física, La Habana, Cuba

Abstract. In this paper we evaluate a new Estimation of Distribution Algorithm (EDA) constructed on top of a very successful Bayesian network learning procedure, Max-Min Hill-Climbing (MMHC). The aim of this paper is to check whether the excellent properties reported for this algorithm in machine learning papers, have some impact on the efficiency and efficacy of EDA based optimization. Our experiments show that the proposed algorithm outperform well-known state of the art EDA like BOA and EBNA in a test bed based on B-functions. On the basis of these results we conclude that the proposed scheme is a promising candidate for challenging real-world applications, specifically, problems related to the areas of Data Mining, Patter Recognition and Artificial Intelligence.

Keywords: Estimation of distribution algorithms · B-functions
Bayesian networks · Dependency learning · Evolutionary optimization

1 Introduction

Nowadays research on Estimation of Distribution Algorithms (EDAs) is a well-established branch of evolutionary computation [3]. The amount and quality of papers reporting both theoretical [1, 4–6] and practical works increases every year, while practitioners have begun to consider the possibility of using EDAs for their challenging real-world applications [2, 3, 8]. However, before EDAs can really impact the optimization market still many theoretical issues have to be addressed and solved.

In this contribution, which is only aimed to present our algorithm, we have focused in just two aspects of the problem: the scalability and efficacy issues. By this we mean the ability of any EDA scheme to preserve its good algorithmic properties as the number of variables of the cost function increases. Let the number of function evaluations and the average time to get to the optimum, play the role of the mentioned properties. We shall show that the algorithm we are about to introduce on average scales better than several of the most famous existing Bayesian EDAs. To do that, we present a set of experiments that support our claim. Also, we will argue that these results extend to a very large class of problems.

Y. Hernández Heredia et al. (Eds.): IWAIPR 2018, LNCS 11047, pp. 26–33, 2018.
https://doi.org/10.1007/978-3-030-01132-1_3

We have chosen for our initial study the Bayesian Optimization Algorithm (BOA) [7] and the Estimation of Bayesian Networks algorithm (EBNA) [3]. These algorithms use a scoring metric to explore the space of Bayesian networks and pick up one that is somehow optimal for modeling the search distributions of a binary optimization problem. For the sake of brevity, we do not discuss any of these algorithms neither make a general presentation about EDAs or Bayesian networks. The interested reader is referred to the literature [1, 3, 4, 6].

The novel optimizer is designed for integer problems. It combines the use of a scoring metric and independence tests in its learning algorithm. Learning is accomplished with the Max-Min Hill Climbing (MMHC) algorithm, which was introduced in [11] and implemented in [10]. The MMHC algorithm has been shown to possess good properties for machine learning problems. According to the reported experimental evaluations, it outperforms on average its predecessors with regard to computational efficiency, scalability and quality of the learned networks. Besides it can be easily parallelized. It is obvious that all these properties are of great value for EDA optimization.

Once one has a MMHC implementation there are two things that one is tempted to do immediately: designing the and afterwards its parallel version. On one hand, we obtain scalability with respect to the amount of functions evaluations. On the other hand, time scalability is added with the parallel version. We have accomplished both tasks but, in this work, we will report only the sequential algorithm.

The outline of the paper is as follows. In the next section the MMHC algorithm is discussed following the presentation made in [9, 11] This section is ended with the introduction of our MMHCEDA algorithm. This is followed by the numerical results (Sect. 3) which are presented using the B-functions benchmark [4, 6]. Finally, some remarks on future works and the conclusions are given.

2   The Max-Min Hill-Climbing Algorithm

The so-called Max-Min Hill Climbing (MMHC) algorithm is a two-stage procedure that combines constraint-based and search-and-score methods for learning Bayesian networks. In stage I, the algorithm computes a collection of candidate sets, PC(T), which contain the parents and children of each problem's variable, T. In stage II, it performs a local search –constrained by the PC(T) sets– and looks for the solution in the space of directed acyclic networks.

According to the reported experimental evaluations, MMHC learning outperforms on average its predecessors with regard to computational efficiency, scalability and quality of the learned networks. In what follows we give just a short overview of the algorithm; we refer the reader to [9, 11] and the references therein for a detailed treatment of the topic.

The computation of the candidate sets is accomplished using a local algorithm for causal discovery called Max-Min Parents and Children (MMPC, algorithm 1).

Given the variable T and the sample database D, MMPC uses also a two-phase scheme to discover the PC(T) [11]. In the forward phase, variables enter sequentially PC(T) by use of a heuristic function that selects the variable that maximizes the association with T conditioned on the subset of the current estimate of PC(T) that minimizes that association (hence the name of the algorithm). All variables with an edge to or from T and possibly more will enter PC(T). All false positives are removed in the second phase.

Algorithm 1. $PC(T) = MMPC(T, D)$.

Phase 1 (Forward)

1. $PC(T) = \emptyset$
2. **REPEAT**
   a. $PC(T) = PC(T) \cup X$ (where X maximizes a heuristic function based on independence tests)
3. **UNTIL** All variables are conditionally independent of T given some subset of $PC(T)$

Phase 2 (Backward)

1. Remove from $PC(T)$ any variable independent of T given some subset of $PC(T)$

The above-mentioned association is a conditional measure that captures the strength of the dependence with respect to D and is denoted by $dep(X_i, X_j|Z)$. MMPC runs χ^2 independence tests with the G^2 statistic in order to decide on the conditional (in)dependence of X_i and X_j given Z and uses the p-value of the test as the association. Our current implementation of the algorithm follows [10]. Under the conditional independence assumption:

$$G^2 = 2 \sum_{ijk} N_{ijk} ln \frac{N_{ijk} N_k}{N_{ik} N_{jk}} \tag{1}$$

where N_{ijk} denotes how many times X_i and X_j take, respectively, their i-th and j-th values, whereas the set of variables Z takes its k-th value. N_{ik}, N_{jk} and N_k are defined similarly. Assuming that there are not structural zeros, G^2 behaves asymptotically as χ^2 with:

$$df = (|X_i| - 1)(|X_j| - 1) \prod_{X_k \in Z} |X_k| \tag{2}$$

degrees of freedom. Here, |X| denotes the cardinality of X.

Once we have an efficient algorithm to learn the local structure of the Bayesian network (MMPC) we can learn the overall network. MMHC starts from a fully disconnected network and uses a greedy hill climbing to look for the Bayesian network that optimizes a given scoring metric (our current implementation is based on the Bayesian information criterion). MMHC uses three local operators: *DeleteArc*, *InvertArc* and *AddArc*. The search is constrained because the addition operator obeys the following restriction: $T \rightarrow Y$ can be added only if $Y \in PC(T)$. It is worth noting, that the $PC(T)$ set is unique only if the distribution of data is faithful to a Bayesian network. The functions of the experimental section of this paper, the B-functions, are such a kind of functions.

Algorithm 1. *MMHC(D).*

---

2. **FORALL** variables X **DO**
   a. $PC(X) = MMPC(X, D)$
3. Start from a fully disconnected network (BN)
4. **REPEAT**
   a. Greedily apply hill-climbing operators: *DeleteArc*, *InvertArc* and *AddArc* ($X \rightarrow Y$ can be added only if $Y \in PC(X)$)
5. **UNTIL** no improvements can be obtained
6. Output the computed Bayesian network structure (BN)

2.1 An EDA Based on the MMHC Algorithm

MMHCEDA is just an EDA whose learning step is based on the MMHC algorithm [4, 5]. Its simplest version is shown in algorithm 3. Among other things, this simple scheme does not include mutation nor elitism. This is enough for our current presentation. The analysis of more elaborated algorithms is left for future papers. Note that although one can use any selection scheme, we have chosen the method of truncation selection for all the simulations of this paper.

Algorithm 3. Simple *MMHCEDA* algorithm.

---

1. Let $t \leftarrow 1$. Generate $N \gg 0$ random points
2. According to a selection method, construct a set, CS, of M points
3. Find the structure of the modeling Bayesian network: $BN = MMHC(CS)$
4. Estimate the parameters of $p^s(x, t)$ using BN and CS
5. Generate N new points from $p(x, t + 1) \approx p^s(x, t)$
6. If the termination criteria are not met, make $t \leftarrow t + 1$ and go to step 2

---

3 Numerical Results

In this section we report our empirical comparison of the algorithms *MMHCEDA*, *BOA* and *EBNA* with the so-called B-functions (details will follow). The aim of the experiments is simple: to show that the *MMHCEDA* is well suited for optimization and that it is competitive with the best algorithms that have been reported so far.

3.1 B-Functions

The B-function benchmark was introduced in [5]. Let us start with the formal definition of B-functions.

Definition 1. (B-functions). Given $n > 0$, let $X_1, X_2, \cdots, X_n$ be arbitrary discrete random variables with joint probability mass function $q(X_1, X_2, \cdots, X_n)$. Denoting $x = (x_1, x_2, \cdots, x_n) \in X = X_1 \times X_2 \times \cdots \times X_n$ and assuming that $\hat{x}$ is one of the modes of $q(X)$, the parametric function:

$$Bf_{q,\eta}(x) = \frac{1}{\eta} \log\left(\frac{q(\hat{x})}{q(x)}\right) \tag{3}$$

is non-negative, additive, has a minimum at the point $\hat{x}$ and is called B-function. The temperature, $\frac{1}{\eta}$, and the distribution, $q(x)$ are called definition parameters of the B-function. It worth noting that this definition can be trivially adapted to deal with continuous variables [6].

Loosely speaking, we say that B-functions are important for research because if a "good enough" EDA algorithm is used to optimize (see Eq. 3), it will see search distributions were the probabilistic relationships existing in the definition distribution q (x) are approximated [6]. At this point we recall that the success of the *MMHC* learning algorithm is affected by the faithfulness of the data.

The B-functions have a number of good properties that make them interesting as a benchmark for EDAs (see [4]). For example, it is possible to construct efficient random function generators for some B-function classes. In the experiments of this paper we use the class of binary polytree B-functions, which have definition distributions with polytree structure (single-connected Bayesian network).

We start our experiments with the function FirstPolytree5 –one of the first polytree functions designed [6]. In this case the old practice of building large problems by concatenation of small ones was followed. However, the remaining functions of the paper were obtained using a random B-functions generator. The B-functions studied were named following [6], thus the reader is referred there for details. Here, we just give a short description of the functions.

BF2B30s4-2312: It stands for the random subclass of binary polytree functions that have 30 variables, each with a maximum of four parents. Each pair of adjacent variables – in the polytree – has mutual information in the interval $[0.2, 0.3]$ and the univariate probabilities lie either in $[0.15, 0.25]$ or in $[0.75, 0.85]$. Note that these intervals are mapped to the same entropic interval.

BF2B30s4-1245: Almost as before but this time the entropic interval corresponds to the probability interval $[0.45, 0.55]$ (very high entropy) and the mutual information of the edges belong to the interval $[0.1, 0.2]$.

BF2Bns0-0034: This class has not correlations at all, thus the fields containing the mutual information bounds and the connectivity constraint should be ignored. In this case the univariate probabilities lie either in $[0.35, 0.45]$ or in $[0.55, 0.65]$.

3.2 MMHCEDA Scales with the Function FirstPolytree5

Our first experiment studies the numerical scalability of the *MMHCEDA* using the function $F_{FP5}(x)$ with 50, 100, 150 and 200 variables. FP5 is a separable additive decomposable function with blocks of length 5. In each block the FirstPolytree5 function is evaluated. It has the following property: its Boltzmann distribution with parameter $\beta \approx 2$ has a polytree structure with edges: $x_1 \rightarrow x_3, x_2 \rightarrow x_3, x_3 \rightarrow x_5, x_4 \rightarrow x_5$. The definition of the subfunction f_5^{Poly} is given in [6] whereas F_{FP5} is computed as follows:

$$F_{FP5}(x) = \sum_{i=1}^{l} f_5^{Poly}(x_{5*i-4}, x_{5*i-3}, x_{5*i-2}, x_{5*i-1}, x_{5*i}) \tag{4}$$

The point $(0, 1, 0, 0, 1, \ldots, 0, 1, 0, 0, 1)$ is the global maximum of this problem where the function takes the value $l * 1.723$, with $n = 5 * l$. The aim of the experiment was to find the critical (minimum) population size that guarantees 100% of success in 30 runs. We used the bisection method to compute this critical value.

Figure 1 shows the average number of function evaluations for the critical population size found. From this figure is easy to conclude that in this problem, *MMHCEDA* scales well with the number of variables.

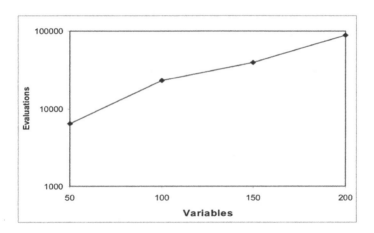

Fig. 1. Scalability of the $CBEDA_{MMHC}$ for the function $F_{FP5}(x)$.

3.3 Minimization of BF2B30s4-2312 and BF2B30s4-1245

In this experiment two B-functions, one with low (BF2B30s4-2312) and another with high univariate entropies (BF2B30s4-1245) were chosen. Later on, the percentage of convergence of each algorithm was obtained for a population size of 100 individuals. When a certain algorithm didn't converge 100%, its population was augmented with 100 individuals until arriving to a population of 500. Note that with the high entropy B-function were necessary population sizes of 1000, 2000, 4000 and 8000.

Table 1. Minimization of the function **BF2B30s4-2312**.

N	UMDA	BOA k=1	BOA k=2	BOA k=3	EBNA	MMHCEDA
100	97	30	0	0	100	46.6
200	100	100	50	23.3	97	100
300	100	100	90	46.6	100	100
400	100	100	100	90	100	100
500	100	10	100	100	100	100

As can be seen from Table 1, the optimization of the function BF2B30s4-2312 is an easy task for all studied algorithms. Again, BOA shows a very strong dependency on the parameter k. A more interesting observation is that *MMHCEDA* is more efficient than EBNA. We draw the attention of the reader to the following fact: with the function BF2B30s4-2312 the critical population sizes of EBNA and $CBEDA_{MMHC}$ were 100 and 200 respectively (see the Table 2). Despite this, $CBEDA_{MMHC}$ makes less functions evaluations than EBNA, so it converges faster and therefore discovers faster the important correlations of the problem.

Table 2. Minimization of the function **BF2B30s4-1245**.

N	UMDA	BOA k=1	BOA k=2	BOA k=3	EBNA	MMHCEDA
100	3.33	0	0	0	13.3	6.67
200	3.33	30	10	0	16.6	23.3
300	3.33	46.6	23.3	13.3	30	40
400	3.33	53.3	43.3	30	30	66.6
500	3.33	50	56.6	43.3	26.6	53.3
1000	3.33	43.3	50	50	40	73.3
4000	3.33	43.3	50	43.3	33.3	100
8000	3.33	43.3	50	50	43.3	100

The B-function BF2B30s4-1245 turns out to be much harder, which confirms what was said in [4, 5] with regard to the entropy of the function. We have included the UMDA in our experiments to highlight this issue: it easily finds the optimum of the low entropy function but fails dramatically with the high entropy one. The good news is that the *MMHCEDA* performs well in both extreme cases. Neither BOA nor EBNA can do that, they fail even with a population of 8000 individuals. In contrast, our *MMHCEDA* already gets 100% success rate with 2000 individuals.

4   Conclusions and Future Work

The evaluated algorithm is based in recent advances in the area of learning of Bayesian networks from data. In particular, the algorithm scales well with high efficiency of data. We have wondered to what extent these features could mean a significant impulse with regard to the quality of the EDAs and their capacities to attack real world problems of large dimensions mainly problems from Data Mining, Pattern Recognition, and Artificial Intelligence fields. Indeed, the comparison of the *MMHCEDA* with the algorithms *BOA* and *EBNA* allows us to conclude that it is a competitive evolutionary optimization algorithm. Keeping in mind the nature of the chosen test functions, we conjecture that similar results will be obtained with many other classes of problems. The research reported here is just a first promising step and thus we continue working in this direction. We are currently developing a parallel version of the algorithm. Another line that we are already approaching is the creation of more efficient models of the learning type used in this report and consequently of new EDAs based on them.

References

1. Ding, C., Ding, L., Peng, W.: Comparison of effects of different learning methods on estimation of distribution algorithms. J. Softw. Eng. **9**(3), 451–468 (2015)
2. Gao, S., Qiu, L., Cao, C.: Solving 0–1 integer programming problem by estimation of distribution algorithms. J. Comput. Intell. Electr. Syst. **3**(1), 65–68 (2014)
3. Larrañaga, P., Lozano, J.A.: Estimation of Distribution Algorithms. A New Tool for Evolutionary Optimization. Kluwer Academic, Boston (2002)
4. Madera, J.: Hacia una Generación Eficiente de Algoritmos Evolutivos con Estimación de Distribuciones: Pruebas de (In)dependencia +Paralelismo. Ph.D. thesis, Instituto de Cibernética, Matemática y Física, La Habana. Adviser: A. Ochoa (2009). (in Spanish)
5. Ochoa, A.: Opportunities for expensive optimization with estimation of distribution algorithms. In: Tenne, Y., Goh, C.-K. (eds.) Computational Intelligence in Expensive Optimization Problems. ALO, vol. 2, pp. 193–218. Springer, Heidelberg (2010). https://doi.org/10.1007/978-3-642-10701-6_8
6. Ochoa, A., Soto, M.: Linking entropy to estimation of distribution algorithms. In: Lozano, J. A., Larrañaga, P., Inza, I., Bengoetxea, E. (eds.) Towards a New Evolutionary Computation: Advances in Estimation of Distribution Algorithms. STUDFUZZ, vol. 192, pp. 1–38. Springer, Heidelberg (2006). https://doi.org/10.1007/3-540-32494-1_1
7. Pelikan, M., Goldberg, D.E., Cantú-Paz, E.: BOA: the Bayesian optimization algorithm. In: Proceedings of the Genetic and Evolutionary Computation Conference GECCO-99, pp. 525–532. Morgan Kaufmann, San Francisco (1999)
8. Pérez-Rodríguez, R., Hernández-Aguirre, A.: An estimation of distribution algorithm-based approach for the order batching problem: an experimental study. In: Handbook of Research on Military, Aeronautical, and Maritime Logistics and Operations. IGI Global (2016)
9. Preetam, N., Hauser, A., Maathuis, M.H.: High-dimensional consistency in score-based and hybrid structure learning. arXiv preprint arXiv:1507.02608 (2018)
10. Scutari, M., Ness, R.: bnlearn: Bayesian network structure learning, parameter learning and inference. R package version 3 (2012)
11. Tsamardinos, I., Brown, L.E., Aliferis, C.F.: The max-min hill-climbing Bayesian network structure learning algorithm. Mach. Learn. **65**(1), 31–78 (2006)

Calcified Plaque Detection in IVUS Sequences: Preliminary Results Using Convolutional Nets

Simone Balocco[1,2], Mauricio González[1], Ricardo Ñanculef[3(✉)], Petia Radeva[1], and Gabriel Thomas[4]

[1] Department of Mathematics and Informatics, University of Barcelona, Barcelona, Spain
balocco.simone@gmail.com
[2] Computer Vision Center, Bellaterra, Spain
[3] Department of Informatics, Federico Santa María Technical University, Valparaíso, Chile
jnancu@inf.utfsm.cl
[4] Department of Computer Science, University of Manitoba, Winnipeg, Canada
gabriel.thomas@umanitoba.ca

Abstract. The manual inspection of intravascular ultrasound (IVUS) images to detect clinically relevant patterns is a difficult and laborious task performed routinely by physicians. In this paper, we present a framework based on convolutional nets for the quick selection of IVUS frames containing arterial calcification, a pattern whose detection plays a vital role in the diagnosis of atherosclerosis. Preliminary experiments on a dataset acquired from eighty patients show that convolutional architectures improve detections of a shallow classifier in terms of F_1-measure, precision and recall.

Keywords: Intravascular ultrasound images · Convolutional nets
Deep learning · Medical image analysis

1 Introduction

Intravascular ultrasound (IVUS) is a catheter-based imaging technique generally used during percutaneous interventions. An IVUS acquisition consists in a sequence of frames (pullback) that reproduce the internal vascular morphology. Despite the large amount of data in a pullback, physicians mainly focus on regions of the vessel characterized by clinically relevant observations (referred to as "clinical events") such as presence of stenosis, characterized by calcifications or lipid pools, indicating potential threats for the patient health (see Fig. 1). The quick identification of these regions is fundamental for the diagnosis and the clinically assisted intervention. The huge number of frames that need to be analyzed, makes this procedure extremely time-consuming.

© Springer Nature Switzerland AG 2018
Y. Hernández Heredia et al. (Eds.): IWAIPR 2018, LNCS 11047, pp. 34–42, 2018.
https://doi.org/10.1007/978-3-030-01132-1_4

Related Work. Several researchers have studied the automatic detection of clinical events in IVUS images using pattern recognition techniques. In [4], a first approach for the automatic detection of markers delimiting clinical events along the vessel (key frames) was proposed. The detection was based on the analysis of vessel morphological profiles extracted using supervised classifiers [5]. Then, the selection of key frames was obtained using the symbolic aggregate approXimation (SAX) algorithm. In another paper, [1], the automatic identification of vascular bifurcations was studied. The approach was based on a Random Forest classifier which computed textural descriptors along angular sectors of the image. In [3] a method for automated selection of vessel segments containing culprit and non-culprit frames was presented. The method uses the LOESS non-parametric regression method to analyze the distribution of atherosclerotic plaque burden. More recently, an approach for the detection of the boundaries and the position of the stent along the pullback has been proposed [2]. In such paper, the measure of likelihood for a frame to contain a stent is computed using a stacked sequential learning classification approach, in which specific stent features were designed [5]. Then, a the representation of the stent presence is obtained applying an iterative approximation of the signal using the SAX algorithm. The main limitation of these approaches is that they require careful design of handcrafted features, which is specific for each clinical event. In general, these features are costly effort to obtain and they are not sufficiently flexible to describe the complicated characteristics of some clinical events.

Contribution. We investigate a novel approach for IVUS sequence analysis based on convolutional neural nets (CNN). This technique is able to automatically learn the optimal set of features for the detection of a clinical event from a dataset where only one label per frame has been provided indicating the presence of the pattern. In this paper, the presence of arterial calcifications has been selected as a exemplar clinical event, since it play a major role in the atherosclerotic appearance and development [3–5]. Our contribution is hence a novel approach to automatically select the sections of a pullback which contain calcification and should be considered for a more detailed inspection. Our preliminary experiments using *in-vivo* image sequences acquired from eighty patients, show that convolutional architectures improve detections of a shallow classifier in terms of F_1-measure, precision and recall.

2   Methodology

We address the problem of selecting the frames in a pullback (X_ℓ) that are relevant for the presence arterial calcification. Our framework has three components depicted in Fig. 2. The first component implements a gating procedure that selects the most stable frames in the pullback, discarding images affected by artifacts due to the heart's contraction/expansion cycle [6]. The second component performs a frame-based analysis of the sequence, producing a temporal signal $(S_\ell) = (S_1, S_2, \ldots, S_L)$, where a high score $S_\ell \in [0, 1]$ indicates that relevant levels of calcification has been detected in X_ℓ, while a low score indicates that

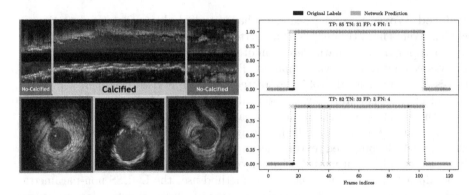

Fig. 1. Left: longitudinal view of an exemplar IVUS pullback having a section containing calcifications. Right: predictions obtained by the proposed pipeline, after step 2 (bottom) and after step 3 (top).

the frame is not relevant for calcification analysis. The last component performs a sequence-based refinement of the temporal signal (S_ℓ) which aims to increase its temporal consistency. As detailed below, these corrected scores are used to select the final set of frames using a optimized thresholding procedure.

To implement the first step of this framework, we use the method introduced by [6]. As for the other components, we adopt a supervised learning approach, that is, we assume that a dataset $D = \{(\boldsymbol{X}_\ell)_n\}$ of N pullbacks has been collected and annotated by an specialist. Ground-truth labels $T = \{(T_\ell)_n\}$ are assumed to be binary, that is, $T_{\ell,n} = 1$ if the frame ℓ of the n-th pullback has been annotated for the presence of calcified plaque and 0 otherwise.

2.1 CNN Classification of IVUS Pullbacks

2.1.1 Convolutional Neural Nets

Given an unknown function $f_0 : \mathbb{X} \to \mathbb{Y}$ that one needs to learn from data, neural networks implement a hypothesis $f : \mathbb{X} \to \mathbb{Y}$ that decomposes as the composition $f = f_1 \circ f_2 \circ \cdots f_M$ of more simple functions f_m referred to as layers. In classic feed-forward nets (FFNs), layers receive as input a vector $\boldsymbol{a}^{(m-1)}$ and compute as output a new feature vector implementing a map of the form $\boldsymbol{a}^{(m)} = g_m(\boldsymbol{W}^{(m)}\boldsymbol{a}^{(m-1)} + \boldsymbol{b}^{(m)})$, where $\boldsymbol{W}^{(m)}$ is a matrix and $g_m(\cdot)$ is a non-linear

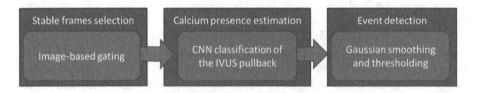

Fig. 2. Schematic representation of the frame selection technique.

function applied component-wise. Compared to FFNs, the early layers of a CNN allow new types of computation: convolution and pooling. Convolutional layers receive as input an image $A^{(m-1)}$ (or multi-dimensional array) and compute as output a new image $A^{(m)}$. The output at channel o is known as *a feature map*, and is computed as in Eq. (1), where $*$ denotes the (2-D) convolution operation, $b_o^{(m)} \in \mathbb{R}$ and $W_{ok}^{(m)}$ is matrix of shape $P_m \times Q_m$ parametrizing a spatial filter that the layer can learn from data to detect or enhance some feature in the incoming image.

$$A_o^{(m)} = g_m \left(\sum_k W_{ok}^{(m)} * A_k^{(m-1)} + b_o^{(m)} \right) . \tag{1}$$

Pooling layers of a CNN implement a spatial dimensionality reduction operation designed to reduce the number of trainable parameters for the next layers and allow them to focus on larger areas of the input pattern. A typical pooling layer with pool sizes $P_m, Q_m \in \mathbb{N}$ divides each channel of the input image into non-overlapping $P_m \times Q_m$ patches and substitute the values in that region by a single value determined by a using a compressing function.

Architecting a deep CNN stands for devising an appropriate succession of layers, as well as determining their hyper-parameters. Typical patterns introduce a pooling layer after one or two convolutional layers, repeating this convolutional block until the size of feature map is small enough to introduce traditional layers.

2.1.2 Training CNN-based Plaque Detectors

Given an annotated dataset for the presence of arterial calcification in IVUS images (for notation, see page 3), we can train frame-wise detectors using a network $f(X)$ which predicts the probability of an image X containing the pattern. This is achieved by using a fully connected output layer with a sigmoid neuron, i.e. a layer f_M implementing the transformation $a^{(M)} = \sigma(W^{(M)} a^{(M-1)} + b^{(M)})$ with $\sigma(\xi) = (1 + \exp(\xi))^{-1}$. The network's parameters Θ can thus be learnt to maximize the log-likelihood

$$J(\Theta) = - \sum_n \sum_\ell Q(T_{\ell,n}, f_\Theta(X_{\ell,n})), \tag{2}$$

where $Q(y, p) = -(1 - y)(1 - p) - yp$ is known as the *cross-entropy* loss.

The optimization of this objective function can be performed using back-propagation [8]. For deep networks, the success of this learning strategy heavily depends on the number and diversity of training instances. Since our dataset consists of few thousands of images, which is quite large for biomedical studies but probably insufficient for training deep nets, we need to enrich the dataset with data augmentation strategies. Concretely, since we expect a high rotational invariance of the calcified plaque detectors, we expanded the original dataset by randomly rotating each image in the range 0–360°. Each rotated image can also be flipped horizontally and vertically. To make this process memory-efficient, we do not expand the dataset before training, but perform the data augmentation operations stochastically during back-propagation learning.

To make the training process even more robust to overfitting, we train the CNN using Dropout [9], a regularization technique recently introduced to improve the generalization ability of deep nets. At each iteration of the learning process, an stochastic binary mask is applied to the output of each layer (each output feature map in the case of convolutional layers). In this way, the next layer is constrained to learn with incomplete information from the previous layer, preventing strong levels of co-adaptation between the feature detectors extracted by the net. To properly handle the stochasticity of the learning signals arising from the use of Dropout and dynamic data augmentation, we used back-propagation with momentum and the bias correction method proposed in [7].

2.2 Sequence-Based Analysis (Smoothing and Thresholding)

2.2.1 Smoothing

Classifying each frame in a pullback independently may be sub-optimal for accurate detection because it does not properly enforce consistenty of predicted labels over time. Ground-truth labels in contrast are temporally consistent, in the sense that the detection of the clinical pattern at time t significantly increases the probability of observing the pattern at times $t+1$ and $t-1$. Incorporating such prior knowledge into the system requires a sequence-based analysis that can be carried out in many different ways. In this paper, we explore the simplest and more efficient of these alternatives, namely, we smooth the probabilities resulting from the first step of our pipeline with a low-pass filter. Formally, if we denote by (S_ℓ) the sequence of predictions obtained by applying the CNN to the frames of a given pullback (X_ℓ), the second step of our pipeline is the sequence (S'_ℓ) obtained as $S'_\ell = \sum_{t=0}^{T-1} S_{\ell+t} K_{T-1-t}$, where (K_ℓ) is the sequence obtained by considering a discrete approximation of a Gaussian kernel with width σ. To obtain a sequence (S'_ℓ) of the same length as the input sequence, (S_ℓ) is first zero-padded conveniently.

2.2.2 Thresholding

The CNN used in our pipeline has been trained to minimize the cross-entropy loss, i.e. to approximate the posterior distribution over the set of labels. For binary classification problems, these probabilities typically translate into a decision by using the rule $Y(X) = I(f(X) \leq \theta)$ with $\theta = 0.5$, which is optimal when $f(X)$ is the true posterior and the classification accuracy is the metric to be optimized. However, in the context of pattern detection on IVUS data, two most frequent measures of performance are precision, recall, and F_1-measure which combines the first two into a single score using its harmonic mean. Compared to accuracy, F_1 increases only marginally as a function of the true negatives (cases correctly identified as not containing the pattern) giving much more relevance to true positives (cases correctly identified as containing the pattern). Unfortunately, training a neural net to directly maximize F-measure is much more difficult than optimizing the cross-entropy. To address this problem, we use here a simple heuristic which consists in choosing θ for a decision rule of the form $Y(\boldsymbol{X}) = I(f(\boldsymbol{X}) \leq \theta)$ in order to maximize the empirical F_1 measure on the training set. Though simple, this method has been found to be effective and is commonly applied in many scenarios such as document retrieval.

3 Materials, Experiments and Results

3.1 Materials

A set of IVUS pullbacks corresponding to 80 patients was collected at the *Germans Trias i Pujol Hospital* in Badalona (Spain), using an iLab echograph with a 40 MHz catheter and a pullback speed of 0.5 mm/s. The data acquisition protocol was approved by the IRB of each clinical center. After the gating procedure (see Sect. 2), obtained sequences were variable in length, with an average of 111.8 frames. A total of 8914 IVUS images were obtained. One expert manually annotated each image for the presence of calcification. The fraction of frames containing the pattern (positives) was 40.65%.

To assess the performance of the different methods, we used a pullback-based partition of the dataset into three disjoint subsets: a training set of 36 pullbacks (4024 images in average), a validation set of 8 pullbacks (1006 images in average) and a test set of 36 pullbacks. These sets were randomly drawn from the complete dataset. The performance measures reported in this section were obtained after 10 train/test splits. It is worth mentioning that a pullback-based partition of the dataset reproduces better the real-world scenario in which a whole new pullback of a patient never seen by the system is acquired and classified. Since a frame-based partition includes images from every patient in the training set, it may contain images of the new pullback, likely producing overly optimistic results.

3.2 Experiments

To assess the efficacy of the CNN used in our pipeline, we experimented with different architectures varying the number of convolutional blocks and filters in each layer. For space constraints we expose here some representative cases summarized in Table 1. The basic convolutional block consists of a convolutional layer with rectifier linear units followed by a max-pooling layer with pooling sizes 2×2 and strides 2×2. We fix the filter size of convolutional layers to 3×3 as preliminary experiments revealed that larger filters produced similar results. This convolutional block was repeated $M = 1, \ldots, 5$ times to obtained models of different depth. The output of the last block was directly passed to the output neuron. For networks of M blocks, the number of convolutional filters was halved every $\lfloor M/2 \rfloor$ layers to keep under control the expressive power of the model. This allowed to reduce the effect of overfitting in larger nets. Dropout was set to a conservative value of $q = 0.1$ (probability of dropping a neuron), except when overfitting issues were observed. Architectural decisions were always taken observing the performance on the training and validation sets.

Table 1. Number of convolutional blocks (M), convolutional filters (F) and total number of trainable parameters (P, K = thousands) in the different architectures.

Model	M F	P	q	Model	M F	P	q
CNN1[a]	1 16	63 K	0.1	CNN1[b]	1 32	127 K	0.1
CNN2[a]	2 64+32	47 K	0.1	CNN3[a]	3 64+32+32	34 K	0.1
CNN3[b]	3 64+64+32	62 K	0.1	CNN4[a]	4 32+32+16+16	17 K	0.1
CNN4[b]	4 64+64+32+32	66 K	0.1	CNN4[c]	4 64+64+32+32	66 K	0.4
CNN5[a]	5 64+64+32+32+16	70 K	0.4	(q = dropout rate, see text for details)			

Table 2. Average precision ($\bar{P}$), recall ($\bar{R}$) and F_1-measure ($\bar{F}_1$) computed among 10 train/test splits. Standard deviations are in parenthesis. For a single fold, the median among the sequences was computed to wave the effect of outliers.

Model (params)	Train			Test		
	$\bar{F}_1$	$\bar{P}$	$\bar{R}$	$\bar{F}_1$	$\bar{P}$	$\bar{R}$
SVM	0.84 (0.14)	0.87 (0.10)	0.83 (0.14)	0.38 (0.03)	0.40 (0.03)	0.58 (0.06)
CNN1[a] (63.665)	0.93 (0.01)	0.94 (0.02)	0.95 (0.02)	0.55 (0.04)	0.67 (0.09)	0.68 (0.08)
CNN1[b] (127.329)	0.81 (0.01)	0.81 (0.06)	0.89 (0.06)	0.61 (0.05)	0.67 (0.03)	0.91 (0.06)
CNN2[a] (47.905)	0.90 (0.02)	0.90 (0.04)	0.94 (0.04)	0.60 (0.03)	0.71 (0.06)	0.76 (0.09)
CNN3[a] (34.625)	0.89 (0.02)	0.92 (0.05)	0.91 (0.03)	0.64 (0.05)	0.78 (0.06)	0.80 (0.05)
CNN3[b] (62.305)	0.92 (0.03)	0.93 (0.05)	0.92 (0.03)	0.60 (0.05)	0.76 (0.11)	0.74 (0.11)
CNN4[a] (17.089)	0.90 (0.03)	0.90 (0.05)	0.93 (0.02)	0.61 (0.06)	0.72 (0.06)	0.82 (0.04)
CNN4[b] (66.433)	0.94 (0.01)	0.95 (0.03)	0.96 (0.01)	0.58 (0.07)	0.67 (0.08)	0.80 (0.05)
CNN4[c] (66.433)	0.87 (0.02)	0.86 (0.05)	0.91 (0.03)	0.65 (0.02)	0.77 (0.06)	0.81 (0.08)
CNN5[a] (70.385)	0.87 (0.02)	0.86 (0.05)	0.90 (0.03)	0.67 (0.04)	0.77 (0.08)	0.83 (0.09)

As mentioned before, we trained the nets using the adaptive stochastic gradient descent method proposed in [7], following author's recommendations to set the parameters. For simplicity, we used a fixed number of 100 SGD iterations (epochs). Parameters σ and θ used in steps 2 and 3 of our pipeline, were determined using a simple 100×100 grid search with a range of $[0.1, 8]$ for σ and $[0.1, 0.9]$ for θ, using the validation set. Statistics on the test set were observed only after the nets were selected and trained. Similarly, for the baseline, a linear SVM trained directly on the pixels of the IVUS images, the regularization parameter C was selected using a logarithmic grid search on the interval $[10^{-5}, 10^3]$ using the validation set to select the best values.

3.3   Results

Table 2 summarizes the average scores obtained by the different models, as well as their standard deviations (in parenthesis). All the CNNs improves on the baseline. The best result ($F_1 = 0.67$) is obtained using a CNN of 5 convolutional blocks, the deepest of the models considered in this paper[1]. This corresponds

---

[1] Note that an average F_1 score computed among 10 trials is not necessarily equal to $2(\bar{P}\bar{R})/(\bar{P} + \bar{R})$ where $\bar{P}$ is the average precision and $\bar{R}$ the average recall.

to an average precision of 77% at an average recall of 83%. A paired t-test showed statistically significant differences between this F_1-measure and all the others, excepting those of the models CNN4^c and CNN3^a with 4 and 3 layers respectively. Depth however is neither a necessary nor a sufficient condition for obtaining good performance. A model using only 1 convolutional block achieves a F_1 of 0.61, similar to the results obtained by models CNN4^a and CNN3^b and CNN2^a with 4, 3 and 2 convolutional layers respectively. On the other hand, a deep model (CNN4^b) achieves a F_1 of 0.58 well below the average. These results are explained by considering the small number of images that are available to train the models. Even if (see Table 1) an increase in depth does not necessarily translate into an increase of the number of parameters, it is often argued that the expressive power of a deep model increases exponentially in the number of layers, making it more prone to overfitting. Indeed, previous experiments (not reported due to space constraints) showed that deep nets trained without data-augmentation achieved high scores in the training set but poorer results in the test set. The use of augmented data helps to alleviate this problem, but it is no always enough. Indeed, the best and second best models (CNN5^a and CNN4^c) use levels of Dropout significantly more aggressive than the other models. Comparing CNN4^c with CNN4^b (whose F_1 is worse than that of shallower models), we can see that a strong level of regularization is necessary to avoid overfitting even using data-augmentation. Moreover, comparing CNN4^b with CNN4^a, we confirm that for using a deep model a reduction of the total number of parameters is a coarse, tough conceivable way to control overfitting in the case of as very small dataset as ours. Finally, it is interesting to point out that even if a shallow model can obtain acceptable performance, this is achieved at expenses of an increase in the number of parameters. For instance, model CNN1^a, which has a number of parameters similar to CNN5^a is among the worst models.

4   Conclusions

We have presented a framework based on convolutional nets for the automatic selection of frames in an IVUS pullback that are relevant for the presence of arterial calcification. This can help a physician to focus on a small subset of the large sequence of frames produced by a typical IVUS data acquisition. Our best results were obtained with a deep model of 5 convolutional layers which outperformed the baseline and shallower CNNs, obtaining an average F_1-measure of 0.67, precision of 0.77 and recall of 0.83. Overall, our experiments suggest that the use of deep architectures for IVUS data analysis is promising even if challenging, due to the scarcity of labelled data. Careful architecting, data augmentation and regularization were essential to obtain good results.

References

1. Alberti, M., et al.: Automatic bifurcation detection in coronary IVUS sequences. IEEE Trans. Biomed. Eng. **59**(4), 1022–1031 (2012)
2. Balocco, S., Ciompi, F., Rigla, J., Carrillo, X., Mauri, J., Radeva, P.: Intra-coronary stent localization in intravascular ultrasound sequences, a preliminary study. In: Cardoso, M., et al. (eds.) LABELS/CVII/STENT -2017. LNCS, vol. 10552, pp. 12–19. Springer, Cham (2017). https://doi.org/10.1007/978-3-319-67534-3_2
3. Chen, Z., et al.: Quantitative comparison of plaque in coronary culprit and non-culprit vessel segments using intravascular ultrasound. In: 17th MICCAI, pp. 28–35 (2014)
4. Ciompi, F., Pujol, O., Balocco, S., Carrillo, X., Mauri-Ferré, J., Radeva, P.: Automatic key frames detection in intravascular ultrasound sequences. In: 14th MICCAI, pp. 78–94 (2011)
5. Ciompi, F., et al.: Holimab: a holistic approach for media-adventitia border detection in intravascular ultrasound. Med. Image Anal. **16**(6), 1085–1100 (2012)
6. Gatta, C., Balocco, S., Ciompi, F., Hemetsberger, R., Leor, O.R., Radeva, P.: Real-time gating of IVUS sequences based on motion blur analysis: method and quantitative validation. In: Jiang, T., Navab, N., Pluim, J.P.W., Viergever, M.A. (eds.) MICCAI 2010. LNCS, vol. 6362, pp. 59–67. Springer, Heidelberg (2010). https://doi.org/10.1007/978-3-642-15745-5_8
7. Kingma, D.P., Ba, J.: Adam: a method for stochastic optimization. arXiv preprint arXiv:1412.6980 (2014)
8. LeCun, Y., et al.: Handwritten digit recognition with a back-propagation network. In: Advances in Neural Information Processing Systems, pp. 396–404 (1990)
9. Srivastava, N., Hinton, G., Krizhevsky, A., Sutskever, I., Salakhutdinov, R.: Dropout: a simple way to prevent neural networks from overfitting. J. Mach. Learn. Res. **15**(1), 1929–1958 (2014)

Multilayer-Based HMM Training to Support Bearing Fault Diagnosis

Jorge Fernández[1(✉)], Andrés Álvarez[1], H. Quintero[2], J. Echeverry[1], and Álvaro Orozco[1]

[1] Automatics Research Group, Pereira, Colombia
jorgeferram17@utp.edu.co
[2] Procesos de Manufactura y Diseño de Máquinas, Universidad Tecnológica de Pereira, Pereira, Colombia

Abstract. The bearings are among the most critical components in rotating machinery. For this reason, fault diagnosis in those elements is essential to avoid economic losses and human casualties. Traditionally, the automatic bearing fault diagnosis has been addressed by approaches based on Hidden Markov Models (HMM). However, the efficiency and reliability of the HMM-based diagnostic systems are still relevant topics for many researchers. In this paper, we present a modified training approach based on multilayer partition to support bearing fault diagnosis, that we called MHMM. The proposed strategy seeks to increase the system efficiency by reducing the number of HMM required to perform a proper diagnosis, making it more intelligent and suitable for this application. For concrete testing, the bearing fault databases from the Western Case Reserve University and the Politecnica Salesiana University were employed to assess the MHMM under a training and testing scheme. Attained results show that the proposed approach can effectively reduce the number of models required to perform the diagnosis while keeping high accuracy ratings when we compare the MHMM with the benchmarks. Also, the diagnosis process time is reduced as well.

Keywords: Computer science · Fault diagnosis
Multilayer partition · HMM · Maintenance

1 Introduction

Rolling bearings are among the most critical components in rotating machinery. Defects in those elements can lead to machine malfunction, sudden collapse, and others, which may cause economic losses and even human casualties. Thus, fault diagnosis in rolling bearing elements plays an essential role, as it allows to detect the fault degradation process and locate the damaged component within the machinery [4]. Nowadays, the methods of fault diagnosis have found important application, due to the extensive spread of condition-based maintenance technology (CBM) and preventive maintenance (PM). In many manufacturing

Y. Hernández Heredia et al. (Eds.): IWAIPR 2018, LNCS 11047, pp. 43–50, 2018.
https://doi.org/10.1007/978-3-030-01132-1_5

industries, the continuous upgrade and development of diagnostic methodologies have become a holistic interest of many researchers, who seek to increase productivity, reliability and to reduce maintenance costs [9]. For rotating machinery, the vibration signals measured by acceleration sensors can efficiently indicate the hallmark of the fault states [5]. Nevertheless, detecting damaged bearings by using their vibration signals is a difficult task, because the signature of a defective bearing is spread across a full frequency band, and can be easily masked by noise or low-frequency effects.

In the last decade, automatic fault detection and diagnosis has been addressed by statistical data-based approaches [2]. In pattern recognition, external sources originate problems such as uncertainty, randomness, and incompleteness. However, it is well known that stochastic models deal with these problems efficiently [8]. Therefore, among these stochastic models, the application of HMMs was motivated due to its robust mathematical structure and proven success to model stationary and non-stationary signals [3]. A well-known problem associated to the usage of HMM in diagnostic systems relies upon the high computational burden associated with these models, which makes the diagnostic process to take a lot of time [4, 7, 10]. Different approaches have been proposed to address this problem, Gao *et al.* [4] demonstrate that the selection of the HMM structure and parameter initialization have massive impact on the model accuracy and iteration speed. Hence, to pursue a fast diagnostic process, they focused on simplifying the HMM structure (i.e., to estimate the number of hidden states). Another approach was developed by Bicego *et al.* in [1], where the authors addressed the parameter selection by introducing a method called the *pruning strategy*. However, to solve this problem, the proposed approaches have never explored the database characteristics in order to reduce the number of models required to perform an adequate diagnosis. Which could make the diagnostic process more efficient as the number of models to train, and evaluate is shortened.

This paper presents a strategy to exploit the bearing fault databases characteristics, in order to make the HMM-based diagnostic systems more efficient, and speed up the diagnostic process, called Multilayer HMM-based diagnostic system. The proposed approach seeks to reduce the number of HMM required to perform a proper diagnosis, by being aware of the database structure, e.g., instead of modelling each bearing symptom (combination of fault and severity level), we model the bearing faults and the bearing severity levels separately. Resulting, in the number of models being a summation, instead of a multiplication; which can speed up the diagnostic process, as the system is more efficient. In turn, we recreate the state-of-the-art diagnostic systems based on HMM and GMM, and compare them to the proposed MHMM regarding accuracy and diagnostic process time. Attained results on the databases from the Western Case Reserve University and the Politecnica Salesiana University demonstrate that the proposed approach training and testing time is significantly lower than the HMM baseline. Therefore in applications where a fast diagnostic process is required, our approach outperforms both HMM and GMM benchmarks concerning the trade-off between time and accuracy.

The rest of the paper is organized as follows: Sect. 2 presents the framework of the proposed approach, Sect. 3 describes the experimental set-up, Sect. 4 experiments and results, and finally, Sect. 5 conclusions.

2 Framework of Modified Modelling Approach Based on Layer Partition for HMM-Based Diagnostic Systems

Let $\{\boldsymbol{Z}_n, y_n\}_{n=1}^N$ be the set holding N vibration signals segments $\boldsymbol{Z}_n \in \mathbb{R}^{W \times T}$, with W row windows $\boldsymbol{z}_{w,n} \in \mathbb{R}^T$ at T time instances ($w \in \{1, 2, \ldots, W\}$), and output labels $y_n \in \{c_{pd}\}$, where $p \in \{1, \ldots, P\}$, $d \in \{1, \ldots, D\}$. The classes c_{pd} are defined by pairing bearings in different health states with different operation conditions (e.g., degradation levels, loads, velocities, etc.). For all the provided windows $\boldsymbol{z}_{w,n}$, some meaningful features are computed to represent the hidden information from the raw data and enhance the discrimination among classes. These features are stored in the row vector $\boldsymbol{x}_{w,n} \in \mathbb{R}^M$ in order to create the feature set $\{\boldsymbol{X}_n, y_n\}_{n=1}^N$. Each sequence $\boldsymbol{X}_n \in \mathbb{R}^{W \times M}$ (being M the number of features extracted), are appropriately distributed according to the cross-validation technique k-folds splitting strategy, to train and test the diagnostic system fairly.

Multilayer Partition. From the resulting training split, the set $\{\boldsymbol{X}'_n, y_n\}_{n=1}^{N'}$, where $N' < N$ is generated. In this part, our proposed Multilayer partition is carried out. This stage aims to take advantage of the database construction to reduce the number of classes to be modelled with HMM. Let $c_{pd} = HS_p \cap OC_d$, where HS: health state and OC: operation condition, accordingly, the total number of classes be $C = P \times D$. As for each health state p there are D operation conditions. Instead of modelling each symptom separately, we are going to model in the first layer all the signals by their health state and in the second layer all signals by their operation condition. Resulting in an uncorrelated pair of sets: $\mathcal{H} = \{\boldsymbol{X}'_n, y_n^\dagger\}_{n=1}^{N'}$, where $y_n^\dagger \in \{1, \ldots, P\}$, and $\mathcal{O} = \{\boldsymbol{X}'_n, y_n^\star\}_{n=1}^{N'}$, where $y_n^\star \in \{1, \ldots, D\}$. Yielding a total of $L = P + D$ class arrangements to be modeled Due to the large number of samples, a Bag of words based down-sampling was considered to select a representative subset of signals for each arrangement. Next, For the reduced sets $\{\boldsymbol{X}'_n, y_n^{(\dagger,\star)}\}_{n=1}^{N_a}$ where $N_a < N'$, the best HMM $\boldsymbol{\lambda}_l^{(\dagger,\star)} = (\Theta, \boldsymbol{A}, \boldsymbol{\pi}, \boldsymbol{B})$ is trained.

Hidden Markov Models. Theoretically, a continuous HMM is a probabilistic sequence modeling tool that describes a stochastic process of $\boldsymbol{O} = O_1, O_2, \ldots, O_T$, with $O_t \in V$, where $V = \mathbb{R}^d$ (i.e., a continuous set of observation symbols), to be an indirect observation of an underlying random process of $\boldsymbol{Q} = Q_1, Q_2, \ldots, Q_T$ with $Q_t \in \Theta$, where $\Theta = \{\theta_1, \theta_2, \ldots, \theta_k\}$ (i.e., a set of hidden states) [1]. The underlying state sequence is assumed to evolve on the Markov process and the transition probability is represented in a matrix $\boldsymbol{A} \in \{A_{ij}\}$, $1 \leq i, j \leq k$, where $A_{ij} = P[Q_{t+1} = \theta_j | Q_t = \theta_i]$. For an HMM, observations are emitted from each state according to the emission probability density function $b(O|\theta_i)$, such that: $\int_V b(O|\theta_i) dO = 1$. In this application, the observations $O \in V$

are the row vectors $\boldsymbol{x}_{w,n}$ in matrix $\boldsymbol{X}'_n$, the emission probability $b(\boldsymbol{x}_{w,n}|\theta_i)$ is modelled as a mixture of Gaussians: $b(\boldsymbol{x}_{w,n}|\theta_i) = \sum_{j=1}^{U_i} c_{ij}\mathcal{N}(\boldsymbol{x}_{w,n}|\boldsymbol{\vartheta}_{i,j}, \boldsymbol{\Sigma}_{i,j})$, where $\mathcal{N}(\boldsymbol{x}_{w,n}|\cdot)$ denotes a Gaussian density with mean $\boldsymbol{\vartheta}_{i,j} \in \mathbb{R}^M$ and covariance $\boldsymbol{\Sigma}_{i,j} \in \mathbb{R}^{M \times M}$. The observations from state θ_i are modelled as samples from a Gaussian mixture with U_i components, with $c_{ij} \in [0,1]$ denoting the mixture weight of the jth component in state θ_i. We let $\boldsymbol{B}$ denote the set of all the mixture parameters (U_i's, $\boldsymbol{\vartheta}_{i,j}$'s and $\boldsymbol{\Sigma}_{i,j}$'s). Together with the initial state probability distribution $\boldsymbol{\pi} = \{\pi(\theta_i)\}$ where $\pi(\theta_i) = P[Q_1 = \theta_i]$ $1 \le i \le k$, an HMM can be represented by the tuple $\boldsymbol{\lambda} = (\Theta, \boldsymbol{A}, \boldsymbol{\pi}, \boldsymbol{B})$ [9].

Successively, an HMM can be trained for each arrangement and a model set $\Lambda = \{\hat{\boldsymbol{\lambda}}_l^{(\dagger,\star)} : l \in \{1,\ldots,L\}\}$ is obtained by adopting the maximum likelihood criterion [1], that is: $\hat{\boldsymbol{\lambda}}_l = \arg\max_{\boldsymbol{\lambda}} P(\boldsymbol{X}'_n|\boldsymbol{\lambda}); \forall\{\boldsymbol{X}'_n : y_n = l^{(\dagger,\star)}\}$. This procedure is known as HMM training. The best known way to implement it is the Baum-Welch algorithm [1]. Once every arrangement is modeled by an optimized HMM, the diagnosis step is carried out. Hence, The test split is conformed by the set $\{\boldsymbol{X}^*_n, y_n\}_{n=1}^{N^*}$, where $N^* < N$. Thus, given a new sequence $\boldsymbol{X}^*_n$, a MHMM-based classification rule is given by: $\hat{y}_n^{\dagger} = \arg\max_{l^{(\dagger)}} P(\boldsymbol{X}^*_n|\boldsymbol{\lambda}_l^{(\dagger)})$ and $\hat{y}_n^{\star} = \arg\max_{l^{(\star)}} P(\boldsymbol{X}^*_n|\boldsymbol{\lambda}_l^{(\star)})$. Finally, the estimated label with the proposed approach is given by: $\hat{y}_n = \hat{y}_n^{\dagger} \cap \hat{y}_n^{\star}$. In summary, Fig. 1. presents the stages for the proposed MHMM-based diagnostic system.

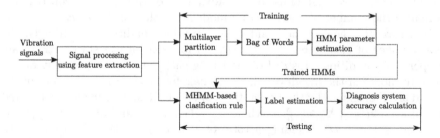

Fig. 1. Sketch of the proposed MHMM-based diagnostic system.

3   Experimental Set-Up

To test and evaluate the performance of the proposed diagnostic system (MHMM), we used the bearing fault vibration databases from the well-known *Western Case Reserve University*[1] (WC-DB) and from the *Politecnica Salesiana University* in Ecuador (PS-DB) [6]. In the WC-DB, the experiments were performed by a single bearing rig, in which various health states were tested under three different fault degradation levels, resulting in 40 signals of 10 s (approximately) from the accelerometer attached to the bearing housing drive end. On

---

[1] Available: https://csegroups.case.edu/bearingdatacenter/pages/download-data-file.

the other hand, in the PS-DB, the experiments were performed by a two bearing rig, in which different failure patterns (combination of bearings in different health states), as well as various velocities and loads, were tested, resulting in 630 signals of 20 s from both accelerometers placed on top of the bearing housings. For both databases, the experimental apparatus used to collect the data was similar and comprises accelerometers, bearings, data acquisition system (48 kHz and 50 kHz respectively), motor, shaft, inverter, tachometer, and flywheels.

Pre-processing and Feature Extraction. For both databases, the vibration signals were divided in segments of quasi-stationarity, i.e., segments of $\varrho = 4096$ points according to [6], generating the matrix $\mathbf{Q} \in \mathbb{R}^{N \times \varrho}$ holding $N \in \{4072, 19215\}$ vibration segments. Afterwards, each segment is divided in 7 time windows using a 1024 points long Hamming window with a 50% overlap, yielding $W = 7$. In each case, the labels are defined by a combination of the bearing health states and operation conditions, that is $C \in \{10, 21\}$ respectively. Finally the set $\{\mathbf{Z}_n, y_n\}_{n=1}^{N}$ is created. Besides, to demonstrate the robustness of our approach, we decided to compute two well-known feature extraction methods. (i) Multi-scale Fractal dimension: The MFD was used to characterize the nonlinear features from the bearing vibration signals. A more detailed explanation of the method is presented in [11]. Thus, we compute 25 MFD features with parameters maximum scale $\epsilon_{max} = 78$ and length of the moving window across scales $\mu = 6$, selected according to the specifications from the same author. (ii) Mel-Frequency Cesptral Coefficients: The MFCC were used to characterize both linear and nonlinear features from the bearing vibration signals. To compute these coefficients, we followed the steps presented in [10]. Consequently, we compute 12 MFC coefficients where the number of filters $R = 12$ was selected empirically. Following the feature extraction with each methodology, we obtained the feature matrix $\mathbf{X}_n \in \mathbb{R}^{W \times M}$ for each case, where $M \in \{25 \text{ MFD}, 12 \text{ MFCC}\}$, creating the set $\{\mathbf{X}_n, y_n\}_{n=1}^{N}$.

MHMM Training. For each database, the number of class arrangements was $L \in \{7, 10\}$, standing for: 4 health states and 3 degradation levels in the first DB and 7 failure patterns and 3 different loads in the second DB. The HMM structure (i.e., the number of states and mixtures) was selected according to the *pruning strategy*, yielding: $k = 2$ and $U_i = 1$, respectively. The validation of the proposal was made by calculating the classifier performance in terms of accuracy and diagnostic process time. Furthermore, the classification accuracy was generated by a 10-fold cross-validation scheme.

As baseline, diagnostic systems based on GMM, [7], and HMM, [8], were used as well to model each class in the database. For the GMM topology, we used three centers according to specifications from the same author. The following experiments were performed using the Matlab software on a Lenovo Y50-70 notebook equipped with a graphics core NVIDIA GEFORCE GTX 960M and an Intel processor Core i7-4710HQ. The HMM toolbox was developed by Murphy *et al.* and is available online[2].

---

[2] http://www.cs.ubc.ca/~murphyk/Bayes/PreMIT/hmm.html.

4   Results and Discussions

In Fig. 2 we present an example of the feature extraction methodologies for a row window $z_{w,n}$. This figure illustrates the windowed characterization from signals of the WC-DB. However, to show all windows in the same figure, the mean and standard deviation through the columns of X_n are presented instead. To create Table 1, we use the WC-DB. This experiment shows the tendency of our approach to reduce the training and testing time of the diagnostic system, due to the parallel computation of the HMMs, i.e., uncorrelated pair of sets (See Sect. 2). While, keeping a competitive accuracy. On the other hand, we used the Bag of words algorithm to select a representative subset of samples for training. In columns 4 and 5 shows the cross-validation results for training HMMs with a subset of 100 and 200 signals per class respectively. A larger number of samples per class for training does not affect the diagnostic systems in terms of accuracy. Whereas, the computation time for the training stage increased considerably. To create Table 2, we use the PS-DB. In this case, the number of classes $C = 21$, yielding $L = 10$. As seen, the model training time demanded for our approach was the lowest in every configuration, while being able to keep the accuracy within acceptable boundaries. From the results of this dataset, the most critical combination is MFD + Accelerometer 2. Therefore, the confusion matrices from the baseline (HMM) and the proposed approach (MHMM) are presented in Fig. 3. From the matrices, the MFD characterization does not enhance the discrimination among symptoms good enough. Specifically, the failure patterns 4 (Bearing 1 with ball fault and Bearing 2 healthy), and 7 (Bearing 1 with outer race fault and Bearing 2 ball fault) are hard to classify from the vibration signals of Accelerometer 2. On the other hand, is hard for the system to classify the operation conditions 2 (1 flywheel) and 3 (2 flywheels). As seen, our approach can keep high accuracy with low variability in the cross-validation scheme, as the computational time decreases, resulting in a methodology suitable to diagnose bearings symptoms through their vibration signal.

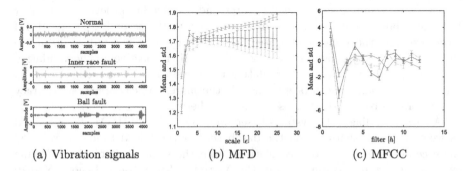

(a) Vibration signals   (b) MFD   (c) MFCC

Fig. 2. Feature extraction from some vibration signals. 2(a) shows some bearing vibration signals, 2(b) and (c) show the mean and standard deviation of the computed windowed feature extraction.

Table 1. Diagnosis performance from different probabilistic modelling tools and configurations in the data base form the *Western University*, as well as the diagnosis process time.

Modeling Tool	Feature extraction	Number of models	C = 10 (100 signals per class for training)			C = 10 (200 signals per class for training)		
			ACC [%]	Training time [s]	Testing time [s]	ACC [%]	Training time [s]	Testing time [s]
GMM	MFD	10	90.79 ± 1.04	6.5 ± 2.2	0.6 ± 0.1	90.57 ± 1.33	6.4 ± 2.2	0.5 ± 0.1
HMM		10	97.35 ± 0.72	29.7 ± 6.3	3.1 ± 0.1	97.64 ± 0.89	54.7 ± 16.1	2.7 ± 0.2
MHMM		7	**90.31 ± 2.19**	**13.2 ± 8.1**	**1.3 ± 0.1**	**90.83 ± 1.66**	**26.0 ± 4.2**	**1.2 ± 0.1**
GMM	MFCC	10	99.23 ± 0.29	2.8 ± 0.2	0.5 ± 0.1	99.18 ± 0.29	2.8 ± 0.2	0.5 ± 0.1
HMM		10	99.85 ± 0.17	29.5 ± 7.7	2.5 ± 0.4	99.85 ± 0.13	48.3 ± 11.2	2.3 ± 0.2
MHMM		7	**99.41 ± 0.52**	**18.2 ± 7.9**	**1.0 ± 0.3**	**99.29 ± 0.57**	**40.1 ± 22.2**	**1.1 ± 0.1**

Table 2. Diagnosis performance from different probabilistic modelling tools and configurations in the PS-DB, as well as the diagnosis process time.

Modeling Tool	Feature extraction	Number of models	C = 21 Accelerometer 1			C = 21 Accelerometer 2		
			ACC [%]	Training time [s]	Testing time [s]	ACC [%]	Training time [s]	Testing time [s]
GMM	MFD	21	67.51 ± 1.22	104.1 ± 28.8	7.6 ± 0.8	49.17 ± 0.84	106.5 ± 32.7	8.2 ± 1.0
HMM		21	98.13 ± 0.34	48.1 ± 6.6	29.8 ± 3.5	82.88 ± 0.98	50.3 ± 9.0	30.6 ± 3.4
MHMM		10	**94.56 ± 0.90**	**33.3 ± 5.8**	**14.7 ± 2.4**	**67.91 ± 2.13**	**42.3 ± 6.7**	**14.9 ± 2.8**
GMM	MFCC	21	94.95 ± 0.21	23.1 ± 5.3	5.2 ± 1.1	93.57 ± 0.36	21.2 ± 4.8	4.7 ± 0.5
HMM		21	99.26 ± 0.34	33.0 ± 5.6	23.4 ± 1.6	99.20 ± 0.26	29.4 ± 3.5	25.1 ± 2.0
MHMM		10	**95.48 ± 1.03**	**22.8 ± 17.3**	**12.9 ± 2.5**	**96.87 ± 0.61**	**20.1 ± 7.1**	**13.0 ± 1.5**

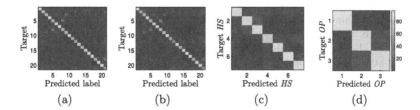

(a)　　　　(b)　　　　(c)　　　　(d)

Fig. 3. Confusion matrices. In 3(a) is shown the CM of the HMM + MFD validation. In 3(b) is shown the CM of the MHMM + MFCC. In 3(c) and (d) is shown the validation of the Multilayer partition.

5   Conclusions

A multilayer-based HMM training approach is introduced to support bearing fault diagnosis (MHMM). Our approach takes advantage of the databases characteristics to reduce the number of HMM from multiplication to a sum of the number of health states and conditions, to perform the diagnosis. Therefore, the proposed MHMM is more efficient than the conventional HMM-based system, as it requires fewer models to achieve a proper diagnosis, allowing to speed up the diagnosis process. Attained results on the well-known WC-DB and the private SP-DB, demonstrated that our proposal outperforms state-of-art results concerning the trade-off between the accuracy achieved and the diagnostic process time. As future work, authors plan to use feature selection/embedding to combine the multiple characterization techniques, to increase the classification performance of the proposed MHMM-based diagnostic system.

Acknowledgments. Under grants provided by the project 1110-669-46074 funded by Colciencias. Also, J. Echeverry is supported by the project 6-16-4, funded by the VIIE-Universidad Tecnologica de Pereira.

References

1. Bicego, M., Murino, V., Figueiredo, M.A.: A sequential pruning strategy for the selection of the number of states in hidden Markov models. Pattern Recognit. Lett. **24**(9–10), 1395–1407 (2003)
2. Boutros, T., Liang, M.: Detection and diagnosis of bearing and cutting tool faults using hidden Markov models. Mech. Syst. Signal Process. **25**(6), 2102–2124 (2011)
3. Gao, Y., Villecco, F., Li, M., Song, W.: Multi-scale permutation entropy based on improved LMD and HMM for rolling bearing diagnosis. Entropy **19**(4), 176 (2017)
4. Gao, Y., Xie, N., Hu, K., Zhu, Y., Wang, L.: An optimized clustering approach using simulated annealing algorithm with HMM coordination for rolling elements bearings' diagnosis. J. Fail. Anal. Prev. **17**(3), 602–619 (2017)
5. Khorasani, A.M., Littlefair, G., Goldberg, M.: Time domain vibration signal processing on milling process for chatter detection. J. Mach. Form. Technol. **6**(1/2), 45 (2014)
6. Li, C., Sánchez, R.V., Zurita, G., Cerrada, M., Cabrera, D.: Fault diagnosis for rotating machinery using vibration measurement deep statistical feature learning. Sensors **16**(6), 895 (2016)
7. Marwala, T.: Condition Monitoring Using Computational Intelligence Methods: Applications in Mechanical and Electrical Systems. Springer, London (2012). https://doi.org/10.1007/978-1-4471-2380-4
8. Sadhu, A., Prakash, G., Narasimhan, S.: A hybrid hidden Markov model towards fault detection of rotating components. J. Vib. Control. **23**(19), 3175–3195 (2017)
9. Yu, J.: Adaptive hidden Markov model-based online learning framework for bearing faulty detection and performance degradation monitoring. Mech. Syst. Signal Process. **83**, 149–162 (2017)
10. Zhai, G., Chen, J., Li, C., Wang, G.: Pattern recognition approach to identify loose particle material based on modified MFCC and HMMs. Neurocomputing **155**, 135–145 (2015)
11. Zhang, P.L., Li, B., Mi, S.S., Zhang, Y.T., Liu, D.S.: Bearing fault detection using multi-scale fractal dimensions based on morphological covers. Shock. Vib. **19**(6), 1373–1383 (2012)

Predictive Model for Specific Energy Consumption in the Turning of AISI 316L Steel

Dagnier-Antonio Curra-Sosa[1](✉), Roberto Pérez-Rodríguez[1], and Ricardo Del-Risco-Alfonso[2]

[1] CAD/CAM Study Center, University of Holguín, 80100 Holguín, Cuba
dcurra85@gmail.com
[2] CEEFREP, University of Camagüey, 70400 Camagüey, Cuba

Abstract. This article presents an approach for the simulation of machining operations through Artificial Intelligence, which guarantees an automatic learning of the distinctive features in the processes of metal cutting. In the research, an Artificial Neural Network was designed, which establishes the relationships between the parameters of cutting regime and the technological indexes of machining, based on the information generated in real experimentation. For the conception of suitable cutting strategies, the following magnitudes were considered for the input of the model: lubrication regime, cutting speed, feed rate and machining time; which determined the behavior of the cutting forces in the turning of the AISI 316L steel, in order to obtain the cutting powers that define the specific energy consumption. Several designs were considered according to the features of Multi-Layer Perceptron architecture and the selected model was evaluated according to the mean square error and the regression coefficient R^2, reflecting high precision in the approximation. The deviation for the error made in the estimation of the cutting force values represents approximately 2% of the average value. These results showed a good level of reliability in the prediction of energy consumption under various machining conditions, in order to adopt relevant saving measures.

Keywords: Specific energy consumption · Turning · AISI 316L steel
Predictive model · Artificial neural network

1 Introduction

The demand for high quality mechanical components, high accuracy and shorter delivery times for high performance systems has increased considerably in recent years worldwide. This fact has led to the development of new technologies applied to machining processes [1]. The energy consumption and the efficiency of processes constitute a matter of great importance for the universities and industry, for which it is necessary that the international organizations have sustainable strategies, that support the decision-making and contribute to mitigate the high prices in energy production and associated environmental problems.

© Springer Nature Switzerland AG 2018
Y. Hernández Heredia et al. (Eds.): IWAIPR 2018, LNCS 11047, pp. 51–58, 2018.
https://doi.org/10.1007/978-3-030-01132-1_6

There is a growing social commitment towards the development of manufacturing systems and strategies with a minimum environmental impact that allows the application of sustainable manufacturing. Preliminary environmental studies for machine-tools in material removal processes (for example: turning, milling, etc.) indicate that more than 99% of the environmental impacts are due to the consumption of electrical energy [2, 3]. Therefore, the reduction of the electric power consumption of the manufacturing processes not only economically benefits the manufacturers but also improves their environmental performance.

Some of the problems that arise in the machining process are related to the lack of data and appropriate models. This situation is exacerbated by the continuous development and introduction of new tools and work materials, as well as changes in machining conditions [4]. In several investigations have been referenced to the computational methods that respond to Machine Learning, and especially, to Artificial Neural Networks (ANN), as non-linear prediction instruments, in the forecasting of indexes based on having databases that characterize the modeled phenomenon.

Among the most used architectures, the Multi-Layer Perceptron (MLP) has proved to be adequate in inference with a high level of precision, as demonstrated [5] when modeling the constitutive flow behavior of stainless austenitic steel under hot deformation. Other more recent results were provided by [6] when modeling the thrust forces in the drilling of AISI 316, [7] in the prediction of cutting conditions in CNC lathes, [8] study the effect of design variables on the measures calculated for sustainable operational machining, [9] model the power consumed in the turning of brass and aluminium, and [10] evaluates the effect of the time-controlled pulse on the roughness of the surface for turning with Minimum Quantity Lubrication (MQL).

From this background, in the research a predictive model was obtained for the Specific Energy Consumption (SEC) in the turning of a stainless steel AISI 316L, based on ANN of the MLP type. For this purpose, it was necessary to investigate the effect of the cut conditions that constituted the inputs of the network formed by a hidden layer with 20 neurons and trained by the Levenberg-Marquardt backpropagation algorithm.

2 Materials and Methods

In this machining process it was considered to use a ceramic cutting tool RNGN 120700E004 JX1 without coating, 12.7 mm in diameter and 7.94 mm in thickness. This selection is attributed to its novelty in the market and be designed to machine heat-resistant alloys in addition to the interest generated in the evaluation of its behavior. In the turning operation for which this tool is intended, a CNC lathe HAAS ST-10 with a maximum capacity of 356×406 mm, 11.2 kW of power and 6000 rpm in the spindle, that meets the characteristics of the work regime, was used according to the values of cutting speed and feed rate (see Fig. 1), in addition to the necessary technical parameters.

An experiment with 3 replicas (54 tests) based on dry and MQL turning operations of a bar of 25 mm in diameter and 100 mm in length was developed, varying the cutting speed in 3 levels (200 m/min, 300 m/min, 400 m/min), the feed rate in 3 levels

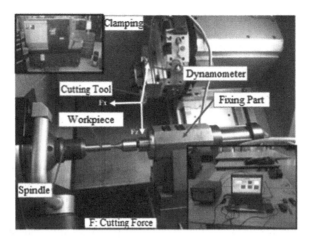

Fig. 1. Experimental station.

(0.1 mm/rev, 0.15 mm/rev, 0.2 mm/rev) and a constant cutting depth of 0.5 mm. The measurements of the force values are made every 0.003 s by the Kistler 9257B dynamometer mounted on the clamping tool, which were then processed through a 5070 multichannel load amplifier connected to a PC, using a program for the data acquisition made on LabVIEW.

In this cutting process, it is necessary to find the dependence between the cutting forces and the parameters of the cutting regime as independent variables, through an ANN that represents this functional relationship. The values of these variables allow obtaining the power consumption of the machine-tools, which is determined by the energy consumption of the spindle system. SEC represents the rate of energy consumed when removing 1 cm^3 of material and to obtain it, is necessary to calculate the cutting powers and the material removal rate through the formulas in [11]:

$$N = \frac{1000 * v_c}{\pi * D} \tag{1}$$

$$T = \frac{L}{N * f} \tag{2}$$

$$SEC = \frac{E_c}{V} = \frac{\int P_i(t)dt}{\int MRR(t)dt} = 60 * \frac{\int (P_c(t) + P_u(N) + P_{ad}(t))dt}{a_{sp} * f * v_c * T} \tag{3}$$

where N denotes the spindle speed, v_c the cutting speed and D the bar diameter in (1). T is the experiment duration, L the bar length and f the feed rate in (2). E_c represents the energy consumed by the spindle system, V the volume of material removed, $P_i(t)$ the input power of the spindle system, $MRR(t)$ the material removal rate, $P_c(t)$ the cutting power of the machining process, $P_u(N)$ the idle power, $P_{ad}(t)$ the additional load loss of the spindle system, a_{sp} the depth of cut and t the machining time in (3). In (4), (5) and (6) the functions $P_c(t)$, $P_u(N)$ y $P_{ad}(t)$ are determined by $F_x(t), F_y(t)$ and $F_z(t)$ as the values of directional cutting force that will be estimated by the neural network designed.

$$P_c(t) = F_c(t) * \frac{v_c}{60} = \sqrt{F_x^2(t) + F_y^2(t) + F_z^2(t)} * \frac{v_c}{60} \tag{4}$$

$$P_u(N) = 1.573 * N + 98 \tag{5}$$

$$P_{ad}(t) = 3 * 10^{-6} * P_c^2(t) + 0.1939 * P_c(t) \tag{6}$$

From the experimental tests, by cutting an austenitic stainless steel that according to the AISI-SAE standard is 316L and whose composition to be used as a biomedical material is established by ASTM F138 standard, records of the parameters of the cutting regime constituted by the values of cutting speed, feed rate and machining time for each lubrication regime was generated in the period of time where the values of cutting forces remain stable with the minimum presence of outliers (see Table 1).

Table 1. Parameters of cutting regime.

Lubrication regime	Cutting speed (m/min)	Feed rate (mm/rev)	Machining time (msec)
MQL/Dry	200	0.1	4001 values
		0.15	2701 values
		0.2	1905 values
	300	0.1	3000 values
		0.15	2500 values
		0.2	1900 values
	400	0.1	1900 values
		0.15	2000 values
		0.2	2000 values

The software used for the processing was MatLab, due to its strengths as a high level programming language with graphic capabilities and to be an interactive environment in the design and exploration of computer models, specifically, those of Machine Learning [12]. The records that are introduced to MatLab constitute tuples formed by the 4 independent variables that represent the parameters of the cutting regime and the 3 dependent variables for the directional cutting forces, as follows:

$$(r_l, v_c, f, t, F_x, F_y, F_z) \tag{7}$$

where r_l denotes the lubrication regime. In correspondence with the wide variety of ANN applications, there are several architectures oriented to the modeling of particular phenomena that require estimation, classification, clustering and forecasting among others. In the case at hand, an MLP type network is used due to its potential in the adjustment of functions. For this, several designs were considered, according to the features of Table 2 that determine their performance:

Table 2. Choices for the design of ANN.

Features	Choices
Number of hidden layers	1 or 2 hidden layers
Number of neurons in the hidden layer(s)	10, 15 or 20 neurons
Transfer functions of neurons in hidden layer(s)	Sigmoid hyperbolic tangent, logarithmic sigmoid
Transfer functions of neurons in output layer	Poslin, Purelin, Softmax
Performance function	Mean Squared Normalized Error, Mean absolute error
Division of the sample for training, validation and testing	{0.6;0.2;0.2}, {0.7;0.2;0.1}, {0.7;0.15;0.15}
Selection of records for training, selection and testing	Random, organized
Training algorithm	Levenberg-Marquardt backpropagation, scaled conjugated gradient

3   Results and Discussions

In the experimentation, most of the possible combinations were considered, as options were discarded due to the poor performance they showed, from identifying in each of these, the best of 10 neural networks obtained with the same initial conditions. It was decided to use a network composed of an input layer with 4 neurons, a hidden layer with 20 neurons and in the output layer 3 neurons as shown in Fig. 2. The transfer functions in the neurons that showed the best results were the Tangent Sigmoid Hyperbolic in the hidden layer and Purelin in the output layer. Although both performance functions offer similar results, the Mean Squared Normalized Error is considered to be more sensitive to the presence of outliers that may appear in the force values due to the work environment.

The 43 814 records distributed as shown in Table 1 were divided into the proportion 60%, 20% and 20% for the training, validation and testing processes respectively; having the lowest value of the approach error than the other two variants. With this division, the random selection was discarded and the organized selection was considered in which, for every 5 consecutive records, 3 of these randomly chosen are taken for training, another one for validation and the last one for the test. With this strategy the learning of the network was more effective. For training, was selected as a supervised algorithm, the Levenberg-Marquardt backpropagation due to a better performance on its counterpart in terms of speed and adaptability.

From several workouts of the selected network architecture, Fig. 3 shows the level of adjustment to the values of the Real Cutting Force (RCF) to the Estimated Cutting Force (ECF) by means of the regression coefficient R, specifying a 99% accuracy. The

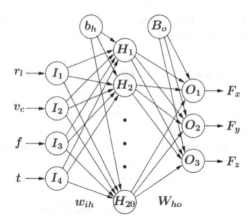

Fig. 2. Multi-layer perceptron architecture.

smallest value obtained from the error function is approximately 47.5832 which means that the deviation for the error made in the estimation of the cutting force values is 6.8981 which represents approximately 2% of the average value.

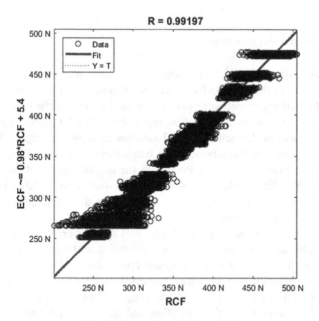

Fig. 3. Regression RCF vs ECF.

In addition to the proximity of the estimated values obtained by the ANN to the real values (see Fig. 4), the trends of this machining operation are confirmed, where the feed rate is decisive in the SEC through the inverse relationship that characterizes it and the slight increase in the values of SEC in the dry cut as shown in Table 3. At this point it is important to emphasize the practical utility of these models in obtaining the engineer's technical notes, so that he/she has an instrument that will support him in the decision-making process regarding the adequate work regime in order to optimize the use of resources and technologies available in their work environment.

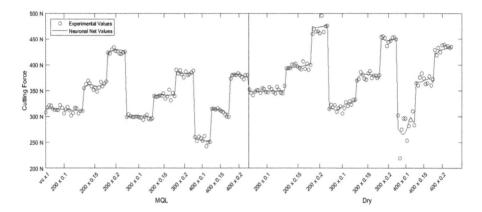

Fig. 4. Experimental values vs neural network values.

Table 3. Experimental SEC and estimated SEC.

Lubrication regime	Cutting speed (m/min)	Feed rate (mm/rev)	Experimental SEC (J/cm^3)	Estimated SEC (J/cm^3)
MQL	200	0.1	32 124 ± 10.3469	32 126 ± 3.2371
		0.15	22 163 ± 10.7764	22 162 ± 4.4847
		0.2	17 434 ± 10.387	17 433 ± 2.5983
	300	0.1	31 612 ± 10.9251	31 612 ± 2.6617
		0.15	21 737 ± 8.0072	21 737 ± 1.4845
		0.2	16 812 ± 11.0832	16 814 ± 2.9042
	400	0.1	30 423 ± 22.1497	30 422 ± 9.0603
		0.15	21 192 ± 15.2873	21 190 ± 8.5544
		0.2	16 722 ± 8.699	16 723 ± 3.9225
Dry	200	0.1	32 976 ± 9.659	32 976 ± 1.5757
		0.15	22 746 ± 11.2969	22 743 ± 4.765
		0.2	17 991 ± 21.4675	17 993 ± 3.0655
	300	0.1	32 097 ± 26.9352	32 100 ± 16.3696
		0.15	22 346 ± 15.3537	22 344 ± 5.704
		0.2	17 596 ± 17.1353	17 596 ± 3.0117
	400	0.1	31 051 ± 89.1983	31 032 ± 48.8941
		0.15	22 133 ± 21.6529	22 132 ± 6.6294
		0.2	17 324 ± 15.1823	17 322 ± 7.4933

4 Conclusions

The article described the instruments used in the experimentation as well as the information obtained regarding the parameters of the cutting regime and the technological indexes of machining considered. The modeling in MatLab is based on the supervised learning algorithms that it implements and among these, an MLP type ANN is designed for the functional adjustment between the considered variables, where the best configuration in terms of performance according to its features is evaluated. The results obtained showed a high precision in the estimation of the cutting force, an aspect that is evident in the values of performance indexes such as the mean square error and the R-adjustment. This allowed obtaining the values of the SEC for each one of the selection variants in the parameters of the cutting rate. Therefore, the predictive model is adequate in terms of energy savings, which help to mitigate the negative consequences caused by the emission of CO_2 into the atmosphere.

References

1. Grzesik, W.: Advanced Machining Processes of Metallic Materials: Theory, Modelling and Applications. Elsevier, New York City (2008). http://www.elsevier.com/wps
2. Kara, S., Li, W.: Unit process energy consumption models for material removal processes. CIRP Ann. Manuf. Technol. **60**, 37–40 (2011)
3. Dornfeld, A.: Moving towards green and sustainable manufacturing. Int. J. Precis. Eng. Manuf. Green Technol. **1**, 63–66 (2014)
4. Arsecularatne, J., Zhang, L., Montross, C.: Wear and tool life of tungsten carbide, PCBN and PCD cutting tools. Int. J. Mach. Tools Manuf. **46**(2), 482–491 (2006)
5. Mandal, S., Sivaprasad, P., Venugopal, S., Murthy, K.: Constitutive flow behaviour of austenitic stainless steel under hot deformation: artificial neural network modelling to understand, evaluate and predict. Modell. Simul. Mater. Sci. Eng. **14**, 1053–1070 (2006)
6. Çiçek, A., Kivak, T., Samtas, G., Çay, Y.: Modelling of thrust forces in drilling of AISI 316 stainless steel using artificial neural network and multiple regression analysis. J. Mech. Eng. **58**, 492–498 (2012)
7. Ahilan, C., Kumanan, S., Sivakumaran, N., Dhas, J.: Modeling and prediction of machining quality in CNC turning process using intelligent hybrid decision making tools. Appl. Soft Comput. **13**(3), 1543–1551 (2013)
8. Koyee, R., Heisel, U., Eisseler, R., Schmauder, S.: Modeling and optimization of turning duplex stainless steels. J. Manuf. Process. **16**, 451–467 (2014)
9. Phate, M., Toney, S.: Formulation of artificial neural network based model for the dry machining of ferrous and non-ferrous materials used in Indian small scale industries. Int. J. Mater. Sci. Eng. **4**(3), 145–160 (2016)
10. Mia, M., et al.: Effect of time-controlled MQL pulsing on surface roughness in hard turning by statistical analysis and artificial neural network. Int. J. Adv. Manuf. Technol. **91**, 3211–3223 (2017)
11. Xie, J., Liu, F., Qiu, H.: An integrated model for predicting the specific energy consumption of manufacturing processes. Int. J. Adv. Manuf. **85**, 1339–1346 (2016)
12. Paluszek, M., Thomas, S.: MATLAB Machine Learning. Apress, New Jersey (2017)

Training Neural Networks by Continuation Particle Swarm Optimization

Jairo Rojas-Delgado$^{(\boxtimes)}$ⓘ and Rafael Trujillo-Rasúaⓘ

Universidad de las Ciencias Informáticas, Havana, Cuba
{jrdelgado,trujillo}@uci.cu

Abstract. Artificial Neural Networks research field is among the areas of major activity in Artificial Intelligence. Conventional training approaches applied to neural networks present several theoretical and computational limitations. In this paper we propose an approach for Artificial Neural Network training based on optimization by continuation and Particle Swarm Optimization algorithm. The objective is to reduce overall execution time of training without causing negative effects in accuracy. Our proposal is compared with Standard Particle Swarm Optimization algorithm using public benchmark datasets. Experimental results show that the optimization by continuation approach reduces execution time required to perform training in about 20%−50% without statistically significant loss of accuracy.

Keywords: Continuation · Optimization · Neural-network · Training

1 Introduction

Artificial Neural Networks (ANNs) are widely used in common applications of image recognition [25], signal processing [21], speech [15] and several other fields. A neural network is trained through the minimization of a surface generated by its set of parameters and an output error obtained by feeding the network with a set of training patterns. The most popular algorithm for training is Stochastic Gradient Descent (SGD) which is a gradient based first order method that has been proven to converge into local minima in the parameter space.

The recent introduction of deep neural networks [9] have raised several difficulties from a theoretical and practical point of view. The error surface of a deep neural network is highly non-convex [13] and presents a poor correspondence between its local and global structure [9]. Also, the number of local minima increases exponentially respect to the number of parameters of the network. In fact, such local minima appear to be saddle points instead of true minima [8] causing a diminution of the convergence speed of optimization, specially for gradient based training algorithms. In general, second-order methods have not obtained better results than first-order methods in this area [9].

© Springer Nature Switzerland AG 2018
Y. Hernández Heredia et al. (Eds.): IWAIPR 2018, LNCS 11047, pp. 59–67, 2018.
https://doi.org/10.1007/978-3-030-01132-1_7

Additionally, first and second order optimization methods require the calculation of derivatives and Hessians for which Automatic Reverse Mode Differentiation (ARMD) have to be used [10]. The parallelization of such methods faces important challenges due to the inherent sequential nature of ARMD.

In recent years, several meta-heuristic algorithms for optimization have been actively used in ANN training. Meta-heuristic algorithms provide features to escape local minima and increase the probability of global convergence. In the literature there are reports of nature-inspired meta-heuristics such as Cuckoo Search [4,23], Firefly Algorithm [11,19], Wolf Search Optimization [1,18], Particle Swarm Optimization (PSO) [3,5] and others.

For current applications, the rule of thumb to obtain higher accuracy have been to increase not only the number of parameters of ANNs but also the amount of training patterns mainly because over-fitting [6,14]. In this scenario, the use of meta-heuristic algorithms is limited by the increased computational complexity of the fitness function evaluation. Additionally, state-of-the-art meta-heuristic algorithms are population based and the fitness function is evaluated for each solution in the population. Hence, a reduction in the computational complexity of the fitness function is of paramount importance.

In this work, we present an approach for ANN training based on optimization by continuation and PSO algorithm. The continuation method heuristic is an optimization approach that aims to start solving an easy problem and progressively change it to the actual complex task [17]. Experimental results show that the optimization by continuation approach reduces execution time required to perform training in about 20%−50% without statistically significant loss of accuracy.

The paper is structured as follows: in Sect. 2 we present some insights on continuation methods and introduce an algorithm to train ANNs based on optimization by continuation and PSO. In Sect. 3 accuracy and execution time results are discussed. Finally, some conclusions and recommendations are given.

2   Optimization by Continuation

A fitness function evaluates the quality of a solution in an optimization problem. Its use may be simplified to perform a discrimination between solutions. Intuitively it can be seen that such quality estimation does not have to be fine-grained to discriminate candidate solutions. Throughout this article we use x for scalars, $\boldsymbol{x}$ for vectors and X for sets.

In practice the fitness function of an ANN can be a sort of loss function such as the Mean Squared Error (MSE) in Eq. (1), where $X = \{\boldsymbol{x}_1, \ldots, \boldsymbol{x}_p\}, \boldsymbol{x}_i \in \mathbb{R}^d$ is the set of training patterns, $\boldsymbol{w} \in \mathbb{R}^n$ contains the neural network parameters and $\hat{y}_i$ and y_i are the expected and real output of the network for the $\boldsymbol{x}_i$ training pattern respectively. For simplicity, we will only consider single-output regression problems.

$$f(\boldsymbol{w}, X) = \frac{\sum_{i=1}^{p} (\hat{y}_i - y_i)^2}{p} \tag{1}$$

In Eq. (1) the computational cost comes from the calculation of the real output y_i that requires the propagation of the training pattern through each layer of the neural network. Actually, the minimization of $f(\boldsymbol{w}, X)$ is an NP-hard optimization problem [16]. Equation (2) formally describes ANN training as an optimization problem.

$$\boldsymbol{w} = argmin_{\boldsymbol{w} \in \mathbb{R}^n} f(\boldsymbol{w}, X) \tag{2}$$

Having an ANN formed by two parameters, its parameter space would look like a landscape with valleys and hills. Since our goal is to find a point in such parameter space near of the global optimum, it is possible to use a coarse-grained representation of the error surface generated by the training patterns. Ideally, such representation would have the most prominent irregularities in its topology, at least from a global point of view.

The principle described above has been explored extensively and is commonly known in optimization field as continuation method [17]. The general idea behind the so-called continuation method heuristic, is to start solving an easy problem and progressively change it to the actual complex task. The major issue here is how to build representations of the error surface, from coarse-grained to fine-grained representations, by presenting training patterns to an ANN.

PSO is a population based meta-heuristic algorithm [2]. PSO has several hyper-parameters such as: population size (r), global contribution (α), local contribution (β), maximum speed (v_{max}) and minimum speed (v_{min}). In ANN training by PSO, the i-th particle in the population represents the ANN parameters vector $\boldsymbol{w}_i$. Let $\boldsymbol{w}^*$ be the position of the particle with the lowest fitness function value in the population and $\boldsymbol{w}_i^*$ be the position where $\boldsymbol{w}_i$ achieved its lowest fitness function value. Each particle $\boldsymbol{w}_i$ moves towards a direction determined by $\boldsymbol{w}^*$, $\boldsymbol{w}_i^*$ and a velocity factor. Particle $\boldsymbol{w}^*$ is also known as *best-global* particle and $\boldsymbol{w}_i^*$ as *best-so-far* particle of $\boldsymbol{w}_i$.

Algorithm 1 describes how to use the continuation PSO for ANN training. The algorithm input is a set of training patterns X and a fitness function in the form of $f(\boldsymbol{w}, X)$. In the first steep of the algorithm, a sequence of subsets of training patterns $\hat{X}_1, \hat{X}_2, \ldots, \hat{X}_k$ is created. The last subset of the sequence, denoted by $\hat{X}_k$, is the entire set of training patterns ($\hat{X}_k = X$) and each subset of training patterns $\hat{X}_i, 1 \leq i \leq k - 1$ is built by randomly selecting a $\beta^\dagger \in [0,1]$ proportion of training patterns from the subset $\hat{X}_{i+1}$. Hence, the sequence holds that $\hat{X}_1 \subset \hat{X}_2 \subset \ldots \subset \hat{X}_k$.

For each $\hat{X}_i$ we update the fitness function value for *best-global* and *best-so-far* particles. This is an important implementation detail reflected in lines 4–5, ensuring that when the optimization surface changes, the fitness function value of the particles changes as well. Line 6 of the algorithm introduces an algorithm hyper-parameter η that controls the number of PSO iterations used to optimize the fitness function $f(\boldsymbol{w}, \hat{X}_i)$.

Notice that in Algorithm 1, $\boldsymbol{w}_j$, $\boldsymbol{w}^*$ and $\boldsymbol{w}_j^*$ are re-used over the iterations of training. That is, for each iteration of Algorithm 1, PSO continues the search using the population from the previous iteration instead of restarting the

---

Algorithm 1. Neural network training by PSO continuation.

Input: Set of training patterns $X = \{x_1, x_2, ..., x_p\}$
Input: Fitness function $f(w, X)$, $w \in \mathbb{R}^n$
Output: Best particle w^*
 1: Build a sequence of subsets of training patterns $\hat{X}_1 \subset \hat{X}_2 \subset ... \subset \hat{X}_k$
 2: Generate initial population $w_1, w_2, ..., w_r$ with $w_j \in \mathbb{R}^n$
 3: **for** i = 1: k **do**
 4:     Update fitness function value of w^* by evaluating $f(w^*, \hat{X}_i)$
 5:     Update fitness function value of w_j^* by evaluating $f(w_j^*, \hat{X}_i)$ for $1 \leq j \leq r$
 6:     Perform a number η of PSO iterations with fitness function $f(w, \hat{X}_i)$
 7: **end for**
 8: **return** best particle w^* in the population

---

population randomly. Hence, the name of *continuation*. Finally, on line 8, the *best-global* particle of the population is returned.

3   Results and Discussion

This section analyzes the experimental results of the proposed continuation approach for ANN training. Generalization error was defined as the MSE on unseen data using 4-folds cross-validation algorithm. The Tibshirani-Tibshirani (TT) bias correction for the minimum error rate in cross validation was considered after performing hyper-parameter optimization [24]. The following benchmark datasets were selected from UCI Machine Learning Repository regression problems:

1. Concrete Compressive Strength Dataset (CCS). Prediction of concrete compressive strength based on its age and ingredients. The dataset contains 1030 training patterns and 9 features [20].
2. Wine Quality Dataset (WQ). Prediction of wine quality based in a series of physics and chemistry features of wine. The dataset contains 4898 training patterns and 12 features [7].
3. Combined Cycle Power Plant Dataset (CCPP). Prediction of the amount of electrical energy that a specific power plant is able to produce each hour. The dataset contains 9568 training patterns and 4 features [22].

We considered network architecture from previous works. A population size $r = 40$ and a search domain $[-10, 10]$ was used for all cases, this means that maximum value for a weight is 10 and the minimum is -10. Hyper-parameters related to PSO were optimized using SMAC [12], an automatic hyper-parameter optimization algorithm. Table 1 shows the selected values of hyper-parameters for each dataset, which can be used to reproduce experimental results.

For standard PSO we used a fixed budget of 4.0×10^4 fitness function evaluations that corresponds to $\eta = 1000$ iterations. For the continuation PSO we used a fixed budget of $4.0 \times 10^4/k$ fitness function evaluations that corresponds to $\eta = 1000/k$ iterations for a total of $\eta = 1000$ iterations considering Algorithm 1.

Table 1. Selected hyper-parameters for each benchmark dataset.

	Standard PSO					Continuation PSO						
	TT	α	β	v_{max}	v_{min}	TT	α	β	v_{max}	v_{min}	k	$\beta^{\dagger}$
CCS	1.37E-3	9.38E-1	3.67E-1	1.25		7.64E-1	4.03E-4	9.11E-1	5.23E-1	1.06	8.03E-1	4	8.18E-1
WQ	2.39E-4	9.38E-1	3.67E-1	1.25		7.64E-1	1.12E-4	7.61E-1	8.83E-1	9.41E-1	7.84E-1	4	5.19E-1
CCPP	1.78E-5	9.38E-1	3.67E-1	1.25		7.64E-1	1.05E-5	6.49E-1	7.18E-1	1.07	8.28E-1	2	4.65E-1

Figure 1 shows the generalization error and training error obtained by the standard and the continuation PSO. The bottom and top lines in the box plots represents the first and third quartiles, the line in the middle represents the median of the measurements and the whiskers represent standard deviation. The small square represents the average of the measurements and the (x) marks represent the maximum and minimum value.

In order to find statistical significant differences between standard and continuation PSO we verified normality hypothesis with Anderson-Darling goodness of fit test. T-test on generalization error revealed statistical difference for two of the datasets CSS (p-value < 0.0001, t-value $= 8.4166$, df $= 98$), WQ (p-value $= 0.0047$, t-value $= 2.8932$, df $= 98$) and no-statistical difference for CCPP (p-value $= 0.8294$, t-value $= 0.2161$, df $= 98$). Despite the small improvement in accuracy for two of the datasets, we must consider the noise introduced by the hyper-parameter optimization algorithm, hence this difference may be meaningless.

Figure 2 presents the execution time of optimization for the benchmark datasets. Empty bars correspond to standard PSO and filled bars correspond to continuation PSO. Execution time was measured in milliseconds in a Core-i3 @2.3GHz personal computer with 4Gb of RAM using a sequential implementation.

As can be seen, the continuation approach for optimization represents a significant diminution in execution time for every benchmark dataset. For all datasets, optimization time was reduced by $20\% - 50\%$ depending on the chosen continuation hyper-parameters.

Table 2 summarizes accuracy and execution time results for further analysis. Measurements are presented in the form of mean($\pm$ standard deviation). It is worth noticing the increase in optimization stability for every dataset considering generalization error and training error standard deviation.

Table 2. Accuracy and execution time results of standard and continuation PSO.

	STANDARD PSO			CONTINUATION PSO		
DATASET	G. ERROR	T. ERROR	TIME (SEC.)	G. ERROR	T. ERROR	TIME (SEC.)
CCS	0.0100(9.9E-4)	0.0069(7.3E-4)	277.80(2.14)	0.0085(7.9E-4)	0.0064(5.7E-4)	217.5(3.32)
WQ	0.0161(2.7E-4)	0.0151(2.7E-4)	1446.4(2.89)	0.0160(2.1E-4)	0.0152(1.5E-4)	709.4(2.86)
CCPP	0.0031(3.7E-5)	0.0030(3.6E-5)	2217.0(10.0)	0.0031(3.1E-5)	0.0031(3.1E-5)	1627.8(9.3)

From an optimization point of view, both approaches obtained similar results. However, it can be observed for every case a small reduction of the gap between generalization error and training error of the continuation PSO respect standard PSO. This suggest a reduced impact of over-fitting and may explain why it seems that when more data is available using similar neural network models, generalization error does not improve. Further analysis should be conducted to study the possible regularization effect of optimization by continuation.

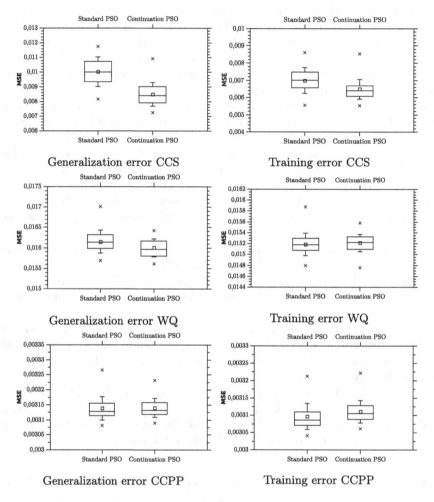

Fig. 1. Comparison of standard and continuation PSO considering generalization and training errors for each dataset.

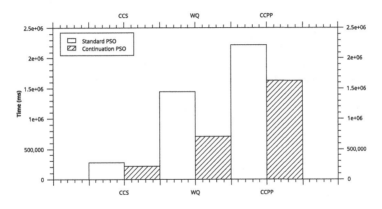

Fig. 2. Sequential execution time of standard and continuation PSO.

4   Conclusions and Recommendations

In this paper we presented an approach for ANN training based on optimization by continuation and PSO algorithm. A considerable diminution in execution time of optimization is observed when using the continuation based PSO. A small but statistical significant improvement in accuracy is observed for some of the benchmark datasets. Further analysis should be conducted to investigate a possible regularization effect of optimization by continuation.

References

1. Ahmed, H.M., Youssef, B.A., Elkorany, A.S., Saleeb, A.A., El-Samie, F.A.: Hybrid gray wolf optimizer-artificial neural network classification approach for magnetic resonance brain images. Appl. Opt. **57**(7), B25–B31 (2018)
2. Bonyadi, M.R., Michalewicz, Z.: Particle swarm optimization for single objective continuous space problems: a review (2017)
3. Chang, P., Yang, J., Yang, J., You, T.: Respiratory signals prediction based on particle swarm optimization and back propagation neural networks. In: AIP Conference Proceedings, vol. 1834, p. 040049. AIP Publishing (2017)
4. Chatterjee, S., Dey, N., Ashour, A.S., Drugarin, C.V.A.: Electrical energy output prediction using cuckoo search based artificial neural network. In: Yang, X.-S., Nagar, A.K., Joshi, A. (eds.) Smart Trends in Systems, Security and Sustainability. LNNS, vol. 18, pp. 277–285. Springer, Singapore (2018). https://doi.org/10.1007/978-981-10-6916-1_26
5. Chen, W., Wang, X.A., Zhang, W., Xu, C.: Phishing detection research based on PSO-BP neural network. In: Barolli, L., Xhafa, F., Javaid, N., Spaho, E., Kolici, V. (eds.) EIDWT 2018. LNDECT, pp. 990–998. Springer, Heidelberg (2018). https://doi.org/10.1007/978-3-319-75928-9_91
6. Chilimbi, T., Suzue, Y., Apacible, J., Kalyanaraman, K.: Project Adam: building an efficient and scalable deep learning training system. In: 11th USENIX Symposium on Operating Systems Design and Implementation (OSDI 2014), pp. 571–582 (2014)

7. Cortez, P., Cerdeira, A., Almeida, F., Matos, T., Reis, J.: Modeling wine preferences by data mining from physicochemical properties. Decis. Support Syst. **47**(4), 547–553 (2009)

8. Dauphin, Y.N., Pascanu, R., Gulcehre, C., Cho, K., Ganguli, S., Bengio, Y.: Identifying and attacking the saddle point problem in high-dimensional non-convex optimization. In: Ghahramani, Z., Welling, M., Cortes, C., Lawrence, N.D., Weinberger, K.Q. (eds.) Advances in Neural Information Processing Systems, vol. 27, pp. 2933–2941. Curran Associates, Inc. (2014)

9. Goodfellow, I., Bengio, Y., Courville, A.: Deep Learning. MIT Press, Cambridge (2016)

10. Griewank, A.: On automatic differentiation. Math. Program.: Recent Dev. Appl. **6**(6), 83–107 (1989)

11. Hashem, M., Hassanein, A.S.: Jaw fracture classification using meta heuristic firefly algorithm with multi-layered associative neural networks. Clust. Comput. 1–8 (2018)

12. Hutter, F., Hoos, H.H., Leyton-Brown, K.: Sequential model-based optimization for general algorithm configuration. LION **5**, 507–523 (2011)

13. Janzamin, M., Sedghi, H., Anandkumar, A.: Beating the perils of non-convexity: guaranteed training of neural networks using tensor methods. CoRR abs/1506.08473 (2015)

14. LeCun, Y., Bengio, Y., Hinton, G.: Deep learning. Nature **521**(7553), 436–444 (2015)

15. Li, K., Mao, S., Li, X., Wu, Z., Meng, H.: Automatic lexical stress and pitch accent detection for L2 English speech using multi-distribution deep neural networks. Speech Commun. **96**, 28–36 (2018)

16. Livni, R., Shalev-Shwartz, S., Shamir, O.: On the computational efficiency of training neural networks. In: Advances in Neural Information Processing Systems, pp. 855–863 (2014)

17. Mobahi, H., Fisher III, J.W.: A theoretical analysis of optimization by Gaussian continuation. In: AAAI, pp. 1205–1211 (2015)

18. Nawi, N.M., Rehman, M., Khan, A.: Ws-bp: an efficient wolf search based backpropagation algorithm. In: International Conference on Mathematics, Engineering And Industrial Applications 2014 (ICoMEIA 2014). vol. 1660, p. 050027. AIP Publishing (2015)

19. Nayak, J., Naik, B., Behera, H.: A novel nature inspired firefly algorithm with higher order neural network: performance analysis. Eng. Sci. Technol. Int. J. **19**, 197–211 (2015)

20. Neeraja, D., Swaroop, G.: Prediction of compressive strength of concrete using artificial neural networks. Res. J. Pharm. Technol. **10**(1), 35–40 (2017)

21. Owaki, S., Fukumoto, Y., Sakamoto, T., Yamamoto, N., Nakamura, M.: Experimental demonstration of SPM compensation based on digital signal processing using a three-layer neural-network for 40-Gbit/s optical 16QAM signal. IEICE Commun. Express **7**(1), 13–18 (2018)

22. Rashid, M., Kamal, K., Zafar, T., Sheikh, Z., Shah, A., Mathavan, S.: Energy prediction of a combined cycle power plant using a particle swarm optimization trained feedforward neural network. In: 2015 International Conference on Mechanical Engineering, Automation and Control Systems (MEACS), pp. 1–5. IEEE (2015)

23. Sreeshakthy, M., Preethi, J.: Classification of human emotion from deap EEG signal using hybrid improved neural networks with cuckoo search. BRAIN. Broad Res. Artif. Intell. Neurosci. 6(3–4), 60–73 (2016)

24. Tibshirani, R.J., Tibshirani, R.: A bias correction for the minimum error rate in cross-validation. Ann. Appl. Stat. **3**, 822–829 (2009)
25. Yu, M., Yang, P., Wei, S.: Railway obstacle detection algorithm using neural network. In: AIP Conference Proceedings. vol. 1967, p. 040017. AIP Publishing (2018)

Intelligent Data Analysis to Calculate the Operational Reliability Coefficient

Zoila Esther Morales Tabares[1(✉)], Alcides Cabrera Campos[1],
Efrén Vázquez Silva[2], and Roberto Antonio Infante Milanés[1]

[1] University of the Informatics Sciences, Havana City, Cuba
{zemorales,alcides,rainfantem}@uci.cu
[2] Salesian Polytechnic University, Cuenca City, Ecuador
evazquez@ups.edu.ec

Abstract. Nowadays the complexity that medical equipment has reached means that not all failure patterns can be easily managed through maintenance activities, carried out after their manufacture and commissioning. For this reason, experts in electromedicine consider that the analysis of failure patterns should be carried out with the tools of reliability engineering, since medical equipment is a technology that is not without risks. Failures in these devices are caused by risks associated mainly with operator malfunctions, impairment of the electrical fluid that causes the stopping of procedures in execution in an unexpected manner and others inherent to the technology. All these risks lead to a dynamic working behaviour of medical equipment, which passes through a finite number of states: running, faulty and broken. As part of the analysis of failure patterns in medical equipment, the CONFEM algorithm is proposed in this manuscript to determine the operational reliability coefficient.

Keywords: Medical equipment · Failure patterns · Risks
Operational reliability coefficient · Algorithm

1 Introduction

The maintenance management through automated systems allows the classification and characterization of the information according to the specific requirements of each user. In addition, it offers the possibility to analyze and make decisions based on globally defined indicators in important processes such as the planning of the demand for spare parts stock. The literature defines a wide range of indicators for assessing maintenance management. The value of these indicators is used as a comparative value or a reference level in order to take corrective, modifying and predictive actions as appropriate.

The most commonly used maintenance indicators in the management of production equipment or services are: mean time between failures (MTBF), mean repair time (MTTR), technical availability, maintenance frequency, failure frequency, operational reliability, among others [17–20]. Reliability has been analyzed for different environments or situations [1–13]. Operational reliability analysis is the fundamental basis of the continuous improvement process, which systematically incorporates advanced tools for diagnosing the current status and predicting the future performance of equipment,

© Springer Nature Switzerland AG 2018
Y. Hernández Heredia et al. (Eds.): IWAIPR 2018, LNCS 11047, pp. 68–76, 2018.
https://doi.org/10.1007/978-3-030-01132-1_8

systems or processes. Its study is carried out through the analysis of fault history or technical status data.

The health sector is one of the areas that must constantly be redirecting its resources to guarantee the operational reliability and technical availability of medical equipment, because medical technology is widely used for the prevention, diagnosis and treatment of various diseases and abnormal physical conditions. It is not without risks, due to the occurrence in clinical practice of failures caused by improper handling by the operator and others related to the technology [15], such as, for example, those related to quality standards; non-compliance with the procedures established by the manufacturers; poor calibration or others related to external causes. All these risks lead to a dynamic working behaviour of medical equipment, which passes through a finite number of states: running, faulty, broken. These states can be absorbent (running, faulty and broken) and non-absorbent (low technique), where when the latter are reached the monitoring process ends. Only absorbent states will be considered in the investigation [23].

This paper presents an algorithm (CONFEM) based on the intelligent analysis of data to obtain the operational reliability coefficient of medical equipment in a health unit, from which it will be possible to carry out adequate maintenance planning (corrective, preventive and predictive) according to the classification categories of medical equipment in order to obtain an adequate relationship between productivity and maintenance cost at the equipment level [14]. The manuscript is divided into two sections. In the first section: Materials and methods, the fundamental concepts used in the development of the algorithm are dealt with, explaining its operation step by step. On the other hand, in the section: Results and discussion, the Equipment Availability and Reliability Sub-module is presented as a practical contribution to the solution. Also, this section presents a detailed analysis of the algorithm's operation to show the reliability of the calculation of the operational reliability coefficient. Finally, Sect. 4 presents the conclusions and future projections made by the authors in relation to the calculation of the operational reliability coefficient.

2 Materials and Methods

Medical equipment requires high safety standards to ensure that the services offered are provided properly and that their operations are carried out in the most appropriate manner. For this reason, a reliability analysis of these medical technologies determines their functionality and availability characteristics, allowing the operator to estimate the deviation of any operating characteristic of a component that may consequently become a failure of the component itself and jeopardize the safety of the medical equipment as a system. Hence, it is defined as the study of reliability: "the probability that an element, device, equipment or system will perform a given function under the correct conditions in a given time" [16, 22]. The following describes the data management process for calculating the operational reliability coefficient of a medical equipment.

2.1   Data Management in the Process of Calculating the Operational Reliability Coefficient

The data used for the process of calculating the operational reliability coefficient came from two different sources: the Management System for Clinical and Electromedical Engineering (SIGICEM) database, which involves current data, and the Reportech software database, which involves historical data [25]. Both databases are available from the National Electromedical Center of Cuba. For this reason, the data were not standardized, so the need arose according to the domain of the problem, to extract the necessary data to locate them in a single source of information (Fig. 1). For this purpose, the extraction, transformation and loading (ETL) processes were performed from SQL statements, which were executed through a script in the MySQL Database Management System, without the need to use tools designed to perform ETL processes, due to the fact that a high degree of transformations, calculations and processing was not required.

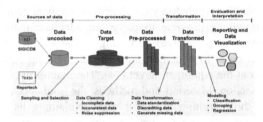

Fig. 1. Data management in the process of calculating the operational reliability coefficient.

Data cleaning was performed according to:

- Incomplete data in attributes of interest or summarized data (equipment_name).
- Existence of noise: errors in the data (equipment_model_attribute).
- Inconsistent data: there is a discrepancy in the values (annual_quantity attribute).

The extraction process consisted of collecting the relevant data from the source databases (SIGICEM and Reportech) to carry out the business component processes. The following transformation techniques were applied to these data:

- Normalize: to avoid data redundancy, data updating problems in the tables and protect their integrity.
- Discrete: transform a continuous value into a discrete one (Equipment states: Running, F; Faulty, D; Broken, R. This transformation allowed the construction of the sequence of absorbing states to obtain the quantitative indicators used in the calculation of the operational reliability coefficient. Another example is the one related to electromedical specialties, where each one was assigned a number in the range of 1 to 12).
- Generation of missing data: by the average of the class to which the object belongs.

After the necessary transformations to improve the quality of the data were carried out, they were loaded into the target database (BD_Stock), which were classified and grouped for better evaluation and interpretation. The population of medical equipment was grouped into non-overlapping and internally homogeneous subpopulations for the performance of the processes that integrate the business component with the use of cluster sampling techniques. To carry out the operational reliability process, the population of medical equipment was stratified into subpopulations by specialty, equipment designation, make and model. These subpopulations were then stratified according to their technical state into three groups of equipment: Running, Faulty and Broken. The classification and grouping of the data allowed the calculation of the operational reliability coefficient based on its evolution over time on continuous variables.

2.2 Process for Calculating the Operational Reliability Coefficient

In the operational field, the operational reliability coefficient (C_0) is calculated as a function of maintenance times:

$$C_o = \frac{MTBF}{MTBF + MTTR} \tag{1}$$

where,
Mean Time Between Failures (*MTBF*).
Mean Time to Repair (*MTTR*).

- *MTBF*: indicates the average time elapsed until the fault event arrives.
- *MTTR*: is the measure of the distribution of the repair time of an equipment or system. This indicator measures the effectiveness of restoring the unit to optimum operating conditions once the unit is out of service due to a failure within a given period of time.

To make up the chain (absorbent states of medical equipment), we rely on historical data from service orders made by the electromedicine specialists of the health units. The service orders contain a set of data related to the management of the equipment, including the technical status (Running, Faulty, Broken). Equipment is managed on the basis of four factors: Equipment Function, Physical Risk Associated with Clinical Application, Maintenance Requirements, and Equipment Trouble History. The first factor has a direct relationship with the equipment and the rest with its level of performance over time [14].

The status chain is constructed by stratifying equipment by specialty, name, brand and model to facilitate the search for reports associated with its operation over time.

Based on the theoretical foundations on operational reliability described above, the sequence of states was constructed to select the dates on which the equipment moves from state F to state D or R until it reaches state F again. Later, the time in days of the occurrences $F \rightarrow (Do'R) \rightarrow F$ is counted, divided by the number of such occurrences present in the chain.

In this manner, the MTBF was calculated:

$$MTBF = \frac{CD\acute{\iota}as_{F \to (D\,o'R) \to F}}{Oc} \qquad (2)$$

where,

$CD\acute{\iota}as$: number of days elapsed in the occurrence $F \to (Do'R) \to F$
Oc: number of occurrences.

The *MTTR* was calculated taking into account the number of days spent on the occurrences $D \to Fo'R \to F$, divided by the number of such occurrences present in the chain.

The numerical value obtained from the relationship between the mean time between faults with the addition of the mean repair time and the mean time between faults is multiplied by 100 for a better interpretation of the operational reliability coefficient in percentage.

2.3   CONFEM Algorithm

The calculation of the operational reliability coefficient shall be performed for n steps. The following describes the operation of the CONFEM algorithm and the MTTR and MTBF functions. It has as input parameters a list with the sequence of states through which a medical equipment passes during its useful life and the instant of time (number of months).

Algorithm 1 CONFEM

> **Input:**
>> listEquipment: List of equipment reported in service orders
>> varLongEq: Equipment list length
>> varSequence: Sequence of states of a device
>> varLongSec: Sequence length
>> varMTBF: Mean Time Between Failures
>> varMTTR: Average repair time
>
> **Output:**
>> varCo: Operational reliability
>
> **Begin:**
>> 1:   **For** i=1 to i< varLongEq **do**
>> 2:   varSequence = GenerateSequence (listEquipment[i])
>> 3:   **If** varLongSec < > 0 **do**
>> 4:   varMTBF = **FunctionMTBF** (varSequence)
>> 5:   varMTTR = **FunctionMTTR** (varSequence)
>> 6:   varCo = varMTBF/ (varMTBF+ varMTTR)
>> 7:   **If not**
>> 8:   "The selected equipment has not been installed"
>> 9:   **End if**
>> 10: **End For**
>> 11: **Return** varCo

In the CONFEM algorithm (Algorithm 1), the methods MTBF Function and MTTTR Function are problem dependent methods, so the complexity of CONFEM was determined from the complexity of these functions. The complexity of MTBF Function is $O(n^2)$ and $O(nlogn)$ is that of MTBF Function. With the application of the summation rule it can be concluded that the complexity of the CONFEM algorithm is $O(n^2)$.

3 Results and Discussion

As a practical contribution of this work, a sub-module was implemented that bears the name Availability and reliability of the equipment, which is integrated with the Prediction and Stock Management Module of the Management System for Clinical Engineering and Electromedicine. This sub-module incorporates the DISTEM algorithm, because the operational reliability and technical availability coefficient is one of the variables considered in the multivariate model for the prediction of spare parts stock for medical equipment.

The CONFEM algorithm was incorporated into the business component of the MPREDSTOCK: Multivariate model for predicting spare parts stock for medical equipment [25]. For this reason, CONFEM receives the same parameters as the MPREDSTOCK as input for its execution. To validate the efficacy of the CONFEM algorithm the experimental method was used on the basis of having each piece independently.

A case database of 385 cases was also designed, which included the entire set of data from 30,843 reports on health center service orders in the national territory in the years 2003 to 2014 available in the Reportech System [26]. The 385 instances were divided into k = 10 training sets, so 356 instances were used for training and 39 for testing. However, only the results for 55 instances are shown in this manuscript because the result achieved with the rest of the instances is similar to the one obtained in Sect. 3.2.

Different combinations of the CONFEM algorithm were executed, such as the execution specified in Sect. 3.1. On the other hand, in Sect. 3.2 it was demonstrated by means of the nonparametric test of the Wilcoxon-signed ranges that the observed operational reliability coefficient does not statistically differ ($p\_value > 0.05$) from the operational reliability coefficient calculated from the theoretical assumptions specified in Sect. 2.3.

3.1 Execution of the CONFEM Algorithm

Medical Equipment

- Specialty: Electro-optical and laboratory
- Equipment designation: Blood gas analyzer
- Mark: ROCHE
- Model: COBAS b121
- Description of the piece: THB/SO2 Module

Sequence of states: FFFFFFFFFFFFFFFFFFFFFFFFFFFFFFFFFFFFFFFFFFFDDDDDDDRRRRRRRRR

The sequence of states of the ROCHE COBAS 121b blood gas analyzer represents 0.17% of the 30, 843 reports made in the service orders of health centers in the national territory. From the sequence of states, the determination matrix of Table 1 and the transition graph between the absorbent states (Fig. 2) were defined with their initial probability vector represented by a 1x3 invariant row vector (π).

Table 1. Parameters used in the experimental analysis.

	Running (F)	Faulty (D)	Broken (R)	Totals
Running (F)	39	1	0	40
Faulty (D)	0	6	1	7
Broken (R)	0	0	8	8
Totals	39	7	9	55

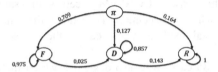

Fig. 2. Transition graph between states of the blood gas analyzing medical equipment.

For a 12-month period, the operational reliability coefficient was 71%, with a technical availability of 52%.

3.2   Application of the Non-parametric Wilcoxon-Signed Range Test

Measurement

- Operational reliability coefficient observed.
- Estimated operational reliability coefficient.

Wilcoxon test hypothesis

H_0: There is no difference between the median of the observed and estimated operational reliability coefficient.

H_1: There are differences between the median of the observed and estimated operational reliability coefficient.

Decision rule: if $p\_value > 0.05$ is not rejected H_0.

Tools used in the analysis: SPSS 13.0 and Weka 3.5.2.

Table 2. Statistics of related samples.

	Median	N	Z	p_value
Coefficient observed	0.7722	55	−0.537	0.592
Estimated coefficient	0.7522			

The experimental results in Table 2 show a $p\_value > 0.05$, so H_0 is not rejected, indicating that there is no statistically significant difference between the median of the observed operational reliability coefficient and the estimated one.

4 Conclusions and Future Projections

The CONFEM algorithm starts from the analysis of the failure patterns of medical equipment for the calculation of the operational reliability coefficient, for which it allows the sequence of states to be extended without altering the adopted model or the temporal complexity of its execution. The results and discussion show that it is satisfactory that the algorithm is based on the distillation of information collected, classified, organized and integrated into the SIGICEM database, and that new information and an appropriate representation of the data for use by the computer system developed is derived. However, the group of authors recommends, in order to achieve greater accuracy in the calculation of the operational reliability coefficient, measuring external effects and states that are not directly visible in the functioning of medical equipment, using more complex methods based on learning, such as the Markov's Hidden Models.

References

1. Yin, H., Wang, K., Qin, Y., Hua, Q., Jiang, Q.: Reliability analysis of subway vehicles based on the data of operational failures. EURASIP J. Wirel. Commun. Netw. (2017). https://doi.org/10.1186/s13638-017-0996-y
2. Pas, J., Rosiński, A.: Selected issues regarding the reliability-operational assessment of electronic transport systems with regard to electromagnetic interference. Eksploat. Niezawodn. Maint. Reliab. **19**(3), 375–381 (2017)
3. Sun, C., He, Z., Cao, H., Zhang, Z., Chen, X., Zuo, M.J.: A non-probabilistic metric derived from condition information for operational reliability assessment of aero-engines. IEEE Trans. Reliab. **64**(1), 167–181 (2015)
4. Carroll, J., McDonald, A., McMillan, D.: Failure rate, repair time and unscheduled O&M cost analysis of offshore wind turbines. University of Strathclyde Glasgow. Wind Energy (2015). https://strathprints.strath.ac.uk/54141/. ISSN 1095-4244
5. Qin, W., Song, J., Han, X., Wang, P.: Operational reliability assessment of power systems based on bus voltage. IET Digit. Libr. **9**(5), 475–482 (2015). https://doi.org/10.1049/iet-gtd.2014.0198. ISSN 1751-8695
6. Garipova, J., Georgiev, A., Papanchev, T., Nikolov, N., Zlatev, D.: Operational reliability assessment of systems containing electronic elements. In: Abraham, A., Kovalev, S., Tarassov, V., Snasel, V., Vasileva, M., Sukhanov, A. (eds.) Proceedings of the Second International Scientific Conference "Intelligent Information Technologies for Industry". Advances in Intelligent Systems and Computing, vol. 68, pp. 340–348. Springer, Cham (2018). https://doi.org/10.1007/978-3-319-68324-9_37

7. González, R., García, R.: Methods and tools for the operational reliability optimization of large-scale industrial wind turbines. In: Xu, J., Nickel, S., Machado, V., Hajiyev, A. (eds.) Proceedings of the Ninth International Conference on Management Science and Engineering Managemen. Advances in Intelligent Systems and Computing, vol. 362, pp. 1175–1188. Springer, Heidelberg (2015). https://doi.org/10.1007/978-3-662-47241-5_99

8. Jacob, J.: Fire safety concerns and operational reliability of automatic sprinkler systems. Int. J. Adv. Eng. **1**(9), 658–660 (2015). ISSN 2394-9279

9. Brusa, E., Stigliani, C., Ferretto, D., Pessa, C.: A model based approach to design for reliability and safety of critical aeronautic systems. In: Proceedings of INCOSE Conference on System Engineering. CIISE, Turin, Italy (2016)

10. Wen, L., Miao-na, C., Xu, J.: Research on comprehensive evaluation model for chemical equipment operation reliability. China Saf. Sci. J. **25**, 139–144 (2015)

11. Díaz, A., Romero, J.A., Cabrera, J., Viego, N.: Operational reliability study to support aeronautical maintenance in Cuba. Engineering **18**(66) (2015). International Microwave Power Institute

12. Zambrano, S., Tarantino, R., Aranguren, S., Agudelo, C.: Critical failure identification methodology in industrial processes based on operational reliability techniques. Colomb. Mag. Adv. Technol. **2**(20), 119–126 (2012). ISSN 1692-7257

13. Guevara, W., Valera Cárdenas, A., Gómez Camperos, J.A.: Metodología para evaluar el factor confiabilidad en la gestión de proyectos de diseño de equipos industriales. Revista Tecnura, 19, 129–141 (2015). https://doi.org/10.14483/udistrital.jour.tecnura.2015.se1.a11

14. World Health Organization (OMS): Introduction to the medical equipment maintenance program. World Health Organization Technical Paper Series on Medical Devices, pp. 47–50. (2012). http://www.who.int/about/licensing/copyright_form/en/index.html

15. Hernández, D.J.: SLD238-SIGICEM: management system for clinical engineering and electromedicine. In: VIII International Congress on Health Informatics. II Congreso Moodle Salud, pp. 1–9 (2011)

16. Espinosa, F.: Operational reliability of equipment: methodologies and tools. University of Talca (2011)

17. Amendola, L.: Human reliability model in asset management. Engineering Management, PMM Institute for Learning, Polytechnic University of Valencia, Spain (2004). www.pmmlearning.com

18. Christensen, H.C.: Maintenance indicators. Maint. Club Mag. **6**(18), 8–9 (2007)

19. Godoy, M.C.: Reliability element interaction model and safety inventory of equipment parts and spare parts through multivariate analysis. M.Sc. thesis, University of Zulia, Maracaibo, Venezuela (2008)

20. Melo, R., Lara, C., Jacobo, F.: Reliability-availability-maintainability estimation by Monte Carlo simulation of a bitter gas compression system during the engineering stage. Tec. Cien. Ed. (IMIQ), vol. 24, no. 2 (2009)

21. Castillo, A.M, Brito, M.L., Fraga, E.: Analysis of criticity personalized. Mech. Eng. J. **12**(3), 1–12 (2009). Redalyc.org. E-ISSN 1815-5944

22. de León, F.C.G.: Industrial Maintenance Technology. University of Murcia, Murcia (1998)

23. Morales, Z.E., Vázquez, E.: Algorithm for prediction of the technical availability of medical equipment. Appl. Math. Sci. **9**(135), 6735–6746 (2015)

24. Morales, Z.E., Vázquez, E., Caballero, Y.: Optimization of spare parts stock for medical equipment. Cuba J. Comput. Sci. **9**, 99–114 (2015)

25. Morales, Z.E., Cabrera, A., Vazquez, E., Caballero, Y.: MPREDSTOCK: multivariate model of spare parts stock prediction for medical equipment. Cuba J. Comput. Sci. **10**(3), 88–104 (2016). ISSN 2227-1899

26. Cabrera, O.: Reportech: medical technology management. In: VII Congress of the Cuban Society of Bioengineering, Havana (2007)

An Integrated Deep Neural Network for Defect Detection in Dynamic Textile Textures

Dirk Siegmund[1,2(✉)], Ashok Prajapati[1,2], Florian Kirchbuchner[1,2], and Arjan Kuijper[1,2]

[1] Fraunhofer Institute for Computer Graphics Research (IGD), Fraunhoferstrasse 5, 64283 Darmstadt, Germany
{dirk.siegmund,ashok.prajapati,
florian.kirchbuchner,arjan.kuijper}@igd.fraunhofer.de
[2] Technische Universität Darmstadt, Karolinenplatz 5, 64289 Darmstadt, Germany

Abstract. This paper presents a comprehensive defect detection method for two common fabric defects groups. Most existing systems require textiles to be spread out in order to detect defects. This method can be applied when the textiles are not spread out and does not require any pre- processing. The deep learning architecture we present is based on transfer learning and localizes and recognizes cuts, holes and stain defects. Classification and localization is combined into a single system combining two different networks. The experiments this paper presents show that even without adding depth information, the network was able to distinguish between stain and shadow. This method has been successful even for textiles in voluminous shape and is less computationally intensive than other state-of-the-art methods.

1 Introduction

Manually detecting defects such as "stain/dirt" or "holes and holes" is a time-consuming and error-prone process. Automated visual inspection can be a reliable and stable solution in this domain. When a defect detection system is used in the manufacturing process, it can ensure a quality product to the consumers. Research on outspread fabrics achieves high accuracy but is not comparable with textiles in voluminous shape. Uneven surface, varying colors, sewing pattern and weaving of different textile fibers like cotton, linen and polyester are some of the challenges in this domain. Automated visual inspection could provide a reliable and stable performance in defect detection. However, its adaptation is still slow, because of the several challenges:

- Similarity of global/local shadow and dark stain defects
- Large variety of fabric surfaces and brightness
- Variation in the appearance of fiber widths, due to the voluminous shape

© Springer Nature Switzerland AG 2018
Y. Hernández Heredia et al. (Eds.): IWAIPR 2018, LNCS 11047, pp. 77–84, 2018.
https://doi.org/10.1007/978-3-030-01132-1_9

- A defect can take any form and color
- Similarity of fibers defects, edges and seams.

In the related work, these challenges were tackled using a decision tree classification process [1,2] and pre-processing [3]. Moreover, to ensure real-time detection, it is necessary that the processing steps are as simple as possible. In this paper a full end-to-end classification method is presented which is computationally efficient, does not require any pre-processing and is robust against the flaws that undergoes during changes. Furthermore, the presented method is able to predict different defects on the same image. The presented deep learning architecture localizes and recognizes cuts, holes and stain defects on images of textiles. In Sect. 2, we summarize the state-of-art that provides an overview of different approaches used for this application. In Sect. 3 the basic building blocks of the algorithm and the technical components are described and the architecture of the Neural Network is mainly discussed. In the results Sect. 4 the conducted experiments and its results are described and the advantages and limitation are discussed.

2   Related Work

Automated visual inspection can play a vital role in textile industry that helps in reducing human inspection, which is time-consuming, inconsistent and inefficient. There are several methods which are intended to be applied in the fabric furling/production where the fabric is spread out [2,4]. Compared to that is the classification of defects in 3D shape more complex and requires algorithms to be robust against folds and shaded areas. In a recent work we compared different classical feature extraction and machine learning methods in order to detect stain on textiles [3]. The texture descriptors: LBP, Color Histogram and SIFT/SURF showed negative impact in recognizing stain defects at shaded regions, seams and borders. Normalizing shaded areas by using a disparity map of the textile-image enabled stain recognition by using a simple color-range threshold. In order to detect fiber defects like holes, more complex models are required. A combination of stereo normalization, SURF [5] key points and Convolutional Neural Networks (CNN)[6] for was proposed in a later work. That method used partially overlapping patches of 32×32 pixels around key points, and used them for training of a slightly modified LeNet-5 [7] CNN. Drawback of this method is the complex pre-processing where a disparity map image needs to be acquired and processed. Furthermore, the need for two synchronized cameras increases the costs and is computationally costly.

3   Methodology

Our approach is based on transfer learning and uses the Faster-RCNN architecture [8] in order to localize and classify the defects 'cuts and holes' and 'stain' (see Fig. 1). It reuses CNN features for proposing regions instead of running localization separately through selective search [9]. Thus, the architecture consists of two networks: A regional proposal network (RPN), that generates the region proposal and a network that uses these proposals to detect objects (see Fig. 1).

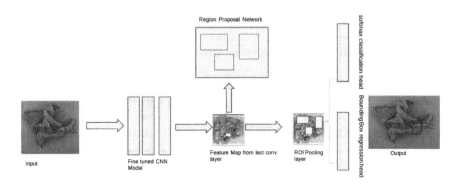

Fig. 1. Processing pipeline

The RPN is a fully convolutional network [10], on top of the convolutional feature map. It slides a small network (sliding window) over the convolutional feature map output of the last shared convolutional layer. The RPN predicts numerous bounding boxes (k) at each location (see Fig. 2). These k reference boxes are actually the anchors which are centered at the sliding window, generating k = 9 anchors at each sliding position where three scales and aspect ratios are used. Faster R-CNN uses a region of interest (RoI) pooling layer that pools the feature map of each proposal into a fixed size (7×7). Thus, defects of arbitrary size can be handled by using that approach.

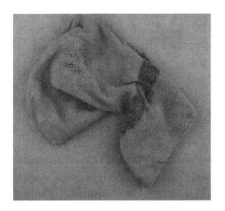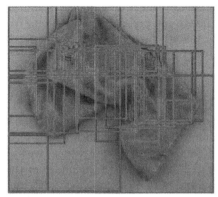

Fig. 2. Left: Input image, Right: Proposed ROI's by RPN

3.1 Feature Extraction Architecture

The Residual Network (Resnet) [11] and the VGG [12] architecture were evaluated to be used to extract features of the fabric in order to use them for the RPN and Fast RCNN. Residual learning framework ease the training of substantially deeper networks and are easy to optimize. It also gains accuracy with the increase in depth. Resnet has been evaluated on imagenet [13] with a depth up to 152 layers which is 8 times deeper than VGG nets but still having lower complexity. VGG uses very small (3×3) convolution filters pushing the ConvNet depth to 16–19 weight layers. VGG uses a fixed-size 224×224 RGB image as it's input during training. It subtracts the mean RGB value in it's input image which is computed over the training images. The convolution stride is set to 1 pixel to preserve the spatial resolution of the convolutional layer. Similarly, it performs max-poling over 2×2 pixel window with two strides of the VGG architecture and uses five max-pooling layer (as shown in Fig. 5). Three fully connected layers follow a stack of convolutional layers, two out of them have 4096 nodes and the third with 1000 nodes performs softmax classification over 1000 class ImageNet database. All hidden layers use ReLU as an activation function.

3.2 Halfway Fusion of Disparity Map

In case of distinguishing between stain and shadow in the image [3], depth information provide complimentary information as shown in our previous work [6]. As an experiment, we try to add the depth information, in the form of a disparity map, to the network in the training process. We want to find out if the trained network learns and benefits from these complementary features in a transfer learning architecture. For the generation of the disparity map, we used the same data as descibed in our previous work [3]. Generally, four fusion models: early fusion, halfway fusion, late fusion and score fusion can be distinguished citeliu2016multispectral. Liu et al. has shown that halfway fusion works well when fusing complimentary information as a thermal image with a regular image for pedestrian detection. We follow that approach and concatenate the original image and the corresponding disparity map at the middle of the ConvNet and before Network in Network.

3.3 Dataset

We evaluated our approach on a extended data-set of dry-cleaned woven cotton cleaning textiles collected in the same way as described here [6]. It consists of 2415 images (out of 306 textiles) with ground truth in Pascal VOC [14] format. In Fig. 3 and 4 are some samples of the defects classes. The data-set is spitted into a train (1549 images), test (286 images) and validation subset (297 images).

In order to remove noise from the background of the disparity map image, simple color masking is applied, as described in [3].

Fig. 3. Left: Input image, Right: Proposed ROI's by RPN

Fig. 4. Left: Input image, Right: Proposed ROI's by RPN

3.4 Experimental Network Designs

We used a pre-trained VGG16, which is composed of 16 layers with 13 convolutional layers and three fully-connected layer. We only use the first 10 convolutional layers (see Fig. 5) and extract the features from the last layer which is passed to the RPN. As training of large input is computational costly, we reduced the image size to a maximum of 600 pixel at the largest side. All presented design experiments use a dropout of 0.5 in the fully-connected layers and are trained using the AdamOptimizer. Resnet showed lower accuracy in all experiments, with the same data and different sets of hyper-parameters, we will therefore not go more into detail when using that network. Our training data was flipped horizontally, vertically and further augmented by adding artificial blur, contrast adjustment and sharpening. This resulted in 10,843 images available for training.

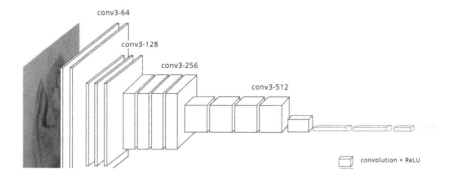

Fig. 5. Adapted neural network design, based on the VGG16 model.

Design 1: All convolutional layers are fine-tuned and two fully-connected layers are used, each with 1024 neurons and ReLU activation functions. A learning rate of 0.001 is used and decayed to 0.0001 after 15 epochs.

Design 2: The first four layers are freezed and the remaining are fine-tuned. This design also uses the first 10 convolutional layers and two fully-connected layer, each with 1024 neurons and ReLU activation functions as in Design 1. The learning rate of 0.0001 and then decay rate at 0.2 is used after 10 epochs.

Design 3: All the convolutional layers are freezed and two fully-connected layers are used each with 1024 neurons and ReLU activation functions. A learning rate of 0.001 is decayed to 0.0001 after 15 epochs as in Design 1.

Design 4 (with Depth): The first four layers are freezed and both RGB and disparity image are passed through them. The features from the fourth ConvNet are concatenated. The dimensionality is reduced to 128 by using Network in Network where 1×1 convolutional filter is used.

Design 5 (with Depth): RGB-D images are generated by concatenating the RGB image and disparity map such that the input to the first convolutional layer is the fourth channel. Batch normalization and dropout are used such that the gradient converges quickly and solves the overfitting problem.

4   Results

The test-set contained 864 images including 379 images without defect, used for computing of the classification accuracy. For the classification of the entire image, the image is labeled as 0 if it contains holes/cuts, 1 if it contains stains, 2 if it contains both cuts/holes and stain, 3 if it does not contain any defect. During evaluation, if the model predicts a defect then it is classified over one of the four fabric class (0,1,2,3) based on either there is only cuts/holes or stains or both or no defect at all. The classification accuracy shown in Table 1 is the overall accuracy i.e correctly predicted class(es). The accuracy is given at the optimal threshold, found by using grid search.

Table 1. Achieved accuracy rates of fiber-defect detection methods.

Methodology	Localization	Recognized defects	Classifier	Accuracy
SURF BoW [6]	Sliding window	Cuts & Holes	AdaBoost	87.99 ± 2.2 %
RI unified LBP [6]	Sliding window	Cuts & Holes	AdaBoost	84.94 ± 3.7 %
SURF+CNN [6]	Around keypoints	Cuts & Holes	CNN	90.15 ± 1.4 %
Stereo-Normalization [3]	Contour	Stain	Color threshold	94.32 ± 0.9 %
Design 1	Bounding box	Cuts & Holes, Stain	RPN & CNN	92.60 %
Design 2	Bounding box	Cuts & Holes, Stain	RPN & CNN	**95.48 %**
Design 3	Bounding box	Cuts & Holes, Stain	RPN & CNN	89.70%
Design 4 with disparity	Bounding box	Cuts & Holes, Stain	RPN & CNN	89.11 %
Design 5 with disparity	Bounding box	Cuts & Holes, Stain	RPN & CNN	87.70%

Fig. 6. Result samples showing detected defects and misclassification.

We observed that the model trained with only RGB image learned the difference between shade and stain even without disparity map. Only in few cases shadow is classified as stain (see Fig. 6) whereas almost no shadow being classified as cuts/holes. By setting a higher threshold, shadow is being classified as stain and edges and colorful areas are getting misclassified as defect. On the other side get images without defect less often misclassified. A threshold of 0.7 showed the lowest equal error rate and best overall classification accuracy. The confusion matrix for the test set shows that, 17 out of 379 defect free images are unclassified. Similarly, all fibers with stain only are predicted correctly while 2 fabrics with cuts and holes are classified as defect free. An overall classification accuracy of 95.48% was achieved by using the "design 2" composition. We noticed a number of small stain defects being undetected. One of the reasons for that could be the number of down-sampling or max pool operations in the CNN. By using disparity, better results than the model trained with just the RGB image were expected. But better results have only been achieved at shaded areas. At some extent it has negative impact over cuts & holes and regions where the fiber shows other color. As the pre-trained network has never seen disparity images we assume that the number of training images needs to be further increased in order to learn complementary relations. We observed that by using data augmentation techniques (blur, contrast etc.), the effect of different illumination can be reduced. That could be further increased by introducing more such data into the training and adding other augmentation approach.

5   Conclusion

In this paper, a transfer learning method for detection of fabric defects on voluminous fabrics was described. A deep neural network architecture was presented, that allowed end-to-end classification and localization. Competitive methods require prepossessing and localize only patch wise. Our object detector can be used to localize and differentiate between various defects like: cuts, holes and stain, even when the fabric shows folds, shaded areas and differently colored fibers. Several network designs were evaluated by adapting the CNN feature extractor VGG and using RGB and RGB+D images. We showed that fusing disparity maps half-way into the network reduces false detection by shadow but also results in lower accuracy at different challenging cases. Our results showed that even without adding additional depth information, the model distinguishes well between stain and shadow on fabrics and achieves state of the art results.

Acknowledgments. This work was supported by the German Federal Ministry of Education and Research (BMBF) as well as by the Hessen State Ministry for Higher Education, Research and the Arts (HMWK) within CRISP.

References

1. Siegmund, D., Kaehm, O., Handtke, D.: Rapid classification of textile fabrics arranged in piles. In: Proceedings of the 13th International Joint Conference on e-Business and Telecommunications, pp. 99–105 (2016)
2. Borghese, N.A., Fomasi, M.: Automatic defect classification on a production line. Intell. Ind. Syst. **1**, 373–393 (2015)
3. Siegmund, D., Kuijper, A., Braun, A.: Stereo-image normalization of voluminous objects improves textile defect recognition. In: Bebis, G., et al. (eds.) ISVC 2016. LNCS, vol. 10072, pp. 181–192. Springer, Cham (2016). https://doi.org/10.1007/978-3-319-50835-1_17
4. Li, Y., Zhao, W., Pan, J.: Deformable patterned fabric defect detection with fisher criterion-based deep learning. IEEE Trans. Autom. Sci. Eng. **14**, 1256–1264 (2017)
5. Bay, H., Tuytelaars, T., Van Gool, L.: SURF: speeded up robust features. In: Leonardis, A., Bischof, H., Pinz, A. (eds.) ECCV 2006. LNCS, vol. 3951, pp. 404–417. Springer, Heidelberg (2006). https://doi.org/10.1007/11744023_32
6. Siegmund, D., Samartzidis, T., Fu, B., Braun, A., Kuijper, A.: Fiber defect detection of inhomogeneous voluminous textiles. In: Carrasco-Ochoa, J.A., Martínez-Trinidad, J.F., Olvera-López, J.A. (eds.) MCPR 2017. LNCS, vol. 10267, pp. 278–287. Springer, Cham (2017). https://doi.org/10.1007/978-3-319-59226-8_27
7. LeCun, Y., Bottou, L., Bengio, Y., Haffner, P.: Gradient-based learning applied to document recognition. Proc. IEEE **86**, 2278–2324 (1998)
8. Ren, S., He, K., Girshick, R., Sun, J.: Faster R-CNN: towards real-time object detection with region proposal networks. In: Advances in Neural Information Processing Systems, pp. 91–99 (2015)
9. Girshick, R.: Fast R-CNN. arXiv preprint arXiv:1504.08083 (2015)
10. Long, J., Shelhamer, E., Darrell, T.: Fully convolutional networks for semantic segmentation. In: Proceedings of the IEEE Conference on Computer Vision and Pattern Recognition, pp. 3431–3440 (2015)
11. He, K., Zhang, X., Ren, S., Sun, J.: Deep residual learning for image recognition. In: Proceedings of the IEEE Conference on Computer Vision and Pattern Recognition, pp. 770–778 (2016)
12. Simonyan, K., Zisserman, A.: Very deep convolutional networks for large-scale image recognition. CoRR abs/1409.1556 (2014)
13. Krizhevsky, A., Sutskever, I., Hinton, G.E.: Imagenet classification with deep convolutional neural networks. In: Advances in Neural Information Processing Systems, pp. 1097–1105 (2012)
14. Everingham, M., Eslami, S.A., Van Gool, L., Williams, C.K., Winn, J., Zisserman, A.: The pascal visual object classes challenge: a retrospective. Int. J. Comput. Vis. **111**, 98–136 (2015)

Biometrics, Image and Video Analysis

Speeding up High Resolution Palmprint Matching by Using Singular Points

Manuel Aguado-Martínez[(⊠)] and José Hernández-Palancar

Advanced Technologies Application Center (CENATAV),
7ma A #21406 e/214 y 216, Siboney, Playa, 12200 Havana, Cuba
{maguado,jpalancar}@cenatav.co.cu
http://www.cenatav.co.cu

Abstract. Applications for palmprints range from civilian scenarios to forensics where palmprints technologies are urgently needed given that they are frequently found in crime scenes. However, for forensic applications, the resolution needed for palmprint images pose a challenging problem due to the factor that matching algorithms are time-consuming. Although widely explored in fingerprints, singular points have not yet received the same attention from palmprint researchers. In this article, an exploratory study is conducted to validate the hypothesis that singular points can be used effectively to speed up palmprint matching systems. Experimentation show how it is possible to accomplish the above while obtaining acceptable recognition rates.

Keywords: Palmprint matching · Singular points · Biometrics
Forensics

1 Introduction

With the rise of the information era, biometric technologies had become a hot research topic. A wide variety of biometric traits that includes face, ear, gait and veins among others has been investigated. Long before that, fingerprints were used in a large number of scenarios that go from civilian applications to law enforcement. Nevertheless, some problems associated to fingerprints in elderly people and manual workers had made that in the last two decades or so researchers started to look with growing interest into the skin patterns of palms. According to [13] palmprints are highly individual, their thesis is supported on the basis of the rich and useful information that can be extracted from the large area of the palm. Furthermore, the urgent need for palmprint applications in forensic scenarios had been clearly stated by several studies cited by [9] regarding the number of latent palmprints found in crime scenes.

Palmprint research can be divided into two groups: methods that employ low-resolution images (150 dpi or less) and methods that employ high-resolution images (500 dpi or more). Low-resolution images (Fig. 1a) are mainly used in civilian applications since the scanner devices are generally less expensive than

Y. Hernández Heredia et al. (Eds.): IWAIPR 2018, LNCS 11047, pp. 87–94, 2018.
https://doi.org/10.1007/978-3-030-01132-1_10

those used to capture higher resolution images. In those cases, features related to texture and principal palm lines are mainly used [1,5,11]. High-resolution images on another hand (Fig. 1b), are used for higher security levels, like the ones required in forensic scenarios and border control for example. At this level of details, just as in fingerprints, minutiae, defined as the terminations an bifurcations of ridges, can be extracted with relative confidence. In addition, singular points, cores, and deltas (Fig. 1b) can also be extracted from high resolution palmprint images.

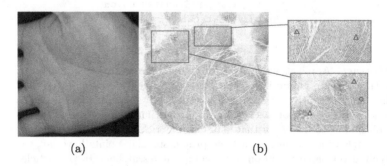

(a)   (b)

Fig. 1. A low resolution palmprint image (a), a high resolution palmprint image (b). Singular points: Core (red circle), Delta (blue triangle) (Color figure online)

Compared to fingerprints the number of minutiae that can be extracted from palmprints can be very large (more than 10 times). Additionally, due to the form of the hand and its large area non-linear distortion can be a highly disruptive factor [3]. In light of these facts, palmprint matching algorithms are very slow because they need to try a high number of minutiae combinations and to compensate for the large non-linear distortion between minutiae of the same palm. Just an example, the number of fingerprint matches that can perform Verifinger [17] per second can be around 15000 while only 3 palmprint matches can be performed per second using the same software [3]. For large biometric systems like forensic systems efficiency is a key factor, and therefore, major improvements in this direction are urgently needed.

This article pretends to explore the viability of using singular points to drastically improve the efficiency of a palmprint matching system. The future goal of this preliminary study is to apply this approach in forensic scenarios. The general idea is to decide whether two palmprint images come from the same hand, by comparing the geometrical distribution of the minutiae in the neighborhoods of singular points of the same type. Experiments show how the matching speed of the proposed system in [8] gets improved by a factor of 34 while obtaining acceptable recognition rates.

In the next subsection, a brief description of the state-of-the-art is given. Section 2 explains in details the proposed system while the experimental setups and obtained results are presented in Sect. 3. Finally, some conclusions and general thoughts will be given in Sect. 4.

1.1   Related Work

Back in 2009 a latent palmprint matching method was proposed in [10]. The authors introduced a fixed-length minutia descriptor named MinutiaCode that encodes the neighborhood of each minutia capturing information regarding ridge quality, texture and surrounding minutiae. The fixed-length descriptor allows overcoming the efficiency drawbacks of matching two minutiae descriptor of variable length. Looking to improve the recognition rates in [4] a multi-feature system was proposed. Using features like density map, ridge orientation and principal lines besides minutiae, the desired improvement in efficacy was obtained, however, this came at cost of a huge efficiency penalization. An orientation-based alignment palmprint algorithm was proposed in [3]. By registering palmprints into the same coordinate system the total computational complexity of the matching process can be reduced. The highly successful Minutia Cylinder-Code in fingerprint applications was introduced for palmprints in [2]. A few modifications were made to the original algorithm to compensate for the intrinsic characteristics of palmprints. In [14] efficiency is addressed by clustering minutiae into similar groups and matching these groups locally to establish some initial correspondences that are lately used to math the entires sets of minutiae. Previous to this work an expanded triangle representation based on the Delaunay triangulation was proposed [8]. It was designed to compensate for spurious and missing minutiae, improving in this way recognition rates from the state-of-the-art methods. However, this proposal like the previous ones lacks of matching speed.

Singular points have been used extensively in fingerprint applications [15, 18, 22]. However, in palmprints and despite the large number of singular points present in palms, this has not been the case. Many authors have pointed out the challenges of palmprint orientation field estimation due to creases which could be one of the causes for this apathy. In palmprints, singular points have been mainly used for classification purpose. In [20] the authors developed a method to extract singular points. Singular points are extracted using the Poincaré Index [12] over a four-direction image. Singular points are only extracted from the hypothenar region. This is the region with the small presence of creases and wrinkles and therefore where the orientation field can be effectively estimated disregarding the negative effects of creases. Palmprints are classified into six classes base on the number of singular points of each type (cores and deltas) in the hypothenar region. Fourteen years later in [16], difficulties for extracting singular points in palmprints caused by creases and wrinkles are again mentioned. In this work, distributions of singularities in the interdigital region are studied. Singular points are manually extracted and 5 classes are defined according to the number and type of them.

2   Proposal

Singular points in palmprints are in great number. From the classes defined in [20] and [16], there is a maximum of three singular points in the hypothenar region and six in the interdigital region, for a maximum total of nine singular points. This last total does not include singular points that can be extracted from the thenar region. In this work, the idea of speeding up palmprint matching system using singular points is explored. Differently, from previous works, singular points are extracted automatically from the entire palmprint. A geometrical triangular local structure is then constructed for each singular point by using the neighboring minutiae. Local structures from singular points of the same type in different palmprints are then matched to find out if both singular points are from the same hand. Following, the automatic procedure for extract singular points from the entire palm is introduced. Singular points neighborhood modeling and matching are presented in the subsequent subsection.

2.1   Singular Points Extraction

Like it was previously stated reliably extracting singular points from palmprints has been a challenging task. Behind this is the fact that in most cases feature extraction methods applied to palmprints are adaptations of those applied to fingerprints. For singular point extraction, an accurate estimation of the ridges orientation field is crucial. In fingerprints, the most widespread methods for orientation field estimation are based on the premise that the direction of a ridge is orthogonal to the gradient phase angle [15]. Creases and wrinkles in palmprints can completely disrupt this assumption. Since the direction of creases can point to the maximum intensity change in the image it is quite difficult to distinguish creases from ridges based only on a local directional criterion. Figure 2 shows two examples of ridge estimation in a local palmprint region with a heavy presence of creases using a gradient-based algorithm. It is quite easy to perceive from these two examples how the global ridge pattern is completely disrupted by creases.

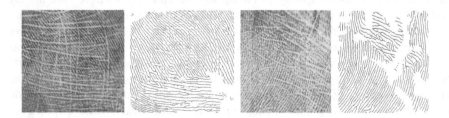

Fig. 2. Ridges estimation using a fingerprint ridge extraction algorithm based on the gradient phase angle.

A few approaches had been proposed to overcome this negative effect [7,10]. The proposed solutions aim to enhance the ridge pattern while suppressing the creases using a bank of Gabor filters. Gabor filters are contextual filters that need the orientation and frequency of the pattern that should be enhanced. Ridge frequency and orientation candidates are estimated first locally from a local Fourier spectrum and them the correct ones are selected by a region growing algorithm that evaluates how these candidates globally fit each other. Although creases are effectively suppressed, the computation complexity of this region growing algorithms is quite high. The hole feature extraction stage can take up to 55–56 s depending on the hardware architecture [2,3]. This drawback, of course, limits the practical applications of these methods.

Recently a new palmprint enhancement algorithm developed in our lab was proposed in [19]. The efficiency of the whole process is drastically improved by introducing a preprocessing step based on the level sets theory which allows reducing the number of extracted candidates from the Fourier spectrum by half. Furthermore, the computational complexity of the region growing algorithm is reduced even more by extrapolating the orientation field using the method proposed in [6]. Reported results improve the recognition rates of the previous methods. So, to reliable extract ridge information, each palmprint image is enhanced using this algorithm before any further feature extraction process.

To extract singular points the Poincaré Index (PI) is used. From the local ridge orientations estimated by the enhancement algorithm and centered at each local area, two different regions represented in Fig. 3a and b are analyzed to compute the PIs pi_1 and pi_2 respectively.

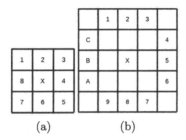

(a)   (b)

Fig. 3. Block regions (a) and (b) to calculate the Poincaré Index.

If $pi_1 * pi_2 > 0$ then there is a singular point in that local area and the type is defined by Eq. 1.

$$SP_{type} = \begin{cases} Core, & pi_1 > 0 \\ Delta, & otherwise \end{cases}.$$ (1)

For a more fine-grain location extraction (pixel level) of the singular points, an orientation field at pixel level should be used. Since creases were suppressed from the palmprint image by the enhancement algorithm the orientations at pixel level can be computed by using the gradient phase angle. Singular points in adjacent local areas are then clustered into only one singular point and its position is selected as the point of maximum curvature in the pixel orientation field in those areas.

2.2   Singular Point Matching

For each singular point, the triangular representation proposed in [8] is constructed for the minutiae in a circular neighborhood of radio r of the singular point. The selection of r will pose a compromise between efficiency and efficacy. For high values of r, more minutiae will be considered in the neighborhood of each singular point increasing the discriminative power of the local structure but decreasing the efficiency. When comparing two palmprints A and B, each one of the singular points of A is compared against the singular points o B using the matching algorithm proposed in [8]. The maximum obtained score is selected as the final decision value.

3   Experiments and Results

Experiments were conducted on the THUPALMLAB database composed for a total of 1280 palmprint images from 80 users [21]. Each hand was recorded 8 times by inking the palm skin pattern on a paper and scanning it at a resolution of 500 dpi. Due to the irregular hand bone structure, a strict protocol must be followed to acquire palmprint images. Failing to do so, will cause a high number of cases were both the central region and the interdigital region will be not completely inked on the paper. This was the case with the THUPALMLAB database were not strict acquisition protocol was followed. As a result, no singular points were detected in 160 images. Since the aim of this work is to explore the possibility of using singular points to speed up palmprint matching algorithms, an identification experiment was designed without considering these 160 images and where a total of 3657 genuine scores and 618917 impostor scores were obtained. To evaluate the effect of each singular point neighborhood size, three different values of r were tested. Results are presented in Tables 1 and 2.

In addition to the previous algorithm in [8], the state-of-the-art algorithms proposed in [10] and [4] were used as reference. As expected, the efficacy of the matching system using singular points increased for bigger values of r. When comparing with the algorithm in [8], the results using singular points are not better. However, results for all three neighborhoods are better than those obtained

Table 1. Verification results on the THUPALMLAB database in terms of Equal Error Rate (EER) and False Match Rates (FMR).

Algorithm	EER	ZeroFMR	FMR1000	FMR100
CPIM [8]	0.05%	0.08%	0.05%	0.05%
Proposed ($r = 170$)	6.51%	9.81%	7.46%	6.83%
Proposed ($r = 250$)	5.58%	8.28%	6.23%	5.82%
Proposed ($r = 500$)	4.09%	5.27%	4.56%	4.15%
Jain and Feng (2009) [10]	5.04%	22.50%	19.43%	17.32%
Dai and Zhou (2011) [4]	2.99%	11.58%	10.45%	8.78%

Table 2. Average matching times in seconds.

Algorithm	Genuine	Impostor
CPIM [8]	0.2018s	0.1868s
Proposed ($r = 170$)	0.0059s	0.0043s
Proposed ($r = 250$)	0.0104s	0.0078s
Proposed ($r = 500$)	0.0691s	0.0465s
Jain and Feng (2009) [10]	2.019s	1.906s
Dai and Zhou (2011) [4]	5.364s	5.158s

with the algorithms in [10] and [4]. Due to the relaxed protocol followed in the acquisition of the THUPALMLAB database, the singular point matching system is badly affected by pairs of genuine palmprints not having coincident singular points. This could explain the gap with the previous algorithm [8]. Nevertheless, even for the biggest neighborhood, the average matching speed was greatly improved. The speed-up factor was in the range of 34 times for genuine matchings and 43 times for impostor matchings, which represents a very important speed gain considering the huge size of palmprint databases in forensic scenarios. Execution times for algorithms in [10] and [4] are only reported as a reference from other algorithms in the state-of-the-art since they were obtained in different architectures. Execution times for the CPIM algorithm and the proposed method were obtained on an Intel i7-4770 @3.40 GHz CPU.

4   Conclusions

All in all, in this paper the feasibility of using singular points to speed up high-resolution palmprint matching systems is explored. Obtained recognition rates look very promising while greatly improving matching speeds. Additionally, the efficacy of the singular point matching system is affected by genuine pairs not having coincident singular points. The last can be easily overcome by implementing and following strict acquisition protocols. Aiming to forensic scenarios, identification test on latent palmprint images are still needed. Singular points can be manually extracted from latent palmprint images by forensic experts when present and used as an alternative to speed-up the search for the latent query in a huge database. Future works will be focused on this direction.

References

1. Alamghtuf, J., Khelifi, F.: Self geometric relationship-based matching for palmprint identification using sift. In: 2017 5th International Workshop on Biometrics and Forensics (IWBF), pp. 1–5. IEEE (2017)
2. Cappelli, R., Ferrara, M., Maio, D.: A fast and accurate palmprint recognition system based on minutiae. IEEE Trans. Syst. Man Cybern. Part B (Cybern.) **42**(3), 956–962 (2012)

3. Dai, J., Feng, J., Zhou, J.: Robust and efficient ridge-based palmprint matching. IEEE Trans. Pattern Anal. Mach. Intell. **34**(8), 1618–1632 (2012)
4. Dai, J., Zhou, J.: Multifeature-based high-resolution palmprint recognition. IEEE Trans. Pattern Anal. Mach. Intell. **33**(5), 945–957 (2011)
5. Fei, L., Xu, Y., Teng, S., Zhang, W., Tang, W., Fang, X.: Local orientation binary pattern with use for palmprint recognition. In: Zhou, J., et al. (eds.) CCBR 2017. LNCS, vol. 10568, pp. 213–220. Springer, Cham (2017). https://doi.org/10.1007/978-3-319-69923-3_23
6. Feng, J., Jain, A.K.: Fingerprint reconstruction: from minutiae to phase. IEEE Trans. Pattern Anal. Mach. Intell. **33**(2), 209–223 (2011)
7. Funada, J., et al.: Feature extraction method for palmprint considering elimination of creases. In: Fourteenth International Conference on Pattern Recognition, Proceedings, vol. 2, pp. 1849–1854. IEEE (1998)
8. Hernandez-Palancar, J., Munoz-Briseno, A., Gago-Alonso, A.: Using a triangular matching approach for latent fingerprint and palmprint identification. Int. J. Pattern Recognit. Artif. Intell. **28**(07), 1460004 (2014)
9. Jain, A., Demirkus, M.: On latent palmprint matching. Technical report 48824, Michigan State University (2008)
10. Jain, A.K., Feng, J.: Latent palmprint matching. IEEE Trans. Pattern Anal. Mach. Intell. **31**(6), 1032–1047 (2009)
11. Jia, W., et al.: Palmprint recognition based on complete direction representation. IEEE Trans. Image Process. **26**, 4483–4498 (2017)
12. Karu, K., Jain, A.K.: Fingerprint classification. Pattern Recognit. **29**(3), 389–404 (1996)
13. Kong, A., Zhang, D., Kamel, M.: Palmprint identification using feature-level fusion. Pattern Recognit. **39**(3), 478–487 (2006)
14. Liu, E., Jain, A.K., Tian, J.: A coarse to fine minutiae-based latent palmprint matching. IEEE Trans. Pattern Anal. Mach. Intell. **35**(10), 2307–2322 (2013)
15. Maltoni, D., Maio, D., Jain, A.K., Prabhakar, S.: Handbook of Fingerprint Recognition. Springer, London (2009). https://doi.org/10.1007/978-1-84882-254-2
16. Morales, A., Kumar, A., Ferrer, M.A.: Interdigital palm region for biometric identification. Comput. Vis. Image Underst. **142**, 125–133 (2016)
17. Neurotechnology-Inc.: Verifinger (sdk) (2012). http://www.neurotechnology.com
18. Peralta, D., Triguero, I., García, S., Saeys, Y., Benitez, J.M., Herrera, F.: On the use of convolutional neural networks for robust classification of multiple fingerprint captures. Int. J. Intell. Syst. **33**(1), 213–230 (2018)
19. Cupull-Gómez, R., Castillo-Rosado, K., Hernóndez-Palancar, J.: Automatic enhancement and segmentation for latent palmprint impressions. In: XVII Convención y Feria Internacional Informática, IV Conferencia Internacional en Ciencias Computacionales e Informáticas (CICCI), p. 10. CICCI (2018)
20. Shu, W., Rong, G., Bian, Z., Zhang, D.: Automatic palmprint verification. Int. J. Image Graph. **1**(01), 135–151 (2001)
21. Yang, X., Feng, J., Zhou, J.: Palmprint indexing based on ridge features. In: 2011 International Joint Conference on Biometrics (IJCB), pp. 1–8. IEEE (2011)
22. Zhu, E., Guo, X., Yin, J.: Walking to singular points of fingerprints. Pattern Recognit. **56**, 116–128 (2016)

Low-Resolution Face Recognition with Deep Convolutional Features in the Dissimilarity Space

Mairelys Hernández-Durán, Yenisel Plasencia-Calaña,
and Heydi Méndez-Vázquez[✉]

Advanced Technologies Application Center, 7ma A # 21406, Playa, Havana, Cuba
{mhduran,yplasencia,hmendez}@cenatav.co.cu

Abstract. In video surveillance and others real-life applications, it is usually needed to match low resolution (LR) face images against high-resolution (HR) gallery images. Although extensive efforts have been made, it is still difficult to find effective representations for low-resolution face recognition due to the degradation in resolution together with facial variations. This paper makes use of alternative representations based on dissimilarities between objects. Unlike previous works, we construct the dissimilarity space on top of deep convolutional features. We obtain a more compact representation by using prototype selection methods. Besides, metric learning methods are used to replace the standard Euclidean distance in the dissimilarity space. Experiments conducted on two data sets particularly designed for low-resolution face recognition showed that the proposal outperforms state-of-the-art methods, including some neural networks designed for this problem.

Keywords: Face recognition · Low-resolution
Dissimilarity representation · Convolutional networks

1 Introduction

Face recognition systems based on good quality and high-resolution images have obtained good results in practical applications [1]. However, high-resolution (HR) images are often not available, especially in real scenarios with uncontrolled conditions. On the contrary, low-resolution (LR) images are usually captured on these environments, which generates the so-called dimensional mismatch problem (different resolutions between gallery/probe images).

Different approaches have been proposed for low-resolution face recognition [2–4]. However, the performance of traditional methods suggests that current feature representation approaches are not enough to cope with the low resolution problem [5]. Recently, alternative representations based on dissimilarities between objects have been explored. It was shown in [6] that discriminative information for classification can be obtained if the LR images are analyzed in

© Springer Nature Switzerland AG 2018
Y. Hernández Heredia et al. (Eds.): IWAIPR 2018, LNCS 11047, pp. 95–103, 2018.
https://doi.org/10.1007/978-3-030-01132-1_11

the context of dissimilarities with other images and good results can be achieved in low-resolution face recognition.

The dissimilarity space (DS) representation brings a proximity information between prototypes and the rest of the training set, instead of representing the characteristics of each object individually [7]. It is necessary a base representation to build a dissimilarity space, unless an expert directly defines it. Intuitively, if more discriminative features are used as basis, the DS will be more effective. Recently, convolutional neural networks (CNNs) have been successfully applied in many domains and also in this context [3]. Taking this into account, we believe that features obtained from a deep architecture could replace traditional features as basis to construct a DS and thus, a more robust representation can be obtained.

In this paper, we propose a method for low-resolution face recognition that builds a DS on top of features learned by a convolutional neural network. We take advantage of a pre-trained network to avoid costs in terms of computer resources, and time in adjusting the parameters of the training stage. We also propose a reduced DS by using prototype selection methods and a learned metric is used in order to improve the classification accuracy in this space. Extensive experimental evaluations are conducted on two complex databases, where our method achieves state-of-the-art results, outperforming previous methods based on dissimilarity representations as well as some others that use deep convolutional features directly.

2   Dissimilarity Space from Deep Convolutional Features

The general scheme of the proposal can be found in Fig. 1. First, the low-high strategy proposed in [6] is used to deal with the dimensional mismatch. Deep convolutional features are obtained by means of the pre-trained VGG-Face [8] network and the DS is constructed on top of these features. Finally, a metric learning is applied to replace the standard Euclidean distance in the DS.

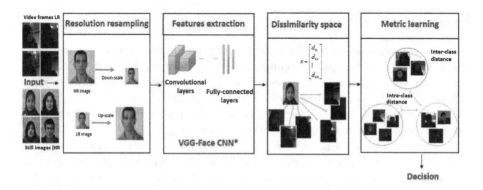

Fig. 1. General flow of the process.

2.1   Deep Convolutional Features Extraction

Recently, CNNs have become the state-of-the-art for many tasks [3]. In deep architectures, feature layers are not manually designed but they have learning procedures focused on general purpose, while specialization is given by the training data of the network. Despite their effectiveness, CNNs are difficult to train because they have many hyper-parameters (learning rate, momentum, etc.). Achieving the best combination requires complex calculations and powerful equipments. However, once the model is learned, it can be used to solve other similar problems without any additional training. Since it is convenient for users who do not have the resources needed for training, the use of intermediate layers from pre-trained networks have been growing recently [9].

Different already trained CNNs models are publicly available. We have selected VGG-Face [8] that currently reports one of the best performances for face recognition. We follow the idea in [9] which suggests that when using a pre-trained network for a given task, intermediate representations may achieve better results for a similar task. Considering this, we get not only the original net-descriptor from the last fully conected layer (dimension 4096), but also an average pooling descriptor obtained from the third convolutional layer of the 8th block (dimension 512).

2.2   Dissimilarity Space and Prototype Selection

Once the deep convolutional features are extracted from face images, cosine similarity is used as the distance measure to create the DS. The DS was first introduced by Pȩkalska and Duin [10]. Let X be the space of objects, let $R = \{r_1, r_2, ..., r_k\}$ be the set of prototypes such that $R \in X$, and let $d : X \times X \to \mathbb{R}^+$ be a suitable dissimilarity measure for the problem. For a finite training set $T = \{x_1, x_2, ..., x_l\}$ such that $T \in X$, a mapping $\phi_R^d : X \to \mathbb{R}^k$ defines the embedding of training and test objects in the DS by the dissimilarities with the prototypes:

$$\phi_R^d(x_i) = [d(x_i, r_1) \ d(x_i, r_2) \ ... \ d(x_i, r_k)]. \tag{1}$$

The prototypes may be chosen based on some criterion or even at random; but they should have good representation capabilities [11]. These methods allow to generate a new space to represent the whole set while keeping or even improving its discriminative power. We will focus on selective schemes since we are interested in exploiting a given dissimilarity matrix computed directly from the initial features. Some methods from this group were evaluated in this work:

Random. The selection of a representation set defines a dissimilarity space in which the entire training set is used to train the classifier. For this reason, even a randomly selected representation can be useful as a basic procedure [7].

Farthest-First Traversal (FFT) [12]. It selects an initial prototype at random from a sample of objects S, being $S = \{X_1, X_2, ..., X_k\} \subset X$; and then, each new prototype is defined as the farthest element of S from all previously chosen prototypes. It stops when it reaches the desired cardinality without any refinement.

kCentres [7]. It groups k-centroid objects from a symmetric distance matrix. These centroids are chosen so that the maximum distance of the objects with their closest centroid is minimized. Initialization can be randomly done. The value of k can alter the representation of the new space, therefore some adjustment would be necessary during the experiments.

Center [7]. As its name indicates, it selects prototypes situated in the center of a given set. Due to their central position all prototypes are structurally similar which may origin redundant prototypes. However, samples at the border are not considered, and thus, the set of prototypes is not negatively influenced by outliers.

Genetic Algorithm (GA) [11]. It is a search method based on heuristics that mimic natural mechanisms, by evolving individuals created after each generation by the best fitted ones. The basic idea is to maintain a population of chromosomes, which represent plausible solutions to a particular problem, and the evolution of this population through a process of competition and controlled variation. We use a variant proposed in [11] (GAsup), in which a stage of clustering is added before the random initialization which guarantees a faster convergence of the method.

2.3   Metric Learning in the Dissimilarity Space

Metric learning algorithms take advantage of prior information in form of labels over standard similarity measures. The effectiveness of using a learned metric to improve the DS representation was shown in [6]. In the present study, we selected two metric learning methods to replace the standard Euclidean distance in the dissimilarity space: LDA (Linear Discriminant Analysis) [13] and LMNN (Large Margin Nearest Neighbor) [14]. LDA computes a linear projection L that maximizes the amount of between-class variance relative to the amount of within-class variance. The linear transformation L is chosen to maximize the ratio of between-class to within-class variance, subject to the constraint that L defines a projection matrix, in a way that better separation between objects of different classes is achieved. In LMNN, the metric is trained following the criterion that the k-nearest neighbors belong to the same class, while samples from different classes are separated by a large margin. These metrics are used in this work to compute distances in the nearest neighbor (1-NN) classification.

3 Experimental Evaluation and Discussion

Two public face datasets designed for low-resolution face recognition evaluation were selected for the experiments. The **COX database** [15] includes 1000 still HR images and 3,000 videos corresponding to 1000 subjects. The still images were captured with a high-resolution camera. Videos were taken simulating a video-protection environment, with three cameras at different locations. Video-to-Still (V2S) and Still-to-Videos (S2V) evaluation protocols are evaluated. On the other hand, **SCFace database** [1] is composed by images captured simulating surveillance scenarios, making this database one of the most suitable set to evaluate LR case. It contains images of 130 subjects including high quality frontal images (mugshot). To capture the LR ones, three distances were used; each one with five video cameras with different qualities and resolutions.

Table 1. Results in Cox with some prototype selection methods.

	Average pooling descriptor			Original net-descriptor		
Method	Camera 1	Camera 2	Camera 3	Camera 1	Camera 2	Camera 3
random	81.56	80.96	90.75	75.45	76.22	86.41
FFT [12]	80.22	82.80	89.43	78.33	81.45	87.65
kcentres [7]	82.36	85.98	90.26	81.34	83.27	90.18
center [7]	86.85	88.58	**95.86**	84.49	86.18	**92.90**
GAsup [11]	84.74	88.36	94.29	82.56	84.22	90.36

3.1 Experiments on COX Database

Considering that COX database has a larger number of subjects, we first conducted an experiment on it, in order to compare the performance of the two network descriptors (the original net-descriptor and the average pooling descriptor) and some prototype selection methods under the proposed scheme. Both networks descriptors are obtained from the pre-trained VGG-Face model. For the prototype selection methods, similar parameters to those used in [11] were selected, with a cardinality equal to 120. For down-scaling and up-scaling the images in the low-high strategy, bicubic interpolation was used. Every video contains a large number of frames, thus we selected 20 frames distributed in a spaced manner to represent the whole video, which are averaged for obtaining the final face descriptor.

We report in Table 1 a comparison between some prototype selection methods to obtain a reduced DS, using LDA metric learning. It shows the recognition rates obtained for 10 random iterations of the V2S protocol, in which three videos from 300 subjects are used for training (900 in total), and the rest 700 videos from each camera are used for testing. We found that a small set of prototypes is sufficient to obtain a good representation. From this comparative study we can see that the *center* method reported the best performance followed by the *GAsup* method with a small difference. We consider *center* is the best in this setup because automatically learned representation are sensitive to outliers, i.e., those objects that are highly deviated from its representation compared with the rest of the dataset. From the results, we can see that the average pooling descriptor reports the best results in comparison with those obtained with the original net-descriptor. This implies that also in the DS, intermediate layers are able to obtain more discriminative representations when a pre-trained network is used. This is an advantage since it brings a much simple and effective representation than the original representation. On the other hand, it can be seen that in general the best results are obtained for Camera 3, the less affected by low resolution.

Table 2. Recognition rates on COX database following the S2V and V2S protocols.

Method	V2S-cam1	V2S-cam2	V2S-cam3	S2V-cam1	S2V-cam2	S2V-cam3
PSCL [15]	38.60	33.20	53.26	36.39	30.87	50.96
VGG-Face [8]	79.10	77.53	79.03	59.31	65.21	74.29
CERML-EG [16]	85.71	82.51	87.23	88.80	85.69	90.99
CERML-EA [16]	86.40	83.13	86.76	**88.97**	85.84	90.26
CERML-ES [16]	86.21	82.66	86.64	88.93	85.37	89.64
Our **center LMNN**	85.33	86.18	88.27	81.66	84.77	90.10
Our GAsup LMNN	80.54	80.96	87.44	81.20	85.44	89.96
Our **center LDA**	**87.54**	**89.04**	**91.91**	86.85	**88.58**	**95.86**
Our GAsup LDA	82.34	81.19	91.59	84.74	88.36	94.29

Considering the above results, we compare the proposal, using the average pooling descriptor and the best prototype selection methods (*center* and *GAsup*), with different state-of-the-art algorithms. We follow the comparison protocol in [15] to also evaluate the performance of the two metric learning methods (LMNN and LDA). Table 2 shows the recognition rates obtained not only in V2S, but also in S2V scenario. It can be seen that in general our proposal achieves higher recognition rates that previous methods evaluated on COX database, including those specially designed for dealing with the dimensional mismatch problem such as Point-to-Set Correlation Learning (PSCL) [15] and the three variants of the Cross Euclidean-to-Riemannian Metric (CERML) [16]. Moreover, when comparing with the results obtained by the original VGG-Face network the obtained improvement is significant. This shows the influence of the proposed pipeline on the classification accuracy, i.e. the use of intermediate layers, the construction of the DS and the use of a metric learning. From the table we can also observe that in general, *center* method performs better than *GAsup* with both metric learning methods. Our result follows the statement in [17] because LDA has a simple closed-form solution that is useful to handle large-scale learning.

3.2 Experiments on SCFace Database

For evaluating the proposal in the SCFace database we follow the protocol used in [3], in which the HR images (mugshot) are used as gallery and the images of distance 1 (the most affected by LR) are used for test. We randomly selected 80 subjects for training and the remaining 50 subjects for testing. For this database, a single video representation was obtained taking the average of 5 images per subject (the database only has 5 images per subject in each distance). In this case only the average pooling descriptor with the *center* method of prototype selection was used, since it was the best performing combination in previous experiments. The results in terms of average recognition rates (10 random iterations) are presented in Table 3. They are compared with state-of-the-art methods reported on this database, also including the original VGG-Face network.

Table 3. Recognition rates in SCFace database.

Method	Recognition rates(%)
MDS [2]	61.14
Proposal in [3]	74.00
VGG-Face [8]	68.75
Our center LDA	92.23
Our center LMNN	**94.96**

In contrast with the results in COX dataset, we found that LMNN metric learning shows better results in comparison with LDA metric learning in SCFace database. It is important to mention that the dimension of the vectors with LDA is always smaller than the number of classes, therefore, for problems with a small number of classes it does not offer good results. We consider this is the reason why in the case of Cox database that contains images from 1000 subjects LDA performs better, while for the SCFace database that only has 130 subjects, the LMNN method exhibits better results than LDA. As shown, the proposed scheme achieves a significantly higher recognition rate (94.96%) than other state-of-the-art methods. When comparing our results with those obtained by the VGG-Face, it is corroborated that the strategy allows us to obtain more robust descriptors from the network and also, the importance of using metric learning to emphasize discriminative information from the descriptors.

4 Conclusions

One important contribution of our work is the proposal of obtaining a dissimilarity representation from deep convolutional features to address low-resolution face recognition. We found that dissimilarity representations constructed from convolutional features are more effective than representations directly obtained from convolutional network, as in the case of the VGG-Face. It was shown that since automatically learned representations are sensitive to outliers, it is convenient the use of prototype selection methods that take into account central objects. On the other hand, it was corroborated that the low-high strategy and the metric learning methods used in previous works are effective for this problem. As future work, we aim at improving our results by using neural networks in two main phases of our approach. First, to address the dimensional mismatch using a super-resolution neural network. Second, trying to find more discriminative descriptors from neural network to construct the dissimilarity space.

References

1. Grgic, M., Delac, K., Grgic, S.: SCface-surveillance cameras face database. Multimed. Tools Appl. **51**(3), 863–879 (2011)
2. Biswas, S., Aggarwal, G., Flynn, P.J., Bowyer, K.W.: Pose-robust recognition of low-resolution face images. IEEE Trans. Pattern Anal. Mach. Intell. **35**(12), 3037–3049 (2013)
3. Zeng, D., Chen, H., Zhao, Q.: Towards resolution invariant face recognition in uncontrolled scenarios. In: 2016 International Conference on Biometrics (ICB), pp. 1–8. IEEE (2016)
4. Lu, T., Xiong, Z., Zhang, Y., Wang, B., Lu, T.: Robust face super-resolution via locality-constrained low-rank representation. IEEE Access **5**, 13103–13117 (2017)
5. Rajawat, A., Pandey, M.K., Rajput, S.S.: Low resolution face recognition techniques: a survey. In: 2017 3rd International Conference on Computational Intelligence and Communication Technology (CICT), pp. 1–4. IEEE (2017)
6. Hernández-Durán, M., Plasencia-Calaña, Y., Méndez-Vázquez, H.: Metric learning in the dissimilarity space to improve low-resolution face recognition. In: Beltrán-Castañón, C., Nyström, I., Famili, F. (eds.) CIARP 2016. LNCS, vol. 10125, pp. 217–224. Springer, Cham (2017). https://doi.org/10.1007/978-3-319-52277-7_27
7. Pękalska, E., Duin, R.P., Paclík, P.: Prototype selection for dissimilarity-based classifiers. Pattern Recognit. **39**(2), 189–208 (2006)
8. Parkhi, O.M., Vedaldi, A., Zisserman, A.: Deep face recognition. BMVC **1**, 6 (2015)
9. López-Avila, L., Plasencia-Calaña, Y., Martínez-Díaz, Y., Méndez-Vázquez, H.: On the use of pre-trained neural networks for different face recognition tasks. In: Mendoza, M., Velastín, S. (eds.) CIARP 2017. LNCS, vol. 10657, pp. 356–364. Springer, Cham (2018). https://doi.org/10.1007/978-3-319-75193-1_43
10. Pękalska, E., Duin, R.: Dissimilarity Representation For Pattern Recognition: Foundations and Applications, vol. 64. World Scientific, Singapore (2005)
11. Plasencia-Calaña, Y., Orozco-Alzate, M., Méndez-Vázquez, H., García-Reyes, E., Duin, R.P.W.: Towards scalable prototype selection by genetic algorithms with fast criteria. In: Fränti, P., Brown, G., Loog, M., Escolano, F., Pelillo, M. (eds.) S+SSPR 2014. LNCS, vol. 8621, pp. 343–352. Springer, Heidelberg (2014). https://doi.org/10.1007/978-3-662-44415-3_35
12. Olivetti, E., Nguyen, T.B., Garyfallidis, E.: The approximation of the dissimilarity projection. In: 2012 International Workshop on Pattern Recognition in NeuroImaging (PRNI), pp. 85–88. IEEE (2012)
13. Hastie, T., Tibshirani, R.: Discriminant adaptive nearest neighbor classification and regression. In: Advances in Neural Information Processing Systems, pp. 409–415 (1996)

14. Weinberger, K.Q., Blitzer, J., Saul, L.K.: Distance metric learning for large margin nearest neighbor classification. In: Advances in neural information processing systems, pp. 1473–1480 (2006)
15. Huang, Z., et al.: A Benchmark and comparative study of video-based face recognition on COX face database. IEEE Trans. Image Process. **24**(12), 5967–5981 (2015)
16. Huang, Z., Wang, R., Van Gool, L., Chen, X., et al.: Cross euclidean-to-riemannian metric learning with application to face recognition from video. In: IEEE Transactions on Pattern Analysis and Machine Intelligence (2017)
17. Liao, S., Lei, Z., Yi, D., Li, S.Z.: A Benchmark study of large-scale unconstrained face recognition. In: 2014 IEEE International Joint Conference on Biometrics (IJCB), pp. 1–8. IEEE (2014)

Exploring Local Deep Representations for Facial Gender Classification in Videos

Fabiola Becerra-Riera[(✉)], Annette Morales-González,
and Heydi Méndez-Vázquez

Advanced Technologies Application Center, 7ma A #21406, Playa, Havana, Cuba
{fbecerra,amorales,hmendez}@cenatav.co.cu

Abstract. Gender recognition in videos is a challenging task that has received limited attention in recent years. To tackle this problem, we propose to explore the use of intermediate features of a Convolutional Neural Network (CNN) with a component-based face representation methodology. With this approach we intend to exploit the gender information provided by different face parts. The features extracted from video key frames are combined with two different strategies to preserve the temporal information, and Random Forest classifiers are employed to obtain a final gender prediction for a video sequence. Our results on the McGill and COX datasets show that our proposal outperforms the end-to-end CNN approach and, in the McGill dataset, 100% of accuracy was obtained.

Keywords: Soft-biometrics · Gender classification
Video face analysis · Deep learning representation

1 Introduction

The estimation of demographic soft-biometrics (gender, race, age) has been an active research topic in recent years because of their application in domains such as biometric identification, video surveillance, marketing, among others. Gender is perhaps the most widely studied demographic attribute in Computer Vision [13]. Although its classification in controlled environments is not trivial because of the ambiguity in the anatomy of each individual, in real scenarios this problem is increased by changes in lighting, pose variations and occlusions, just to mention some examples. Recognizing gender on videos is even more challenging due to the frequently poor resolution and the presence of blurriness in the video frames. However, limited attention has been given to this problem [7,8,17].

Automatic gender estimation from faces usually goes through several steps: face detection, pre-processing, feature extraction and classification. Feature extraction is, maybe, the most critical step in order to achieve good performance. Traditional approaches employ different types of single low-level features, or computational expensive algorithms that explore multiple combinations of them to

© Springer Nature Switzerland AG 2018
Y. Hernández Heredia et al. (Eds.): IWAIPR 2018, LNCS 11047, pp. 104–112, 2018.
https://doi.org/10.1007/978-3-030-01132-1_12

find one that satisfies the needs of a specific scenario. Although combining low-level features has shown promising results [4], usually the selection of the initial set is the result of an empirical process influenced by the expertise of researchers. In recent years the scientific community has focused on Deep Learning-based approaches, which have shown impressive results and are the state-of-the-art on face attribute classification [11,21]. Most of the Deep Learning-based proposals use information from the upper layers to train classifiers or employ deep networks that handle both feature extraction and classification; however, some studies have shown that the use of intermediate representations, encoding different layers of visual information, may be more useful to describe the data [20,21]. In particular, considering the local information (from sub-regions or local patches) in the designing of deep architectures, has shown very good results for gender classification [12,15].

Motivated by the good results obtained by component-based gender classification methods [2,3,15], we propose a pipeline for gender estimation from videos applying a component-based face representation methodology , which takes into account that different parts of the face can provide different information about the gender of a person. Each facial region is described by features from intermediate layers of a trained Convolutional Neural Network. A global representation of the regions from selected video frames is constructed and a Random Forest (RF) classifier is trained to predict gender for each video frame. Different combination strategies among frame predictions are analyzed to obtain the best performance on gender estimation in the entire video.

The rest of this paper is organized as follows. Section 2 summarizes previous related works. Section 3 introduces the proposal. Section 4 presents experimental analysis. Finally, Sect. 5 concludes the paper.

2   Related Work

Among the most recent deep learning approaches for gender and age estimation from face images, two CNNs stand out for their simplicity and yet good results. The first one, proposed by Levi and Hassner [10], has a simple convolutional architecture that can be used even when the training set is limited. Their results provided a baseline for other Deep Learning approaches and showed that learning representations can boost the accuracy in the classification of gender. The second CNN, proposed by Rothe et al. [16], is a more elaborated solution based on the popular VGG-16 architecture [14]. Although their original proposal is devoted to estimate age from face images, the gender model released by the authors[1] shows impressive results for gender classification, outperforming the Levi and Hassner CNN. Based on this, we chose the second CNN, called DEX by the authors, to explore the use of intermediate representations obtained from the network.

In order to exploit the information related to different local face parts we base our proposal in the work of [2]. In that work, face images are subdivided into eight regions and the most discriminative ones for gender and age estimation are

---

[1] https://data.vision.ee.ethz.ch/cvl/rrothe/imdb-wiki/.

determined. The authors show the benefits of this region-based approach when face images are affected by occlusions (e.g., caps, eyeglasses or scarves), which is a crucial problem in real scenarios.

The aforementioned approaches focus on gender classification in still images. In the present work we focus on gender estimation from face videos instead of images, which suppose more complex scenarios. We redefine the facial regions proposed in [2] in order to incorporate valuable information discarded before and to take into account the temporal information of the video sequence.

In the literature there are few works related to gender classification from faces in videos. The first one was proposed by [18], employing Haar-like features and Adaboost for feature selection. In order to combine the classification of individual frames, they use a decision criterion that takes into account the adjacent frames classification output through a weighted voting function and a quality function. They evaluate their proposal on videos of 30 subjects collected from the internet. The proposals of [6,7] introduce probabilistic graphical models to represent temporal dependencies and the classification of a face at a specific time is conditioned on features from previous frames of the video sequence. In these papers authors use their own McGill Faces dataset [8]. A temporal-coherent feature for gender classification in videos was proposed by [19]. They build a pixel-intensity feature for a single frame, and the individual frame features are concatenated in order to classify the entire video at once. Selim et al. [17] proposed a CNN very similar to the one of [10] to classify each frame of a video sequence. Based on a quality criterion, they separate frames into different quality groups and they train a model for each of them. These last two works [17,19] also employ the McGill dataset, each one improving the existing results.

Nevertheless, as we will show in Sect. 4, we were able to confirm with our experiments that the use of the DEX CNN practically solves the problems posed in the McGill dataset, outperforming all the other state-of-the-art results in this dataset. This is why we are proposing to use this CNN to explore the intermediate representation for video gender classification.

3   Proposed Approach

The general flowchart of our proposal is presented in Fig. 1. The two main novelties of the proposed pipeline are: (1) The component-based feature extraction using a pre-trained neural network and (2) the combination strategies considered for obtaining the final video classification. First, an efficient method to obtain key frames from a given face sequence is applied [5]. Then, following the proposal in [2], face regions are extracted with the aim of exploiting the impact of each one separately for gender estimation. Besides the eight regions used in [2], we include hair and contour regions since visual information surrounding the face in an image could be of high importance for gender classification, especially when the facial features are ambiguous [1], which is a common problem in real-world videos. Each region is represented by extracting features from a pre-trained CNN and finally, a strategy for integrating the temporal information is used. In the following subsections we explain in details how the face regions are represented and the different strategies used for considering information coming from different frames.

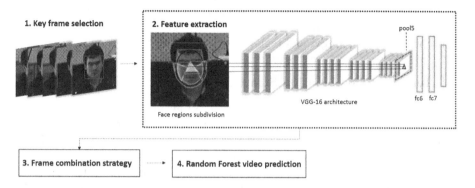

Fig. 1. Proposed general pipeline for gender estimation on videos.

3.1 Face Region Representation

We explore the use of visual information from intermediate layers of CNNs to represent face regions. As we mentioned before, we consider a recent network proposed for age and gender estimation in the wild (DEX CNN [16]), which is based on the VGG-Face network [14] and pre-trained in the IMDB-WIKI dataset.

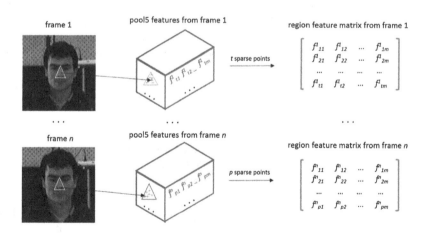

Fig. 2. Face region representation.

Face regions for one frame are first represented by a set of sparse points. A bijection between each of these points in the input frame and the corresponding points in the CNN layer is then performed, and a set of visual features is obtained from the pool5 layer (average pooling after the last convolutional layer). The process of obtaining these features for one region is illustrated in Fig. 2. We extract the visual features for each region from the selected key frames (step 2 of the pipeline) and they can be used independently or aggregated into one vector, depending on the temporal combination strategy selected. We concatenate the feature vectors of the individual regions as the final representation.

3.2   Temporal Combination Strategies

In order to incorporate the temporal information available in videos, we follow two strategies. The first one considers feature aggregation over the best key frames selected. In other words, the corresponding intermediate features of the CNN for every region are averaged within the entire volume of frames. The second strategy is majority voting, employed by several related works [7,17,18], where each frame provides a single prediction and the overall video prediction is given by the predominant label among all frames.

For both strategies, a Random Forest (RF) classifier is used. The contribution of each video region for gender classification is analyzed by training and testing different classifiers for single regions and their possible combinations.

4   Experimental Analysis and Discussion

We conduct experiments in the McGill and the COX databases for evaluating our proposal. The McGill dataset [8] has 60 videos of 31 female and 29 male subjects. Currently, only a subset of 35 videos is available (13 males and 22 females). We performed a 3-fold cross validation following the protocol of [17]. The COX database [9], camera 3 subset, has 1000 identity videos simulating a surveillance environment. This dataset does not provide gender labels, therefore we performed the manual labeling of 561 female and 439 male subjects. We ran a 5-fold cross validation in this dataset. Sample frames from one subject of each dataset are shown in Fig. 3.

We compare the impact of our component-based approach, with the use of intermediate features alone. For that aim, besides extracting features from the pool5 layer with the regions strategy explained on Sect. 3.1, we evaluate features obtained from fc6 and fc7 layers of the DEX CNN, which empirically displayed better results in [16]. For the aggregation strategy in this case, we averaged the corresponding 4096 feature vectors obtained for the best key frames.

In Table 1 we show the average classification accuracy obtained with the DEX end-to-end CNN, compared to the results of the fc6 and fc7 layers of this same network and with our proposed component-based methodology (DEX-pool5 + Regions), considering the two temporal combination strategies (aggregation and majority voting). For DEX-pool5 + Regions we report the results for the best region combination: nose alone reported our best results in the McGill dataset

Fig. 3. Video examples from COX and McGill datasets.

Table 1. Gender classification accuracy on McGill and COX datasets.

	McGill dataset		COX dataset	
	Aggregation	Majority voting	Aggregation	Majority voting
Wang et al. 2015 [19]	71.4%	-	-	-
Selim et al. 2018 [17]	-	90.4%	-	-
DEX CNN [16]	-	97.9%	-	90.3%
DEX-fc6	91.2%	91.1%	95.2%	95.8%
DEX-fc7	92.3%	86%	95.1%	95%
DEX-pool5 + Regions	**100%**	**100%**	**95.9%**	**96.1%**

and the eyes-nose-face-hair combination achieved the higher accuracy in the COX dataset.

As can be seen in Table 1, the best prior result on the McGill dataset was 90.4% and an improvement to 97.9% was obtained by employing the end-to-end DEX CNN. Nevertheless, by using our component-based proposal, 388 region combinations (8 of them containing only one or two face regions) already obtained 100% of accuracy with the aggregation of frames. An interesting remark is that using the nose alone 100% of effectiveness was achieved with the two temporal strategies. Therefore, with this result, our approach completely solved the gender estimation problem in this dataset. The COX database, which is bigger and presents higher complexity, is still a challenge. We can see that the use of intermediate layer features (fc6, fc7 and our proposal) outperformed in 5% or more the end-to-end network output. Our results were slightly better than those of fc6 in COX, but it is worth noting that in the McGill dataset our proposal outperformed fc6 and fc7 in 8%. We believe that this is due to the "curse of dimensionality" since the McGill dataset is small and fc6 and fc7 are high-dimensional vectors. This means that for this case, our proposal is a better choice.

We also performed an experimental analysis of the best region combinations using our DEX-pool5 + Regions pipeline. We took into account the classification accuracy of each gender class separately, and we compared them to the results achieved by the end-to-end network. Table 2 includes our best 5 region combinations codified by DEX-pool5 features with the aggregation strategy in the COX database. As can be seen, the proposed component-based method not only outperforms the end-to-end CNN in general, but it also shows a better inter-class balance. These 5 region combinations in which the eyes, nose, face and hair seem to be the more important ones, achieved a better commitment between male and female classification.

Table 2. Gender classification accuracy for our best 5 region combinations and the end-to-end DEX network in the COX dataset.

	Accuracy		
	General	Male	Female
eyes-nose-face-hair	95.9%	95.2%	96.4%
eyes-face-mouth	95.8%	94.5%	96.7%
eyes-face-hair	95.8%	94.9%	96.4%
eyes-forehead-nose-eyebrows	95.8%	94.7%	96.6%
eyes-cheeks-nose-eyebrows-hair	95.8%	94.5%	96.7%
DEX CNN [16]	90.3%	98.8%	83.6%

5   Conclusions

In this work we explored the use of features from intermediate layers of a trained CNN and we exploit the information from different face regions to tackle gender estimation on real-world videos. Our proposal showed its effectiveness obtaining superior results than the end-to-end approach and also than fc6 and fc7 layers in both databases (McGill and COX), by means of two different strategies to incorporate the temporal information in videos. In the McGill dataset our approach completely solved the gender estimation problem obtaining 100% of accuracy and outperforming other state-of-the-art methods. In the COX dataset our proposal showed a better inter-class balance with respect to the original CNN, achieving a better general accuracy.

References

1. Afifi, M., Abdelhamed, A.: Afif4: deep gender classification based on adaboost-based fusion of isolated facial features and foggy faces. arXiv preprint arXiv:1706.04277 (2017)
2. Becerra-Riera, F., Méndez-Vázquez, H., Morales-González, A., Tistarelli, M.: Age and gender classification using local appearance descriptors from facial components. In: International Joint Conference on Biometrics (IJCB), pp. 799–804. IEEE (2017)

3. Castrillón-Santana, M., Lorenzo-Navarro, J., Ramón-Balmaseda, E.: Descriptors and regions of interest fusion for in- and cross-database gender classification in the wild. Image Vis. Comput. **57**(C), 15–24 (2017)
4. Castrillón-Santana, M., Marsico, M.D., Nappi, M., Riccio, D.: MEG: texture operators for multi-expert gender classification. Comput. Vis. Image Underst. **156**, 4–18 (2017)
5. Chang, L., Rodés, I., Méndez, H., del Toro, E.: Best-shot selection for video face recognition using FPGA. In: Ruiz-Shulcloper, J., Kropatsch, W.G. (eds.) CIARP 2008. LNCS, vol. 5197, pp. 543–550. Springer, Heidelberg (2008). https://doi.org/10.1007/978-3-540-85920-8_66
6. Demirkus, M., Precup, D., Clark, J.J., Arbel, T.: Hierarchical spatio-temporal probabilistic graphical model with multiple feature fusion for binary facial attribute classification in real-world face videos. IEEE Trans. Pattern Anal. Mach. Intell. **38**(6), 1185–1203 (2016)
7. Demirkus, M., Toews, M., Clark, J.J., Arbel, T.: Gender classification from unconstrained video sequences. In: 2010 IEEE Computer Society Conference on Computer Vision and Pattern Recognition - Workshops, pp. 55–62, June 2010
8. Demirkus, M., Precup, D., Clark, J.J., Arbel, T.: Hierarchical temporal graphical model for head pose estimation and subsequent attribute classification in real-world videos. Comput. Vis. Image Underst. **136**, 128–145 (2015)
9. Huang, Z., et al.: A benchmark and comparative study of video-based face recognition on COX face database. IEEE Trans. Image Process. **24**(12), 5967–5981 (2015)
10. Levi, G., Hassner, T.: Age and gender classification using convolutional neural networks. In: Conference on Computer Vision and Pattern Recognition (CVPR) Workshops, pp. 34–42. IEEE (2015)
11. Liu, Z., Luo, P., Wang, X., Tang, X.: Deep learning face attributes in the wild. In: International Conference on Computer Vision (ICCV), pp. 3730–3738. IEEE (2015)
12. Mansanet, J., Albiol, A., Paredes, R.: Local deep neural networks for gender recognition. Pattern Recognit. Lett. (PRLetters) **70**(C), 80–86 (2016)
13. Ng, C.B., Tay, Y.H., Goi, B.-M.: Recognizing human gender in computer vision: a survey. In: Anthony, P., Ishizuka, M., Lukose, D. (eds.) PRICAI 2012. LNCS (LNAI), vol. 7458, pp. 335–346. Springer, Heidelberg (2012). https://doi.org/10.1007/978-3-642-32695-0_31
14. Parkhi, O.M., Vedaldi, A., Zisserman, A.: Deep face recognition. In: BMVC, vol. 1, p. 6 (2015)
15. Rodríguez, P., Cucurull, G., Gonfaus, J.M., Roca, F.X., González, J.: Age and gender recognition in the wild with deep attention. Pattern Recognit. (PR) **72**(C), 563–571 (2017)
16. Rothe, R., Timofte, R., Gool, L.V.: Deep expectation of real and apparent age from a single image without facial landmarks. Int. J. Comput. Vis. (IJCV) **126**, 144–157 (2016)
17. Selim, M., Sundararajan, S., Pagani, A., Stricker, D.: Image quality-aware deep networks ensemble for efficient gender recognition in the wild. In: Proceedings of the 13th International Joint Conference on Computer Vision, Imaging and Computer Graphics Theory and Applications (VISIGRAPP 2018), vol. 5 (2018)
18. Shakhnarovich, G., Viola, P.A., Moghaddam, B.: A unified learning framework for real time face detection and classification. In: Proceedings of the Fifth IEEE International Conference on Automatic Face and Gesture Recognition, FGR 2002, p. 16. IEEE Computer Society (2002)

19. Wang, W.C., Hsu, R.Y., Huang, C.R., Syu, L.Y.: Video gender recognition using temporal coherent face descriptor. In: 16th IEEE/ACIS International Conference on Software Engineering, Artificial Intelligence, Networking and Parallel/Distributed Computing, SNPD 2015, pp. 113–118. IEEE (2015)
20. Wang, X., Guo, R., Kambhamettu, C.: Deeply-learned feature for age estimation. In: Winter Conference on Applications of Computer Vision (WACV), pp. 534–541 (2015)
21. Zhong, Y., Sullivan, J., Li, H.: Face attribute prediction using off-the-shelf deep learning networks. In: International Conference on Biometrics (ICB). IEEE (2016)

Individual Finger Movement Recognition Based on sEMG and Classification Techniques

Laura Stella Vega-Escobar, Andrés Eduardo Castro-Ospina[✉],
and Leonardo Duque-Muñoz

Instituto Tecnológico Metropolitano, Medellín, Colombia
andrescastro@itm.edu.co

Abstract. Hand gesture recognition is an active research area of human machine interfaces in which the person performs a hand gesture and a machine recognize the actual movement. However, the gestures can be seen as combination of individual finger movements, and recognizing the individual finger movements could improve the gesture recognition. This work presents a framework for finger movement recognition based on the feature extraction of the superficial electromiographic signals generated in the arm. We acquired a dataset with 54 subjects, and eight signals (channels) per subject. Then, features extracted in three types of domains were analized namely, time, frequency, and time-frequency forming a feature set of 720 features. A subset of features were selected and a support vector machine and k-NN classifiers were trained with a 10-fold cross-validation to prevent overfitting. We reached an accuracy over 90% implying that our proposed framework facilitates the finger movement recognition.

Keywords: Acquisition · Classification · Feature selection
Finger movement recognition · sEMG · Validation

1 Introduction

Muscle Computer Interface (MuCI) is a growing area of Human Machine Interfaces (HMI) that makes use of surface electromyographic (sEMG) signals, records of electric activity in the muscles, which is controlled by the nervous system and produced during muscle contraction. Such signals are then translated into computer instructions to allow MuCI [5].

Two currently active research areas in MuCI are hand gesture recognition, and finger movement recognition, both applied in robotics [9], biomedical [14], sign language [10], medicine [27], among others. To discriminate fingers movements and gestures of the hand, several feature estimators and classifiers have been used, such features are divided into three domains, time, frequency and time-frequency domains. The former domain includes features extracted from

© Springer Nature Switzerland AG 2018
Y. Hernández Heredia et al. (Eds.): IWAIPR 2018, LNCS 11047, pp. 113–121, 2018.
https://doi.org/10.1007/978-3-030-01132-1_13

the entire record as Mean Absolute Value (MAV), Waveform Length (WL), Zero Crossings (ZC), Slope Sign Changes (SSC), Willison Amplitude (WAMP), among others [3,19,22,23]. In the second domain, the most used features are Frequency Mean (FMN), Frequency Median (FDM), Modified Frequency Mean (MFMN), Frequency Ratio (FR), among others [17,26]. Finally, in the time-frequency domain the Short Time Fourier Transform (STFT) and Discrete Wavelet Transform (DWT) are the most used [8,16,18].

The most widely used learning approach in the field of processing sEMG signals is supervised learning, which takes advantage of pre-established labels to train a classifier, comparisons have been made among different classification techniques, such as decision trees, k-nearest neighbors (k-NN) [20], Support Vector Machines (SVM) [11], and deep learning [25]. A feature reduction stage improves the performance of the classifier and the computational time. To achieve this, Principal Component Analysis (PCA) and the Independent Components Analysis (ICA) have been used, and selection methods as Sequential Forward Selection, Sequential Backward Selection, among others [4].

Besides, in the state-of-the art the feature estimation techniques and classifiers used by researchers have been applied over hand gesture recognition databases, in which the person perform the gesture following a visual stimuli. These databases contain few gestures, that can be seen as combinations of multiple finger movements. Thus by recognizing multiple individual finger movements, it could be possible to recognize several gestures. On the other hand, some of these labeling methods can present errors. For example, the movements performed by a subject can differ from the ones suggested by the visual stimuli, forcing to carry out a process of data relabeling [1,6,7].

In this work a methodology to automatically recognize finger movements is presented. The sEMG signals recorded of individual finger movement were aquired with a wireless armband, and its integration with flexible sensors aims to perform an automatic labeling of data. Several features estimators were applied in time, frequency and time-frequency domains. Then a feature reduction stage is performed with Sequential Forward Selection (SFS). Finally, the recognition is made with Support Vector Machines (SVM), and k-Nearest Neighbors (k-NN) classifiers. Achieved results show that proposed methodology facilitates the finger movement recognition, with a moderate performance for k-NN since achieves low sensitivity, but on the other hand, reaching a outstanding performance for SVM in terms of four performance measures above 90% for all classes.

2   Materials and Methods

Feature Estimation Techniques. Features in time domain are fast and easy to implement, because these features do not require any transformation and are stationary, therefore, they are widely used [3,23]. Features in the time-frequency domain as well as the time features are widely used [17,26], the most used time-frequency technique is the DWT, which decomposes the signal into different approximation and detail components that are related with different frequency bands.

Sequential Forward Selection (SFS). The objective of feature selection algorithms is to choose a number of features from the extracted feature set that yields minimum classification error, i.e., obtain the most discriminant features from the feature set. In this sense, SFS algorithm use a bottom-up search procedure which start from an empty feature set S and gradually add features selected by some evaluation function, that minimizes the mean squared error (MSE). At each iteration, the feature to be included to S is selected among the remaining available features and is the one with greater weight [21].

k-nearest neighbors (k-NN). Is a non parametric method of supervised learning which has as its main argument the distance between samples. The classifier compare a new sample with all the training samples. The output is a class membership. A sample is classified by a majority vote of its k-neighbors, with the sample being assigned to the most common class between them. The value of k can be selected having a radius of comparison or using Voronoi diagrams [2].

Support Vector Machine (SVM). Support vector machines are binary classifiers. The SVM produces a hyperplane which discriminates the data at hand into its corresponding classes. However, it is not always possible to separate them correctly, if so, the outcome of the model can not be generalized to other data. This is known as overfitting. To allow some errors and reduce overfitting, the SVM handle a C parameter that controls the trade-off between training errors and rigid margins, creating a soft margin which allows some misclassification Eq. (1). SVM cost function can be expressed as:

$$\tau(\boldsymbol{w}) = \text{minimize} \frac{1}{2}\|\boldsymbol{w}\|^2 + C \sum_{i=1}^{n} \varepsilon_i \tag{1}$$

where $\boldsymbol{w}$ is a normal vector to the hyperplane and ε_i represents the penalty for i-th example not satisfying the margin constraint. More details on Soft Margin SVM can be found in [15].

3 Experimental Setup

Methodology used in this manuscript is depicted in Fig. 1 and consists on four stages, data acquisition and pre-processing with the Myo Armband® device, feature estimation in time, frequency and time-frequency domains; dimension reduction with SFS; and classification with SVMs and k-nn classifiers. A brief description of the stages follows.

3.1 Signal Acquisition and Pre-processing

Dataset. sEMG were obtained from 54 subjects, 31 men and 23 women between 20–35 years, healthy and voluntary without motor or physiological problems, the subjects signed an informed consent to take part of the study, the study was approved by an ethics committee.

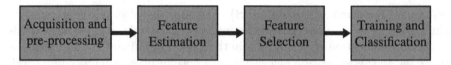

Fig. 1. Methodology proposed for individual movements of fingers of the hands recognition

sEMG signals are recorded by a Myo Armband®, this device contains 8 electrodes of stainless steel and its communication is wireless. Each subject is asked to be seated with both arms resting on a table, the most comfortable way without any distraction that could disturb its attention during the execution of motor tasks. Then, the device Myo is located at the right arm of the subject, ensuring that channel four is in the lower forearm followed by channel 3 in a clockwise direction and the fifth channel in counterclockwise sense, see Fig. 2(a).

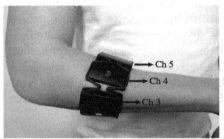 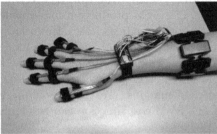

(a) Location of Myo Armband® device on the arm

(b) Location of flexible sensor on the fingers of the hand

Fig. 2. Acquisition prototype

The subject is asked to perform 6 movements, namely the flexion of *(i)* thumb, *(ii)* index finger, *(iii)* middle finger, *(iv)* ring finger, *(v)* pinky finger, and finally *(vi)* resting state, each movement is repeated 5 times and the execution is not necessarily performed in this order.

Five flexible sensor model SEN0628 56 mm, one per finger of the hand, are used for subsequent automatic database labeling, this sensor allows recognition from the resistance variation when it is flexed, where its resistance is inversely proportional to the applied bending, see Fig. 2(b).

Myo Armband® device signals are sent wirelessly to a Feather fruit-32U4 microcontroller, and in turn, the signals acquired by flexible sensors are sent to the same microcontroller, this with the objective that both signals are synchronized for auto-tagging the individual finger movements.

Pre-processing. A filtering step is carried out in order to minimize the noise or artifacts as power noise (60 Hz). A pass band Butterworth filter of order 2 is

Table 1. Features estimated from sEMG signals. For more information, see [19]

Time domain	Frequency domain	Time-frequency domain
Integrated EMG (IEMG)	Frequency Median (FMD)	Discrete Wavelet Transform (DWT) [24]
Mean Value	Frequency Mean	—Family : Daubechies8
Standard deviation		—Levels : 8
Difference Absolute Standard Deviation Value (DASDV)	Modified Frequency Median (MFMD)	*Features estimated from coefficients:*
Mean Absolute Value (MAV)		—Shannon energy
Modified Mean Absolute Value 1 (MMAV1)	Modified Frequency Mean (MFMN)	—Teager energy
Modified Mean Absolute Value 2 (MMAV2)		—Squared energy
		—Mean
Root Mean Square (RMS)	Frequency Ratio (FR)	—Variance
Variance (VAR)		—Standard deviation
Waveform Length (WL)	Signal to noise ratio (SNR)	—Kurtosis
Zero Crossings (ZC)		
Slope Sign Changes (SSC)	Peak Frequency (Hz)	
Willison Amplitude (WAMP)		
Simple Square Integral (SSI)	Mean Power (Volts/Hz)	
Myopulse Percentage Rate (MYOP)		

used with a sampling frequency of 200 Hz, low cutoff frequency of 58 Hz and a high cutoff frequency of 62 Hz. In addition, the signal is smoothed with a low pass filter with a cutoff frequency of 20 Hz, reducing signal noise [12].

3.2 Feature Estimation

This step consists in computing representative information from the signals producing a set of features. The features were computed from three domains: time, frequency and time-frequency, which are widely documented in the literature [3,17,19,22,23,26]. Estimated features are summarized in Table 1.

From this step we obtained a feature matrix with 324 samples (rows) or instances and 720 features (columns). Threshold value for the time domain features ZC, SSC, WA, MYOP empirically was used as three times the standard deviation of the signal. For the frequency domain a sampling frequency of 200 Hz was used, since it is the sample frequency of the Myo Armband device.

3.3 Feature Selection

Sequential Forward Selection (SFS) was used for the feature reduction stage, this in order to select a subset of features that provide the most relevant information from the ones at hand avoiding redundancy among them and removing irrelevant ones, thus reducing the dimensionality of the learning problem which could lead to a reduction of computational time and even to improve the classification performance.

3.4 Training and Classification

The classification process aims to identify the labels of the instances in a test set (unknown instances to the classifier) based only on the obtained features of the signals, i.e., the classifier gathers the sEMG signal features and associates them with a motor action, in this case to each individual finger movements. As supervised learning techniques we used one-against-all k-NN and SVM and to avoid overfitting of such classification models, a ten fold cross-validation is performed, the number of neighbors (k) for k-NN was empirically set to 3, a linear kernel was used for the SVM classifier and a C value of 1. Both classifiers and the feature selection technique were used from Balu toolbox [13]. Finally, to evaluate the classification performance accuracy, sensitivity, specificity and geometric mean measures were used.

4   Results and Discussion

The dimensionality of the problem was reduced by means of SFS to retain the most discriminative features. The number of retained features was set from 10% to 90% of the total of data in steps of 10%. According to the results, reducing the dimensionality to its 30% achieves suitable classification performances both for k-NN and SVM. Selected features with the higher relevant information were mostly from the time-frequency and time domain, highlighting the importance of these domains in MuCI tasks.

The classification results achieved with the selected feature subset for individual finger movement recognition are shown in Fig. 3. Specifically, in Fig. 3(a) can be seen the mean values of accuracy, sensitivity, specificity and geometric mean for the k-NN classifier for the selected subset and their corresponding standar values. X-axis represents the six classes, i.e., the six finger movements, while Y-axis the percentage classification performance. According to the bars it can be concluded that while k-NN reaches a proper accuracy performance and high specificity (around 80%), it also presents moderate sensitivity values (around 50%), such trade-off becomes clear on the geometric mean values. It can be concluded that k-NN is not suitable at recognizing the individual finger movements of the hand.

In Fig. 3(b) are depicted the SVM performances with the same selected subset of features used with k-NN. Achieved results outperform those of k-NN, reaching high mean values of accuracy, sensitivity, specificity and geometric mean (around 97%), improving the identification of the six classes, being class one and two the most improved.

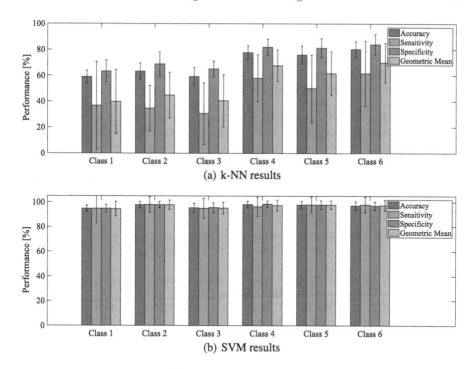

Fig. 3. Achieved results for k-NN and SVM classifiers with a feature reduction to 30%

5 Conclusions

A methodology for the recognition of the individual movement of the fingers was proposed. Feature estimation techniques were used in time, frequency and time-frequency domains, furthermore, k-NN and Support Vector Machines classifiers were used as supervised learning methods. The obtained results show that the performance of the proposed methodology is overall 90% for all classes with the SVM classifier, while the k-NN classifier achieves 70%, therefore, it is not suitable for recognizing the individual movements of the fingers of the hand.

As future work, we will include in our acquisition system the sensors embedded in the Myo Armband device (accelerometer, magnetometer and gyroscope) that we did not use in this work. With those sensors we will study if this information could improve the performance achieved with our methodology. We will increase the number of subjects in the database in order to be able to use learning techniques that require more data such as deep learning, besides, adapt the methodology to perform real time recognition and translate the movements to an exoskeleton or a robotic arm.

References

1. Atzori, M., Muller, H.: The Ninapro database: a resource for sEMG naturally controlled robotic hand prosthetics. In: 2015 37th Annual International Conference of the IEEE Engineering in Medicine and Biology Society, pp. 7151–7154. IEEE (2015)
2. Azaripasand, P., Maleki, A., Fallah, A.: Classification of ADLs using muscle activation waveform versus thirteen EMG features. In: 2015 22nd Iranian Conference on Biomedical Engineering, pp. 189–193. IEEE, November 2015
3. Bian, F., Li, R., Liang, P.: SVM based simultaneous hand movements classification using sEMG signals. In: 2017 IEEE International Conference on Mechatronics and Automation, pp. 427–432. IEEE (2017)
4. Chandrashekar, G., Sahin, F.: A survey on feature selection methods. Comput. Electr. Eng. **40**(1), 16–28 (2014)
5. Chowdhury, A., Ramadas, R., Karmakar, S.: Muscle computer interface: a review. In: Chakrabarti, A., Prakash, R. (eds.) ICoRD 2013. LNME, pp. 411–421. Springer, India (2013)
6. Côté-Allard, U., et al.: Deep learning for electromyographic hand gesture signal classification by leveraging transfer learning (2018)
7. Du, Y., Jin, W., Wei, W., Hu, Y., Geng, W.: Surface EMG-based inter-session gesture recognition enhanced by deep domain adaptation. Sensors **17**(3), 458 (2017)
8. Duan, F., Dai, L., Chang, W., Chen, Z., Zhu, C., Li, W.: sEMG-based identification of hand motion commands using wavelet neural network combined with discrete wavelet transform. IEEE Trans. Ind. Electron. **63**(3), 1923–1934 (2016)
9. Feng, N., Shi, Q., Wang, H., Gong, J., Liu, C., Lu, Z.: A soft robotic hand: design, analysis, sEMG control, and experiment. Int. J. Adv. Manuf. Technol. **97**, 319–333 (2018)
10. Hirafuji Neiva, D., Zanchettin, C.: Gesture recognition: a review focusing on sign language in a mobile context. Expert Syst. Appl. **103**, 159–183 (2018)
11. Hu, X., Kan, J., Li, W.: Classification of surface electromyogram signals based on directed acyclic graphs and support vector machines. Turk. J. Electr. Eng. Comput. Sci. **26**(2), 732–742 (2018)
12. Kieliba, P., Tropea, P., Pirondini, E., Coscia, M., Micera, S., Artoni, F.: How are muscle synergies affected by electromyography pre-processing? IEEE Trans. Neural Syst. Rehabil. Eng. **26**(4), 882–893 (2018)
13. Mery, D.: BALU: A Matlab toolbox for computer vision, pattern recognition and image processing (2011). http://dmery.ing.puc.cl/index.php/balu
14. Muñoz-Cardona, J.E., Henao-Gallo, O.A., López-Herrera, J.F.: Sistema de Rehabilitación basado en el Uso de Análisis Biomecánico y Videojuegos mediante el Sensor Kinect. TecnoLógicas, p. 43, November 2013
15. Naik, G.R., Kumar, D.K., Jayadeva: Twin SVM for gesture classification using the surface electromyogram. IEEE Trans. Inf. Technol. Biomed. **14**(2), 301–308 (2010)
16. Naik, G.R.: Applications, Challenges, and Advancements in Electromyography Signal Processing. Advances in Medical Technologies and Clinical Practice. IGI Global, Hershey (2014)
17. Oleinikov, A., Abibullaev, B., Shintemirov, A., Folgheraiter, M.: Feature extraction and real-time recognition of hand motion intentions from EMGs via artificial neural networks. In: 2018 6th International Conference on Brain-Computer Interface, pp. 1–5. IEEE (2018)

18. Phinyomark, A., Quaine, F., Charbonnier, S., Serviere, C., Tarpin-Bernard, F., Laurillau, Y.: EMG feature evaluation for improving myoelectric pattern recognition robustness. Expert Syst. Appl. **40**(12), 4832–4840 (2013)
19. Phinyomark, A., Scheme, E.: A feature extraction issue for myoelectric control based on wearable EMG sensors. In: 2018 IEEE Sensors Applications Symposium, pp. 1–6. IEEE, March 2018
20. Purushothaman, G., Vikas, R.: Identification of a feature selection based pattern recognition scheme for finger movement recognition from multichannel EMG signals. Australas. Phys. Eng. Sci. Med. **41**(2), 549–559 (2018)
21. Rodriguez-Galiano, V.F., Luque-Espinar, J.A., Chica-Olmo, M., Mendes, M.P.: Feature selection approaches for predictive modelling of groundwater nitrate pollution: an evaluation of filters, embedded and wrapper methods. Sci. Total Environ. **624**, 661–672 (2018)
22. Shi, W.T., Lyu, Z.J., Tang, S.T., Chia, T.L., Yang, C.Y.: A bionic hand controlled by hand gesture recognition based on surface EMG signals: a preliminary study. Biocybern. Biomed. Eng. **38**(1), 126–135 (2018)
23. Tosin, M.C., Majolo, M., Chedid, R., Cene, V.H., Balbinot, A.: sEMG feature selection and classification using SVM-RFE. In: 2017 39th Annual International Conference of the IEEE Engineering in Medicine and Biology Society, pp. 390–393. IEEE, July 2017
24. Vallejo, M., Gallego, C.J., Duque-Muñoz, L., Delgado-Trejos, E.: Neuromuscular disease detection by neural networks and fuzzy entropy on time-frequency analysis of electromyography signals. Expert. Syst. **35**(4), e12274 (2018)
25. Wang, X., Wang, Y., Wang, Z., Wang, C., Li, Y.: Hand gesture recognition using sparse autoencoder-based deep neural network based on electromyography measurements. In: Varadan, V.K. (ed.) Nano-, Bio-, Info-Tech Sensors, 3D System II, p. 42. SPIE, March 2018
26. Wu, Y., Liang, S., Zhang, L., Chai, Z., Cao, C., Wang, S.: Gesture recognition method based on a single-channel sEMG envelope signal. EURASIP J. Wirel. Commun. Netw. **2018**(1), 35 (2018)
27. Xu, Y., Zhang, D., Wang, Y., Feng, J., Xu, W.: Two ways to improve myoelectric control for a transhumeral amputee after targeted muscle reinnervation: a case study. J. Neuroeng. Rehabil. **15**(1), 37 (2018)

Watermarking Based on Krawtchouk Moments for Handwritten Document Images

Ernesto Avila-Domenech[(✉)] and Anier Soria-Lorente

Universidad de Granma, Carretera Central vía Holguín Km 1/2,
Bayamo, Granma, Cuba
eadomenech@gmail.com, asorial1983@gmail.com

Abstract. In this paper, a digital watermarking technique for copyright protection based on the concept of embed a digital watermark and modifying coefficients in Krawtchouk moments domain is presented. This technique is specifically for handwritten document images using a QR code as a digital watermark. It consists in dividing the image into 8×8 pixels blocks, where the number of selected blocks is equal to the number of watermark bits. The Krawtchouk moments of each selected block are determined. After that, one coefficient is modified using Dither modulation. In addition, the results obtained in terms of perceptual quality (PSNR) and robustness (BER) show that the proposed technique is robust to JPEG compression attacks keeping imperceptibility.

Keywords: Digital watermarking · Genetic algorithm
Hadwritten documents · Krawtchouk moments · QR code

1 Introduction

The rapid evolution of the digital world has facilitated the manipulation and transmission of digital media, such as text, images, audio, video and 3D models. Easy access and replication have led to serious problems with copyright protection of media. Therefore, the scientific community has developed several techniques to ensure the protection of copyright and the information in general.

One of the more used techniques in the Information Hiding field is the Digital watermarking. It is defined as the process of embedding information into a noise-tolerant digital signal to identify the copyright ownership of the media [11].

There is an extensive literature about watermarking techniques applied to various types of host content, such as audio [3, 7], image [9, 10, 15] and video [14].

Recently, the scientists developed the orthogonal moments, which use as kernel functions orthogonal polynomials that constitute orthogonal basis. This property of orthogonality, gives to the corresponding moments the feature of minimum information redundancy, meaning that different moment orders describe different image content. Some representative moment families are the Tchebichef, dual Hahn, Racah and Krawtchouk moments [13].

© Springer Nature Switzerland AG 2018
Y. Hernández Heredia et al. (Eds.): IWAIPR 2018, LNCS 11047, pp. 122–129, 2018.
https://doi.org/10.1007/978-3-030-01132-1_14

The main advantage of the orthogonal moments is their ability to uniquely describe the content of an image by permitting the full reconstruction of the image they describe. The information embedment through moments' domain in conjunction with the minimum reconstruction error of the final watermarked image, makes image moments an attractive and useful tool in watermarking applications [12].

In this paper, we propose a new digital watermarking schema based on the set of Krawtchouk moments. The rest of the paper is organized as follows. Section 2 covers the background of this work in three subsections. The approaches followed in the proposed system are discussed in Sect. 3. Finally, experimental results and discussions are given in Sect. 4.

2 Background

Arnold Transform

The Arnold transform is a invertible method that can be used for pixel scrambling, and has been adopted in various watermarking schemes. By using the Arnold transform, the high pixel correlation can be disrupted. The Arnold transform is shown in Eq. 1, where p and q are positive integers, $det(A) = 1$, and (x', y') are the new coordinates of the pixel after Arnold transform is applied to a pixel at position (x, y) [6]. The transform changes the position of two pixels, and if it is done several times, a disordered image can be generated. Because of Arnold transform of periodicity, the original image will be recovered.

$$\begin{bmatrix} x' \\ y' \end{bmatrix} = A \begin{bmatrix} x \\ y \end{bmatrix} \bmod N = \begin{bmatrix} 1 & p \\ q & pq+1 \end{bmatrix} \begin{bmatrix} x \\ y \end{bmatrix} \bmod N. \tag{1}$$

In Fig. 1, on the left, original watermark, in the center, scrambled watermark image using Arnold transform 20 times (with $p = 1$, $q = 1$ and $N = 62$) and in the right, the recovered watermark image using Arnold transform 10 times more because for $N = 62$ the periodicity is 30.

Krawtchouk Moments

The Krawtchouk moments were introduced by Yap in [16]. These orthogonal moments satisfy the following recurrence relation

$$\alpha_n(Np - 2np + n - x)\overline{K}_n^{p,N}(x)$$
$$= p(n - N)\overline{K}_{n+1}^{p,N}(x) + \beta_n n(1 - p)\overline{K}_{n-1}^{p,N}(x), \quad n \geq 1,$$

Fig. 1. Watermark image, scrambled image and recovered image.

with initial conditions

$$\overline{K}_0^{p,N}(x) = \sqrt{w^{p,N}(x)p^{-1}},$$

and

$$\overline{K}_1^{p,N}(x) = (Np - x)(Np)^{-1}\sqrt{w^{p,N}(x)(1-p)(Np)^{-1}},$$

where $\alpha_n = \sqrt{\frac{(1-p)(n+1)}{p(N-n)}}$, $\beta_n = \sqrt{\frac{(1-p)^2(n+1)n}{p^2(N-n)_2}}$, $w^{p,N}(x) = \binom{N}{x}p^x(1-p)^{N-x}$ and $0 < p < 1$.

The Krawtchouk moment of order $(m+n)$ of an image $f(x,y)$ with $M \times N$ pixels is defined as

$$K_{mn} = \sum_{x=0}^{M-1}\sum_{y=0}^{N-1} f(x,y)\overline{K}_m^{p,M}(x)\overline{K}_n^{q,N}(y), \qquad (2)$$

where $m \in [0, M-1]$ and $n \in [0, N-1]$.

The image $f(x,y)$ can be reconstructed using

$$f(x,y) = \sum_{m=0}^{M-1}\sum_{n=0}^{N-1} K_{mn}\overline{K}_m^{p,M}(x)\overline{K}_n^{q,N}(y), \qquad (3)$$

where $x \in [0, M-1]$ and $y \in [0, N-1]$.

The lower order Krawtchouk moments store information of a specific region-of-interest of an image, the higher order moments store information of the rest of the image. Therefore, by reconstructing the image from the lower order moments and discarding the higher order moments, a sub-image can be extracted from the subject image. For each additional moment used in reconstructing the image, the square error of the reconstructed image is reduced [16].

The set of lower order Krawtchouk moments is generally the set of perceptually significant components of the image. This choice ensures that the watermark is robust to attacks [17].

Dither Modulation Quantization

Dither modulation quantization technique is one of the most popular in the watermarking. It has good performance on following requirements of watermarking: perceptibility ratio, data payload, robustness, and blind extraction. The combination of dither modulation quantization with different transformation domain watermarking methods also improves watermark extraction capability [5].

One bit of the watermark can be embedded as

$$|C_0'(k_1, k_2)| = \begin{cases} 2\Delta \times round(\frac{|C_0(k_1,k_2)|}{2\Delta}) + \frac{\Delta}{2}, & if\ W(i,j) = 1 \\ 2\Delta \times round(\frac{|C_0(k_1,k_2)|}{2\Delta}) - \frac{\Delta}{2} & if\ W(i,j) = 0 \end{cases}, \qquad (4)$$

where Δ is the quantization step controlling the embedding strength of the watermark bit, $|\cdot|$ is the absolute operator, $round(\cdot)$ denotes the rounding operation to the nearest integer, $W(i,j)$ is the watermark bit at the position (i,j) and $C_0'(k_1,k_2)$ is the modified block.

To extract the watermark it is used

$$W^*(i,j) = arg_{\sigma \in \{0,1\}} min(|C_0''(k_1,k_2)|_\sigma - |C_0^*(k_1,k_2)|)), \tag{5}$$

where $C_0^*(k_1,k_2)$ is the extracted watermark and $|C_0''(k_1,k_2)|_\sigma$ is defined as

$$|C_0''(k_1,k_2)|_\sigma = \begin{cases} 2\Delta \times round(\frac{|C_0^*(k_1,k_2)|}{2\Delta}) + \frac{\Delta}{2}, & if\ \sigma = 1 \\ 2\Delta \times round(\frac{|C_0^*(k_1,k_2)|}{2\Delta}) - \frac{\Delta}{2} & if\ \sigma = 0 \end{cases}. \tag{6}$$

3 Materials and Methods

Watermark Embedding Scheme (see Fig. 2)

✓ The binary watermark image (QR code) is scrambled using Arnold transform (see Eq. 1).
✓ The cover image is transformed from RGB to YCbCr color space, and the Y component, corresponding to the luminance information, is divided into small image blocks of 8×8 pixels.
✓ The Krawtchouk moments of selected blocks are determined by Eq. 2.
✓ Watermark bit is embedded in the selected block moments using Dither modulation (see Eq. 4).
✓ Watermarked blocks can be obtained using Eq. 3.
✓ The last step is to transform the YCbCr to RGB space to obtain RGB watermarked image.

Watermark Extraction (see Fig. 2)

✓ The watermarked image is transformed from the RGB to the YCbCr color space and the Y component is divided into 8×8 pixels blocks.
✓ The Krawtchouk moments of selected blocks are determined.
✓ Scrambled watermark bits are obtained with the selected block moments using Dither modulation (see Eq. 5).
✓ Finally, QR code watermark is constructed with the scrambled bits using Arnold transform.

Optimization Against JPEG Compression Attacks

Recently, metaheuristic optimization algorithms have been used [1,4] to improve the performance of watermarking methods in solving the conflict between quality and robustness. Metaheuristic algorithms are used to find parameters that can be used to increase robustness but maintaining the imperceptibility parameters. Some watermarking methods use the metaheuristic algorithm to optimize a single objective, such as robustness or quality, while the other objective is considered through predetermined inclusion parameters or evaluated in an adaptive way.

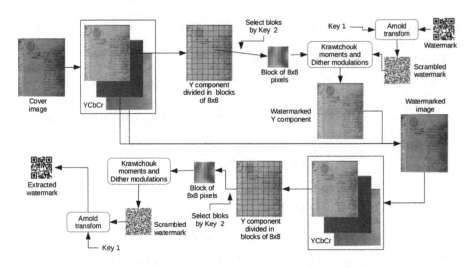

Fig. 2. Watermark embedding and extraction scheme.

Fig. 3. Handwritten document images (1.jpg and 2.jpg, left to right).

In this proposal, using the images represented in Fig. 3, a similar genetic algorithm as the one used in [4] was applied to determine the ideal parameters with the purpose of guaranteeing the performance between imperceptibility and robustness.

In the parameters obtained for both images, the coefficient to be used is the same as the applied attack. It can be observed that in the JPEG 20% attack, the optimum coefficient to be used for both images is 19 and Δ for one case is 128 and in other case 141. Taking into account the four attacks, the one with the 20% is the most aggressive, the 19 coefficient is taken as reference because it is the same for both images. Considering that the bit error rate generates acceptable values, 128 is considered as Δ value, because it is the lowest value for JPEG 20% attack in both images (see Tables 1 and 2).

Table 1. Optimized parameters for 1.jpg image.

Attack	FA	Coefficient	Δ	PSNR	BER	QR decoded
JPEG 75%	0.829307	43	35	54.0657677342	0.00104058272633	Yes
JPEG 50%	0.817445	43	72	49.2058749843	0.00520291363163	Yes
JPEG 20%	0.805757	19	128	43.2630691126	0.00312174817898	Yes
Guetzli 85% [2]	0.819719	28	49	49.4777158275	0.0	Yes

Table 2. Optimized parameters for 2.jpg image.

Attack	FA	Coefficient	Δ	PSNR	BER	QR decoded
JPEG 75%	0.826590	43	35	53.9286245147	0.00728407908429	Yes
JPEG 50%	0.809593	43	75	48.4338108172	0.0239334027055	Yes
JPEG 20%	0.804583	19	141	42.5328352352	0.00208116545265	Yes
Guetzli 85% [2]	0.819719	28	49	49.4777158275	0.0	Yes

4   Results and Discussion

For the evaluation of results the logarithmic value of ratio between signal and noise (PSNR), and the bit error rate (BER) are used.

The PSNR value is calculated using the equation

$$PSNR = 10\log_{10}\left(\frac{MAX^2}{MSE}\right) = 20\log_{10}\left(\frac{MAX}{\sqrt{MSE}}\right), \tag{7}$$

where MAX is the maximum possible pixel value of the image and MSE represent a mean square error.

$$MSE = \frac{1}{MN}\sum_{i=1}^{M}\sum_{j=1}^{N}[f'(m,n) - f(m,n)]^2, \tag{8}$$

where $M \times N$ is the size of the image, $f(m,n)$ is a cover image and $f'(m,n)$ is a watermarked image.

The BER value is calculated using the equation

$$BER = \frac{1}{B}\sum_{n=0}^{B-1}\begin{cases}1 & \text{if } w'(n) \neq w(n) \\ 0 & \text{if } w'(n) = w(n)\end{cases}, \tag{9}$$

where $w(n)$ y $w'(n)$ are binary bits (0 or 1) of the original watermark and extracted watermark. B is the number of pixels of the watermark.

With the optimized parameters, 60 images that belong to [8] were evaluated. The values obtained for all images were acceptable because in 100% of cases the watermark was decoded. Besides the PSNR values were between 44 dB and 46 dB (see Fig. 4), it means the nonexistence of visual differences between the watermarked and original images. Moreover, Fig. 5 shows the obtained result for BER corresponding to these images for the four types of JPEG compression attacks. As it can be observed, values under 0.005% were achieved, being decoded all QR watermark codes.

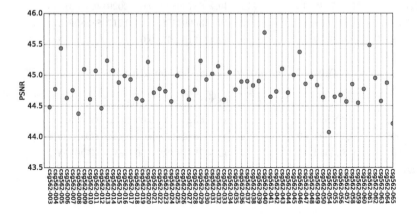

Fig. 4. PSNR values for Saint Gall database watermarked images.

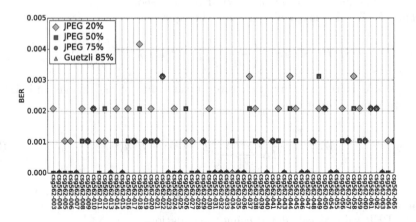

Fig. 5. BER values under different JPEG compression attacks.

5   Conclusions

In this paper, a digital watermarking technique based on Krawtchouk moments was implemented, and it was optimized by a genetic algorithm for manuscript document images. The results show a BER less than 0.005%, so the extracted QR codes were decoded in 100% of the 60 analyzed images. In addition, the values of PSNR in all cases exceeded 44 dB. Thus, there is no visual difference between the original and watermarked images.

References

1. Abdelhakim, A.M., Saad, M.H., Sayed, M., et al.: Optimized SVD-based robust watermarking in the fractional Fourier domain. Multimed. Tools Appl. 1–23 (2018). https://doi.org/10.1007/s11042-018-6014-5
2. Alakuijala, J., Obryk, R., Stoliarchuk, O., Szabadka, Z., Vandevenne, L., Wassenberg, J.: Guetzli: perceptually guided JPEG encoder, pp. 1–13 (2017)
3. Ali, G., et al.: Audio watermarking by hybridization of DWT-DCT. Int. J. Comput. Sci. Netw. Secur. **17**(8), 19–27 (2017)
4. Avila-Domenech, E.: Marca de agua digital basada en DWT-DCT para imágenes de documentos manuscritos: optimización contra ataques de compresión JPEG. Rev. Cuba. Ciencias Inform. **12**(2), 30–43 (2018)
5. Chen, B., Wornell, G.W.: Quantization index modulation: a class of provably good methods for digital watermarking and information embedding. IEEE Trans. Inf. Theory **47**(4), 1423–1443 (2001)
6. Chow, Y.-W., Susilo, W., Tonien, J., Zong, W.: A QR code watermarking approach based on the DWT-DCT technique. In: Pieprzyk, J., Suriadi, S. (eds.) ACISP 2017. LNCS, vol. 10343, pp. 314–331. Springer, Cham (2017). https://doi.org/10.1007/978-3-319-59870-3_18
7. Dhar, P.K., Shimamura, T.: Blind audio watermarking in transform domain based on singular value decomposition and exponential-log operations. In: Signals, pp. 552–561 (2017). https://doi.org/10.13164/re.2017.0552
8. Fischer, A., Frinken, V., Fornés, A., Bunke, H.: Transcription alignment of Latin manuscripts using hidden Markov models. In: Proceedings of the 2011 Workshop on Historical Document Imaging and Processing, pp. 29–36. ACM (2011)
9. Ghazvini, M., Hachrood, E.M., Mirzadi, M.: An improved image watermarking method in frequency domain. J. Appl. Secur. Res. **12**(2), 260–275 (2017). https://doi.org/10.1080/19361610.2017.1277878
10. Juarez-Sandoval, O.U., Cedillo-hernandez, M., Nakano-Miyatake, M., Cedillo-Hernandez, A., Perez-Meana, H.: Digital image ownership authentication via camouflaged unseen-visible watermarking. Multimed. Tools Appl. **77**, 26601–26634 (2018)
11. Nin, J., Ricciardi, S.: Digital watermarking techniques and security issues in the information and communication society. In: 2013 27th International Conference on Advanced Information Networking and Applications Workshops (WAINA), pp. 1553–1558. IEEE (2013)
12. Papakostas, G.A., Tsougenis, E.D., Koulouriotis, D.E.: Moment-based local image watermarking via genetic optimization. Appl. Math. Comput. **227**, 222–236 (2014). https://doi.org/10.1016/j.amc.2013.11.036
13. Papakostas, G.A., Koulouriotis, D.E., Karakasis, E.G.: Computation strategies of orthogonal image moments: a comparative study. Appl. Math. Comput. **216**(1), 1–17 (2010)
14. Sake, A., Tirumala, R.: Bi-orthogonal wavelet transform based video watermarking using optimization techniques. Mater. Today: Proc. **5**(1), 1470–1477 (2018)
15. Su, Q., Chen, B.: Robust color image watermarking technique in the spatial domain. Soft Comput. (2017). https://doi.org/10.1007/s00500-017-2489-7
16. Yap, P., Paramesran, R., Ong, S.H.: Image analysis by Krawtchouk moments. IEEE Trans. Image Process. **12**(11), 1367–1377 (2003)
17. Yap, P.T., Paramesran, R.: Local watermarks based on Krawtchouk moments. In: TENCON 2004. 2004 IEEE Region 10 Conference, pp. 73–76. IEEE (2004)

Data Mining and Applications

Multi-graph Frequent Approximate Subgraph Mining for Image Clustering

Niusvel Acosta-Mendoza[1,2(✉)], Jesús Ariel Carrasco-Ochoa[2],
Andrés Gago-Alonso[1], José Francisco Martínez-Trinidad[2],
and José Eladio Medina-Pagola[3]

[1] Advanced Technologies Application Center (CENATAV),
7a # 21406 e/ 214 and 216 Siboney, Playa, 12200 Havana, Cuba
{nacosta,agago}@cenatav.co.cu
[2] Instituto Nacional de Astrofísica, Óptica y Electrónica (INAOE),
Luis Enrique Erro No. 1, Sta. Mar ía Tonantzintla, 72840 Puebla, Mexico
{nacosta,ariel,fmartine}@ccc.inaoep.mx
[3] Universidad de las Ciencias Informáticas (UCI),
Carretera San Antonio, Km 2 1/2, Torrens, La Lisa, 19370 Havana, Cuba
jmedina@cenatav.co.cu,jmedinap@uci.cu

Abstract. In data mining, frequent approximate subgraph (FAS) mining techniques has taken the full attention of several applications, where some approximations are allowed between graphs for identifying important patterns. In the last four years, the application of FAS mining algorithms over multi-graphs has reported relevant results in different pattern recognition tasks like supervised classification and object identification. However, to the best of our knowledge, there is no reported work where the patterns identified by a FAS mining algorithm over multi-graph collections are used for image clustering. Thus, in this paper, we explore the use of multi-graph FASs for image clustering. Some experiments are performed over image collections for showing that by using multi-graph FASs under the bag of features image approach, the image clustering results reported by using simple-graph FAS can be improved.

Keywords: Approximate multi-graph matching
Approximate multi-graph mining · Multi-graph clustering

1 Introduction

Representing images as graphs, we can take into account some spatial relations between objects for different pattern recognition and data mining tasks [1]. This spatial information cannot be obtained by any other kind of representation.

The identification of frequent pattern from the graph representation, specially the mining of those frequent approximate subgraphs (FASs), has been an important topic in data mining, which has taken the full attention of several works [2–5]. In these works, the fact of allowing approximations between vertex

© Springer Nature Switzerland AG 2018
Y. Hernández Heredia et al. (Eds.): IWAIPR 2018, LNCS 11047, pp. 133–140, 2018.
https://doi.org/10.1007/978-3-030-01132-1_15

and edge labels in the graph matching process has reported better results than exact graph matching approaches. These results have been obtained by using FASs in supervised classification tasks, but for graph clustering tasks, the use of the FAS mining techniques is not well explored.

In the literature, there are only few works for image clustering based on FAS mining techniques, where the mined FASs have been used as features [6,7]. In these works, each image is represented as a simple-graph and FASs mined by MaxAFG [8] and VEAM [9] algorithms respectively, are used for building a vector representation, where the similarity based on edit distance [10] between each FAS and each image is stored. The graph clustering approach proposed in [6] is based on algorithms for mining FASs on a single-graph, where approximations in vertex and edge labels, as well as in the graph structure are allowed. In this way, the FASs are mined separately into every single graph, obtaining local representative patterns in a graph collection. On the other hand, the approach proposed in [7] is based on algorithms for mining FASs over graph collections, allowing variations only in vertex and graph labels. In this approach, the common part among different graphs that are not frequent inside any of them are taking into account, identifying global representative patterns in a graph collection.

In the last years, several authors claim that, in several real world applications, could be more than one spatial relation, and in these cases, a multi-graph representation is the best option [11,12]. Then, the FASs identified on multi-graph representation have been successfully used in different pattern recognition tasks [13–16]. In these applications, the fact to identifying FASs, which contain approximations in multi-graphs, allows to obtain useful patterns. However, to the best of our knowledge, the use of multi-graph FASs has been not explored for identifying information useful for data clustering. Thus, in this paper, unlike in [6,7], we explore the use of the multi-graph FASs for image clustering.

The organization of this paper is the following. In Sect. 2, our proposed method based on multi-graph FAS mining for image clustering is introduced. In Sect. 3, our experimentation is presented. Finally, our conclusions and future work directions are discussed in Sect. 4.

2   Our Proposal

The image clustering method introduced in this section is an adaptation of the FAS-based image clustering method proposed in [7]. Given a set of images where each image is represented as a multi-graph, the main idea of our image clustering method based on multi-graph FAS mining consists in finding a set of patterns over a multi-graph collection to be used as attributes in a vectorial representation for describing all images. Then, using this vectorial representation, a traditional clustering algorithm can be used for separating the images in groups according to their similarity.

Following the idea mentioned above, there are several steps to achieve the final clustering results starting by the representation of each image as a multi-graph. In this paper, we propose using a multi-graph representation and FAS miners which work with multi-graph collections (see Fig. 1). Our image clustering method based on multi-graph FAS mining comprises four steps: (1) multi-graph representation, (2) multi-graph FAS mining, (3) FAS vector representation, and (4) clustering.

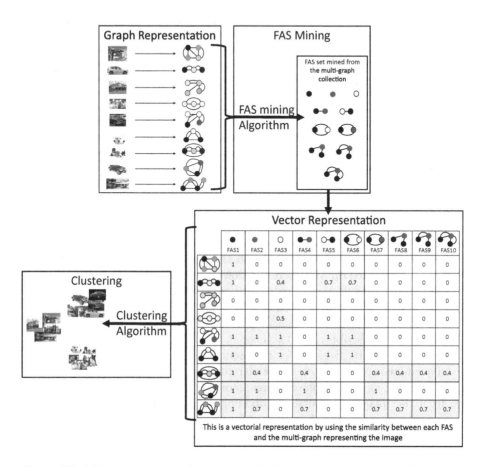

Fig. 1. Workflow of our image clustering method based on multi-graph FAS mining.

In the multi-graph representation step, we represented each image of a collection as a multi-graph. Several algorithms have been reported in the literature for representing images as graphs [9,12], which we can use as tools for representing images as multi-graphs.

For mining patterns from images represented as multi-graphs, any of the reported multi-graph FAS algorithms can be used. Once we have the mined multi-graph FASs, we can use them to generate a vector representation for each multi-graph (image). Then, by applying the bag of features [17], the FASs mined from the multi-graph collection are used as attributes in a vectorial representation for each image, where each element of an image vectorial representation has the similarity between a FAS and the multi-graph which represents the image; resulting a bag of multi-graph FAS approach. This similarity is computed according to the similarity function used in the approximate graph matching process of the multi-graph FAS mining algorithm applied. Next, using the vectorial representation of each image, a traditional clustering algorithm is applied. In this way, images are clustering according to the similarities obtained from the multi-graph FAS representation.

In summary, once we have each image in the collection represented as a multi-graph, the patterns are obtained by using a multi-graph FAS miner. Then, a FAS vector representation of the original images is built using the identified patterns. Thus, the dimension of the vectors is determined by the number of multi-graph FASs. Finally, these attribute vectors are given to a clustering algorithm for computing the resultant clusters.

3   Experiments

In this section, we show the experimental results obtained over two image collections, following our clustering method (see Sect. 2). In this way, we show the usefulness of the use of multi-graph FASs in a clustering task. All our experiments were carried out on a personal computer with an Intel(R) Core(TM) i5-3317U CPU @1.70 GHz with 8 GB of RAM. All the algorithms were implemented in ANSI-C and executed on Microsoft Windows 10.

The two image collections used in our experiments are CoenenDB-200 and CoenenDB-6000, which were used in [7]. CoenenDB-200 is composed by 200 images with two classes (100 images per class) and CoenenDB-6000 contains 6000 images also distributed in two classes. For our experiments, the class was not used as attribute. Besides, for representing an image as a multi-graph, we used a quad-tree approach [18], where we represent each image as it was proposed in [9], but using more than one relation among vertices. First, we obtain a quad-tree from the image by recursively dividing it in quadrants; stopping when a uniform color or a predefined number (4 for our experiments) of levels is reached (see Fig. 2(a-b)). Then, each leaf of the quad-tree is represented as a vertex of a multi-graph; where the most frequent color, in the corresponding quadrant, is used as label (see Fig. 2(c)). Vertices corresponding to adjacent quadrants are connected by two edges labeled as follows. For one edge, the smallest angle formed between the line that connects the centers of the two adjacent quadrants and the horizontal axis is used as label. An example of this angle is shown in Fig. 3, where we have two angles (α and β) between the horizontal line and the line connecting the quadrants. In this example, α is selected as the edge label, since $\alpha < \beta$. For the other edge, the distance between the centers of the two adjacent quadrants is used as label; d in Fig. 3(b). Since there could be a large number of different values for these edge labels, the angle and distance values were discretized into 24 equal bins for each one, as it was suggested in [9]. Finally, in the 200 multi-graphs of CoenenDB-200, the average size of the multi-graphs is 20 vertices and 70 edges. In the 6000 multi-graphs of CoenenDB-6000, the average size of the multi-graphs is 8 vertices and 24 edges.

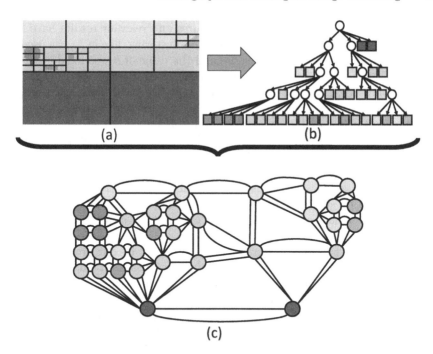

Fig. 2. Example of how an image is represented as a multi-graph by using the quad-tree approach.

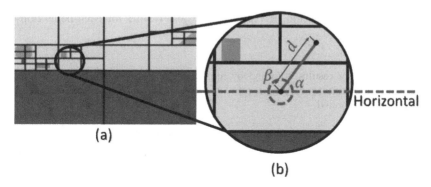

Fig. 3. Example of the angles formed between the line that connects the centers of the two adjacent quadrants and the horizontal axis in the multi-graph representation for an image.

In our experiments, we use two multi-graph FAS algorithms: AMgMiner [14] for mining all FASs, and GenCloMgVEAM [16] for mining a set of representative FASs. We decide to use AMgMiner because is the fastest reported multi-graph FAS algorithm, and GenCloMgVEAM is the only one reported in the literature for mining representative multi-graph FASs. These algorithms allow label approximations preserving the graph structures and relevant results have been reported by using them. On the other hand, for clustering, like in [7], we used the WEKA implementation of k-means [19], and the value of k was fixed according to the number of classes in the used image collections. Besides, in order to validate and compare our clustering results, we apply the rand index measure [20]. We apply the rand index measure because we know the real classes of the image collections and it is a well know cluster quality index.

In our experiments, we compare the results obtained by our proposal against those reported in [7], in which results obtained by using the simple-graph FASs separately mined from single graphs and results obtained by using the simple-graph FASs over graph collections were shown, as well as results obtained by a method based on spatial pyramid matching. We perform this comparison for showing the usefulness of the multi-graph FAS mining in an image clustering task.

In Table 1, we show the clustering results obtained by our proposal, as well as using an approach based on separately mining FASs from single graphs [6], and the method proposed in [21]. In this table, the first column shows the graph collection identifier; the second one shows the clustering results, in terms of Rand Index, obtained by using the method proposed in [21]; the third column shows the clustering results, in terms of Rand Index, obtained by using the method proposed in [6]; and the last column shows the clustering results obtained by applying our proposal. The cells with "–" means that the method proposed in [6] cannot be applied since, due to the size of the collection, it was unable to mine the FASs after a weak; while our proposal only used less of two hours for processing this collection. In Table 1, the best results for each collection are highlighted in bold.

Table 1. Clustering results obtained by applying the k-means algorithm, evaluated with the rand index measure. The symbol "–" means that the corresponding method was unable to be applied.

Compared methods	Image collections	
	CoenenDB-200	CoenenDB-6000
The method proposed in [21]	0.657	0.705
The single graph method [6]	0.768	–
The graph collection method [7]	0.805	0.948
Our proposal by using all multi-graph FASs	**0.851**	0.959
Our proposal by using a subset of multi-graph FASs	0.847	**0.966**

As we can see in Table 1, the clustering results obtained by our proposal are better than other ones. In this way, we show the usefulness of the use of multi-graph FAS mining for clustering tasks. Based on these results, the best option is our proposal based on the subset of multi-graph FASs mined by Gen-CloMgVEAM, because we achieved very good clustering results but obtaining up to 66% of the total number of FASs.

4   Conclusions and Future Work

In this paper, we introduce a multi-graph FAS based image clustering method, with the aim of explore the usefulness of the multi-graph FASs for image clustering tasks. For this aim, we performed experiments over two image collections, and the achieved results were compared against those results of different clustering methods reported in the literature.

Based on our experiments, we conclude that using multi-graph FASs as attributes, it is possible to obtain better results than those obtained by a method based on pyramid matching [21] and by using simple-graph FASs [6,7]. On the other hand, in our experiments, we have shown that using a representative subset of all multi-graph FASs as attributes, it is possible to obtain relevant results but reducing the number of patterns used for representing the images.

As future work, our intention is to verify our conclusions performing experiments over different and largest image collections.

Acknowledgment. This work was partly supported by the National Council of Science and Technology of Mexico (CONACyT) through the scholarship grant 287045.

References

1. Muñoz-Briseño, A., Lara-Alvarez, G., Gago-Alonso, A., Hernández-Palancar, J.: A novel geometric graph miner and its applications. Pattern Recognit. Lett. **84**, 208–214 (2016)
2. Ozaki, T., Etoh, M.: Closed and maximal subgraph mining in internally and externally weighted graph databases. In: Proceedings of the IEEE Workshops of International Conference on Advanced Information Networking and Applications, pp. 626–631. IEEE Computer Society (2011)
3. Jia, Y., Zhang, J., Huan, J.: An efficient graph-mining method for complicated and noisy data with real-world applications. Knowl. Inf. Syst. **28**(2), 423–447 (2011)
4. Morales-González, A., Acosta-Mendoza, N., Gago-Alonso, A., García-Reyes, E., Medina-Pagola, J.: A new proposal for graph-based image classification using frequent approximate subgraphs. Pattern Recognit. **47**(1), 169–177 (2014)
5. Li, R., Wang, W.: REAFUM: representative approximate frequent subgraph mining. In: SIAM International Conference on Data Mining, Vancouver, BC, Canada, pp. 757–765. SIAM (2015)
6. Flores-Garrido, M., Carrasco-Ochoa, J., Martínez-Trinidad, J.: Graph clustering via inexact patterns. In: Bayro-Corrochano, E., Hancock, E. (eds.) Progress in Pattern Recognition, Image Analysis, Computer Vision, and Applications, pp. 391–398. Springer International Publishing, Cham (2014)

7. Acosta-Mendoza, N., Carrasco-Ochoa, J.A., Martínez-Trinidad, J.F., Gago-Alonso, A., Medina-Pagola, J.E.: Image clustering based on frequent approximate subgraph mining. In: Martínez-Trinidad, J.F., Carrasco-Ochoa, J.A., Olvera-López, J.A., Sarkar, S. (eds.) MCPR 2018. LNCS, vol. 10880, pp. 189–198. Springer, Cham (2018). https://doi.org/10.1007/978-3-319-92198-3_19

8. Flores-Garrido, M., Carrasco-Ochoa, J., Martínez-Trinidad, J.: Mining maximal frequent patterns in a single graph using inexact matching. Knowl.-Based Syst. **66**, 166–177 (2014)

9. Acosta-Mendoza, N., Gago-Alonso, A., Medina-Pagola, J.: Frequent approximate subgraphs as features for graph-based image classification. Knowl.-Based Syst. **27**, 381–392 (2012)

10. Neuhaus, M., Bunke, H.: Automatic learning of cost functions for graph edit distance. Inf. Sci. **177**(1), 239–247 (2007)

11. Kropatsch, W., Haxhimusa, Y., Pizlo, Z., Langs, G.: Vision pyramids that do not grow too high. Pattern Recognit. Lett. **26**, 319–337 (2005)

12. Morales-González, A., García-Reyes, E.B.: Simple object recognition based on spatial relations and visual features represented using irregular pyramids. Multimed. Tools Appl. **63**(3), 875–897 (2013)

13. Acosta-Mendoza, N., Gago-Alonso, A., Carrasco-Ochoa, J., Martínez-Trinidad, J., Medina-Pagola, J.: Extension of canonical adjacency matrices for frequent approximate subgraph mining on multi-graph collections. Int. J. Pattern Recognit. Artif. Intell. **31**(7), 25 (2017)

14. Acosta-Mendoza, N., Gago-Alonso, A., Carrasco-Ochoa, J., Martínez-Trinidad, J., Medina-Pagola, J.: A new algorithm for approximate pattern mining in multi-graph collections. Knowl.-Based Syst. **109**, 198–207 (2016)

15. Acosta-Mendoza, N., Carrasco-Ochoa, J.A., Martínez-Trinidad, J.F., Gago-Alonso, A., Medina-Pagola, J.E.: A new method based on graph transformation for FAS mining in multi-graph collections. In: Carrasco-Ochoa, J.A., Martínez-Trinidad, J.F., Sossa-Azuela, J.H., Olvera López, J.A., Famili, F. (eds.) MCPR 2015. LNCS, vol. 9116, pp. 13–22. Springer, Cham (2015). https://doi.org/10.1007/978-3-319-19264-2_2

16. Acosta-Mendoza, N., Gago-Alonso, A., Carrasco-Ochoa, J.A., Martínez-Trinidad, J.F., Medina-Pagola, J.E.: Mining generalized closed patterns from multi-graph collections. In: Mendoza, M., Velastín, S. (eds.) CIARP 2017. LNCS, vol. 10657, pp. 10–18. Springer, Cham (2018). https://doi.org/10.1007/978-3-319-75193-1_2

17. O'Hara, S., Draper, B.: Introduction to the bag of features paradigm for image classification and retrieval. Computing Research Repository (CoRR) abs/1101.3354 (2011)

18. Finkel, R., Bentley, J.: Quad trees: a data structure for retrieval on composite keys. Acta Inform. **4**, 1–9 (1974)

19. Arthur, D., Vassilvitskii, S.: K-means: the advantages of carefull seeding. In: Proceedings of the eighteenth Annual ACM-SIAM Symposium on Discrete Algorithms, pp. 1027–1035. ACM (2007)

20. Rand, M.: Objective criteria for the evaluation of clustering methods. J. Am. Stat. Assoc. **66**(336), 846–850 (1971)

21. Lazebnik, S., Schmid, C., Ponce, J.: Beyond bags of features: spatial pyramid matching for recognizing natural scene categories. In: IEEE Computer Society Conference on Computer Vision and Pattern Recognition (CVPR), pp. 1–8. IEEE (2006)

Data Mining Techniques in Normal or Pathological Infant Cry

Yadisbel Martinez-Cañete$^{(\boxtimes)}$ (ID), Sergio Daniel Cano-Ortiz (ID),
Lienys Lombardía-Legrá, Ernesto Rodríguez-Fernández,
and Liette Veranes-Vicet

Universidad de Oriente, Las Américas Ave., 90900 Santiago de Cuba, Cuba
{ymartinez, scano, lienys, ernesto,
liette.veranes}@uo.edu.cu

Abstract. The infant cry is the only means of communication of a baby and carries information about its physical and mental state. The analysis of the acoustic infant cry waveform opens the possibility of extracting this information, useful in supporting the diagnosis of pathologies since the first days of birth.

In order to obtain this useful information, it is first necessary to acquire and to process the cry signal, being the latter an arduous and tedious process if performed manually. Because of this, it is necessary to develop a system that allows the extraction of the information present in the cry, automatically, that greatly facilitates the work of pediatricians and specialist doctors.

The present work evaluates some data mining techniques in standard configurations, for the classification of normal or pathological infant cry in support of the diagnosis of diseases in the Central Nervous System.

Evaluation is performed comparing seven classifiers: Naïve Bayes, Simple Logistic, SMO, IBk, Decision Table, J48 and Random Forest, on acoustic attributes Linear Prediction Coefficients and Mel Frequency Cepstral Coefficients and two different testing options: 10-fold cross-validation, and Supplied test set.

Best results are obtained with the IBk and Random Forest methods, with receiver operating characteristics (ROC) areas of .923 and .956, respectively.

Keywords: Infant cry analysis · Data mining · MFCC · LPC
Supervised classification

1 Introduction

Crying is an acoustic event that contains information about the functioning of the central nervous system. It is, in turn, the natural means of communication of the baby with the environment that surround him/her, this being the only way to express their physical and/or emotional state.

According to specialists in the area of health, the baby's cry wave is a carrier of useful information, both to determine the mood of the baby, and to detect certain major physical pathologies, mainly cerebral, from very early stages [1].

© Springer Nature Switzerland AG 2018
Y. Hernández Heredia et al. (Eds.): IWAIPR 2018, LNCS 11047, pp. 141–148, 2018.
https://doi.org/10.1007/978-3-030-01132-1_16

Since the beginning of the 20th century, efforts have been made to research infants' crying in order to discover how much information is "hidden" within the sound [2].

Many research have been conducted to find approaches for automatically predicting an infant's state of health based on acoustic infant cry features. Several classification model approaches originating from mathematical or computer science disciplines were applied to the infant cry [3].

In the review by Fuhr et al. [3], had been identified nine different types of classification models for infant cry classification.

Bayes Classifier model in Amaro-Camargo and Reyes-Garcia [4], Hidden Markov Model in Aucouturier et al., Lederman et al., Lederman et al., Abdulaziz and Ahmad, Honda et al., Singh et al. [5–10]. Linear Discriminant Analysis (LDA) in Fuller [11], Fuzzy Logic in Cano-Ortiz et al., Kia et al., Reyes-Galaviz et al., Santiago-Sanchez et al., Barajas and Reyes [12–16], Decision Tree in Amaro-Camargo and Reyes-Garcia, Etz et al. [4, 17], K-Nearest Neighbour (KNN) in Cohen and Lavner [18], Weighted Rough Set Framework in Own and Abraham [19].

The classification models were applied to the reference dataset and rated according to the rating scheme, the results for each classification model are:

The best k-nearest neighbor model reached an accuracy value of 91.48%. The Bayes classifier had an accuracy of 80.68% on the test dataset. Linear discriminant analysis achieved 79.55% accuracy on the test dataset resulting. Decision Tree, Accuracy on the test dataset varied between 69.32% and 98.64%. The best logistic regression model reached 69.89% accuracy on the test dataset. The best support vector machine model only reached an accuracy of 53.98% on the test dataset resulting.

Two types of artificial neural networks were trained, multilayer perceptron based network and radial basis function based network. Accuracy values for these two types of models were 79.50% and 73.90%, respectively, on the test dataset [3].

Orlandi et al. (2016) were exploiting differences between full-term and preterm infant cry with robust automatic acoustical analysis and data mining techniques. The best results were obtained with the Random Forest method (receiver operating characteristic area, 0.94) [20].

The development of different methods of analysis and digital signal processing has allowed a better characterization of the parameters of the crying signal, although so far no medical routine based on analysis of infant crying has been used as a diagnostic tool in a clinical environment.

Based on the above, the scientific problem that is to be solved can be stated as the insufficiency in the application of classification methods of infant crying in support of the diagnosis of diseases in the Central Nervous System (CNS).

The general objective of the research is to evaluate data mining techniques on the Linear Prediction Coefficients (LPC) and Mel Frequency Cepstral Coefficients (MFCC) in infant cry signal for classification in support of medical diagnosis.

2 Materials and Methods

The process of automatic recognition baby's cry wave can be generally seen in three stages, the first, where the acoustic analysis of the signal is carried out: consisting of eliminating the stimulus signal and performing segmentations into frames of 1 s length, varying the amount thereof; in the second stage, the characteristic vectors are obtained, cleaning the resulting files and creating the data matrices to analyze, the third stage is where the type of crying is identified by a classifier.

2.1 GPV Database

The crying recordings were made at the Materno Este Hospital in Santiago de Cuba. The crying was induced by a standardized stimulus: a touch of the index finger on the infant's heel. The children were in supine position, open and extended legs, and were not crying at the time of the stimulus. 12 s of crying were recorded for each infant with a SONY CFS-210 device. A PHILIPS SBC-3040 microphone located at a distance from the child's lips of about 17 cm was used. Then these cries were digitized by the PCVOX speech acquisition system. The original files have the extension.MST and are coded to 16 bits and sampled at 8000 Hz, with a total of 26 cases, 13 normal and 13 pathological. The original files were converted to the .WAV format.

The main interest is to detect the anomalies that distinguish two classes: normal and pathological in which the pathological class includes pathologies of the Central Nervous System with hypoxia background.

The pathological class is concerned with four Pathological Specific Groups: Hypoxia, Delay in Intra-Uterine Growth (DIUG), Hypoxia with Aggravating Factors (HAF) and Hyperbilirubinaemia, respectively.

The age range of babies is from the first 15 days of born to six months approximately.

2.2 Baby Chillanto Database

The database used was downloaded from the website http://ingenieria.uatx.mx/orionfrg/cry, is the so-called Baby Chillanto database and is owned by the National Institute of Optical and Electronic Astrophysics (INAOE) - CONACYT, Mexico. The database is described in [21]. Baby Chillanto consists of 21 normal crying signals, 52 crying signals from deaf children (hypo-acoustic), 6 signs of asphyxia crying, 34 crying signals from hungry children and 25 crying signals from children with pain. The samples used in this database are complete signals with approximately 12 s or less. The normal cry signals are recorded from 5 babies; the recorded mute cry signals from 6 babies and the recorded asphyxia cry signals from 6 babies. For this analysis, we took the 21 normal crying signals and the 34 crying cues from hungry children to create a normal class and we took the 52 crying signals from deaf children (hypo-acoustic), the 6 signs of asphyxia crying and the 25 crying signals of children with pain to create a pathological class. The infant sampling frequency crying signals is set at 8000 Hz.

2.3 Acoustic Analysis of Infant Cry

The acoustic analysis is done to extract the most important characteristics of the baby's crying in the time domain. The kind of acoustic analysis used consists of taking the complete signal and obtaining segments of 1 s, first a thorough process of excluding the crying stimulus signal ("ya" signal) was carried out, as well as reducing the duration of each signal based on having a normalized and ordered sample of data.

It is defined as the process of Pre-processing to:

- Delete the stimulus signal from each of the crying signals.
- Segment the previous signals in 11, 10 and 8 s respectively.

The characteristic vectors were formed by extracting the LPC and MFCC, coefficients in Praat software.

The samples already segmented in one second were divided into windows of 50 ms. The resulting vector contains 304 coefficients for both LPC and MFCC for each sample of one second because 16 LPC and 16 MFCC are extracted from each window as defined in the commands declared above.

For each type of sample, GPV database and Baby Chillanto database, 9.arff files were created for their study, 3 for each pre-processing, performed in the acoustic analysis of the signals, of 11, 10 and 8 s respectively.

The number of feature is between 16 and 32, these numbers are given by the number of attributes that have the files chosen for the analysis: 16 MFCC coefficients, 16 LPC coefficients or the merge of the 16 MFCC coefficients with the 16 LPC coefficients; in addition to the sampling window and the feature that represents the class: normal class (NC) and pathological class (PC).

The number of instances varies from the type of pre-processing performed by the acoustic analysis of the signal, as can be seen in the following Table 1:

Table 1. Number of instances per pre-processed and per class

GPV database			
Pre-processing	#Instances	NC	PC
Pre-processing 11 s	5225	2717	2508
Pre-processing 10 s	4750	2470	2280
Pre-processing 8 s	3952	1976	1976
Baby Chillanto database			
Pre-processing 11 s	28842	11495	17347
Pre-processing 10 s	26220	10450	15770
Pre-processing 8 s	20976	8360	12616

2.4 Infant Cry Classification

The selected methods make a general representation of each of the existing data mining techniques in Weka. In the representation of Bayesian techniques, the Bayesian classifier Naive: Naive Bayes was used. For the parametric statistical modeling techniques, the logistic regression was used: Simple Logistic; in those based on support vector machines, the Sequential Minimum Optimization (SMO) algorithm was used; with the techniques based on distance, the nearest k-neighbors method was used: IBk. In the techniques based on decision trees, two methods were used, the algorithm C4.5: J48 and the Random Forest: Random Forest (RF); and for those based on rule learning systems, the Decision Table was applied: Decision Table.

For the configuration of some of the methods, the following parameters were changed:

NaiveBayes => useKernelEstimator = True
Use a core density estimator to model the numerical attributes instead of a normal distribution.
DecisionTable => useIbk = True
Use the nearest neighbor algorithm (IBk) instead of the majority class.
J48 => confidenceFactor = 0.05 (5%)
Establish the confidence factor for tree pruning.

The evaluation of the performance of classifiers is done only in two ways:

Cross-validation: From the 9 study files for each type of sample, the cross-validation technique was applied equally to 10 subsets (10-Cross-validation).

Supplied test set: Taking randomly the 80% of instances for the training set, and 20% for testing, it was created from the 9 study files.

3   Results and Discussion

The first step was to evaluate the best feature considering the LPC, MFCC and the joint LPC & MFCC coefficients, in such manner to obtain a better classification rate.

Table 2 summarizes the accuracy estimation (%) obtained with the LPC, MFCC and LPC & MFCC attributes applying the classifiers IBk, RF, J48 and SMO.

Table 2. Feature evaluation GPV database

GPV database								
	IBk	IBk	RF	RF	J48	J48	SMO	SMO
	CV%	ST%	ST%	CV%	ST%	CV%	ST%	CV%
LPC	80.1	80.4	77.0	78.5	72.3	71.4	67.6	63.8
MFCC	88.8	88.2	81.6	81.8	77.9	79.6	71.6	69.4
LPC & MFCC	88.8	89.3	83.0	83.5	78.8	79.3	72.3	72.8
Baby Chillanto database								
	IBk	IBk	RF	RF	J48	J48	SMO	SMO
	CV%	ST%	ST%	CV%	ST%	CV%	ST%	CV%
LPC	84.4	85.9	83.7	82.3	78.1	77.7	67.6	67.9
MFCC	92.7	93.6	89.8	88.7	84.6	83.7	76.9	75.0
LPC & MFCC	93.1	94.0	90.3	89.7	86.3	85.1	78.6	77.3

For testing evaluation, we used the following options: 10-Folds Cross-validation (CV) and Supplied test set (ST).

When using the classifiers, the best results were obtained when using the IBk method with 89.3% of correct answers in most cases of the study files in the GPV database and 94% in the Baby Chillanto database.

The Random Forest algorithm classified the correct normal class number fairly closely and the percentage of total hits remained above 83.5% for the GPV database and 90.3% for the Baby Chillanto database.

Finally, it was possible to see that in the analysis files where the MFCC coefficients and the LPC coefficients are joined, the percentage level rises significantly in comparison with the other files, and the best result, in most of the classification methods were obtained with preprocessing signal of 11 s.

To assess the results, the following classification algorithms were compared: IBk, Random Forest, J48, SMO. These methods were tested with cross validation and supplied test (80% training) method. Again, the best results were obtained applying the IBk classifier though with slight differences with the other approaches. The results are reported in Table 3. The ROC area bests results were 0.956 and 0.923 is highlighted in bold.

Table 3. Classifier result with Baby Chillanto database and supplied test evaluation

Classifier	TP rate	FP rate	Precision	F-measure	ROC area
IBk	0.930	0.073	0.931	0.931	**0.923**
RandomForest	0.895	0.103	0.897	0.895	**0.956**
J48	0.850	0.156	0.851	0.851	0.851
SMO	0.771	0.240	0.773	0.771	0.765
Simple Logistic	0.766	0.260	0.764	0.765	0.844
Naïve Bayes	0.715	0.281	0.726	0.717	0.793
Decision Table	0.720	0.273	0.732	0.723	0.784

For supplied test evaluation methods, the classification results have higher accuracy than 10-Folds cross validation.

The high and consistent results obtained with the IBk model, supported by the different performance measures applied show that the proposed approach is reliable.

4   Conclusions

Summarizing, this paper presents an evaluation of classification models for infant cry classification with data mining techniques, for the classification in normal or pathological infant cry.

Certainly, the merger of MFCC and LPC coefficients in the acoustic analysis of the crying of the baby is a better option to extract characteristics of the signal and to classify between the normal and pathological crying.

In the classification of infant crying, the percentage of correctness of the techniques used varies in each study file, with the IBk and Random Forest methods giving better results with 0.923 and 0.956 ROC areas, respectively and these proved to better predict the class.

Although these classifiers have reported good results in normal conditions, the bibliography reports classifiers based on Bayesian Networks that can be more robust to noise factors; also to improve the classification using methods of reduction of instances and features can be used to improve the classification.

Acknowledgements. The authors would like to thank Carlos Alberto Reyes Garcia, PhD Researcher, CCC-INAOE, Mexico for providing infant cry database. Part of this research was made thanks to the financial support derived from the Web Project (WebIND) in collaboration with the University of Applied Sciences from Dusseldorf.

References

1. Orozco, J., Reyes, C.: Extraction and analysis of acoustic characteristics of baby crying for automatic recognition based on neural networks. Ph.D. dissertation, Master's thesis, INAOE, Puebla, Mexico (2002)
2. Galaviz, O.F.R.: Classification of baby crying for identification of hypoacuse and asphyxia by means of a hybrid system (genetic-neuronal). Master's thesis on Computer Science, Apizaco Institute of Technology (ITA) (2005)
3. Fuhr, T., Reetz, H., Wegener, C.: Comparison of supervised-learning models for infant cry classification/vergleich von klassifikations modellen zur säuglingsschrei analyse. Int. J. Health Prof. **2**(1), 4–15 (2015)
4. Amaro-Camargo, E., Reyes-Garcia, C.A.: Applying statistical vectors of acoustic characteristics for the automatic classification of infant cry. Adv. Pattern Recognit. **4681**, 1078–1085 (2007)
5. Aucouturier, J.-J., Nonaka, Y., Katahira, K., Okanoya, K.: Segmentation of expiratory and inspiratory sounds in baby cry audio recordings using hidden Markov models. J. Acoust. Soc. Am. **130**(5), 2969–2977 (2011)
6. Lederman, D., Cohen, A., Zmora, E., Wermke, K., Hauschildt, S., Stellzig-Eisenhauer, A.: On the use of hidden Markov models in infants' cry classification. In: 22nd Convention of Electrical and Electronics Engineers proceedings, Israel, pp. 350–352 (2002)
7. Lederman, D., Zmora, E., Hauschildt, S., Stellzig-Eisenhauer, A., Wermke, K.: Classification of cries of infants with cleft-palate using parallel hidden Markov models. Med. Biol. Eng. Comput. **46**(10), 965–975 (2008)
8. Abdulaziz, Y., Ahmad, S.: An accurate infant cry classification system based on continuous hidden Markov Model. In: International Symposium on Information Technology (ITSim), vol. 3, pp. 1648–1652 (2010)
9. Honda, K., Kitahara, K., Matsunaga, S., Yamashita, M., Shinohara, K.: Emotion classification of infant cries with consideration for local and global features. In: Signal Information Processing Association Annual Summit and Conference (APSIPA ASC), Asia-Pacific, pp. 1–4 (2012)
10. Singh, A.K., Mukhopadhyay, J., Rao, K.: Classification of infant cries using epoch and spectral features. In: National Conference on Communications (NCC), pp. 1–5 (2013)

11. Fuller, B.F.: Acoustic discrimination of three types of infant cries. Nurs. Res. **40**(3), 156–160 (1991)
12. Cano-Ortiz, S.D., Reyes-Garcia, C.A., Reyes-Galaviz, O.F., Escobedo-Beceiro, D.I., Cano-Otero, J.D.: Emergence of a new alternative on cry analysis: the fuzzy approach. In: 5th Latin American Congress on Biomedical Engineering (claib2011): Sustainable Technologies for the Health of all, Pts 1 and 2, vol. 33, no. (1–2), pp. 846–849 (2013)
13. Kia, M., Kia, S., Davoudi, N., Biniazan, R.: A detection system of infant cry using fuzzy classification including dialing alarm calls function. In: Second International Conference on Innovative Computing Technology (INTECH), pp. 224–229 (2012)
14. Reyes Galaviz, O.F., Reyes Garcia, C.A.: Infant cry classification to identify hypoacoustics and asphyxia with neural networks. In: Monroy, R., Arroyo-Figueroa, G., Sucar, L.E., Sossa, H. (eds.) MICAI 2004. LNCS (LNAI), vol. 2972, pp. 69–78. Springer, Heidelberg (2004). https://doi.org/10.1007/978-3-540-24694-7_8
15. Santiago-Sanchez, K., Reyes-Garcia, C.A., Gomez-Gil, P.: Type-2 fuzzy sets applied to pattern matching for the classification of cries of infants under neurological risk. Adv. Pattern Recogn. **5754**, 201–210 (2009)
16. Barajas, S.E., Reyes, C.A.: Your fuzzy relational neural network parameters optimization with a genetic algorithm. In: FUZZ-IEEE: Proceedings of the IEEE International Conference on Fuzzy Systems: Biggest Little Conference in the World, pp. 684–689 (2005)
17. Etz, T., Reetz, H., Wegener, C.: A classification model for infant cries with hearing impairment and unilateral cleft lip and palate. Folia Phoniatr. Logop. **64**(5), 254–261 (2012)
18. Cohen, R., Lavner, Y.: Infant cry analysis and detection. In: 2012 IEEE 27th Convention of Electrical Electronics Engineers in Israel (IEEEI), Israel, pp. 1–5 (2012)
19. Own, H.S., Abraham, A.: A new weighted rough set framework based classification for Egyptian NeoNatal Jaundice. Appl. Soft Comput. **12**(3), 999–1005 (2012)
20. Orlandi, S., Garcia, C.A.R., Bandini, A., Donzelli, G., Manfredi, C.: Application of pattern recognition techniques to the classification of full-term and preterm infant cry. J. Voice **30**(6), 656–663 (2016)
21. Reyes-Galaviz, O.F., Cano-Ortiz, S., Reyes-Garcia, C.: Evolutionary-neural system to classify infant cry units for pathologies identification in recently born babies. In: Proceedings of the 8th Mexican International Conference on Artificial Intelligence. MICAI 2009, Guanajuato, Mexico, pp. 330–335 (2009)

Angle-Based Model for Interactive Dimensionality Reduction and Data Visualization

Cielo K. Basante-Villota[1], Carlos M. Ortega-Castillo[1(✉)],
Diego F. Peña-Unigarro[1], E. Javier Revelo-Fuelagán[1],
Jose A. Salazar-Castro[1,2], MacArthur Ortega-Bustamante[3],
Paul Rosero-Montalvo[3,4,5], Laura Stella Vega-Escobar[6],
and Diego H. Peluffo-Ordóñez[2,7]

[1] Universidad de Nariño, Pasto, Colombia
[2] Corporación Universitaria Autónoma de Nariño, Pasto, Colombia
karlosmaor@hotmail.com
[3] Universidad Técnica del Norte, Ibarra, Ecuador
[4] Universidad de Salamanca, Salamanca, Spain
[5] Instituto Tecnológico Superior 17 de Julio, Ibarra, Ecuador
[6] Instituto Tecnológico Metropolitano (ITM), Medellín, Colombia
[7] Yachay Tech, Urcuquí, Ecuador

Abstract. In recent times, an undeniable fact is that the amount of data available has increased dramatically due mainly to the advance of new technologies allowing for storage and communication of enormous volumes of information. In consequence, there is an important need for finding the relevant information within the raw data through the application of novel data visualization techniques that permit the correct manipulation of data. This issue has motivated the development of graphic forms for visually representing and analyzing high-dimensional data. Particularly, in this work, we propose a graphical approach, which, allows the combination of dimensionality reduction (DR) methods using an angle-based model, making the data visualization more intelligible. Such approach is designed for a readily use, so that the input parameters are interactively given by the user within a user-friendly environment. The proposed approach enables users (even those being non-experts) to intuitively select a particular DR method or perform a mixture of methods. The experimental results prove that the interactive manipulation enabled by the here-proposed model-due to its ability of displaying a variety of embedded spaces-makes the task of selecting a embedded space simpler and more adequately fitted for a specific need.

Keywords: Dimensionality reduction · Data visualization
Kernel PCA · Pairwise similarity

© Springer Nature Switzerland AG 2018
Y. Hernández Heredia et al. (Eds.): IWAIPR 2018, LNCS 11047, pp. 149–157, 2018.
https://doi.org/10.1007/978-3-030-01132-1_17

1   Introduction

Given the existence of new sources of information (sensors, mobile phone, emails, social networks, the internet in general, and among others), the emerging term so-named Big Data has taken place, which is a relatively new concept attained to encompass big volumes of data coming from several sources as well as technologies able to deal with such data. The main issues that Big Data concerns are: volume, visualization, variability and speed. Therefore, this research field has increasingly become an area of great interest in computer science and data analytics. This research is focused on the concept of data visualization through dimensionality reduction techniques. The mapping of high-dimensional data into a smaller version that depicts the most relevant information from the original data is a widely studied research area [8,12], given its ability to reduce the computational cost or improve the performance of pattern recognition and information visualization systems [9,10]. Despite the existence of tools that achieve the efficient indicators in terms of computational performance, exploration and representation of high-dimensional data, they do not take into account properties such as interactivity and controllability. Therefore, an improvement in these aspects is required [9]. In consequence, there is a gap between the knowledge of the users and the database to be analyzed [12]. In this connection, there is a need for an interface wherein users can obtain an overview of the data to draw conclusions and make decisions [12]. This paper proposes an interactive model, which is based on the geometry of a triangle, using mainly the theorem of internal and external angles of the Euclidean geometry. Each vertex of the triangle represents a DR method. Therefore, the vertex with the greatest angle will represent the highest model value as well as the maximum application of one particular DR method. Spectral DR methods are implementing through kernel approximations [7,8], which are combined to reach a final kernel matrix. Finally, such a kernel matrix feeds a generalized algorithm of kernel principal component analysis (KPCA) [7]. The benefit of this approach is that user may utilize DR methods over the data, even with no knowledge about the theoretical foundations behind them. The user controls the results simply by exploring an intuitive interface based on the angles of a triangle. The angle-based model proposed in this paper is evaluated using three DR methods, namely: locally linear embedding (LLE) [11], multidimensional classical scaling (CMD) [3] and laplacian eigenmaps (LE) [2]. The experiments are performed over a real databases (images of objects - MNIST) and two artificial data-set (Swiss roll and letter S in 3D) [1]. The DR performance is quantified by a scaled version of the average agreement rate between K-ary neighborhoods explained in [6]. This paper is organized as follows: Sect. 2 describes the Proposed angle-based model for the combination of DR methods. Experimental setup and results are presented in Sects. 3 and 4, respectively. Finally, some final remarks are drawn in Sect. 5.

2   Proposed Model for Interactive Dimensionality Reduction Using a Angle-Based Approach

This section describes the proposed model, here named, angle-based model that allows an interactive combination of three different unsupervised DR spectral methods, in order to obtain an improvement of the data visualization process. A suitable and versatile approximation for DR spectral methods are kernel matrices because they make possible a linear combination [7,8].

Our interactive model allows the mixing of kernel matrices in an intuitive way. First, the kernel matrices obtained by applying the DR methods in high-dimensional data are linearly combined, after the angle-based model is applied a new kernel matrix is created which contains a weighted combination of three different types of DR methods with the purpose of reach several low-dimensional spaces. Therefore, user can easily and intuitively select a both a unique DR method or a combination of three different DR methods in order to get a suitable data representation of one specific task by simply exploring the different positions that can be obtained. Since we are aiming at combining three DR methods, we propose to use a triangle, where each vertex represents a DR method. This triangle is within in a square since this geometric figure allows us to obtain angles close to 180°. The model proposed in this paper is based on the geometry of a triangle, using the external and internal angle theorem of Euclidean geometry, which say that every exterior angle of a triangle is equal to the sum of the two Non-adjacent interior angles, as shown in Fig. 1(a) $\sphericalangle D = \sphericalangle C + \sphericalangle A$, it can be intuitively demonstrated that $\sphericalangle D + \sphericalangle B = 180°$ and therefore $\sphericalangle C + \sphericalangle A + \sphericalangle B = 180°$.

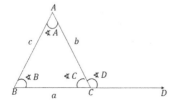

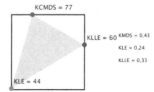

(a) *Illustration of the triangle geometry*

(b) *Illustration of angle-based model.*

Fig. 1. Illustration of the construction of the interaction model.

The user has the freedom to move each one of the vertices that are represented by three spheres of different colors around the square, thus changing the measure of the angles and consequently the factors of each of the methods. 180° illustrates a normalized value of 1, so the percentage corresponding to each method depicts the mixture configuration of the kernel matrices. Figure 1(b) shows a graph of the model proposed.

For data visualization purposes through DR methods, the terms to be combined are the kernel matrices corresponding to the considered DR methods. Therefore, we obtain a resultant kernel matrix $\widehat{K}$ as the mixture of M kernel matrices $\{K^{(1)}, \cdots, K^{(M)}\}$ so: $\widehat{K} = \sum_{m=1}^{M} \alpha_m K^{(m)}$, where α_m is the coefficient or weighting factor corresponding to method m and $\alpha = \{\alpha_1, \cdots, \alpha_m\}$ is weighting vector. In this work $m = 3$ and the relationship between the points within the surface and the coefficients of linear combination α_m are given by the angular measure of each vertex that makes up the triangle. Nevertheless, this interactive model differs from other approaches as [14,15] due to the fact that angle base model has the ability to expand the number of dimensionality reduction methods which can be combined. Thus, the proposed model can be adapted into a polygonal approach, if new kernel representations are proposed, in order to increase the number of embedded spaces which can improve tasks as data visualization, pattern recognition, data mining, among others.

3   Experimental Setup

Data-Sets: Experiments are carried out over three conventional data sets. The first data set is a letter **S** in 3D ($N = 1000$ data points and $D = 3$). The second data set is a toy set here called Swiss roll (N = 3000 data points and D = 3). The third data set is a randomly selected subset of the MNIST image bank, which is formed by 6000 gray-level images of each of the 10 digits ($N = 1500$ data points –150 instances for all 10 digits– and $D = 24^2$). Figure 2 depicts examples of the considered data sets.

(a) *Letter S in 3D*   (b) *Swiss Roll*   (c) *MNIST*

Fig. 2. The three considered datasets.

Methods: Dimensionality reduction allows the extraction of relevant information from high-dimensional data sets aimed at improving the performance of a pattern recognition system or that facilitates the visualization and analysis of data. In mathematical terms, the goal of dimensionality reduction is to embed a high dimensional data matrix $Y = [y_i]_{1 \le i \le N}$, such that $y_i \in \mathbb{R}^D$ into a low-dimensional, latent data matrix $X = [x_i]_{1 \le i \le N}$ being $x_i \in \mathbb{R}^d$, where $d < D$ [12,13]. Three spectral DR approaches are considered, namely: classical multidimensional scalling (CMDS) [3], locally linear embedding (LLE) [11], and graph Laplacian eigenmaps (LE) [2]. They are all performed in their standard algorithms. Also, in order to evaluate our framework, kernel approximations are also considered. CMDS kernel is the double centered distance matrix $D \in \mathbb{R}^{N \times N}$ so $K^{(1)} = K_{CMDS} = -\frac{1}{2}(I - 1_N 1_N^\top)D(I - 1_N 1_N^\top)$, where the ij entry of D is given by $d_{ij} = \|y_i - y_j\|_2^2$. A kernel for LLE can be approximated from a quadratic form in terms of the matrix W holding linear coefficients that sum to 1 and optimally reconstruct observed data. Define a matrix $M \in \mathbb{R}^{N \times N}$ as $M = (I_N - W)(I_N - W^\top)$ and λ_{max} as the largest eigenvalue of M. Kernel matrix for LLE is in the form $K^{(2)} = K_{LLE} = \lambda_{max} I_N - M$. Since kernel PCA is a maximization of the high-dimensional covariance represented by a kernel, a feasible kernel for LE can be represented as the pseudo-inverse of the graph Laplacian L: $K^{(3)} = K_{LE} = L^\dagger$, where $L = D - S$, S is a similarity matrix and $D = \text{Diag}(S 1_N)$ is the degree matrix. All previously mentioned kernels are widely described in [5]. The similarity matrices are formed in such a way that the relative bandwidth parameter is estimated keeping the entropy over neighbor distribution as roughly $\log K$ where K is the given number of neighbors as explained in [4]. For all methods, input data is embedded into a 2-dimensional space, then $d = 2$. The number of neighbors is established as $K = 30$ for all considered data sets.

Quality Measures: To quantify the performance of studied methods, the scaled version of the average agreement rate $R_{NX}(K)$ introduced in [6] is used, which is ranged within the interval $[0, 1]$. Since $R_{NX}(K)$ is calculated at each perplexity value from 2 to $N - 1$, a numerical indicator of the overall performance can be obtained by calculating its area under the curve (AUC). The AUC assesses the dimension reduction quality at all scales, with the most appropriate weights.

Experiment Description: To assess the performance of the interactive visualization interface, a testing were done by moving the vertices of the triangle through the square. Doing so a collection of weighting factors are established to consequently carry out the mixture. In Fig. 3 the weighting factors configuration for the experiment are defined.

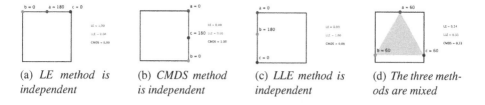

(a) *LE method is independent*

(b) *CMDS method is independent*

(c) *LLE method independent*

(d) *The three methods are mixed*

Fig. 3. The chosen positions for the experiment.

4   Results and Discussion

In the experiment we considered three DR methods that are mixed through the angle-based model. We tested the interactive model in four positions as shown in Fig. 3. Three of the positions represent one single DR method and in the last configuration the three methods are combined with the same percentage of participation. The results are shown in Figs. 4, 5 and 6. In the results we can see the embedded data and several curves that give a notion to the user about the performance of the low-dimensional space and the preservation of the neighbors in the high dimensional-space. If the value of the area under the curve is greater, the performance of the integrated data will be better. Therefore, we affirm that the sphere Fig. 4 obtains embedded data with greater preservation of relevant information. In the Figs. 5 and 6 we observe that some DR methods have better performance in one or another data-set depending on their nature.

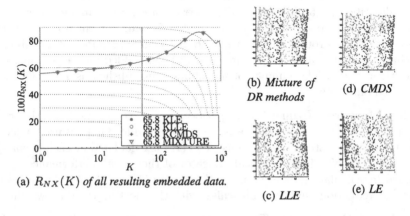

Fig. 4. Results for the letter-S data-set.

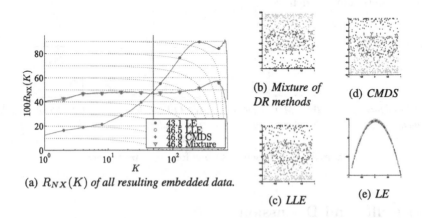

Fig. 5. Results for the Swiss roll data-set.

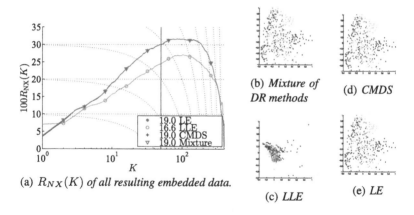

(a) $R_{NX}(K)$ *of all resulting embedded data.*

(b) *Mixture of DR methods*

(c) *LLE*

(d) *CMDS*

(e) *LE*

Fig. 6. Results for MNIST dataset.

To facilitate the management of our interactive model, we implemented an interface in the NetBeans software, which allows the calculation of the DR methods and the visualization of their results through scatter plots. In order to create an attractive visual analysis environment. Figure 7 shows a view of the implemented interface. Therefore, a powerful tool is provided to make decisions about the most appropriate representation of the original data, as well as, the combination of the most appropriate DR methods, with the purpose of to users (even non-expert) can intuitively interact with the DR methods and its feasible combinations.

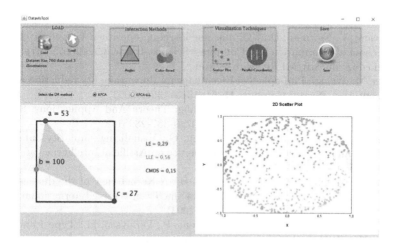

Fig. 7. View of the interface implemented on NetBeans software.

5   Conclusions and Future Work

The angle-based interaction model successfully generates the mixing coefficients, since it allows the three DR methods to be combined satisfactorily in any position that is required. In addition, the model allows the use of independently implemented DR methods. It is important to mention that the interaction model can be used in other types of mixtures that are based on linear combinations. The development of the interactive interface facilitates the use of the interaction model for users without experience in DR methods, due to all the results are shown graphically, allowing a more intuitive understanding of the data. The angles of the triangle turn out to be easy to understand and therefore attractive for interaction with the interface. In this sense, the user might fulfill their specific needs and parameter criteria by moving the vertices of the triangle. As future work, other DR methods could be included for mixing, since our approach has a suitable adaptation capability for the mixture of more than three kernel matrices in order to improve the results of the dimensionality reduction. Furthermore, several developed and interactive models can be explored to optimize and accelerate the interface and its performance.

Acknowledgments. This work is supported by the Smart Data Analysis Systems (SDAS) Research Group (http://sdas-group.com), as well as the *"Grupo de Investigación en Ingeniería Eléctrica y Electrónica - GIIEE"* from Universidad de Nariño. Also, the authors acknowledge to the research project: *"Desarrollo de una metodología de visualización interactiva y eficaz de información en Big Data"* supported by Agreement No. 18 November 1st, 2016 by VIPRI from Universidad de Nariño.

References

1. Asuncion, A., Newman, D.: UCI machine learning repository. University of california, School of Information and Computer Science, Irvine, CA (2007). http://www.ics.uci.edu/~mlearn/MLRepository.html
2. Belkin, M., Niyogi, P.: Laplacian Eigenmaps for dimensionality reduction and data representation. Neural Comput. **15**(6), 1373–1396 (2003)
3. Borg, I.: Modern Multidimensional Scaling: Theory And Applications. Springer, New York (2005). https://doi.org/10.1007/0-387-28981-X
4. Cook, J., Sutskever, I., Mnih, A., Hinton, G.: Visualizing similarity data with a mixture of maps. In: International Conference on Artificial Intelligence and Statistics, pp. 67–74 (2007)
5. Ham, J., Lee, D.D., Mika, S., Schölkopf, B.: A Kernel view of the dimensionality reduction of manifolds. In: Proceedings of the Twenty-First International Conference on Machine learning, p. 47. ACM (2004)
6. Lee, J.A., Renard, E., Bernard, G., Dupont, P., Verleysen, M.: Type 1 and 2 mixtures of Kullback-Leibler divergences as cost functions in dimensionality reduction based on similarity preservation. Neurocomputing **112**, 92–108 (2013)
7. Peluffo-Ordonez, D.H., Aldo Lee, J., Verleysen, M.: Generalized Kernel framework for unsupervised spectral methods of dimensionality reduction. In: 2014 IEEE Symposium on Computational Intelligence and Data Mining (CIDM), pp. 171–177. IEEE (2014)

8. Peluffo-Ordóñez, D.H., Castro-Ospina, A.E., Alvarado-Pérez, J.C., Revelo-Fuelagán, E.J.: Multiple Kernel learning for spectral dimensionality reduction. Progress in Pattern Recognition, Image Analysis, Computer Vision, and Applications. LNCS, vol. 9423, pp. 626–634. Springer, Cham (2015). https://doi.org/10.1007/978-3-319-25751-8_75

9. Peluffo-Ordóñez, D.H., Lee, J.A., Verleysen, M.: Recent methods for dimensionality reduction: a brief comparative analysis. In: European Symposium on Artificial Neural Networks (ESANN). Citeseer (2014)

10. Peluffo-Ordóñez, D.H., Lee, J.A., Verleysen, M.: Short review of dimensionality reduction methods based on stochastic neighbour embedding. In: Villmann, T., Schleif, F.-M., Kaden, M., Lange, M. (eds.) Advances in Self-Organizing Maps and Learning Vector Quantization. AISC, vol. 295, pp. 65–74. Springer, Cham (2014). https://doi.org/10.1007/978-3-319-07695-9_6

11. Roweis, S.T., Saul, L.K.: Nonlinear dimensionality reduction by locally linear embedding. Science **290**(5500), 2323–2326 (2000)

12. Sedlmair, M., Aupetit, M.: Data-driven evaluation of visual quality measures. Comput. Graph. Forum **34**, 201–210 (2015)

13. Sedlmair, M., Brehmer, M., Ingram, S., Munzner, T.: Dimensionality reduction in the wild: gaps and guidance. Department of Computer Science, University of British Columbia, Vancouver, BC, Canada, Technical report TR-2012-03 (2012)

14. Peña-Unigarro, D.F., et al.: Interactive data visualization using dimensionality reduction and dissimilarity-based representations. In: Yin, H., et al. (eds.) IDEAL 2017. LNCS, vol. 10585, pp. 461–469. Springer, Cham (2017). https://doi.org/10.1007/978-3-319-68935-7_50

15. Rosero-Montalvo, P.D., Peña-Unigarro, D.F., Peluffo, D.H., Castro-Silva, J.A., Umaquinga, A., Rosero-Rosero, E.A.: Interactive visualization methodology of high-dimensional data with a color-based model for dimensionality reduction. Biomed. Appl. Based Nat. Artif. Comput. **10338**, 289 (2017)

Irony Detection Based on Character Language Model Classifiers

Yisel Clavel Quintero[1,2(✉)] and Leticia Arco García[2]

[1] Universidad de Holguín, Avenida XX Aniversario, Vía Guardalavaca,
Piedra Blanca, Holguín, Cuba
yclavelq@uho.edu.cu
[2] Universidad Central "Marta Abreu" de Las Villas, Carretera a Camajuaní,
Km 5 ½, Santa Clara, Villa Clara, Cuba
leticiaa@uclv.edu.cu

Abstract. With the development of social networks and e-commerce, these media became regular spaces for ironic or sarcastic opinions. The detection of ironic opinions can help companies and government to improve products and services. Reliably identifying sarcasm and irony in text can improve the performance of natural language processing techniques applied to opinion mining, sentiment analysis and summarization. There are two main ways to detect irony in texts: features based classification and text classification without features. Most researchers focus their studies on the features creation that characterizes irony. However, there are new approaches that classify irony directly without feature creation. In this paper, we propose a new approach to detect irony by applying character language model classifiers without any feature engineering. We evaluated some algorithms from API LingPipe on Twitter and Amazon datasets including the SemEval-2018 Task 3 dataset for irony detection of English tweets. Several experiments were developed for analyzing the performance of each algorithm per each balanced and unbalanced collections created from the original datasets. The proposal obtained competitive values of accuracy, precision, recall and F1-measure.

Keywords: Irony classification · Machine learning · Supervised learning

1 Introduction

Irony is a resource very used in philosophy, literature and everyday life, mainly in politics and press. With the development of social networks and e-commerce platforms, these media became in regular spaces for ironic or sarcastic opinions.

Governments and companies are becoming more interested to know the opinions that are being published about them on the Internet for security reasons or to improve products and services being offered. However, the Poe's Law [15] says that without a clear indicator of the author's intent such as an emoticon or other display of humor, it is impossible to distinguish between a parody of extreme views and a sincere expression of the parodied views [5].

© Springer Nature Switzerland AG 2018
Y. Hernández Heredia et al. (Eds.): IWAIPR 2018, LNCS 11047, pp. 158–165, 2018.
https://doi.org/10.1007/978-3-030-01132-1_18

Irony is "the expression of one's meaning by using language that normally signifies the opposite, typically for humorous or emphatic effect"[1]. Sarcasm is a special case of irony; it is "the use of irony to mock or convey contempt"[2]. There are two main types of irony: verbal and situational [4, 17]. Some authors distinguish other types such as dramatic [1], discourse [11] and tragic irony [3].

The detection of figurative language like irony requires complex pragmatic abilities and the comprehension of context. There are some abilities that the receptor must have to deduce correctly the presence of irony and the real meaning of an ironic opinion. The irony detection in texts is a difficult task since it does not take into consideration the verbal (tone, timbre, etc.) and no verbal (gestures, facial expressions, etc.) communication. On the other hand, texts found in social media have specific characteristics; they are informal and they use ill-formed language and unstructured content. Usually, social media texts contain spelling mistakes, abbreviations and slang [7].

Reliably identifying sarcasm and irony in text can improve the performance of the Natural Language Processing (NLP) techniques applied to opinion mining, sentiment analysis, summarization, etc. [4]. Irony and sarcasm detection is a text classification task that has become an important challenge in areas such as opinion mining because its recognition changes the polarity of the opinion drastically [18]. Recently, it is been defined the Task 3: Irony detection in English tweets in the 12th International Workshop on Semantic Evaluation (SemEval-2018) [6].

Most researchers focus on the features creation that characterizes irony (linguistic, syntactic, semantic and statistic features) [2, 12, 16–18]. Others use word embeddings to construct an irony lexicon [9, 14] that it is applied to the unsupervised or supervised classification task. However, there are new approaches that classify directly without feature creation [9] in case of irony-labeled datasets [10]. Following this idea, this paper proposes to detect irony by applying character language model classifiers without any feature engineering and word embeddings.

The rest of this paper is organized as follows. In Sect. 2 we review previous irony detection approaches. In Sect. 3 we show our proposal and the applied classifiers. In Sect. 4 we described the experiments realized, the corpora used and the obtained results. We conclude in Sect. 5.

2 Irony Detection Approaches

There are two main ways to detect irony: features based classification and text classification without features. The first and most common way is based on construct features of irony such as the contrast of sentiment polarity, intensifiers, interjections, punctuations marks, quotes, ellipsis, capitalization, emoticons, abbreviators, onomatopoeias, user profile and negation, among others [2, 7, 12, 16–18].

---

[1] English Oxford Living Dictionaries: Irony, https://en.oxforddictionaries.com/definition/irony, last accessed 2018/04/28.

[2] English Oxford Living Dictionaries: Sarcasm, https://en.oxforddictionaries.com/definition/sarcasm, last accessed 2018/04/28.

In [16], the authors proposed a model based on four types of conceptual features: signatures, unexpectedness, style and emotional scenarios. The model is evaluated on 40000 tweets by considering the appropriateness or representativeness of different patterns to irony detection and by considering the empirical performance of the model on a tweet classification task with a balanced (50% of ironic texts and 50% of non-ironic texts) and unbalanced distribution (30% of ironic texts and 70% of non-ironic texts). The highest F-measure obtained was 0.77 in the balanced corpus with the decision trees algorithm.

In [17], a set of features is proposed to represent humor and irony in short online texts. This approach was validated by using a corpus of 50000 tweets with the hashtags: *#irony, #humor, #politics* and *#technology*. Concerning humor, the authors are focused on evaluating features based on ambiguity. With respect to irony, they propose more abstract features to represent favorable and unfavorable ironic contexts based on profiled polarity, unexpectedness and emotional scenarios. Several experiments were performed to evaluate the capabilities of discriminating between humorous and ironic texts achieving the best results (F-measure = 0.93) the classifier with the four features designed regarding humor.

The authors of [2] presented a supervised classification approach using the Amazon review corpus "SarcasmCorpus" [4]. They proposed a feature set such as word polarity imbalance, hyperboles, polarity, punctuation, ellipsis, quotes, interjection and emoticons. The dataset consists of 437 ironic texts and 817 non-ironic. The best result was achieved by using the star-rating with bag-of-words and specific features with a logistic regression approach (F1-measure = 0.74).

In [7], an approach was proposed for both identifying irony and calculating the polarity. Authors proposed a group of features: categorical and dimensional models of emotions and textual markers (such as punctuation marks, part-of-speech labels, emoticons, and specific Twitter's markers). The authors experimented with the SemEval-2015 Task 11 dataset and they used as evaluation measures the cosine similarity (cosSim) and the Mean-Squared-Error (MSE), achieving 0.71 and 2.50 respectively as best results for sentiment analysis with irony detection.

In [18], new features that allowed characterizing ironic texts and therefore discriminate between classes were created. It was mainly based on specific and general patterns, ambiguity, contextual imbalance, statistics on word appearances and contrast in the text. A module, which allows the effective irony detection from the created features and others selected from the literature, was developed applying supervised learning techniques. The corpora of Twitter texts were tested in a balanced and unbalanced distribution and some algorithms of Weka toolkit were evaluated with the implemented features. The better result for balanced corpora was obtained by SMO (F-measure = 0.93) and Random Forest was the best in the unbalanced corpora (F-measure = 0.98). The feature creation achieved an F-measure = 0.92.

A text classification without features was presented in [9], where three different deep learning models, Convolutional Neural Network (CNN), Recurrent Neural Network (RNN) and Attentive RNN, were explored on Twitter datasets. Authors used word embeddings to represent texts. In the preprocessing step, the hashtags and username mentions were removed, and hyperlinks and out-of-vocabulary words were treated as special tokens. The skip-gram word2vec vectors pre-trained by Google were used. The proposed Attentive RNN achieved the best performance with no further feature engineering (F1-measure = 0.89).

The organizers of Task 3 of SemEval-2018 [6] propose two different subtasks for the automatic irony detection on Twitter: (A) determine whether a tweet is ironic or not and (B) to predict one out of four labels describing verbal irony realized through a polarity contrast, verbal irony without such a polarity contrast, descriptions of situational irony and non-irony. For the subtask A they present a corpus of 1911 ironic tweets and 1923 regular tweets collected using the hashtags *#irony, #sarcasm* and *#not*. Using this corpus, the better irony detection results (F1-measure = 0.71) were obtained with a densely connected Long Short-Term Memory (LSTM) method based on (pre-trained) word embeddings, sentiment features using the AffectiveTweet package [13] and syntactic features [6]. This corpus will be used to validate our approach, which will allow the comparison with others published results.

3 New Proposal for Irony Detection

We dealt with irony detection task as a text classification problem to classify in "ironic" and "no ironic" categories. We trained a set of character based language models (one per category) on the opinion texts to explore if they are capable of learning without applying any NLP technique. This allows to avoid any loss of useful information that may help classifiers distinguish between ironic and non-ironic texts, such as numbers, emoticons, capitalization, punctuation marks and others signs of irony.

The API LingPipe 4.0.1[3], a tool kit for processing text using computational linguistics, was used for classification and evaluation tasks. The following LingPipe algorithms were consider in our proposal because they have achieved good results in text mining tasks as recommended by the LingPipe tutorial[4]:

- Dynamic Language Model (DLM): It accepts training events of categorized character sequences. Training is based on a multivariate estimator for the category distribution and dynamic language models for the per-category character sequence estimators.
- Naïve Bayes (NB): It is a trainable Naïve Bayes text classifier with tokens as features. A classifier is constructed from a set of categories and a tokenizer factory. The token estimator is a unigram token language model with a uniform whitespace model and an optional n-gram character language model for smoothing unknown tokens.
- Traditional Naïve Bayes (TNB): It is a traditional token-based approach to Naïve Bayes text classification. It converts character sequences into sequences of tokens and estimates a multinomial distribution over categories. For each category, Naïve Bayes estimates a multinomial distribution over words, indicating the dependence of the probability of words on categories. This classifier uses the token counts (bag-

---

[3] http://alias-i.com/.

[4] Alias-i: LingPipe API Tutorials, http://alias-i.com/lingpipe/demos/tutorial/read-me.html, last accessed 2018/04/28 (2011).

of-words) sequence that is actually being classified, not the raw character sequence input (See footnote 4).

Character language models estimate the likelihood of a given text. They are trained using samples of the text, and then, they are able to match other similar text. Character language models are used in LingPipe for classification problems (topic, subjectivity and polarity classification), tagging (part-of-speech tagging and named entity recognition) and Spelling Correction (See footnote 4).

4 Experiments

We performed various experiments in LingPipe to explore the classification results of the proposed algorithms. We use labeled datasets from Twitter and Amazon, which contain commonly many ironic texts. The texts messages in Twitter (tweets) are short; therefore, figurative language is expressed in a very concise manner [7]. In Amazon the texts are bigger, where the users write product reviews usually in several paragraphs.

Since irony and sarcasm are not frequent in sentiment expressions some researchers proposed reflect this in datasets using a small set of ironic texts [10], representing the 10% or the 30% [16, 17] of the training corpus. Others used a balanced dataset [6] with good result as well.

4.1 Datasets and Evaluation Settings

We use three different collections for evaluating our proposal, collected for previous research, which allow us to compare our approach with others previously published. The selected collections contains English opinions representing various domains and different textual characteristics, useful for improving the training step without features in the classification process. The first one contains 2713 tweets (1439 ironic and 1274 non-ironic), obtained by the union of 721 ironic tweets and 691 non-ironic tweets collected by [12] and the collection of 718 ironic tweets and 583 non-ironic tweets of 10 states of USA collected by [18]. These collections were obtained by using both the Twitter API and the twitter4j library[5] for download tweets from hashtags. Both twitter collections were joined in order to have a bigger collection (T). The second collection (A), named "SarcasmCorpus"[6], is a collection of Amazon reviews presented by [4], which contains 437 ironic texts and 817 regular texts. Finally, the third collection (SE) considered in our study is available in SemEval-2018 Task 3 Subtask A[7] which consists of 1911 ironic tweets and 1923 non-ironic tweets. This collection was not joined with collection T, even when it is about tweets, because we want to evaluate the SemEval dataset in order to be able to compare it with other approaches of this competition.

---

[5] http://twitter4j.org/en/.

[6] http://storm.cis.fordham.edu/ ~ filatova/SarcasmCorpus.rar.

[7] https://github.com/Cyvhee/SemEval2018-Task3/tree/master/datasets/train/SemEval2018-T3-train-taskA.txt.

Collections A and SE are previously classified by experts. Texts in collection T were previously classified in "ironic" if they have the presence of hashtag indicators of irony (#irony #ironic #not #sarcasm #sarcastic) and "no ironic" if not, which may not be completely trusted because the hashtags are posted by common users, not experts. In the preprocessing corpus stage for Twitter corpora, the hashtags indicators of irony and the URL were removed, the retweets (marked with "RT") and publicity tweets (with an URL corresponding to an image or video) were removed; as proposed by [6–8].

Several experiments were developed for analyzing the performance of each algorithm per each dataset. From the three collections were formed new datasets, three for each one: a balanced dataset and two unbalanced datasets with 10% and 30% of ironic texts. The texts were chosen randomly. The Table 1 shows the distribution of texts in datasets created for the experiments. It was specified a training dataset of 20% of the collection and a testing dataset with the rest.

Table 1. Distribution of datasets used. The datasets names are show with type (B: balanced, U: unbalanced) and percent of ironic texts (30 or 10% of ironic texts).

	TB	TU30	TU10	AB	AU30	AU10	SEB	SEU30	SEU10
Ironic texts	1439	548	142	437	350	91	1911	824	214
No ironic texts	1274	1274	1274	817	817	817	1923	1923	1923
Total	2713	1822	1416	1254	1167	908	3834	2747	2137

Two categories "ironic" and "no ironic" were defined for training classifiers and a size of n-gram character sequences of six as recommend by LingPipe. For TNB, we had to define the prior count for categories (a multinomial distribution over categories) and the prior count for tokens per category (a multinomial distribution over words) as a standard value of 0.5. For this algorithm we had to specify a length normalization, for which we train with the values 5, 10 and 20, recommended as typical by the authors of LingPipe, obtaining the best accuracy with 20. For the evaluation the 10-fold cross-validation was performed with a confidence of 95%.

4.2 Irony Detection Results

Tables 2, 3, and 4 show the experimental results by considering the average measure results of the 10-fold cross-validation. The validation measures included in our study are accuracy (Acc) and macro average F1-measure (maF1).

DLM, NB and TNB classifiers work better with short texts as tweets. DLM obtained the best results in all experiments. The best F1-measure values obtained with the Twitter dataset T are competitive than the ones obtained in approaches on Twitter corpora with and without feature construction mentioned in Sect. 2. The DLM and NB results with balanced dataset and 30% of ironic texts are better respect to the F1 = 0.77 reported in [15], but they do not improve the other values reported by the literature. The best F1-measure values obtained with Amazon dataset are competitive than the F1-measure value 0.74 obtained in [2] with the same collection [4] that we used, with the advantage of there is no need to create any feature and to do any preprocess task. The results obtained with SemEval dataset are worse than the F1-measure = 0.71 reported as better by SemEval-2018 competition. Accuracy increases in unbalanced datasets, but recall and consequently F1-measure values decrease significantly. The unbalanced collections require a future analysis by using algorithms robust to imbalance.

Table 2. Irony classification results by using collection T.

Algorithm	AccB	maF1B	AccU30	maF1U30	AccU10	maF1U10
DLM	0.8183	0.8155	0.8952	0.8755	0.9322	0.7656
NB	0.8021	0.7972	0.8705	0.8336	0.9103	0.5909
TNB	0.7796	0.7629	0.7398	0.5391	0.8998	–

Table 3. Irony classification results by using collection A.

Algorithm	AccB	maF1B	AccU30	maF1U30	AccU10	maF1U10
DLM	0.7353	0.6766	0.7583	0.6448	0.8943	–
NB	0.6627	0.4659	0.7026	0.4564	0.8998	–
TNB	0.6516	–	0.7014	–	0.7326	–

Table 4. Irony classification results by using collection SE.

Algorithm	AccB	maF1B	AccU30	maF1U30	AccU10	maF1U10
DLM	0.6510	0.6506	0.7135	0.6018	0.8947	0.5187
NB	0.6369	0.6365	0.7077	0.5205	0.9013	0.5000
TNB	0.6270	0.6051	0.7000	–	0.8999	–

5   Conclusions

In this paper we presented a new proposal for irony detection without features engineering with the character language model classifiers of LingPipe. This approach consumes less time since it is not necessary to construct features neither apply complex preprocess techniques before training the classifiers. The effectiveness of this kind of classifiers in irony detection is shown in the experimental results, obtaining competitive results than other state-of-the-art approaches by using similar collections. The better results were achieved on the Twitter datasets. We plan to increase the corpora and to prove other datasets. Also, we will evaluate other text classification algorithms with this proposal to compare the performance.

References

1. Attardo, S.: Irony as relevant inappropriateness. In: Irony in Language and Thought, pp. 135–174. Taylor and Francis Group (2007)
2. Buschmeier, K., Cimiano, P., Klinger, R.: An impact analysis of features in a classification approach to irony detection in product reviews. In: 5th Workshop on Computational Approaches to Subjectivity, Sentiment and Social Media Analysis, pp. 42–49. Association for Computational Linguistics, Baltimore (2014)
3. Colston, H.: On necessary conditions for verbal irony comprehension, pp. 97–134. Taylor and Francis Group (2007)
4. Filatova, E.: Irony and sarcasm: corpus generation and analysis using crowdsourcing. In: The International Conference on Language Resources and Evaluation LREC. European Language Resources Association (ELRA), New York (2012)
5. Grey, E.: Can't take a Joke? That's just Poe's law, 2017's most important internet phenomenon (2017)
6. Van Hee, C., Lefever, E., Hoste, V.: SemEval-2018 task 3: irony detection in English tweets. In: 12th International Workshop on Semantic Evaluation (SemEval 2018), New Orleans, LA, USA (2018)
7. Farías, H., Irazu, D.: Irony and sarcasm detection in Twitter: the role of affective content. Doctoral thesis. Universitat Politècnica de València (2017)
8. Huang, H.-H., Chen, C.-C., Chen, H.-H.: Disambiguating false-alarm hashtag usages in tweets for irony detection. In: 55th Annual Meeting of the Association for Computational Linguistics (ACL), Vancouver, Canada (2017)
9. Huang, Y.-H., Huang, H.-H., Chen, H.-H.: Irony detection with attentive recurrent neural networks. In: Jose, J.M., et al. (eds.) ECIR 2017. LNCS, vol. 10193, pp. 534–540. Springer, Cham (2017). https://doi.org/10.1007/978-3-319-56608-5_45
10. Joshi, A., Bhattacharyya, P., Carman, M.J.: Automatic sarcasm detection: a survey. ACM Comput. Surv. **50**, 5 (2016)
11. Kumon-Nakamura, S., Glucksberg, S., Brown, M.: How about another piece of pie: the allusional pretense theory of discourse irony. In: Irony in Language and Thought, pp. 57–96. Taylor and Francis Group (2007)
12. Ling, J., Klinger, R.: An empirical, quantitative analysis of the differences between sarcasm and irony. In: Semantic Sentiment and Emotion Workshop ESWC, Crete, Greece (2016)
13. Mohammad, S., Bravo-Marquez, F.: Emotion intensities in tweets. In: Proceedings of the 6th Joint Conference on Lexical and Computational Semantics, *SEM@ACM 2017, pp. 65–77 (2017)
14. Nozza, D., Fersini, E., Messina, E.: Unsupervised irony detection: a probabilistic model with word embeddings. In: 8th International Joint Conference on Knowledge Discovery, Knowledge Engineering and Knowledge Management (IC3K 2016), pp. 68–76 (2016)
15. Poe, N.: Big contradictions in the evolution theory (2005)
16. Reyes, A., Rosso, P., Buscaldi, D.: From humor recognition to irony detection: the figurative language of social media. Data Knowl. Eng. **74**, 1–12 (2012)
17. Reyes, A., Rosso, P., Veale, T.: A multidimensional approach for detecting irony in Twitter. Lang. Resour. Eval. **47**, 239–268 (2013)
18. Sotolongo, A., Arco, L., Rodríguez, A.: Detección de ironía en textos cortos enfocada a la minería de opinión. In: IV Conferencia Internacional en Ciencias Computacionales e Informáticas (CICCI' 2018), XVII Convención y Feria Internacional Informática 2018, La Habana (2018)

Identifying Twitter Users Influence and Open Mindedness Using Anomaly Detection

Mario Alfonso Prado-Romero$^{(\boxtimes)}$ (iD), Alberto Fernández Oliva,
and Lucina García Hernández

University of Havana, Sán Lázaro and L, Vedado, 10400 Havana, Cuba
{mario.prado,afdez,lucina}matcom.uh.cu

Abstract. Social networks help us to connect and share our thoughts with family and friends. Businesses want to take advantage of social media to better reach their customers, but traditional advertising results annoying for most social network users. As a result, the use of influencers to help a message reach their target audience has become a topic of great interest. Despite the many works in this field, detecting influence in social networks is still an open topic. In this work we propose to use anomaly detection for finding "influential" and "open minded" individuals in the Twitter network. Targeting these users can help advertisers to reach closed communities and to increase the spread of their message.

Keywords: Anomaly detection · Twitter · Influencer
Social networks

1 Introduction

Nowadays, social networks are part of our lives, helping people to stay in touch with family and friends, businesses to reach their customers and researchers to better understand society. Social networks give users the possibility to spread information and potentially reach millions of people and have been successfully used by public figures like celebrities and politicians to engage their followers. For this reason developing strategies to reach the target audience in social networks has become a critical task.

With more than 280 million monthly active users, Twitter is one of the most popular social networks of today [1]. This online micro-blogging service allows users to publicly discuss any topic from politics to everyday-life issues using small messages called tweets. A user can follow another user to see his tweets and can retweet one of these tweets to share it with his followers. Also, It is possible for users to mention other users in their tweets adding expressions of the type @UserName and to tag tweets with key words called hashtags. Most of all Fortune 500 companies have created a Twitter account, but while many businesses have an online presence, they may not be effectively communicating

© Springer Nature Switzerland AG 2018
Y. Hernández Heredia et al. (Eds.): IWAIPR 2018, LNCS 11047, pp. 166–173, 2018.
https://doi.org/10.1007/978-3-030-01132-1_19

with their target market and most users are annoyed by online advertisements [2]. To be more effective, marketers look for influencers to promote their marketing campaigns making the product propaganda go viral through the social network [3].

Studying influence patterns can help us to better understand why certain trends or innovations are adopted faster than others and how we could help advertisers and marketers to design more effective campaigns [4]. It is possible to define many influence indicators on Twitter and each one leads to a different user ranking [5]. In this work we are interested in two particular kinds of users, those whose influence goes beyond their own community and those who are more receptive to opinions coming from outside their own community. These kinds of users can help business to spread information more easily and to reach their target audience. Most users prefer to connect with people having similar points of views and liking similar topics, for this reason our target users can be seen as anomalies.

Anomaly detection refers to the problem of finding patterns in data that do not conform to expected behavior [6]. Techniques to detect anomalies in networks can be used to identify telecoms fraud, money laundering, and people with unusual behaviors in human groups. We propose to use anomaly detection for identifying influential and open minded users in Twitter. The main contributions of our work are:

- **To propose a novel algorithm to identify users "influence" and "open mindedness":** We designed an unsupervised anomaly detection algorithm to analyze the Twitter network and identify users with influence in communities beyond their own and those more prone to consider external opinions.
- **It uses only structural information of the network:** There are many works focused on analyzing Twitter user behavior and sentiment analysis. Most of these works analyze the content of tweets, users profile and even information external to Twitter, but our proposal only needs structural information, this is useful in scenarios with more privacy restriction on content.

The remainder of this paper is structured as follows: In Sect. 2, we explain how our work is related to state of the art. In Sect. 3 our proposal is presented. In Sect. 4, we analyze the results of our algorithm on Twitter data. Finally, in Sect. 5, we present conclusions and some open challenges are discussed.

2 Related Work

Influence detection on Twitter is an open task and there are many works focused on it, using different approaches and detecting different kinds of influence. Some of these studies focus on structural properties of the network. In [4] the ability of the number of followers, re-tweets and mentions to predict influence are analyzed. A new measure combining these properties is proposed in [5]. Furthermore, the problem is seen as an information propagation one by [3]. None of these works consider the community of the users in their analysis.

Some works analyze the content of the messages to help in identifying influence. In [7] this information is used to identify five different roles among influencers. An approach based on Machine Learning techniques and Social Network Analysis is proposed by [1]. Also, the authors use some structural measures that consider the community of the user, but they analyze it from a global perspective. A recommender system to identify users more prone to spread information given a request from a stranger is proposed by [8].

None of the previously mentioned works analyze the users in its community and do not take into consideration that all highest ranking influencers can be members of the same community. To overcome this problem we rank influence and open mindedness by community, identifying those individuals that can help to spread the desired message among different communities. To the best of our knowledge, ours is the first work approaching influence detection problem as an anomaly detection one.

There is much research focused on anomaly detection, but most of them are focused on vector data [6]. Due to the expressiveness of networks the interest in detecting anomalies in graphs has increased [9]. Only a small number of works are targeted to identify graph anomalies, analyzing each element in its community [10–13], but these works are focused on identifying anomalous vertices with numeric attributes and are not suitable for our problem. Our proposal is based on the InterScore algorithm [14], which was designed to discover mixing accounts in the Bitcoin network, but differentiates from it taking into consideration edge direction, and the sign of the dissimilarity among elements. In the next section we explain our proposal in detail.

3   Identifying Influence and Open Mindedness

Twitter is a mainly content-oriented social network, with communities evolving around topics instead of people, where retweets are the main content-based interaction [5]. For our analysis we use the retweet network where users are vertices and there is an edge from vertex v to vertex u if user v retweeted a tweet from u. Usually, people form communities of like-minded individuals and have a tendency to share more those tweets that are interesting from the community perspective and to ignore other points of view. This behavior can be a problem if we want to use a reduced number of individuals to spread a message that reaches even the small communities.

Our proposal to solve this problem is based on the InterScore anomaly detection algorithm [14] but deviates from it in two major aspects. First, the direction of edges has a semantical difference in Twitter. Users with an anomalous number of out-edges with users from other communities are more open to opinions external to its own group. On the other hand, users with an anomalous number of incoming edges from other communities are people whose opinions are interesting for people beyond the frontiers of its group. Second, a user can be anomalous if it has a number of inter-community edges far greater or far lower than the rest of the members from its community, but for the problem we are targeting only matter the users with an anomalous high number of inter-community edges. To tackle these two issues we propose a new algorithm called InterScoreDS which analyzes the inter-community links of vertices and considers edge direction and the sign of the difference in the outlierness score function. Due to the differences among user groups our algorithm analyzes each user in its community in an unsupervised fashion. As a result it returns an outlierness ranking of Twitter users.

Definition 1 (Outlier ranking). *An outlier ranking from a graph G is a set $R = \{(v, r)|v \in V, r \in [0, 1]\}$ of tuples, each one containing a vertex from G and its outlierness score.*

The input of our algorithm is a user graph G_U and two boolean values *in_edges_analysis* and *negative_anomalies*. These boolean values allow analysts to control the behavior of the algorithm and to better focus on the kind of outliers they want to identify, thus reducing false positives. In the first stage, the Louvain community detection method [15] is used on G_U to detect groups of related users, returning a clustering C of vertices from G_U. Any state-of-the-art graph clustering algorithm could be used in this stage. We selected the Louvain method based in its performance and applicability to large graphs.

In the second stage, our algorithm iterates over each community $C_i \in C$ and for each vertex calculates the number of inter-community links it has, using a function $l : V \to \mathbb{R}$. Then, for each community C_i we compute the mean difference among the number of inter-community links from its elements as defined below:

$$IMD(C_i) = \frac{\sum_{v_j \in C_i} \sum_{v_k \in C_i, v_j \neq v_k} |l(v_j) - l(v_k)|}{|C_i|} \qquad (1)$$

Depending on analysts choice a function l_{in} to count inter-community in-edges or a function l_{out} for counting inter-community out-edges will be used. Thus, we obtain two different functions $IMD_{in}(C_i)$ and $IMD_{out}(C_i)$ respectively. Then, in the third stage, our algorithm iterates over the elements of each C_i and determines its anomaly score using the following function:

$$r(v, C_i) = \frac{\sum_{u \in C_i, u \neq v} d(v, u, C_i)}{|C_i|} \qquad (2)$$

where $d : V \times V \times 2^V \to \{0, 1\}$ is a function that determines if the inter-community links difference between two vertices is greater than its community mean. Depending on analysts choice, to focus on elements with an atypically large or low number of inter-community links, one of the functions defined below will be used:

$$d_{high}(v, u, C_i) = \begin{cases} 0 & \text{if } |l(v) - l(u)| \leq IMD(C_i) \land (l(v) - l(u)) < 0, \\ 1 & \text{if } |l(v) - l(u)| > IMD(C_i) \land (l(v) - l(u)) \geq 0. \end{cases} \qquad (3)$$

$$d_{low}(v, u, C_i) = \begin{cases} 0 & \text{if } |l(v) - l(u)| \leq IMD(C_i) \wedge (l(v) - l(u)) \geq 0, \\ 1 & \text{if } |l(v) - l(u)| > IMD(C_i) \wedge (l(v) - l(u)) < 0. \end{cases} \quad (4)$$

These score functions measure with how percent of the community a user has a difference in the amount of inter-community links greater than the mean difference for that community. Furthermore, they take into consideration if the number of inter-community links is greater or lower than the mean. These functions adaptively rank users outlierness according to their context, and detect anomalies that cannot be identified from a global point of view. In Algorithm 1, the steps of the InterScoreDS method can be observed in more detail.

Algorithm 1: InterScoreDS

Input: A users network G_U
Input: Boolean value $in\_edges\_analysis$
Input: Boolean value $negative\_anomalies$
Output: An outlier ranking R of the vertices from G_U

```
 1  R ← ∅
 2  C ← Clustering(G_U)
 3  foreach community C_i ∈ C do
 4      if in_edges_analysis then
 5          | m ← IMD_in(C_i)
 6      else
 7          | m ← IMD_out(C_i)
 8      end
 9      foreach user v ∈ C_i do
10          r_v ← 0
11          foreach user u ∈ C_i with u ≠ v do
12              if negative_anomalies then
13                  | r_v ← r_v + d_low(v, u, C_i)
14              else
15                  | r_v ← r_v + d_high(v, u, C_i)
16              end
17          end
18          r_v ← r_v/|C_i|
19          R ← R ∪ {r_v}
20      end
21  end
22  return R
```

The InterScoreDS algorithm has the same $O(V^2)$ computational complexity as the InterScore algorithm, where the outlierness score function is the most expensive stage of the algorithm. Despite that, because the quadratic scoring is performed independently on each community and social networks have many communities, in real scenarios the algorithm performs better than the quadratic worst case.

4   Experimental Results

In this section, we analyze the results of our algorithm on real data, using a set of tweets about 2016 United States presidential elections. Because re-tweets are the most important content-oriented interaction in Twitter [5], we used the tweets from the mentioned dataset to build the re-tweet network[1]. In our network, vertices represent users and there is an edge from vertex v to vertex u if the user v re-tweeted a tweet from user u. Furthermore, edges have a weight indicating how many times user v has re-tweeted user u. In Table 1, some properties of the network are displayed.

Table 1. Network properties

Network property	Value	Network property	Value
Tweets	320 791	Communities	7581
Users	154 475	Smallest community size	2
Edges	204 608	Largest community size	16834
Re-tweets	213 723	Mean community size	20

The re-tweet network is a sparse graph with a high number of communities. The difference of size among communities is also significant with big ones grouping most users, and small ones with only a few members. We have not a labeled dataset of influential users for using as ground truth. Because different measures lead to different perspectives about influence [4], we decided to use a Gaussian anomaly detection algorithm on the number of re-tweets as baseline for our comparisons.

In Fig. 1, we compare the inter-community in-edges and the in-degree from the top 20 outliers detected using InterScoreDS and the baseline Gaussian algorithm. It can be appreciated that our proposal in general detects users with a higher amount of re-tweets and inter-community links (notice scale difference in Fig. 1). This is because it gives analysts the option to focus only on those users with an abnormally large amount of inter-community links. On the other hand, the baseline algorithm also considers users with few re-tweets.

We analyzed the Top 10 outlying users identified by each algorithm and got interesting insights. InterScoreDS rated as influent users like ABC News Politics, CNN Politics, Huff Post Politics, and the presidential candidate Hillary Clinton. On the other hand, the Gaussian algorithm rated as most influent users like CNN Breaking News, The Wall Street Journal, and presidential candidate Bernie Sanders. These differences in ranking are because sites like CNN Breaking News and The Wall Street journal are sites with great influence, but in the politics domain they are consulted only by some communities while sites like CNN Politics influence more communities in the elections topic. Furthermore, the presidential candidate Hillary Clinton made a campaign based in diversity and targeting people from many social groups, while candidate Bernie Sanders was very influent but its influence reached only some communities.

---

[1] Data set available at https://drive.google.com/drive/folders/1f5IazToQKAIgFx1kssiKOTSYLyf7jPNV?usp=sharing.

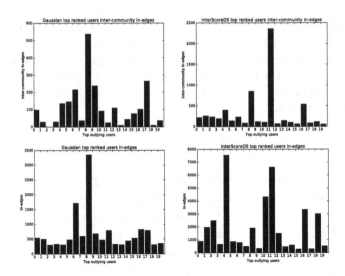

Fig. 1. Comparison of in-degree and inter-community links from the top 20 outliers

The analysis of top 10 open minded users identified by each algorithm is more difficult because in most cases these users are not famous or well known. The most curious finding is that InterScoreDS finds more users self-identified as liberals or progressive compared to the Gaussian algorithm. Also, the Gaussian algorithm identified a user with only one tweet. These differences are due to our algorithm considering users who re-tweet tweets from other communities being people more open minded while the Gaussian algorithm only identify people who re-tweet a lot. Also, our algorithm focused on users performing an abnormally large number of re-tweets, ignoring users with almost not re-tweets.

Experiments show how InterScoreDS can identify influencers with the power to reach many communities. The algorithm gives more options to analysts for focusing on the outliers that are really interesting for them and to overcome some problems of traditional anomaly detection methods.

5   Conclusions

We proposed inter-community links as a measure to identify influence and open mindedness in Twitter users and designed a new anomaly detection algorithm for identifying those users in an unsupervised fashion and analyzing each user in its community. Furthermore, the algorithm was tested on real data and the different results between our approach and Gaussian anomaly detection were discussed.

We will focus on some challenges in future work like parallelizing our algorithm to increase the performance. Also, InterScoreDS can be applied in other social networks and other problems like spammer and bot detection, these are all interesting domains for future work.

References

1. Cossu, J.V., Dugué, N., Labatut, V.: Detecting real-world influence through Twitter. In: 2015 Second European Network Intelligence Conference (ENIC) (2015)
2. Pikas, B., Sorrentino, G.: The effectiveness of online advertising: consumer's perceptions of ads on Facebook, Twitter and Youtube. J. Appl. Bus. Econ. **16**, 70 (2014)
3. Jendoubi, S., Martin, A., Liétard, L., Hadji, H.B., Yaghlane, B.B.: Two evidential data based models for influence maximization in Twitter. Knowl.-Based Syst. **121**, 58–70 (2017)
4. Cha, M., Haddadi, H., Benevenuto, F., Gummadi, P.K.: Measuring user influence in Twitter: the million follower fallacy. Icwsm **10**, 30 (2010)
5. Anger, I., Kittl, C.: Measuring influence on Twitter. In: Proceedings of the 11th International Conference on Knowledge Management and Knowledge Technologies (2011)
6. Chandola, V., Banerjee, A., Kumar, V.: Anomaly detection: a survey. ACM Comput. Surv. (CSUR) **41**, 15 (2009)
7. Chen, C., Gao, D., Li, W., Hou, Y.: Inferring topic-dependent influence roles of Twitter users. In: Proceedings of the 37th International ACM SIGIR Conference on Research & Development in Information Retrieval (2014)
8. Lee, K., Mahmud, J., Chen, J., Zhou, M., Nichols, J.: Who will retweet this?: Automatically identifying and engaging strangers on Twitter to spread information. In: Proceedings of the 19th International Conference on Intelligent User Interfaces (2014)
9. Akoglu, L., Tong, H., Koutra, D.: Graph based anomaly detection and description: a survey. Data Min. Knowl. Discov. **29**, 626–688 (2015)
10. Gao, J., Liang, F., Fan, W., Wang, C., Sun, Y., Han, J.: On community outliers and their efficient detection in information networks. In: Proceedings of the 16th ACM SIGKDD International Conference on Knowledge Discovery and Data Mining (2010)
11. Müller, E., Sánchez, P.I., Mülle, Y., Böhm, K.: Ranking outlier nodes in subspaces of attributed graphs. In: 2013 IEEE 29th International Conference on Data Engineering Data Engineering Workshops (ICDEW) (2013)
12. Prado-Romero, M.A., Gago-Alonso, A.: Detecting contextual collective anomalies at a glance. In: Proceedings of the 23rd International Conference on Pattern Recognition (ICPR). (2016)
13. Prado-Romero, M.A., Gago-Alonso, A.: Community feature selection for anomaly detection in attributed graphs. In: Beltrán-Castañón, C., Nyström, I., Famili, F. (eds.) CIARP 2016. LNCS, vol. 10125, pp. 109–116. Springer, Cham (2017). https://doi.org/10.1007/978-3-319-52277-7_14
14. Prado-Romero, M.A., Doerr, C., Gago-Alonso, A.: Discovering bitcoin mixing using anomaly detection. In: Mendoza, M., Velastín, S. (eds.) CIARP 2017. LNCS, vol. 10657, pp. 534–541. Springer, Cham (2018). https://doi.org/10.1007/978-3-319-75193-1_64
15. Blondel, V.D., Guillaume, J.L., Lambiotte, R., Lefebvre, E.: Fast unfolding of communities in large networks. J. Stat. Mech.: Theory Exp. **2008**, P10008 (2008)

Semantic Loss in Autoencoder Tree Reconstruction Based on Different Tuple-Based Algorithms

Hiram Calvo[✉], Ramón Rivera-Camacho, and Ricardo Barrón-Fernndez

Centro de Investigación en Computación (CIC), Instituto Politécnico Nacional (IPN), Av. JD Bátiz e/ MO de Mendizábal, 07738 Mexico City, Mexico
hcalvo@cic.ipn.mx

Abstract. Current natural language processing analysis is mainly based on two different kinds of representation: structured data or word embeddings (WE). Modern applications also develop some kind of processing after based on these latter representations. Several works choose to structure data by building WE-based semantic trees that hold the maximum amount of semantic information. Many different approaches have been explores, but only a few comparisons have been performed. In this work we developed a compatible tuple base representation for Stanford dependency trees that allows us to compared two different ways of constructing tuples. Our measures mainly comprise tree reconstruction error, mean error over batches of given trees and performance on training stage.

Keywords: Semantic reconstruction · Parsing
Structuring word embeddings

1 Introduction

Almost every Natural Language Processing (NLP) task has a scenario where a phrase has to be parsed. Syntactic parsing is concerned on knowing and representing syntactic features of a sentence. Even simple methods, like word or n-gram counting may be outperformed if syntactic information is added [12].

Much work related to automatic syntactic parsing analysis is grounded on grammar or lexicon approaches with underlying rules based on context-free grammars [9], tree-adjoining grammars [4,6], among others, to express a sentence as a tree that holds syntactic relationships between words. However, to manually create rules that define the grammar is not a preferred option.

At certain point we can realize that a simple phrase could be interpreted on many ways, so, we have to determine as well which parsing tree describes better

We thank the support of Instituto Politécnico Nacional, SIP-IPN, COFAA-IPN. Partially funded by CONACyT (Language Technologies Thematic Network projects 260178, 271622).

© Springer Nature Switzerland AG 2018
Y. Hernández Heredia et al. (Eds.): IWAIPR 2018, LNCS 11047, pp. 174–181, 2018.
https://doi.org/10.1007/978-3-030-01132-1_20

each phrase. This problem of ambiguity is especially hard when the grammar is not bounded to a lexical domain and it has to adapt to several contexts.

Some parsers use generative probabilistic models to deal with this ambiguity and bind the parsing task to a domain. Statistical parsers are supported with some heuristics and large amounts of data. Many techniques are used to tackle this task, like pattern recognition, Markov processes, among others. Nevertheless, when training data is not enough or is out-of-domain, the final model is degraded, having to rely on other sentence features like similarities or sentence dependencies [10].

Modern learning methods, such as deep learning techniques, try to omit feature excessive manipulation by doing one or more phases of unsupervised pre-training that provide good initial distribution of data and capture dependencies between parameters [3]. Those phases have proved to increment accuracy on different NLP tasks.

Is desirable that words could provide us with the relationship between them and their context, instead of using them just as a shot on the entire corpus (i.e., one-hot representation). Word embedding models provide us with this information. After the embedding process we are able to represent a word as a n-dimension vector. Word vectorization, could be used to find relationships between other words, such as similarities or semantic distance between them.

Popular word embedding implementations are based on deep neural networks [2] or skip-gram models [7] trained over huge datasets. As well as in other tasks this pre-training phase gives us meaningful representation on main tasks such as Part-Of-Speech (POS), Language Modelling, Name Entity Recognition (NER), among others.

Even when a word-embedding representation is used, there is a need to structure sentence information. [5,13], among others propose several techniques to build semantic trees according to maximum semantic models based on ordered tuple reconstruction. They point that using traditional parsers is an option, but do not provide more information about the process.

The main objective of building semantic trees is that they hold as much semantic information as possible. We develop a way to compare performance between a traditional parser model and an ordered tuple model.

This paper is divided in the following sections. First, in Sect. 2, we describe our proposal based on deep learning techniques to build semantic trees. For the parsing approach we rely on Stanford parser to generate dependency trees to pair with the ordered tuple approach. Then, in Sect. 3, we present some results of the evaluation for tuples' reconstruction, overall tree reconstruction and performance along with details on implementation of the proposal. Finally, in Sect. 4, we draw our conclusions.

2   Proposal

The main goal of the present work is to develop a way to measure the semantic loss when building a semantic tree.

As different words are related together in different phrases they acquired more meaning as a unit. When we build a semantic tree we make those relationships in a better predictable way that can be expressed as an energy function. If after building a semantic tree we try to reconstruct the former phrase, we can also find how much energy is lost in the process.

By using Energy Based Models (EBMs) we can measure how much energy the construction has lost. We use an autoencoder since they work in a deterministic way and can be fast trained as well as they also present fast inference compared with probabilistic EBMs [14]. We compare the performance on the reconstruction stage of greedy trees based on ordered word tuples and Stanford parser[1] trees using the process described by Socher [13].

2.1   Autoencoder

An Autoencoder (AE) is an artificial neural network that solves its own function and are used to learn representations on a process of encoding and decoding [1]. This process is carried in two stages. The encoder stage on Eq. 1, where it maps on a deterministic way the input vector x to a hidden representation y by a non-linearity. And the reverse process, the decoder stage on Eq. 2, which maps back the hidden y representation to a reconstructed z vector also by a non-linearity.

$$f_\theta(x) = \sigma(Wx + b) \tag{1}$$

$$g_{\theta'}(x) = \sigma(W'x + b') \tag{2}$$

where $\theta = \{W, b\}$ and $\theta' = \{W', b'\}$ are parameters of the neural network [15]. We map each phrase into a vector form using both structures to compare.

2.2   Ordered Tuple Construction

In order to obtain ordered tuples, we build semantic trees with the process described by Socher [13] and Huang [5] based on two-length ordered tuples. We split phrases on words and join them by pairs, we use an AE to produce and rebuild representations that provides us how much semantic loss we obtain. Basically, we join two vectorized words of $1 \times n$, having a $1 \times 2n$ vector representation to produce $1 \times n$ coded production.

We repeat this process until we have just one tuple that represents our entire phrase. The criterion for choosing the next tuple is greedy, that is, we just choose the next minimum reconstruction error. The process is depicted on Fig. 1a.

2.3   Parsing Approach

We use Stanford parser to get dependency trees. As a result, tuples are now eligible by structure. We have to point that Stanford parser does not always produce binary trees, so we choose them on a parent-child manner to use AE on the same way that the ordered tuple approach does. This process is shown in Fig. 1b.

---

[1] http://nlp.stanford.edu/software/lex-parser.shtml.

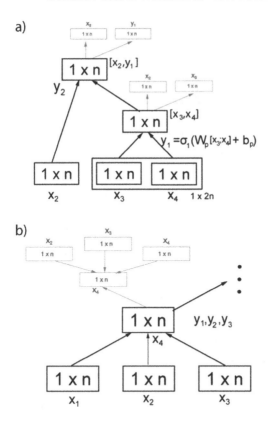

Fig. 1. (a) Ordered 2-length tuple reconstruction process. (b) Stanford parser approach tuple reconstruction.

We use a bottom-up recursive manner algorithm based on Depth First Search (DFS).

3 Experiments and Results

We use a compound methodology to develop our results stage. We split our corpus on a 5:1:1 relation for training, validation and testing. This validation scenario gives us the possibility to avoid overfitting while training [8]. Our testing schema is depicted on Fig. 2.

As a summary, we use training data to train our AE while validation data is tested every n number of epochs to check the method's performance. Once this step ends we proceed to the test stage.

Our results considered four main measures:

i. **Average tuple reconstruction MSE for validation among epochs.**
   It proves the capability of the method to create significant tuple values to be used while training. The better those values are, the better the reconstruction of values is. The same happens for AE convergence.

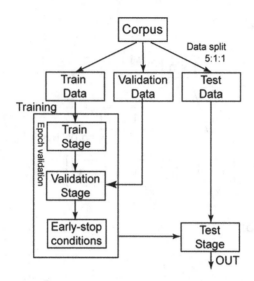

Fig. 2. Training-test methodology based on epoch validation and early stop conditions.

ii. **Measure of MSE on reconstruction stage for testing trees against tree word length.** The less the error becomes, the better reconstruction we have, so, we can say that we can hold more semantic information.

iii. **Covariance between tree length and error reconstruction.** Farther values from zero are expected when variables' linear relationship becomes greater.

iv. **Overall reconstruction on test stage.** We provide the mean reconstruction error of all test trees.

On our word-embedding phase we use Mikolov's method based on CBOW skip-gram model which has outperformed other state of the art embedding models on accuracy and speed for typical NLP tasks like POS, NER, etc. [11].

For our experiment we used text information obtained from the Experience Project[2] site with a Python crawler. This corpus exhibits many kinds of misspelling errors as well as non-text features like images, videos, html tags, etc. It contains phrases from 5 to 100 word-length paragraphs with up to four sentences, a total of ∼3K phrases. The ratio of unknown words over all corpus is ∼15%.

We perform text preprocessing on the simplest form, we just remove those non-text characteristics and split simple sentences over paragraphs. Finally, after splitting with a ratio of 5:1:1, we have ∼2K phrases for training purposes and ∼400 phrases for each validation and testing stages.

We show the reconstruction scenario for both methods in Fig. 3.

On the tuple reconstruction stage we can see that the ordered tuple method has better performance as well as faster convergence to a minimum with early

---

[2] http://www.experienceproject.com/.

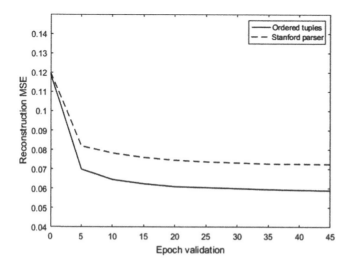

Fig. 3. Validation stage on tuple AE for ordered tuple approach (straight line) and parsers approach (dashed line).

stop conditions, reporting a minimum of ∼0.0595 on epoch 45 while the parser approach reports a minimum of ∼0.0718 for the same epoch.

In order to analyze the relationship between the tree length and the reconstruction error we use the covariance which is a measure of linear dependency of variables. We experimented with batches of 20 phrases each for quicker, easier to read results. We have a total of ∼18 batches for the testing set. Results of absolute covariance values are shown on Fig. 4.

In the ordered tuple approach, we can see covariance values are nearer to zero because the reconstruction error is lower. It means, this method's performance is not affected by the phrase length as much as in the parsing approach. Moreover, on this latter greater values are seen.

This could be justified by tuple dispersion; the main goal of the parsing approach is to show the rules of a given semantic tree that are degraded by misspelling and grammar errors while the tuple approach does not rely on such structures. Covariance fluctuates around 0.04 units for the ordered tuple method while the Stanford approach reports higher values that oscillate around 0.15 units.

Finally, the ordered tuple method exceeds on overall tree reconstruction with a mean of ∼0.102 against ∼0.199 for the parsing approach.

Table 1. Error measures in tuple reconstruction (smaller is better)

	Ordered tuple	Parser
Tuple reconstruction	**0.0595**	0.0718
Covariance fluctuation	**0.04**	0.15
Overall tree reconstruction	**0.102**	0.199

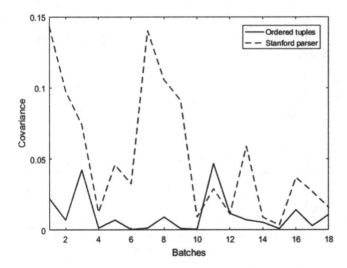

Fig. 4. Over a batch of 20 phrases. Absolute covariance between tree reconstruction error and word length of phrases for ordered tuple approach (straight line) and parsers approach (dashed line).

Table 1 summarizes the performance for the complete test scenario of our experiment. As seen, a better performance is obtained by the ordered tuple approach. Using the parser's method as baseline, the ordered tuple approach exceeds it by 17.1% for tuple reconstruction. Ordered tuple is also remarkably better against covariance fluctuations with 73.3%, which means better reconstruction regardless of the tree size. Finally, in overall tree reconstruction performance the ordered tuple approach still excels with 48.7%.

4   Conclusions

We compared two methods for building trees based on ordered tuples and based on Stanford parser. We found a better overall performance of the tuple approach appreciable on an scenario where misspelling and poorly grammar structure is present. This behavior is justifiable mainly because of the parsing nature to find structures of phrases which get less accuracy when text is not well structured, and secondly because basically a parser has to deal with grammar rules which are not present on poorly expressed text.

The behavior of tree reconstruction according to phrase length was described. Similarly, in both methods we found an important increment of the reconstruction error in trees with the highest length. As tuples become more complex, we found less probability of they being found and trained. When tree rebuilding is in its first steps, we only have to join simple words, while on the final steps these tuples now contain several words or even tuples inside it, that increment the complexity of the reconstruction process.

References

1. Bengio, Y.: Learning deep architectures for AI. Found. Trends Mach. Learn. **2**(1), 1–127 (2009)
2. Collobert, R., Weston, J.: A unified architecture for natural language processing: deep neural networks with multitask learning. In: Proceedings of the 25th International Conference on Machine Learning, pp. 160–167. ACM (2008)
3. Erhan, D., Bengio, Y., Courville, A., Manzagol, P.A., Vincent, P., Bengio, S.: Why does unsupervised pre-training help deep learning? J. Mach. Learn. Res. **11**(Feb), 625–660 (2010)
4. Gardent, C., Kallmeyer, L.: Semantic construction in feature-based TAG. In: Proceedings of the Tenth Conference on European Chapter of the Association for Computational Linguistics, vol. 1, pp. 123–130. Association for Computational Linguistics (2003)
5. Huang, E.: Paraphrase detection using recursive autoencoder (2011). http://nlp. stanford.edu/courses/cs224n/2011/reports/ehhuang.pdf
6. Kallmeyer, L.: Using an enriched tag derivation structure as basis for semantics. In: Proceedings of TAG+ 6 Workshop, pp. 127–136. Citeseer (2002)
7. Mikolov, T., Chen, K., Corrado, G., Dean, J.: Efficient estimation of word representations in vector space. arXiv preprint arXiv:1301.3781 (2013)
8. Prechelt, L.: Early stopping - but when? In: Orr, G.B., Müller, K.-R. (eds.) Neural Networks: Tricks of the Trade. LNCS, vol. 1524, pp. 55–69. Springer, Heidelberg (1998). https://doi.org/10.1007/3-540-49430-8_3
9. Pulman, S.G.: Basic parsing techniques: an introductory survey. In: Encyclopedia of Linguistics (1991)
10. Rush, A.M., Reichart, R., Collins, M., Globerson, A.: Improved parsing and POS tagging using inter-sentence consistency constraints. In: Proceedings of the 2012 Joint Conference on Empirical Methods in Natural Language Processing and Computational Natural Language Learning, pp. 1434–1444. Association for Computational Linguistics (2012)
11. Schnabel, T., Labutov, I., Mimno, D., Joachims, T.: Evaluation methods for unsupervised word embeddings. In: Proceedings of the Empirical Methods in Natural Language Processing (2015)
12. Sidorov, G., Velasquez, F., Stamatatos, E., Gelbukh, A., Chanona-Hernández, L.: Syntactic n-grams as machine learning features for natural language processing. Expert. Syst. Appl. **41**(3), 853–860 (2014)
13. Socher, R., Pennington, J., Huang, E.H., Ng, A.Y., Manning, C.D.: Semi-supervised recursive autoencoders for predicting sentiment distributions. In: Proceedings of the Conference on Empirical Methods in Natural Language Processing, pp. 151–161. Association for Computational Linguistics (2011)
14. Swersky, K., Buchman, D., Freitas, N.D., Marlin, B.M., et al.: On autoencoders and score matching for energy based models. In: Proceedings of the 28th International Conference on Machine Learning (ICML 2011), pp. 1201–1208 (2011)
15. Vincent, P., Larochelle, H., Lajoie, I., Bengio, Y., Manzagol, P.A.: Stacked denoising autoencoders: learning useful representations in a deep network with a local denoising criterion. J. Mach. Learn. Res. **11**(Dec), 3371–3408 (2010)

Machine Learning Theory and Applications

Robust K-SVD: A Novel Approach for Dictionary Learning

Carlos A. Loza$^{(\boxtimes)}$ (iD)

Department of Mathematics, Universidad San Francisco de Quito, Quito, Ecuador
cloza@usfq.edu.ec

Abstract. A novel criterion to the well-known dictionary learning technique, K-SVD, is proposed. The approach exploits the L1-norm as the cost function for the dictionary update stage of K-SVD in order to provide robustness against impulsive noise and outlier input samples. The optimization algorithm successfully retrieves the first principal component of the input samples via greedy search methods and a parameter-free implementation. The final product is Robust K-SVD, a fast, reliable and intuitive algorithm. The results thoroughly detail how, under a wide range of noisy scenarios, the proposed technique outperforms K-SVD in terms of dictionary estimation and processing time. Recovery of Discrete Cosine Transform (DCT) bases and estimation of intrinsic dictionaries from noisy grayscale patches highlight the enhanced performance of Robust K-SVD and illustrate the circumvention of a misplaced assumption in sparse modeling problems: the availability of untampered, noiseless, and outlier-free input samples for training.

Keywords: Dictionary learning · K-SVD · Robust estimation

1 Introduction

Sparse modeling constitutes an advantageous framework for applications where sparsity and parsimonious representations are favored, e.g. data compression, image processing and high-dimensional statistics are some of the fields that exploit its inherent concepts. The modeling itself is usually compartmentalized into two very distinctive stages: sparse coding and dictionary learning; while the former strives to represent the input signal as a combination (usually linear) of a few elements, known as bases or atoms (e.g. the JPEG compression standard), the latter learns the set of such overcomplete generating atoms, i.e. a dictionary, in a data-driven scheme.

The sparse coding problem is usually solved by either exploiting a surrogate of the L0-pseudonorm that characterizes sparse decompositions, e.g. L1-norm-based convex optimization programs, such as Basis Pursuit [4], or a greedy approach that usually yields a suboptimal, but rather more tractable, solution: Matching Pursuit (MP) or any of its variants [13,15]. The dictionary learning estimation is generally solved via probabilistic approaches [11] or generalized

© Springer Nature Switzerland AG 2018
Y. Hernández Heredia et al. (Eds.): IWAIPR 2018, LNCS 11047, pp. 185–192, 2018.
https://doi.org/10.1007/978-3-030-01132-1_21

clustering [1,7]. K-SVD, one of the clustering-based methods, is arguably the most widely utilized and recognized dictionary learning algorithm in the literature [3,6,12]. Its core optimization can be summarized as an alternation between sparse coding and dictionary update stages.

However, K-SVD implicitly relies on second-order statistics via the Singular Value Decomposition (SVD) or Principal Component Analysis (PCA) alternating update stage. This approach, although principled and practical, might yield erroneous estimations under the presence of additive non-Gaussian noise, e.g. impulsive noise. In addition, outlier samples can easily bias the dictionaries due to the equal weight policy of the Minimum Squared Error (MSE) criterion. A well-known alternative against outliers is to substitute MSE fidelity terms by L1-norms of the estimation errors. Therefore, the main contribution of this manuscript is to incorporate robustness into the dictionary learning framework by exploiting the L1-norm as the optimization criterion in the SVD update stage of K-SVD.

In practical terms, unlike regular SVD, L1-norm-based PCA does not have a closed form solution and numerical methods are usually required. Ding et al. proposed R1-PCA in a successful attempt to obtain robust principal components, however, the method is highly dependent on the dimension m of a surrogate subspace [5]. On the other hand, in [2,9], the authors exploit a probabilistic approach with Laplacian priors to perform a L1-norm-based decomposition; nevertheless, they are both limited in practice due to reliance on particular heuristics or use of linear and quadratic programs, respectively. In terms of sparse modeling, Mukherjee et al. developed a L1-based K-SVD variant by solving a reweighted L2-norm problem; yet, the comparison to baseline K-SVD might be biased due to the disparity in sparse coding algorithms, i.e. iteratively reweighted least squares (IRLS) for the proposed method and Orthogonal Matching Pursuit (OMP) for K-SVD [14]. In the present work, the fact that K-SVD needs to only estimate the first principal component (for each atom) is exploited by using the algorithm proposed by Kwak [10]; this technique provides a fast, efficient and reliable methodology to estimate the eigenvector with largest L1 dispersion (in feature space). In this way, the proposed final dictionary learning technique, known as Robust K-SVD, is able to estimate overcomplete patterns in a robust and fast scheme that empirically seems to even alleviate the computational burdens that the state of the art entails.

The rest of the paper is organized as follows: Sect. 2 introduces the concept of robustness to the K-SVD formulation and details the necessary conditions, optimization criteria and algorithms. Section 3 focuses on two types of experiments alongside their results and discussion. Lastly, Sect. 4 concludes the paper.

2   Robust K-SVD

Let $X = [\mathbf{x_1}, \ldots, \mathbf{x_n}] \in \mathbb{R}^{d \times n}$ be the collection of n zero-mean d-dimensional vectors. L2-norm-based PCA attempts to find an m-dimensional linear subspace $(m < d)$, such that the variance is maximized (or the MSE is minimized); this task is accomplished by solving (1):

$$J_2(W, V) = \|X - WV\|_2^2 \tag{1}$$

where $W \in \mathbb{R}^{d \times m}$ is a projection matrix with columns $\{\mathbf{w}_k\}_{k=1}^m$ known as bases of the m-dimensional subspace, i.e. feature space. $V \in \mathbb{R}^{m \times n}$ is the corresponding coefficient matrix, and $\| \cdot \|_2$ denotes the L2-norm operator. The global minimum of (1) is achieved via SVD which also corresponds to the solution of the dual problem:

$$W^* = \arg\max_W \|W^T S_x W\|_2 = \arg\max_W \|W^T X\|_2$$
$$\text{subject to} \quad W^T W = I_m \tag{2}$$

where S_x is the covariance matrix of X and I_m is the $m \times m$ identity matrix. Usually, the solution of (2) is proper and tractable. Nevertheless, it is well-known that the squared L2-norm is sensitive to outliers; thus, it is necessary to appeal to L1-norm-based optimization to mitigate such effect.

2.1   SVD Based on L1-Norm Maximization

Instead of minimizing the squared L2-norm of the error, the following criterion is adopted:

$$J_1(W, V) = \|X - WV\|_1 \tag{3}$$

where $\| \cdot \|_1$ denotes the L1-norm operator. In [10] it was noted that optimizing (3) is rather difficult; thus, it is posited that instead of minimizing J_1 in the original d-dimensional input space, it would be more advantageous to maximize the L1 dispersion in the feature space as follows:

$$W^* = \arg\max_W \|W^T X\|_1$$
$$\text{subject to} \quad W^T W = I_m \tag{4}$$

To obtain a local minimizer, [10] proposes a greedy method where, for $m = 1$, Eq. (4) becomes:

$$\mathbf{w}^* = \arg\max_{\mathbf{w}} \|\mathbf{w}^T X\|_1 = \arg\max_{\mathbf{w}} \sum_{i=1}^n |\mathbf{w}^T \mathbf{x}_i|$$
$$\text{subject to} \quad \|\mathbf{w}\|_2 = 1 \tag{5}$$

For the remaining $m - 1$ principal components, another greedy search is proposed, however, it is not addressed here. Algorithm 1 guarantees finding a local minimizer of (5) by leveraging the fact that $\sum_{i=1}^n |\mathbf{w}^T(t)\mathbf{x}_i|$ is a non-decreasing function of t (for further details, refer to [10]). In practice, a stopping threshold that tracks the norm of successive estimations is utilized.

Algorithm 1. PCA-L1 [10].

Input: $X = [\mathbf{x}_1, \ldots, \mathbf{x}_n] \in \mathbb{R}^{d \times n}$
Output: $\mathbf{w} \in \mathbb{R}^d$

  $\mathbf{w}(0) \leftarrow \mathbf{w}(0)/\|\mathbf{w}(0)\|$ $t \leftarrow 0$
  repeat
    for $i = 1, \ldots, n$ **do**
      if $\mathbf{w}^T(t)\mathbf{x}_i < 0$ **then**
        $p_i(t) = -1$
      else
        $p_i(t) = 1$
      end if
    end for
    $t \leftarrow t + 1$
    $\mathbf{w}(t) = \sum_{i=1}^{n} p_i(t-1)\mathbf{x}_i$
    $\mathbf{w}(t) \leftarrow \mathbf{w}(t)/\|\mathbf{w}(t)\|_2$
  until convergence

2.2 Robust L1-norm-based Dictionary Learning

K-SVD was proposed by Aharon et al. as a generalization of K-means [1]. Given a set of observations $Y = \{\mathbf{y}_i\}_{i=1}^{N}$, $(\mathbf{y}_i \in \mathbb{R}^n)$, the estimation objective is to find a set of overcomplete patterns, atoms, or bases, i.e. a dictionary $D \in \mathbb{R}^{n \times K}$, that is able to sparsely encode the inputs (in a linear fashion):

$$\min_{D,X}\{\|Y - DX\|_2^2\} \quad \text{subject to} \quad \forall i, \ \|\mathbf{x}_i\|_0 \leq T_0 \tag{6}$$

where T_0 denotes the number of non-zero entries in the sparse representation vector $\mathbf{x}_i$, i.e. i-th column of X. Likewise K-means, K-SVD alternates between input assignment and centroids update stages. The former utilizes any of the standard sparse coding algorithms, e.g. MP, OMP, while the latter updates the dictionary atoms via SVD operations. The update stage assumes that both X and $k - 1$ columns of D are fixed, then, the atom in question, $\mathbf{d}_k$, alongside its support in X, i.e. $\mathbf{x}_T^k$ (k-th row in X) are jointly updated as follows:

$$\|Y - DX\|_2^2 = \left\| Y - \sum_{j=1}^{K} \mathbf{d}_j \mathbf{x}_T^j \right\|_2^2 = \left\| (Y - \sum_{j \neq k} \mathbf{d}_j \mathbf{x}_T^j) - \mathbf{d}_k \mathbf{x}_T^k \right\|_2^2 = \|E_k - \mathbf{d}_k \mathbf{x}_T^k\|_2^2$$
$$\tag{7}$$

where E_k is the error when the k-th atom is removed. In order to preserve the sparsity of the solution, it is necessary to restrict the support of E_k to the columns that are currently using the atom $\mathbf{d}_k$; this shrinking operation results in E_k^R which is the matrix to be linearly decomposed via SVD. The resulting updated atom is the first eigenvector (sorted by largest variance). In order to guarantee robustness against impulsive noise and outliers, the MSE criterion is replaced by the L1-norm-based PCA algorithm described in the previous subsection [10]. The final result, Robust K-SVD, is summarized in Algorithm 2.

Algorithm 2. Robust K-SVD

Input: $Y \in \mathbb{R}^{n \times N}, D \in \mathbb{R}^{n \times K}, T_0$
Output: $D \in \mathbb{R}^{n \times K}$

   repeat
      Sparse Coding Stage (standard algorithms can be utilized, e.g. MP, OMP):
      $X \leftarrow \mathrm{SpCod}(Y, D, T_0)$
      Dictionary Update Stage:
      for $k = 1, 2 \ldots K$ **do**
         $w_k \leftarrow \{i | 1 \leq i \leq N, \mathbf{x}_T^k(i) \neq 0\}$
         $E_k \leftarrow Y - \sum_{j \neq k} \mathbf{d}_j \mathbf{x}_T^j$
         $\Omega_k \in \mathbb{R}^{N \times |w_k|}$ s.t. $\Omega_k(w_k(i), i) = 1$
         $E_k^R \leftarrow E_k \Omega_k$
         $\mathbf{d}_k \leftarrow \mathrm{PCA\text{-}L1}(E_k^R)$
      end for
   until convergence

In practice, the algorithm stops after either surpassing a threshold in successive estimations or reaching a fixed number of iterations. One of the main advantages of the proposed approach is that K-SVD, by only exploiting the first eigenvector, does not require the remaining $m - 1$ bases, which is exactly what Algorithm 1 provides in a fast and efficient implementation. This suggests a clear leverage over other techniques that require the full estimation of the bases.

3 Results and Discussion

3.1 Recovery of Orthogonal Bases

The first set of experiments focuses on linear combinations of 16-dimensional DCT bases. Specifically, the atoms are linearly combined ($T_0 = 4$) in a random fashion using coefficients from a uniform distribution between -1 and 1. Out of the 5000 generated samples, impulsive noise is added to 10% of them (SNR from $-30\,$dB to $-15\,$dB). Then, both K-SVD and Robust K-SVD estimate the dictionary with the following model parameters: $K = 16$, $T_0 = 4$, 10^{-3} as convergence criterion for PCA-L1, 20 alternate iterations between sparse coding and dictionary update stages, and 25 different trials for each noise scenario. Figure 1 displays the average normalized cross-correlation coefficient for all the noise cases and combinations between sparse coding mechanisms and dictionary update approaches. It is clear that Robust K-SVD outperforms K-SVD and provides a principled scheme to deal with impulsive noise.

The second scenario fixes the impulsive noise SNR to $-20\,$dB and varies the impulsive noise rate. Again, Fig. 1 confirms that Robust K-SVD is less sensitive to outlier-like, contaminated samples. It is worth mentioning that these comparisons are not biased by the choice of sparse coding mechanisms, i.e. both MP and OMP are used for both dictionary learning techniques; thus, it is explicit that the improved performance is solely due to the Robust K-SVD algorithm.

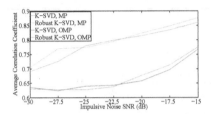 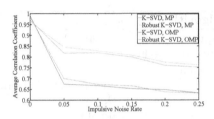

Fig. 1. Recovery of DCT bases. Average normalized cross-correlation between original and estimated dictionaries under impulsive noise. Left: Variable SNR, noise rate of 0.1. Right: Variable rates, noise SNR $= -20$ dB.

Also for this case, there is marginal differences between MP and OMP because the original generating dictionary is orthogonal, i.e. MP reduces to OMP.

3.2   Dictionary Learning on Grayscale Image Patches

The second set of experiments utilizes the Yale Face Database [8] to extract 10000 random 8×8 grayscale patches in order to estimate an intrinsic generating dictionary. For this case, outlier samples were simulated by blocks of salt and pepper noise, i.e. blocks with black and white pixels. The size of the outlier blocks was varied from 1×1 (only one pixel is affected in the sample) until 8×8 (all pixels in the sample are distorted). The number of outlier samples are modified as well for rate values between 0 (no noise), until 0.25 (25 % of the samples are perturbed by noise). In addition, each 8×8 grayscale patch is vectorized into a 64-dimensional zero-mean sample. Lastly, out of the 10000 available blocks, 80% go under the salt and pepper noise treatment, while the remaining clean 20% are reserved for testing and model quantification.

Both K-SVD and Robust K-SVD begin the estimation process with the same initial seed dictionary and utilize the same sparse coding algorithm (OMP). Values of $K = 400$ and $T_0 = 10$ are set. A total of 20 trials per noise scenario are simulated. Lastly, 30 sequential sparse coding and dictionary update stages are ran for each case. The normalized L2-norm of the reconstruction error on the test set is chosen as the metric of success. Figure 2 illustrates the effect of outliers in the dictionary learning process for the 1×1 and 8×8 noisy blocks cases: K-SVD is clearly more biased than Robust K-SVD when outliers are present. The size of the outlier block has a clear effect on the estimation as well. Lastly, it is remarkable how Robust K-SVD outperforms the baseline even for the 0 rate case (no salt and pepper noise), i.e. the proposed method is even able to discard the effect of potential outliers inherent to real-world signals. This clearly suggests that Robust K-SVD is a suitable alternative to K-SVD even when no impulsive noise is explicitly present.

Table 1 summarizes the results for the rest of the noisy block sizes and a particular outlier rate. Again, Robust K-SVD outperforms the corresponding baseline case and shows a natural degradation as the outlier samples grow in influence. It is worth mentioning that Robust K-SVD consistently showcased a

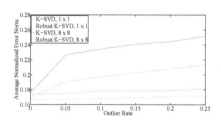

Fig. 2. Estimation of intrinsic dictionary for grayscale image patches. Average L2-norm of reconstruction error (normalized by L2-norm of input) as function of sizes of salt and pepper noisy blocks and rates.

faster processing time that regular K-SVD; e.g. in the 8×8 case, K-SVD needed an average of 1.58 s in the dictionary update stage (*svds* MATLAB routine) while Robust K-SVD spent 0.59 s in the same task (iMac 2.7 GHz Intel Core i5, 8 GB memory). This empirically suggests that Robust K-SVD is not only superior in performance, but also less computationally demanding than the state of the art. In the spirit of openness, the MATLAB code of the proposed algorithm can be found in https://github.com/carlosloza/Robust_KSVD.

Table 1. Average L2-norm of reconstruction error as function of sizes of salt and pepper noisy blocks (0.1 rate case).

Noisy block size	1×1	2×2	3×3	4×4	5×5	6×6	7×7	8×8
K-SVD	0.178	0.183	0.189	0.199	0.209	0.220	0.229	0.234
Robust K-SVD	0.168	0.169	0.171	0.175	0.182	0.190	0.195	0.197

4 Conclusion

Robust K-SVD is able to incorporate robustness into the sparse modeling framework by substituting MSE-based SVD operations with robust and fast estimation of principal components via L1-norm optimization. The results not only illustrate the expected safeguard against impulsive noise and outliers, but they also indicate that Robust K-SVD is suitable for problems framed as noiseless. In addition, we empirically prove that Robust K-SVD is faster and computationally less demanding than K-SVD. This opens the possibility of exploiting the proposed algorithm in high-dimensional scenarios where SVD computations are clearly prohibitive.

References

1. Aharon, M., Elad, M., Bruckstein, A.: K-SVD: an algorithm for designing overcomplete dictionaries for sparse representation. IEEE Trans. Signal Process. **54**(11), 4311–4322 (2006). https://doi.org/10.1109/TSP.2006.881199
2. Baccini, A., Besse, P., Falguerolles, A.: A L1-norm PCA and a heuristic approach. Ordinal Symb. Data Anal. **1**(1), 359–368 (1996)
3. Bryt, O., Elad, M.: Compression of facial images using the K-SVD algorithm. J. Vis. Commun. Image Represent. **19**(4), 270–282 (2008). https://doi.org/10.1016/j.jvcir.2008.03.001
4. Chen, S., Donoho, D., Saunders, M.: Atomic decomposition by basis pursuit. SIAM Rev. **43**(1), 129–159 (2001). https://doi.org/10.1137/S003614450037906X
5. Ding, C., Zhou, D., He, X., Zha, H.: R1-PCA: rotational invariant L1-norm principal component analysis for robust subspace factorization. In: Proceedings of the 23rd International Conference on Machine Learning, pp. 281–288. ACM (2006). https://doi.org/10.1145/1143844.1143880
6. Elad, M., Aharon, M.: Image denoising via sparse and redundant representations over learned dictionaries. IEEE Trans. Image Process. **15**(12), 3736–3745 (2006). https://doi.org/10.1109/TIP.2006.881969
7. Engan, K., Aase, S.O., Husoy, J.H.: Method of optimal directions for frame design. In: Proceedings of the 1999 IEEE International Conference on Acoustics, Speech, and Signal Processing, vol. 5, pp. 2443–2446. IEEE (1999). https://doi.org/10.1109/ICASSP.1999.760624
8. Georghiades, A.S., Belhumeur, P.N., Kriegman, D.J.: From few to many: Illumination cone models for face recognition under variable lighting and pose. IEEE Trans. Pattern Anal. Mach. Intell. **23**(6), 643–660 (2001). https://doi.org/10.1109/34.927464
9. Ke, Q., Kanade, T.: Robust L1 norm factorization in the presence of outliers and missing data by alternative convex programming. In: 2005 IEEE Computer Society Conference on Computer Vision and Pattern Recognition, CVPR 2005, vol. 1, pp. 739–746. IEEE (2005). https://doi.org/10.1109/CVPR.2005.309
10. Kwak, N.: Principal component analysis based on L1-norm maximization. IEEE Trans. Pattern Anal. Mach. Intell. **30**(9), 1672–1680 (2008). https://doi.org/10.1109/TPAMI.2008.114
11. Lewicki, M.S., Olshausen, B.A.: Probabilistic framework for the adaptation and comparison of image codes. JOSA A **16**(7), 1587–1601 (1999). https://doi.org/10.1364/JOSAA.16.001587
12. Loza, C.A., Principe, J.C.: A robust maximum correntropy criterion for dictionary learning. In: 2016 IEEE 26th International Workshop on Machine Learning for Signal Processing (MLSP), pp. 1–6. IEEE (2016). https://doi.org/10.1109/MLSP.2016.7738898
13. Mallat, S.G., Zhang, Z.: Matching pursuits with time-frequency dictionaries. IEEE Trans. Signal Process. **41**(12), 3397–3415 (1993). https://doi.org/10.1109/78.258082
14. Mukherjee, S., Basu, R., Seelamantula, C.S.: L1-K-SVD: a robust dictionary learning algorithm with simultaneous update. Signal Process. **123**, 42–52 (2016). https://doi.org/10.1016/j.sigpro.2015.12.008
15. Tropp, J.A., Gilbert, A.C.: Signal recovery from random measurements via orthogonal matching pursuit. IEEE Trans. Inf. Theory **53**(12), 4655–4666 (2007). https://doi.org/10.1109/TIT.2007.909108

Customer Segmentation Using Multiple Instance Clustering and Purchasing Behaviors

Ivett Fuentes[1,2](✉), Gonzalo Nápoles[2], Leticia Arco[1,2], and Koen Vanhoof[2]

[1] Computer Science Department, Central University of Las Villas, Santa Clara, Cuba
ivett@uclv.cu
[2] Faculty of Business Economics, Hasselt University, Hasselt, Belgium

Abstract. On-line companies usually maintain complex information systems for capturing records about Customer Purchasing Behaviors (CPBs) in a cost-effective manner. Building prediction models from this data is considered a crucial step of most Decision Support Systems used in business informatics. Segmentation of similar CPB is an example of such an analysis. However, existing methods do not consider a strategy for quantifying the interactions between customers taking into account all entities involved in the problem. To tackle this issue, we propose a customer segmentation approach based on their CPB profile and multiple instance clustering. More specifically, we model each customer as an ordered bag comprised of instances, where each instance represents a transaction (order). Internal measures and modularity are adopted to evaluate the resultant segmentation, thus supporting the reliability of our model in business marketing analysis.

Keywords: Multiple instance clustering
Customer Purchasing Behaviors · Decision Support Systems

1 Introduction

The analysis of Customer Purchasing Behaviors (CPBs) plays an important role not only in promotion and marketing strategies, but also in the design of more effective loyalty strategies [3]. For that reason, in recent years CPB analysis is regarded as a crucial step of most current Decision Support Systems (DSSs) [3,15]. However, a deep understanding of underlying patterns is difficult due to the fact that many entities are included, such as products, customers, transactions and revenues [3]. Which is why this research field has been attaining more and more attention in recent years [11,12,15].

In [12] the authors proposed an approach to support loyalty program managers in customizing their segment-specific target marketing activities on a product category level. They obtained a customer segmentation and selected attractive categories for deriving segment-specific, targeted category level promotion

© Springer Nature Switzerland AG 2018
Y. Hernández Heredia et al. (Eds.): IWAIPR 2018, LNCS 11047, pp. 193–200, 2018.
https://doi.org/10.1007/978-3-030-01132-1_22

campaigns. However, they do not explicitly study the relation between the customer behaviors and their purchasing patterns, like their transactions. Besides, they use a classical clustering algorithm for segmentation, which constitutes another one disadvantage. Another DSS to predict CPB is proposed in [3]. However, this proposal only includes a limited number of customer groups and cannot totally capture the interactions between customers.

Although some of these approaches cover partially the solution of the CPB problems, the results are still insufficient. In other words, if we cannot measure what we need, we cannot expect our inferences to be correct [9]. Therefore, it is necessary to identify other measures that guarantee to quantify theses interactions. The above challenges suggest that further research is required to model and analyze the CPB problems. To tackle this issue, we propose a customer segmentation model based on multiple instance clustering where customers are denoted by bags of orders. The advantage of this model is that it better captures the dynamics behind the customers when purchasing.

The remainder of this paper is structured as follows. In Sect. 2, we describe the problem to be solved in detail. Section 3 surveys previous works devoted to clustering multiple instance objects. The proposed approach for clustering customers based on the distance among their bags is described in Sect. 4, whereas the experimental results are discussed in Sect. 5. Conclusions and future research aspects are given in Sect. 6.

2 Cluster Analysis of CPB Profiles

Customer purchasing data comprise a set of orders where each order is a multiset, in which the multiplicity of each element is the number of a purchased product in a specific order. Existing works only approach this problem using classical clustering [7,12]. A simple way to do that is taking into account the total amount of products purchased by customers. However, this approach does not allow totally capturing the interactions between customers, which could be existing in the CPB [3,7]. Moreover, it does not take into account the co-occurrence relationships of products in the orders [8]. Other approaches only consider the individual analysis of purchasing behaviors, and consequently, they cannot reveal various preferences and behaviors of the set of purchasing orders [15].

The definition of dissimilarity or similarity between orders is a key component in all CPB-based segmentation approaches. For example, the overlap between two orders allows quantifying their similarity by considering the purchased products. For that reason, in this research we are interested in the $MSJaccard$ similarity measure [14] given by the Eq. 1. In short, $MSJaccard$ computes the ratio between the intersection and the union of orders, where $multi_{p_k}(o_i)$ denotes the multiplicity of the product p_k in the order o_i.

$$MSJaccard(o_i, o_j) = \frac{|o_i \bar\cap o_j|}{|o_i \uplus o_j|} = \frac{\sum_{p_k \in (o_i \cap o_j)} min(multi_{p_k}(o_i), multi_{p_k}(o_j))}{\sum_{p_k \in (o_i \cup o_j)} max(multi_{p_k}(o_i), multi_{p_k}(o_j))} \quad (1)$$

As already mentioned, our approach is more complex given the fact that an object is characterize by an order bag. Therefore, a practical question would be: how to measure the dissimilarity or similarity between customers i and j, taking into account all purchasing background? In this paper, we apply the multiple instance clustering techniques for solving this problem. Being more specific, we model a customer as a bag $X = \{x_1, \ldots, x_N\}$, where N is the number of orders and x_i is the feature vector (called instance) describing the i-th order. Recall that each bag may have a different size, which means that the value N can vary among the bags in the dataset. In the following section, we further elaborate on the multiple instance clustering problem for gathering CPB profiles.

3   Multiple Instance Clustering Approaches

There are many application domains, in which the complexity demands a richer object representation than single feature vectors [2]. In these scenarios, an object is often described as a set of feature vectors or a multiple instance (MI) object. As a result, the research community started to develop techniques for multiple instance learning that where capable to analyse MI objects [1].

The first MI clustering algorithm is named BAMIC (BAg-level Multi-Instance Clustering) [17]. Concretely, BAMIC splits the unlabeled training bags into k disjoint groups of bags, where several forms of Hausdorff metric [5] are utilized to measure distances among bags. Experimental results show that BAMIC could effectively reveal the inherent structure of the MI dataset. In [16], the authors formulate a Maximum Margin Multiple Instance Clustering (M3IC) problem based on Maximum Margin Clustering (MMC), but the formulation of M3IC involves a nonconvex optimization problem. BAMIC uses a distance measure for comparing bags, so the selection of a meaningful distance measure has an important impact of the resulting clustering. The distance measures used by BAMIC compare the bags by considering their individual instances, thus contributing to cluster with respect to the similarity. Another characteristic of this algorithm is that it requires a fixed number of clusters to operate.

At the first glance, the MI clustering problem might be regarded as a simple extension of classical clustering task where the objects to be gathered are sets instead of being single instances. However, the task of clustering MI bags has its own characteristics. For example, in order to cluster objects described by sets of instances, the most intuitive strategy is to allow the instances contained in one set contribute equally to the clustering process. In the MI clustering context, this kind of strategy may not be appropriate since the instances comprising the bag usually exhibit different characteristics.

4   Multiple Instance Customer Clustering Approach

In this section, we introduce a general approach to apply MI clustering algorithms based on distances between bags, which performs the clustering process by considering the CPB data related to customers. Our approach is described by a general procedure that follows the next steps, which allows obtaining clusters of customers with similar CPB features.

1. **Data pre-processing.** Recover customer background (i.e., customer, product and order information) and apply data pre-processing steps to remove irrelevant transaction records. It should be remarked that the selection of transaction background is subject to a specific period; time intervals in the context of business applications can be typical years, seasons or months. The segmentation of the transactions background depends on relevant business goals, for example the frequency of orders.
2. **Data representation.** Build a proper representation of the cleaned data considering the orders and the desired bag granularity.
3. **Distance selection.** Specify the distance metric to be used for comparing bags. More explicitly, we use the Hausdorff distances to determine the extent to which one bag differs from another. This can be done considering the dissimilarity between two instances as the complement of the overlap between two orders (i.e., $1 - MSJaccard$). This would allow gathering customers with similar CPB profiles, although it is possible to apply other distances for comparing bags (customers) and instances (orders).
4. **Apply a MI clustering algorithm.** We suggest using the BAMIC algorithm since it uses the distances between bags, thus being more suitable to compare the orders that make up the bags. Due to the very high computational complexity found in some problem domains, we suggest to apply Fast Greedy Optimization (FGO) [4] and Label Propagation (LP) [10] algorithms for obtaining the optimal number of clusters. In general, this approach can be extended to other clustering algorithms, which consider the dissimilarity matrix by using MI distances between customers.

5   A Case of Study on Belgian Store Data

Aiming at illustrating the soundness of the proposed clustering procedure, we examine the customer data provided by an anonymous online shop in Belgium. The original transaction dataset comprises 207,376 product transactions, which belong to 11,959 orders that have been purchased by 64,382 customers. If customer C_i purchased product p_k in a certain chain store one day, it is treated as a transaction and stored in the transaction dataset. Product information includes product ID, product subclass, price and mark, among others. Complete and Churn Rate filters are applied in the first step. The first one, eliminates all empty transactions, corresponding to incomplete or not paid orders. The last one, eliminates those customers who do not make more purchases within a given time period. We eliminate customers who were not active the whole year.

As a result, we only include in our study those customers that have an order frequency higher than five. We applied the MI clustering approach to the resulting transaction dataset, which comprises 18,407 transactions, which belong to 6,432 orders that have been purchased by 731 customers.

We first apply BAMIC clustering algorithm. Three multiple instance distances (MI distances) were used for comparing bags [17]: Minimal Hausdorff distance (MINH), Maximal Hausdorff distance (MAXH) and Average Hausdorff distance (AVEH). The number of clusters was varied from two to ten clusters. We used internal measures for evaluating the clustering solutions since we have no knowledge about optimal clustering structure required by the external indexes [6]. The internal indices consider in this research to measure the *goodness* of the clustering structure are Silhouette and Dunn indices [13]. Figure 1 shows the results achieved by the BAMIC algorithm using the three forms of Hausdorff distance when clustering the consumers of our case study. The x-axis denotes the number of clusters while the y-axis represents the analysed validity index. Best values were obtained for $k = 5$ and $k = 7$ using AVEH and MINH respectively.

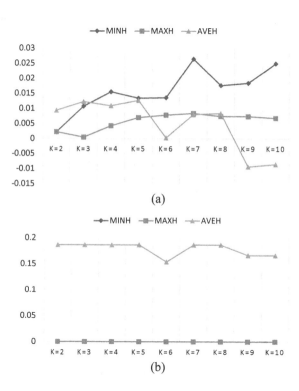

Fig. 1. Performance clustering comparison among forms of Hausdorff distance based on (a) Silhouette index and (b) Dunn index.

Aiming at exploring the clustering process itsel—which does not optimize the number of clusters to keep the computational complexity low—we apply FGO and LP clustering algorithms. For applying both, it is necessary to define the network, from which the communities (i.e., clusters) are discovered. Each consumer is considered as a node and two nodes are connected if their similarity is greater than zero. Each edge is weighted by the similarity $(1 - d(i, j))$ between the customers i and j, such that $d(i, j)$ represents the MI distance between them. FGO works by greedily optimizing the modularity and is considerably faster than other general algorithms. Besides, it allows to extend the segmentation analysis to customer data that was considered too large to be tractable [4]. The LP method is initialized with a unique label, so each node adopts the most popular label associated with its neighbors in that iteration. Figure 2 depicts the histogram and cumulative frequency related to the number of connections impacting each node, where the x-axis represents the node degrees. Moreover, this histogram indicates the presence of node with a much higher connections than most other nodes. Due to the classical clustering approach ignores the topological information and the flow between customers, the above validation indexes obtain lower values. For that reason, it is necessary to take into account both the similarity and the structural information in terms of network linkages between objects in study. Notice that our evaluation strategy resembles the way that communities are evaluated.

For the evaluation of cluster solutions we use the modularity, which can be roughly defined as the number of edges falling within groups minus the expected number in an equivalent network with randomly selected edges. The modularity can be either positive or negative, where positive values indicate the possible presence of community structure. Figure 3 shows that FGO has the best modularity values for the three Hausdorff distances. Figure 4 shows the clustering conformation, the x-axis represents the number of clusters while the y-axis denotes the number of customers. We can see that as was concluded above the best performing is obtained for FGO which allows to form more compact groups, due to this algorithm reached to split the first cluster in more compact subclusters.

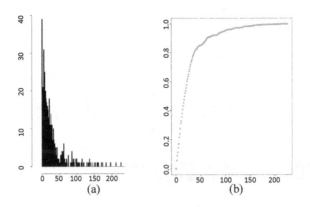

Fig. 2. Histogram and cumulative frequency of node degrees.

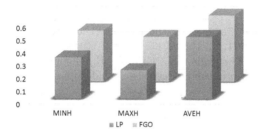

Fig. 3. Modularity values.

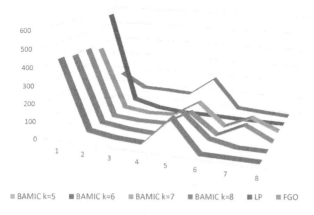

Fig. 4. Clustering conformation for BAMIC, LP and FGO based on minimum Hausdorff distance.

6 Conclusions and Future Work

In this paper, we presented a MI clustering approach for tackling the CPB segmentation problem. This approach was applied on real-life data concerning to a Belgian online shop. Our solution comprises the following advantages: (1) it allows obtaining different segmentation results using different distance functions to compare sets of elements, (2) it allows considering different clustering objectives. The internal validity indices were used to measure the quality of clustering results and evaluate our clustering solutions, which were obtained using BAMIC and modularity for FGO and LP. In most cases, the average and the minimum Hausdorff distances reported the best results while FGO achieved the best results regardless the adopted Hausdorff distance. The future work will be oriented to obtaining a distance function capable of reflecting the structural differences between the bags associated to customers.

References

1. Amores, J.: Multiple instance classification: review, taxonomy and comparative study. Artif. Intell. **201**, 81–105 (2013)
2. Carbonneau, M.A., Cheplygina, V., Granger, E., Gagnon, G.: Multiple instance learning: a survey of problem characteristics and applications. Pattern Recognit. **77**, 329–353 (2018)
3. Chan, S., Ip, W.: A dynamic decision support system to predict the value of customer for new product development. Decis. Support. Syst. **52**(1), 178–188 (2011)
4. Clauset, A., Newman, M.E.J., Moore, C.: Finding community structure in very large networks. Phys. Rev. E **70**, 066111 (2004)
5. Dietterich, T.G., Lathrop, R.H., Lozano-Prez, T.: Solving the multiple instance problem with axis-parallel rectangles. Artif. Intell. **89**(1), 31–71 (1997)
6. Dudoit, S., Fridlyand, J.: A prediction-based resampling method for estimating the number of clusters in a dataset. Genome Biol. **3**(7), research0036-1 (2002)
7. Jiang, T., Tuzhilin, A.: Segmenting customers from population to individuals: does 1-to-1 keep your customers forever? IEEE Trans. Knowl. Data Eng. **18**(10), 1297–1311 (2006)
8. Kim, H.K., Kim, J.K., Chen, Q.Y.: A product network analysis for extending the market basket analysis. Expert. Syst. Appl. **39**(8), 7403–7410 (2012)
9. Ochoa, A., Arco, L.: Differential betweenness in complex networks clustering. In: Ruiz-Shulcloper, J., Kropatsch, W.G. (eds.) CIARP 2008. LNCS, vol. 5197, pp. 227–234. Springer, Heidelberg (2008). https://doi.org/10.1007/978-3-540-85920-8_28
10. Raghavan, U.N., Albert, R., Kumara, S.: Near linear time algorithm to detect community structures in large-scale networks. Phys. Rev. E **76**, 036106 (2007)
11. Ren, H., Huang, T.: Modeling customer bounded rationality in operations management: a review and research opportunities. Comput. Oper. Res. **91**, 48–58 (2018)
12. Reutterer, T., Hornik, K., March, N., Gruber, K.: A data mining framework for targeted category promotions. J. Bus. Econ. **87**(3), 337–358 (2017)
13. Thalamuthu, A., Mukhopadhyay, I., Zheng, X., Tseng, G.C.: Evaluation and comparison of gene clustering methods in microarray analysis. Bioinformatics **22**(19), 2405–2412 (2006)
14. Theobald, M., Siddharth, J., Paepcke, A.: SpotSigs: robust and efficient near duplicate detection in large web collections. In: Proceedings of the 31st Annual International Conference on Research and Development in Information Retrieval, pp. 563–570. ACM (2008)
15. Valero-Fernandez, R., Collins, D.J., Lam, K.P., Rigby, C., Bailey, J.: Towards accurate predictions of customer purchasing patterns. In: Proceedings of the International Conference on Computer and Information Technology (CIT), pp. 157–161. IEEE, August 2017
16. Zhang, D., Wang, F., Si, L., Li, T.: M3IC: maximum margin multiple instance clustering. In: Proceedings of the 21st International Joint Conference on Artificial Intelligence (IJCAI), vol. 9, pp. 1339–1344 (2009)
17. Zhang, M.L., Zhou, Z.H.: Multi-instance clustering with applications to multi-instance prediction. Appl. Intell. **31**(1), 47–68 (2009)

Multimodal Alzheimer Diagnosis Using Instance-Based Data Representation and Multiple Kernel Learning

Diego Collazos-Huertas$^{(\boxtimes)}$, David Cárdenas-Peña,
and German Castellanos-Dominguez

Signal Processing and Recognition Group, Universidad Nacional de Colombia,
Km 9 Vía al Aeropuerto la Nubia, Manizales, Colombia
{dfcollazosh,dcardenasp,cgcastellanosd}@unal.edu.co

Abstract. In biomarker-based Alzheimer diagnostic problems, the combination of different sources of information (modalities) as is a challenging task. Often, the simple data combination lacks diagnostic improvement due to neglecting the correlation among modalities. To deal with this issue, we introduce an approach to discriminate healthy control subjects, mild cognitive impairment patients, and Alzheimer's patients from the neurophysiological test and structural MRI data. To this end, the instance-based feature mapping composes an enhanced data representation based on clinical assessment scores and morphological measures of each brain structure. Then, the extracted multiple feature sets are combined into a single representation through the convex combination of its reproducing kernels. The weighting parameters per feature set are tuned based on the maximization of the centered-kernel alignment criterion. The proposed methodology is evaluated on the well known Alzheimer's Disease Neuroimaging Initiative (ADNI) database into multi-class and bi-class diagnosis tasks. The experimental results indicate that our proposal improves the diagnosis, enhancing data representation with a better class separability. Proposed MKL achieves the best performance in both, the multi-class task (76.6%) and the two-class task (83.1%).

Keywords: Alzheimer's disease · Multiple-instance learning
Metric learning · Multiple kernel learning · Centered kernel alingment

1 Introduction

Alzheimer's disease (AD), the most prevalent form of dementia, is an irreversible neurodegenerative pathology that progressively reduces cognitive and memory functions. An estimated 17% of people aging over 65 and 32% over 80 are suffering AD, 20 and this prevalence tends to rise as the average life expectancy increases [2]. An accurate diagnosis and prediction of disease progression would facilitate optimal decision-making for clinicians and patients. Although studies have applied machine learning methods for the computer-aided diagnosis (CAD)

© Springer Nature Switzerland AG 2018
Y. Hernández Heredia et al. (Eds.): IWAIPR 2018, LNCS 11047, pp. 201–209, 2018.
https://doi.org/10.1007/978-3-030-01132-1_23

of the AD, a bottleneck in the diagnostic performance was shown in previous methods, due to the lacking of efficient strategies for representing biomarkers information [15].

Several biomarkers have shown association with the AD, including brain atrophy measured through structural MRI, hypometabolism, associated with AD measured via FDG-PET, and proteins measured in the CSF. These biomarkers yield complementary information, i.e., different modalities capture disease information from different nature, thereby improving understanding of the disease pattern over that presented by one single modality [11]. In recent years, a large number of studies have been published on the multimodal computer-aided classification of the AD and its prodromal stage, mild cognitive impairment (MCI). Among recent studies, in [12], Tang et al. used volumetric, shape, and diffusion features of the hippocampus and amygdala for AD classification. They used PCA and Student's t-test for reducing the feature set, and LDA and SVM for classification. In the same way, the combination of structural MRI with demographics, cognitive tests, and genetic data has also explored in a few studies. Moradi et al. in [10] used GM density maps, age, and cognitive tests as features, and employed classification algorithms such as low-density separation and random forest for AD conversion prediction. CSF and PET biomarkers are also used jointly to structural MRI features to support AD diagnosis. Nonetheless, due to the simplicity of straightforward concatenation, these methods suffer from a major drawback because it treats all features as equivalent, without an appropriate consideration of the correlation among modalities [8].

In order to lead with the above issue, some approaches ensures that the complementary information found across all modalities is still used. These strategies may either combine the results of classification rules trained on the individual modalities holding the original data representation or use special combination rules to combine features before training providing a new feature representation space. In this context, regional GM volume, regional average FDG-PET intensity, and CSF biomarkers were used as features for AD and MCI classification along with multi-kernel learning [14] and multi-task learning [13]. In recent studies, Korolev et al. [7] and Clark et al. [4], used MRI morphological measures along with demography information, clinical scores and plasma measures for AD conversion prediction. In the first study, the authors used mutual information criterion for feature selection and probabilistic multi-kernel learning for classification. Clark et al., propose a feature selection approach using random forest, and used an ensemble of random forests of conditional trees, SVM, naive Bayes, and multilayer perceptrons for classification.

In this paper, we propose a multimodal computer-aided diagnosis methodology for support AD diagnosis. For this purpose, we introduce an enhanced data representation scenario based on instance-based features that feed a multiple kernel learning (MKL), improving the classification performance into the discrimination tasks between HC patients, MCI, and AD subjects. Using the morphology of anatomical brain structures extracted from MRI data and the cognitive test scores provided by the specialists, we perform the instance-based feature mapping by introducing the use of dissimilarity representations. Every patient-dependent set of feature mappings that has a diverse nature is optimized using a supervised metric learning based on centered kernel alignment (CKA) similarity function yielding a more discriminative feature representation. Furthermore, each enhanced representation scenario per modality is associated with their convex kernel combination by a CKA-based MKL algorithm. The resulting combined feature space is used to support AD classification into two diagnosis tasks, multi-class, and bi-class.

2   Methods

2.1   Instance-Based Feature Mapping

In two-class problems, multiple-instance learning (MIL) assumes that there is, at least, one positive instance in a positive bag, while negative bags only hold negative instances. Thus, the MIL approaches imply a set of N training bags as $\{\boldsymbol{B}_i \in \mathbb{R}^{n_i \times P} : \forall i \in N\}$, where i-th bag comprises n_i instance vectors, $\boldsymbol{x}_{ij} \in \mathbb{R}^P$ with $j \in n_i$. To put into effect the *concept* that makes a bag label either positive or negative ($l_i \in \{+1, -1\}$), the instance-based embedding is intended to map each bag into a vector space through the conditional probability of c-th *concept*, $\boldsymbol{x}_c \in \mathcal{C}$, which is described as $p_{ic} = P(\boldsymbol{x}_c | \boldsymbol{B}_i)$ for a given bag. Aiming to describe conditional distribution $P(\boldsymbol{x}_c | \boldsymbol{B}_i)$ within the Diverse Density framework, multiple concepts (positive and negative) are extracted from the training dataset under the assumption that the bags are conditionally independent of the target concept as follows [9]:

$$P(\boldsymbol{x}_c | \boldsymbol{B}_i) \propto s(\boldsymbol{x}_c | \boldsymbol{B}_i) = \max_{\forall j \in N_i} \exp\left(-\|\boldsymbol{x}_{ij} - \boldsymbol{x}_c\|_2^2 / \sigma^2\right) \qquad (1)$$

where $\sigma \in \mathbb{R}^+$ stands for the bandwidth of an exponentiated square function, notation $\|\cdot\|_2$ stands for ℓ_2-norm, and $s(\boldsymbol{x}_c, \boldsymbol{B}_i)$ is a measure of similarity between *concept* $\boldsymbol{x}_c$ and bag $\boldsymbol{B}_i$. All similarity function assessments in Eq. (1), performed between the training set bags, returns the matrix representation $\boldsymbol{S} = \{s(\boldsymbol{x}_1, \boldsymbol{B}_1), \ldots, (\boldsymbol{x}_C, \boldsymbol{B}_N)\}$, with $\boldsymbol{S} \in \mathbb{R}^{C \times N}$, having rows and columns that denote features and bags, respectively. Note that, by mapping the bags into a *concept*-wise feature space, a single vector representation is produced, so that it computation depends on the fixed number of *concepts*, C, rather than on the varying number of instances, n_i.

2.2   Multiple Kernel Learning in Bag Classification Tasks

For each pair of rows $\boldsymbol{s}_i, \boldsymbol{s}_j \in \mathbb{R}^C$, the generalized inner product measures the similarity between bags through the kernel function $\kappa(\boldsymbol{B}_i, \boldsymbol{B}_j) = \langle \varphi(\boldsymbol{s}_i), \varphi(\boldsymbol{s}_j) \rangle$; $\forall i, j \in N$, where $\varphi(\cdot) : \mathbb{R}^M \rightarrow \mathcal{H}$, which maps from the instance-based feature space $\mathbb{R}^M$ into a Reproduced Kernel Hilbert Space (RKHS) $\mathcal{H}$, so that $|\mathcal{H}| \gg M$. Notation $\langle \cdot, \cdot \rangle$ stands for the inner product. In the MKL framework, bags provided with multiple feature sets are mapped into different concept-wise feature spaces. Therefore, the generating set of kernel functions $\{\kappa_d(\cdot,\cdot) : d \in D\}$ must be merged into a single kernel framework for computing the pairwise similarity between bags. To this end, the MKL approaches attempt to condense several reproduced spaces into a single representation through a convex sum of kernels, relying on the following pair of properties [6]: (i) The positive kernel weights are directly proportional to the relative importance of the combined kernels, (ii) Imposed on the weights, the nonnegative constraint corresponds to concatenate the scaled version of the feature spaces to build the combined representation.

Consequently, we suggest tackling the kernel heterogeneity issue, relying on the following linear, feature combination:

$$\kappa(\boldsymbol{B}_i, \boldsymbol{B}_j; \boldsymbol{\mu}) = \sum_{d \in D} \mu_d \kappa_d \left(\boldsymbol{B}_i^d, \boldsymbol{B}_j^d\right), \tag{2a}$$

$$\text{s.t.:} \sum_{d \in D} \mu_d = 1, \; \mu_d \in \mathbb{R}^+ \tag{2b}$$

where $\boldsymbol{B}_i^d$ stands for i-th bag, which holds P_d-dimensional instances $\boldsymbol{x}_{ij}^d \in \mathbb{R}^{P_d}$ sampled from the d-th input feature space. $\kappa_d : \mathbb{R}^M \times \mathbb{R}^M \to \mathbb{R}$ is the kernel function that maps a bag from d-th instance-based feature representation, $\boldsymbol{s}^d$, to d-th RKHS. $\boldsymbol{\mu} \in \mathbb{R}^D$ is the vector of mixture weights that must be optimized to improve discrimination between classes across the label set. Under the constraints in Eq. (2b) to reproduce a convex function in Eq. (2a), optimization of $\boldsymbol{\mu}$ is carried out by the maximization of Centered Kernel Alignment. As a result, each instance-based feature set is weighted according to its discrimination capability: the higher the weight, the more significant its contribution to the classifier performance.

3   Experimental Setup

3.1   Database and Biomarker Modalities

Alzheimer's Disease Neuroimaging Initiative (ADNI) provided the data used in the preparation of this article[1]. ADNI combines imaging, clinical, and neuropsychological assessments to measure the progression of MCI and early AD in patients. According to the diagnoses along the follow-up visits, the following three patient groups hold: (i) healthy control (HC) subjects that never developed MCI nor AD, (ii) subjects diagnosed as MCI without a change along the follow-up visits, and (iii) subjects diagnosed with the AD at any time during the study. To develop the proposed automated AD diagnosis, we consider two clinical modalities from ADNI, namely, *cognitive tests* and *morphological assessment.*

The *cognitive test* data comprises several neuropsychological evaluations performed by clinicians to assess skills as the general cognition, memory, language,

---

[1] adni.loni.usc.edu.

and vision. The test gives an overall sense of whether the subject is aware of its symptoms and its surrounding environment, as well as the subject remembers word lists, follows instructions and does simple calculations. This study considers the ADAS11, ADAS13, MMSE, RAVLT immediate, RAVLT learning, and RAVLT forgetting cognitive test scores (six feature sets) from 1728 subjects along 8650 follow-up visits. The *morphological assessments* include three kinds of measures from segmented brain structures: *(i)* volume *(ii)* cortical thicknesses and *(iii)* surface area. Such assessments result from processing brain MRI with the FreeSurfer software package[2], with a high test-retest reliability across scanner manufacturers and field strengths. For the same 1728 subjects, FreeSurfer computes features from 64 brain structures on 7165 MRIs, yielding 303 morphological measures of cross-sectional data. Therefore, the input data set includes 70 feature sets (64 structures and six cognitive tests), which are computed from each follow-up visit for each subject in the selected ADNI cohort.

3.2 Data Representation and Metrics of Performance Assessment

For evaluation purposes, we split the dataset into a test subset that holds 30% of the patients for blindfolded assessment of the performance, and a training subset that holds the remaining 70% for tuning the diagnosis system. From the method above described, the following representation scenarios are defined:

1. Raw data representation (RAW): CKA measures the degree of alignment between the labels and raw features from each structure and cognitive tests, ranking the 70 feature sets from the most to the least discriminative one.
2. Metric learning representation (ML): Structure-wise and cognitive tests features are linearly mapped into a new space that maximizes CKA, aiming to improve the discrimination capability of each structure and test.
3. Multiple-instance learning representation (MIL): For each feature set, we treat each follow-up visit as an instance, so that a subject becomes a bag. Therefore, the instance-based feature mapping builds a single feature vector for each subject, allowing to provide a subject-wise diagnosis based on all its visits.
4. Metric Learning on the Multiple-instance learning representation (ML^2): A linear projection from the instance-based feature mapping is computed by maximizing CKA, so that each input feature set improves its discrimination performance by using all the subject's visits.
5. Multiple-kernel learning representation (MKL): The convex combination of kernels gathers the bags resulting from the input feature sets into a single representation space so that the combination weights determine the biomarkers discriminating patient groups.

For the described representation scenarios, the kernel alignment demand two kernels: one that encodes the clinical examinations and another – the supervised

---

[2] freesurfer.nmr.mgh.harvard.edu.

information. In the former case, the feature sets are projected into an RKHS using a Gaussian kernel due to its universal approximating property, estimating its bandwidth parameter $\sigma \in \mathbb{R}^+$ as proposed by [1]. For the latter kernel, a label similarity measure is defined as $L(i,j) = \delta(l_i - l_j)$, where $\delta(l_i - l_j) = 1$ if $l_i = l_j$. Otherwise, $\delta(l_i - l_j) = 0$. Then, the above representation scenarios are evaluated in four classification tasks, namely, multi-class diagnosis (i.e., HC vs. MCI vs. AD), HC vs. MCI, HC vs. AD, and MCI vs. AD. To this end, the Kernel k-Nearest Neighbors (Kernel k-NN) classifier is tuned by maximizing the average validation accuracy (a_c) through an exhaustive search algorithm. Finally, the reported a_c and 95% confidence interval (CI) are provided by a bootstrapping procedure on the test set with 1000 re-samples as suggested in [3].

4   Results and Discussion

This paper introduces a new data representation based on the multiple-kernel learning from the optimized instance-based feature mappings explained above in Sect. 3.2, to support discrimination of AD groups. To this end, we assess firstly on the above-described data representation scenarios, the similarity between each feature set and the given diagnosis by the CKA similarity measure. Figure 1 displays the CKA measure (ρ) on the training subset achieved by the most relevant cognitive tests and the anatomical structures into the four considered representation scenarios. In general, the ADAS13 test $(\rho = 0.40)$ and ADAS11 $(\rho = 0.38)$ highlight as the most relevant feature sets. It is worth noting that ML and ML2 perform the same as RAW and MIL for the cognitive tests, respectively, due to the lack of linear mappings on one-dimensional feature sets. Regarding the metric learning representation, ML outperforms the RAW representation, while ML^2 outperforms MIL, due to learning a linear mapping using supervised information maximizes the group discrimination. In turn, both MIL-based representations (MIL and ML^2) increase the alignment in comparison with RAW and ML. Such a fact proves that taking into account all the follow-up visits of a subject increases the discriminative capability of the reproduced space. Further, ML^2 attains the maximum CKA achieves the largest CKA for all feature sets, where the Amygdala and Hippocampus $(\rho = 0.22)$, as well as, the Middle temporal $(\rho = 0.21)$ compose the most relevant brain structures, which are clinically related to the neurodegenerative process of the AD [5]. As a result, the combination of ML and MIL, i.e., ML^2, provides a data representation with improved group separability.

Further, the resulting ML^2 representations for each feature set are combined using MKL to build a classifier for the considered classification tasks. Table 1 compares the classification results for the proposed MKL against the most relevant feature sets. Regarding the multi-class diagnosis task, the Amygdala feature set performs the best classification accuracy among the anatomical structures $(a_c = 46.7\%)$, while the ADAS feature sets are the most discriminant cognitive scores $(a_c = 66.6\%)$, which is according to the CKA measure in Fig. 1. In addition, proposed MKL approach yields and evaluation accuracy of $a_c = 76.6$,

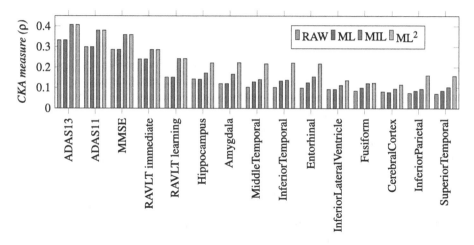

Fig. 1. CKA-based similarity measure for the most relevant feature sets ordered in descending form according to the RAW data representation. Namely, the five clinical scores and the ten anatomical structures with the highest (ρ) values for considered data representation scenarios.

outperforming the ADAS scores by $\sim$10% points. In terms of the bi-class diagnosis, HC vs. AD task presents the highest values of accuracy rates, meaning that such a classification is easier to perform. In contrast, HC vs. MCI results in the more challenging bi-class task yielding the lower classification performance ($a_c = 73.5$). In turn, performance of ADAS13 and the proposal are similar for MCI vs. AD. Therefore, the use of CKA-based metric learning to optimize both, the multi-instance feature mapping and the MKL combination, enhances the classification of multi-class and each considered bi-class diagnosis task.

Table 1. Accuracy performance measures of MKL approach for both scenarios on the test subsets compared with the six most relevant feature sets for supporting diagnosis of AD.

a_c(CI)[%]	HC vs. MCI vs. AD	HC vs. AD	HC vs. MCI	MCI vs. AD
ADAS11	66.6(62.4–70.5)	92.8(89.2–94.9)	72.9(68.0–77.4)	77.3(73.0–81.6)
ADAS13	66.6(62.5–70.7)	94.0(90.7–96.1)	73.2(68.0–77.4)	**81.3(77.0–85.0)**
MMSE	63.5(59.1–67.4)	89.5(85.6–91.9)	63.1(57.0–67.4)	78.9(74.3–82.4)
Hippocampus	22.2(19.1–25.9)	58.6(52.9–63.4)	52.7(47.3–57.9)	47.6(42.2–52.4)
Amygdala	46.7(42.3–51.0)	56.8(51.1–61.9)	52.7(47.3–57.9)	48.4(43.0–53.2)
Middle Temporal	32.8(29.2–36.7)	57.7(51.7–62.8)	53.0(47.6–58.2)	53.7(48.1–58.3)
Proposed MKL	**76.6(72.8–79.9)**	**94.9(91.9–96.7)**	**73.5(68.3–77.7)**	81.0(77.0–84.8)

5 Concluding Remarks and Future Work

This study proposes a multimodal data framework composed of neuropsychological tests and morphological measures of brain structures to support the AD diagnosis and its prodromal stage. The proposed methodology employs an instance-based feature mapping and multiple kernel learning for building a more discriminative data representation space that improves data classification. Evaluation results on ADNI subjects prove that introduced feature mapping based on multi-instance learning (MIL) combined with CKA-based metric learning (ML) enhances data representation with improved group separability. Generally speaking, the convex combination based on CKA metric learning of multiple feature kernels improves the results of the best single feature set in multi-class and three bi-class diagnosis tasks. As an additional benefit, the automatic ranking identifies the brain structures related to memory and learning functions, as well as, the main clinical assessment scores as the most relevant for discriminating HC, MCI, and AD subjects [5]. As a future work, we plan to extend the multimodal MKL-based AD diagnosis methodology to other biomarkers, including information from CSF, PET, and demographic variables, that improve the AD diagnosis and conversion prediction to other stages of disease (e.g., MCI to AD prediction), holding valuable information about the steady and conversion concepts.

Acknowledgments. This work was supported by Doctorados Nacionales 2017, conv. 785 and is developed within the research project 111077757982, funded by COLCIENCIAS.

References

1. Álvarez-Meza, A.M., Cárdenas-Peña, D., Castellanos-Dominguez, G.: Unsupervised kernel function building using maximization of information potential variability. In: Bayro-Corrochano, E., Hancock, E. (eds.) CIARP 2014. LNCS, vol. 8827, pp. 335–342. Springer, Cham (2014). https://doi.org/10.1007/978-3-319-12568-8_41

2. Alzheimer's Association: 2017 Alzheimer's disease facts and figures. Alzheimer's Dement. **13**(4), 325–373 (2017). https://doi.org/10.1016/J.JALZ.2017.02.001

3. Bron, E.E., Smits, M., van der Flier, W.M., Vrenken, H., Barkhof, F., et al.: Standardized evaluation of algorithms for computer-aided diagnosis of dementia based on structural MRI: The CADDementia challenge. NeuroImage **111**, 562–579 (2015)

4. Clark, D.G., et al.: Novel verbal fluency scores and structural brain imaging for prediction of cognitive outcome in mild cognitive impairment. Alzheimer's Dement.: Diagn. Assess. Dis. Monit. **2**, 113–122 (2016)

5. Dimitriadis, S.I., Liparas, D., Tsolaki, M.: Random forest feature selection, fusion and ensemble strategy: combining multiple morphological MRI measures to discriminate among healhy elderly, MCI, cMCI and Alzheimer's disease patients: from the Alzheimer's disease neuroimaging initiative (ADNI) database. J. Neurosci. Methods **302**, 14–23 (2018)

6. Gönen, M., Alpaydin, E.: Multiple kernel learning algorithms. J. Mach. Learn. Res. **12**, 2211–2268 (2011)

7. Korolev, I.O., Symonds, L.L., Bozoki, A.C., Initiative, A.D.N.: Predicting progression from mild cognitive impairment to Alzheimer's dementia using clinical, MRI, and plasma biomarkers via probabilistic pattern classification. PloS One **11**(2), e0138866 (2016)
8. Liu, F., Zhou, L., Shen, C., Yin, J.: Multiple kernel learning in the primal for multimodal Alzheimer's disease classification. IEEE J. Biomed. Health Inform. **18**(3), 984–990 (2014). https://doi.org/10.1109/JBHI.2013.2285378
9. Maron, O., Lozano-Pérez, T.: A framework for multiple-instance learning. In: Jordan, M.I., Kearns, M.J., Solla, S.A. (eds.) Advances in Neural Information Processing Systems, vol. 10, pp. 570–576. MIT Press, Cambridge (1998)
10. Moradi, E., Pepe, A., Gaser, C., Huttunen, H., Tohka, J.: Machine learning framework for early MRI-based Alzheimer's conversion prediction in MCI subjects. NeuroImage **104**, 398–412 (2015). https://doi.org/10.1016/j.neuroimage.2014.10.002
11. Rathore, S., Habes, M., Iftikhar, M.A., Shacklett, A., Davatzikos, C.: A review on neuroimaging-based classification studies and associated feature extraction methods for Alzheimer's disease and its prodromal stages. NeuroImage **155**, 530–548 (2017). https://doi.org/10.1016/j.neuroimage.2017.03.057
12. Tang, X., Qin, Y., Wu, J., Zhang, M., Zhu, W., Miller, M.I.: Shape and diffusion tensor imaging based integrative analysis of the hippocampus and the amygdala in Alzheimer's disease. Magn. Reson. Imaging **34**(8), 1087–1099 (2016). https://doi.org/10.1016/j.mri.2016.05.001
13. Yu, G., Liu, Y., Shen, D.: Graph-guided joint prediction of class label and clinical scores for the Alzheimer's disease. Brain Struct. Funct. **221**(7), 3787–3801 (2016). https://doi.org/10.1007/s00429-015-1132-6
14. Zhang, D., Shen, D.: Multi-modal multi-task learning for joint prediction of clinical scores in Alzheimer's disease. In: Liu, T., Shen, D., Ibanez, L., Tao, X. (eds.) MBIA 2011. LNCS, vol. 7012, pp. 60–67. Springer, Heidelberg (2011). https://doi.org/10.1007/978-3-642-24446-9_8
15. Zhu, X., Suk, H.I., Lee, S.W., Shen, D.: Canonical feature selection for joint regression and multi-class identification in Alzheimer's disease diagnosis. Brain Imaging Behav. **10**(3), 818–828 (2016). https://doi.org/10.1007/s11682-015-9430-4

Relevance of Filter Bank Common Spatial Patterns Using Multiple Kernel Learning in Motor Imagery

Daniel G. García-Murillo[✉], David Cárdenas-Peña,
and Germán Castellanos-Dominguez

Signal Processing and Recognition Group, Universidad Nacional de Colombia,
Km 9 Vía al Aeropuerto la Nubia, Manizales, Colombia
{dggarciam,dcardenasp,cgcastellanosd}@unal.edu.co

Abstract. Brain-Computer Interfaces directly communicate the human brain and machines through the analysis of sensorimotor activity, relying on the Motor Imagery paradigm of cognitive neuroscience. Conventional BCI systems use electroencephalographic signals due to its high temporal resolution, portability, and easiness to implement, for which the filter-banked analysis works as the characterization baseline. Due to such analysis yields to highly dimensional representation spaces leading to overtrained systems, we propose to combine the multiple spectral bands into a single representation space through the maximization of the centered kernel alignment criterion. As a result, the similarity between the measured EEG data and the available label sets is maximized, with the additional benefit of enhancing the spectral interpretation of the subject performance. The proposed κ-FB is evaluated in the dataset IIa of the BCI competition IV for a binary classification task. Attained accuracy proves that κ-FB outperforms other filter-banked representations without compromising the system confidence.

Keywords: Brain computer interfaces · Common spatial patterns
Multiple kernel learning

1 Introduction

Brain-Computer Interfaces (BCI) take advantage of the extracted information from brain activity signals to set direct communication between the human brain and machines. BCI is used to help people with disability through the analysis of human sensorimotor functions, relying on the Motor Imagery (MI) paradigm of cognitive neuroscience. Among the non-invasive techniques for measuring brain activity, like magnetoencephalography (MEG), electroencephalography (EEG) is preferred due to its portability, easiness to implement, and higher temporal resolution.

Nonetheless, BCI systems are heavily dependent on useful feature extraction from EEG data, being Common spatial patterns (CSP) the most popular technique for MI classification tasks. CSP technique constructs a set of spatial filters

© Springer Nature Switzerland AG 2018
Y. Hernández Heredia et al. (Eds.): IWAIPR 2018, LNCS 11047, pp. 210–218, 2018.
https://doi.org/10.1007/978-3-030-01132-1_24

that maximize the variance in a specific class, minimizing at the same time the variance of another class. Generally, classification accuracy depends on each subject, which may have different spectral behavior. To overcome this issue, Filter Bank Common Spatial Patterns (FB) approach is employed, however, at the cost of providing larger feature sets, which may lead to the curse of dimensionality effect.

Aiming to solve the issue as mentioned above, some spectral band selection algorithms can be applied: discriminant FBCSP (DFBCSP) using Fisher ratio [9], sliding window discriminative CSP (SWDCSP) by exploiting affinity propagation [8], sparse regression to select the significant CSP features according to the provided labels [12] or its extended approach sparse Bayesian learning (SBLFB) scheme [11]. Nevertheless, most of these feature selection methods are still computationally expensive. Moreover, in most of the cases, there is not a suitable validation framework that allows ensuring a generalized performance, leading to overtrained systems [10].

Here, we introduce a CSP spectral band selection method that computes the discriminative relevance of spectral band features, reflecting their contribution to discriminate the considered motor imagery classes. Instead of selecting one specific kernel function to encode the whole spectral band information, the proposed Multiple kernel learning (κ-FB) combines several single kernels (i.e., one kernel per spectral band) through a weighted sum, attempting to maximize the similarity between the measured EEG data and the available set of labels (i.e., prior knowledge). Using a kernel alignment algorithm to match the training spaces, the resulting relevance weights are interpreted as the contribution of each spectral band for improving the performance of the motor imagery task classification.

2   Materials and Methods

2.1   Feature Extraction Using Common Spatial Patterns

In binary classification tasks, CSP finds a spatial filter matrix $\boldsymbol{W} \in \mathbb{R}^{C \times 2K}$ to linearly map the EEG channel signals $\boldsymbol{X} \in \mathbb{R}^{C \times T}$ onto a space $\tilde{\boldsymbol{X}} = \boldsymbol{W}^\top \boldsymbol{X}$, so that variance of the mapped signal is maximized for one class while the variance of another class is minimized. The spatial filters $\boldsymbol{w}^* \in \mathbb{R}^C$ to extract MI features are the solution of maximizing the Rayleigh quotient:

$$\boldsymbol{w}^* = \max_{\boldsymbol{w}} \frac{\boldsymbol{w}^\top \boldsymbol{\Sigma}^- \boldsymbol{w}}{\boldsymbol{w}^\top \boldsymbol{\Sigma}^+ \boldsymbol{w}}, \text{ s.t.: } \|\boldsymbol{w}\|_2 = 1 \tag{1}$$

the spatial covariance matrix of the class $l \in \{-, +\}$ is estimated as $\boldsymbol{\Sigma}^l = \mathbb{E}\left\{\boldsymbol{X}_n \boldsymbol{X}_n^\top : n \in N_l\right\}$, being N_l the number of trials in class l. Notations $\|\cdot\|_2$ and $\mathbb{E}\{\cdot\}$ stand for ℓ_2-norm and expectation operator, respectively.

The optimization framework in Eq. (1) can be equivalently transformed into the generalized eigenvalue problem $\boldsymbol{\Sigma}^- \boldsymbol{w}^* = \lambda \boldsymbol{\Sigma}^+ \boldsymbol{w}^*$ with $\lambda \in \mathbb{R}^+$. Thus, a set of spatial filters $\boldsymbol{W}^* = [\boldsymbol{w}_1^* \dots \boldsymbol{w}_{2K}^*]$ can be obtained by collecting eigenvectors corresponding to the K largest and smallest eigenvalues of the generalized eigenvalue problem. To account further for brain activity at different spectral bandwidths, each n-trial of input MI data is bandpass filtered within a set of F frequency bands $\{\boldsymbol{X}_{n,f}:f\in F\}$. The CSP feature vector is then formed as $\boldsymbol{\xi} = [\xi_k:k\in 2K]$ with $\boldsymbol{\xi}\in\mathbb{R}^{2FK}$, having entries $\xi_{n,k}^f = \ln(\mathrm{var}\{\boldsymbol{w}_k^{*\top}\boldsymbol{X}_{n,f}\})$, where $\mathrm{var}\{\cdot\}$ stands for the variance operator.

2.2   Multiple Kernel Learning for Filter-Bank Representation

To measure the pairwise proximity between trials at frequency band f, we perform the dot product-based kernel function as a measure of similarity between functionals, resulting in a set of kernels $\{\kappa(\boldsymbol{\xi}_n^f,\boldsymbol{\xi}_m^f)\in\mathbb{R}^+:f\in F\}$ that must be properly combined to work out a unique similarity value for each pairwise trial comparison. We address this issue through a Multiple Kernel Learning (MKL) framework by the following weighted sum [5]:

$$\kappa(\boldsymbol{\xi}_n,\boldsymbol{\xi}_m;\boldsymbol{\mu}) = \sum_{f\in F}\mu_f\kappa(\boldsymbol{\xi}_n^f,\boldsymbol{\xi}_m^f), \tag{2a}$$

$$\text{s.t.:}\ \sum_{f\in F}\mu_f = 1,\ \mu_f \geq 0 \tag{2b}$$

where vector $\boldsymbol{\mu}\in\mathbb{R}^F$ holds the mixture weights that must be optimized to improve discrimination between classes across the label set. Under the constraints in Eq. (2b) to reproduce a convex function in Eq. (2a), optimization of $\boldsymbol{\mu}$ is carried out by the maximization of Centered Kernel Alignment, so that each CSP feature set is weighted according to its discrimination capability: the higher the weight, the more significant its contribution to the classifier performance.

As a result, the proposed approach using Multiple kernel learning for filter-bank representation in Eqs. (2a) and (2b) (noted as κ-FB) allows selecting the CSP feature sets extracted from the most relevant frequency bands for discriminating a motor imagery task at hand.

3   Experimental Set-Up

3.1   EEG Dataset and Preprocessing

The κ-FB approach is evaluated on a BCI competition IV dataset IIa[1], holding EEG data recorded by 22-electrode montage. Nine subjects were instructed to perform four MI tasks ("left hand","right hand", "both feet", and"tongue"). On different days, each subject completed two sessions, each one including six runs to perform 48 trials (i.e., 12 trials per class) and resulting in 288 trials per sitting. Here, we consider just the bi-class classification task: "left" versus"right hand".

---

[1] available at http://www.bbci.de/competition/iv/.

In the preprocessing stage, all EEG recordings are band-pass filtered between [0.5–100] Hz and sampled at 250 Hz, followed by a fifth order Butterworth band-pass filter to remove noises over 40 Hz and slow baseline signal under 4 Hz. Sub-band decomposition of each channel is further performed, for which the linearly distributed filters have been heuristically adjusted to 7 Hz bandwidth and 90% overlap. In total, we calculate 42 fifth-order Butterworth band-pass filters as to cover the whole bandwidth from4 to 40 Hz. To focus on the learning part of the MI task, each trial recording is temporarily segmented, extracting for analysis the interval that ranges from 0.5 s to 4.5 s. Lastly, CSP-based feature extraction is accomplished from the preprocessed recordings, yielding 42 feature vectors of dimension 22 per trial. However, we only take the first and the last three vectors [3].

3.2 Evaluation Scheme and Performance Assessment

Due to the provided universal approximating property, the κ-FB approach is implemented by a Gaussian kernel, for which the bandwidth parameter is computed as in [1]. For the sake of comparison, κ-FB is contrasted with a couple of similar approaches: The baseline Filter Bank Common Spatial Pattern (or FB) that aims to perform the selection of critical spatio-temporal discriminative characteristics from diverse frequency bands [2]; and its spare version (s-FB) that implements a sparse regression of filter-bank CSP features to predict the trial labels [12].

The classifier is evaluated on a kernelized k-nearest neighbors (Kk-NN) machine, for which the number of neighbors is tuned by an exhaustive search of the best average validation performance. As a measure of classifier performance, we estimate the average accuracy (a_c) by a five-fold cross-validation scheme.

4   Results and Discussion

By handling a convex combination of introduced functional kernels, here, the feature selection of Filter Bank Common Spatial Patterns is performed for improving the discrimination capability in Motor Imagery tasks. During validation of κ-FB approach, the following findings come out from the experiments:

To improve discrimination across MI classes, a multiple kernel learning framework is devised for optimizing the mixture weights to work out a unique similarity value between trials at each frequency band. Optimization includes the maximization of Centered Kernel Alignment to highlight a relevant CSP feature set by learning a mapping matrix that matches the best all extracted feature vectors with the provided binary-class label set. As seen in Fig. 1, the proposed κ-FB approach outperforms the classifier accuracy reached by other compared methods in most of the subjects. Moreover, the accuracy averaged across all subjects is as follows: FB - 82.7 ± 5.8, s-FB - 82.7 ± 5.5, and κ-FB 84.9 ± 5.9. Note that the proposal improves the average accuracy without compromising the standard deviation (i.e., confidence) of presented results.

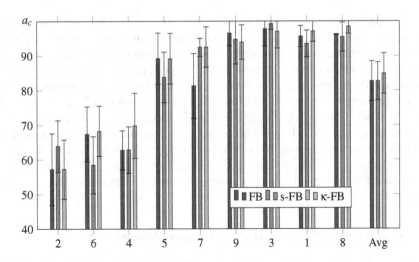

Fig. 1. Testing accuracy results per subject on the test set for all considered CSP-based approaches for motor imagery classification task.

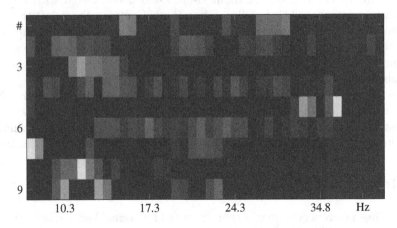

Fig. 2. MKL weights along the frequency bands computed per subject.

The estimated mixing vector allows improving the interpretability, identifying the relevant frequency bands regarding the classifier accuracy. For the sake of illustration, Fig. 2 visually depicts the relative relevance magnitude of each spectral band per subject. Thus, those subjects focalizing the relevance on a less number of frequency bands achieve a better MI discrimination, namely, #8, # 3, #1. At the same time, the subject #5 holds an entirely different spectral behavior, suggesting that he manages the MI task differently. By contrast, the subjects noted as #6, #4, #2 yield a worse accuracy, spreading the relevance contribution on a more considerable amount of frequency bands.

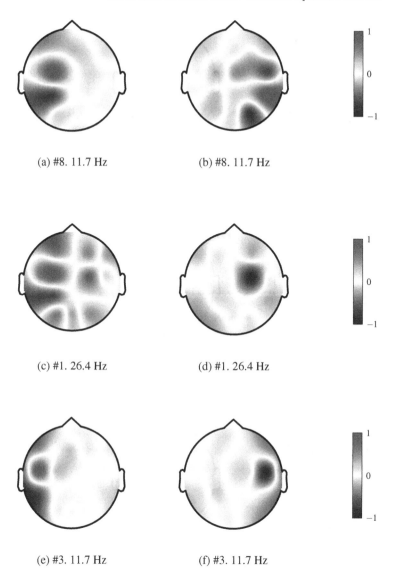

(a) #8. 11.7 Hz   (b) #8. 11.7 Hz

(c) #1. 26.4 Hz   (d) #1. 26.4 Hz

(e) #3. 11.7 Hz   (f) #3. 11.7 Hz

Fig. 3. Estimated spatial filters for the best performing subjects (#8, #1, #3) in the most weighted frequency band. Left: first filter ($k = 1$). Right: last filter ($k = 2K$).

As seen from the topoplots in Fig. 3, the proposed κ-FB method highlights more discriminative information contained in the μ band, more precisely, localized around of the central cortex; this brain region has been associated before with planning and executing of voluntary movements [7]. Besides, the activation surrounding the frontoparietal area ($FC3$, $FC4$, $CP3$, and $CP4$) is related to the subject thinking strategy during MI tasks [6]. On the contrary, the topoplots

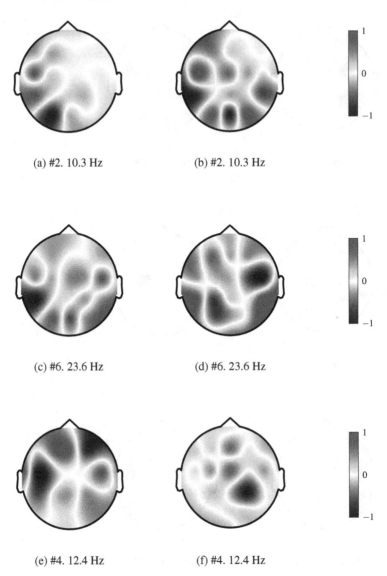

(a) #2. 10.3 Hz

(b) #2. 10.3 Hz

(c) #6. 23.6 Hz

(d) #6. 23.6 Hz

(e) #4. 12.4 Hz

(f) #4. 12.4 Hz

Fig. 4. Estimated spatial filters for the worst performing subjects (#2, #6, #4) in the most weighted frequency band. Left: first filter ($k = 1$). Right: last filter ($k = 2K$).

Fig. 4 reveal that the spatial filters associated with the largest-weighted frequency band involve most of the brain areas for the worst performing subjects. This fact is due to the lack of discriminant information in the motor cortex, which may be related to disconnected electrodes, signal artifacts, and subject tiredness or lack of attention [4].

As a concluding remark, the proposed κ-FB reflects the contribution of each frequency band to highlight the spatial filters that better discriminate the MI task, instead of selecting a single band that may not encode all the contribution of the CSP feature set. The use of the kernel alignment to match data and label spaces results in a set of relevance weights that provide enhanced interpretability of performed accuracy by each subject.

For the future work, we plan to extend the kernel learning to other augmented representations, by instance, the one that includes some sliding windowing strategies, aiming to more adequately extract information from time-varying event-related potentials and improving the discrimination of MI tasks. Also, other kernel combination strategies, as tensor-based, can be explored to interpret discriminating information extracted from subjects with a complicated execution of MI tasks. Finally, we plan to improve the parameter tuning stage using methods as Bayesian or heuristic optimization.

Acknowledgment. This work was developed under the funding of the research project 111077757982, and the *"Convocatoria Nacional Jóvenes Investigadores E Innovadores Por La Paz 2017"*, both granted by COLCIENCIAS.

References

1. Álvarez-Meza, A.M., Cárdenas-Peña, D., Castellanos-Dominguez, G.: Unsupervised kernel function building using maximization of information potential variability. In: Bayro-Corrochano, E., Hancock, E. (eds.) CIARP 2014. LNCS, vol. 8827, pp. 335–342. Springer, Cham (2014). https://doi.org/10.1007/978-3-319-12568-8_41
2. Ang, K.K., Chin, Z.Y., Zhang, H., Guan, C.: Filter bank common spatial pattern (FBCSP) in brain-computer interface. In: IEEE International Joint Conference on Neural Networks, IJCNN 2008. (IEEE World Congress on Computational Intelligence), pp. 2390–2397. IEEE (2008)
3. Blankertz, B., Tomioka, R., Lemm, S., Kawanabe, M., Muller, K.R.: Optimizing spatial filters for robust EEG single-trial analysis. IEEE Signal Process. Mag. **25**(1), 41–56 (2008)
4. Dornhege, G.: Toward Brain-Computer Interfacing. MIT Press, Cambridge (2007)
5. Gönen, M., Alpaydın, E.: Multiple kernel learning algorithms. J. Mach. Learn. Res. **12**(Jul), 2211–2268 (2011)
6. Hanakawa, T., Immisch, I., Toma, K., Dimyan, M.A., Van Gelderen, P., Hallett, M.: Functional properties of brain areas associated with motor execution and imagery. J. Neurophysiol. **89**(2), 989–1002 (2003)
7. Jeannerod, M., Jeannerod, M.: The Cognitive Neuroscience of Action, vol. 1997. Blackwell, Oxford (1997)
8. Sun, G., Hu, J., Wu, G.: A novel frequency band selection method for common spatial pattern in motor imagery based brain computer interface. In: The 2010 International Joint Conference on Neural Networks (IJCNN), pp. 1–6. IEEE (2010)
9. Thomas, K.P., Guan, C., Lau, C.T., Vinod, A.P., Ang, K.K.: A new discriminative common spatial pattern method for motor imagery brain-computer interfaces. IEEE Trans. Biomed. Eng. **56**(11), 2730–2733 (2009)

10. Velásquez-Martínez, L.F., Álvarez-Meza, A.M., Castellanos-Domínguez, C.G.: Motor imagery classification for BCI using common spatial patterns and feature relevance analysis. In: Ferrández Vicente, J.M., Álvarez Sánchez, J.R., de la Paz López, F., Toledo Moreo, F.J. (eds.) IWINAC 2013. LNCS, vol. 7931, pp. 365–374. Springer, Heidelberg (2013). https://doi.org/10.1007/978-3-642-38622-0_38
11. Zhang, W., Sun, F., Tan, C., Liu, S.: Low-rank linear dynamical systems for motor imagery EEG. Comput. Intell. Neurosci. **2016** (2016)
12. Zhang, Y., Zhou, G., Jin, J., Wang, X., Cichocki, A.: Optimizing spatial patterns with sparse filter bands for motor-imagery based brain-computer interface. J. Neurosci. Methods **255**, 85–91 (2015)

Accelerated Proximal Gradient Descent in Metric Learning for Kernel Regression

Hector Gonzalez[1(✉)], Carlos Morell[2], and Francesc J. Ferri[3]

[1] Universidad de las Ciencias Informaticas (UCI), Havana, Cuba
hglez@uci.cu
[2] Universidad Central Marta Abreu (UCLV), Santa Clara, Villa Clara, Cuba
cmorellp@uclv.edu.cu
[3] Dept. Informàtica, Universitat de València, València, Spain
Francesc.Ferri@uv.es

Abstract. The purpose of this paper is to learn a specific distance function for the Nadayara Watson estimator to be applied as a non-linear classifier. The idea of transforming the predictor variables and learning a kernel function based on Mahalanobis pseudo distance througth an low rank structure in the distance function will help us to lead the development of this problem. In context of metric learning for kernel regression, we introduce an Accelerated Proximal Gradient to solve the non-convex optimization problem with better convergence rate than gradient descent. An extensive experiment and the corresponding discussion tries to show that our strategie its a competitive solution in relation to previously proposed approaches. Preliminary results suggest that this line of work can deal with others regularization approach in order to improve the kernel regression problem.

Keywords: Kernel regression · Accelerated proximal gradient
Metric learning · Nadayara watson estimator

1 Introduction

In metric learning for kernel regression, Nadayara Watson (NW) [5] estimator has been widely applied for non-linear regression problems. This estimator use the weighted average output of local information around the Gaussian kernel $K(\boldsymbol{x}_i, \boldsymbol{x}_j)$ over set of the training dataset $\mathcal{D} = \{(\boldsymbol{x}_1, y_1) \ldots (\boldsymbol{x}_n, y_n)\}$ with predictors variables $\boldsymbol{x}_i \in \mathbb{R}^p$ and response variable $y_i \in \mathbb{R}$. The output variables estimator in kernel regression are:

$$\hat{y}(x) = \frac{\sum_{i=1}^{n} K(\boldsymbol{x}_i, x) y_i}{\sum_{i=1}^{n} K(\boldsymbol{x}_i, x)} \tag{1}$$

This work has been partially funded by FEDER and Spanish MEC through project TIN2014-59641-C2-1-P and INV17-01-15-03.

© Springer Nature Switzerland AG 2018
Y. Hernández Heredia et al. (Eds.): IWAIPR 2018, LNCS 11047, pp. 219–227, 2018.
https://doi.org/10.1007/978-3-030-01132-1_25

Among domain applications considered in kernel regression, we can cite short-term traffic flow forecasting [14], image recognition and restoration [6,10], traffic congestion detection [17] or more recently in neural network and deep learning field [16]

The first work in kernel regression are very old [1]. However, Metric learning for kernel regression was introduced thereupon in [20] as unconstrained optimization problem. The main idea in metric learning its to learn a Mahalanobis (pseudo-)metric over the input space in which two near vectors in the output space imply that these should be nearest in the input space [9]. The problem [20] does not contain a regularization mechanism that guarantees the generalization of the learning model. On the other hand, the proposal developed in [8] employs a regularization scheme that is based on norm ℓ_{21} in similar way to [7,21]. Using this norm, as a regularization mechanism, has the advantage of learning an structure for the distance function with rows completely nulled, which is equivalent to eliminate irrelevant variables. In the same way, other regularization mechanisms can have significant effects on the learning matrix for distance function, such as structures with low rank when using the nuclear norm.

To solve the problems previously described in [8,20], the decomposition of the Mahalanobis matrix in $M = L^T L$ has been used, which leads to a problem of non-convex optimization. This element has been little discussed in the modeling of these problems, resolved through gradient descent. Additionally, we must point out that the rate of convergence of the gradient descent method is very poor compared to Accelerated proximal gradient.

Motivated by the elements described above, we summarize ours contributions in this work as:

- We extend the distance metric learning for kernel regression proposed by Weinberger and Tesauro [20], based on introduce a low rank matrix, controlled by the nuclear norm as regularizer function.
- The Mahalanobis matrix is decomposed in the way $M = L^T L$, where L transform linearly the input space of data to improve the prediction.
- The formulation, as non-convex and unconstrained optimization problem, has been treated rigurously trought the correction of Accelerated Proximal Gradient algorithm for non-convex program defined in [11].

Our metric learning model learn a particular pseudo-distance that consistently leads to improvements according to the empirical validation carried out in Sect. 4. In the next Section, the general notation and formalization are stablish while Sect. 3 contains the proposal itself. A final Section with conclusions and further work closes the present paper.

2   General Notation and Formalization

Let $x = [x_1, \ldots, x_p] \in \mathbb{R}^p$, a random input vector and $y \in \mathbb{R}$ a dependent real valued variable. The training dataset is written as $\mathcal{D} = \{(x_1, y_1), \ldots, (x_n, y_n)\}$. The corresponding Kernel Regression model consists of estimating a predictor

$h : \mathbb{R}^n \times \mathbb{R}^n \rightarrow \mathbb{R}$ follow the Eq. (1). The norms are denoted as $\|.\|_2$ for Euclidean norm and nuclear norm as $\|.\|_*$. The trace of matrix are the operator Tr(.). The Mahalanobis matrix learned are a symmetric positive semi-definite real matrix $M \succeq 0$. The Mahalanobis matrix can be decomposed in the matrix transformation L in the way $M = L^T L$ [18–20] or as in [13] $M = A^T W A$ [13] with A an arbitrary square matrix and W as a diagonal matrix to learn.

In classical distance metric learning, the aim its to learn a pseudo-distance Mahalanobis function $d_M(.,.) : M \succeq 0$ equivalent to transform the input data space to improve the correlation between the input and output variables. To ensure that the distance function satisfy the properties of being a metric, it must be fulfiled that the matrix learned are semidefinite positive. Finally, the distance between two vector in input space are:

$$d_M(\boldsymbol{x}_i, \boldsymbol{x}_j) = (\boldsymbol{x}_i - \boldsymbol{x}_j)^T M (\boldsymbol{x}_i - \boldsymbol{x}_j) \tag{2}$$

using the matrix transformation decomposition we can write the distance function in term to L with the decomposition $M = L^T L$

$$d_L(\boldsymbol{x}_i, \boldsymbol{x}_j) = \|L(\boldsymbol{x}_i - \boldsymbol{x}_j)\|_2^2 = \|(\hat{\boldsymbol{x}}_i - \hat{\boldsymbol{x}}_j)\|_2^2 \tag{3}$$

where the mapping transformation of input variables are denoted by $\hat{\boldsymbol{x}} = L\boldsymbol{x}$

The exponential and nonnegative kernel function based on NW are formulated dependent of the Mahalanobis distance function $d_L(\boldsymbol{x}_i, \boldsymbol{x}_j)$ as follow:

$$K(\boldsymbol{x}_i, \boldsymbol{x}_j) = \frac{1}{\sigma\sqrt{2\pi}} \exp^{-\frac{d_L(\boldsymbol{x}_i, \boldsymbol{x}_j)}{2\sigma}} \tag{4}$$

In general, for metric learning problem it's possible to estimate the distance function M (squared of dimension p) trough unconstrained optimization problem as a sum of the loss function $\mathcal{L}(M)$ and the regularized function $\mathcal{R}(M)$.

$$\hat{M} = \underset{M}{\operatorname{argmin}} \frac{1}{2N} \mathcal{L}(M) + \lambda \mathcal{R}(M) \tag{5}$$

Generally, in metric learning based on kernel regression, the loss function is the Mean Square Error (MSE) between the real outputs variables and the predictions $\|y - \hat{y}\|_2^2$ follow NW estimator expressed in Eq. (1). In another hand, the regularization function $\mathcal{R}(M)$ depend of the structure of the coefficient matrix that we want to learn. For example, in single sparser structure (attribute selection) we can use ℓ_1 as a regularization function or for ignore the irrelevant variables ℓ_{21}. Another possibility its to learn the low rank structures for matrix transformation of input mapping variables, them we can use nuclear norm as a regularization.

For an general problem that can be decompose in the sum as follow.

$$\hat{X} = \underset{X}{\operatorname{argmin}} f(X) + g(X) \tag{6}$$

where $f : \mathbb{R}^{n \times p} \rightarrow \mathbb{R}$ and $g : \mathbb{R}^{n \times p} \rightarrow \mathbb{R} \bigcup \{+\infty\}$ are closed proper convex and f is differentiable but g its not differentiable. In this form, we split the objective into two terms, one of which is differentiable and Lipschitz continuous with constant L. This splitting is not unique, so different splittings lead to different implementations of the proximal gradient method for the same original problem [15].

On the other hand, the problem of the proximal gradient can be tackled computationally by an approximation of f through the linearisation of the g function. In this kind of problem the proximal gradient method notation are introduced as:

$$X^{t+1} := \operatorname*{prox}_{s_t,g}(X^t - s_t \nabla f(X^t)) \tag{7}$$

In order to estimate an specifies the step size s^t which can be appropriately determined by iteratively increasing its value until the inequality in (7) holds. This procedure is commonly referred as line search proximal operator.

$$f(X^{t+1}) \le f(X^t) + \langle \nabla f(X^t), X - X^t \rangle + \frac{1}{2s_t}\|X - X^t\|_F^2 \tag{8}$$

3 Proximal Gradient Descent in Metric Learning for Kernel Regression (PG_MLKR)

Many different criteria and approaches have been proposed to learn distances for classification but all of them share the same rationale: a distance is good if it keeps same-class points close and puts points from other classes far away. In the kernel regression approach this idea is modeled as an unconstrained optimization problem where the MSE is minimized between the real values and the estimated values for all data in the training set.

In contrast to classification problems, it is far from obvious that similar ideas are to be useful in regression problems without introducing more information about both input and output spaces.

We formulate an optimization problem to learn an input distance based on NW kernel regression estimator by following an approach similar to the one in [20] that has been followed by many other authors like [7,8]. The goal is to obtain a Mahalanobis like distance, parametrized by a matrix, $M = L^T L$, which minimize the MSE and the regularizer term at the same time. In our particular case we have:

$$\hat{L} = \operatorname*{argmin}_{L} \frac{1}{2N}\|y - \hat{y}(L)\|_2^2 + \lambda\|L\|_* \tag{9}$$

$\hat{y}$ depend of distance matrix according to Eq. (1) through the kernel function defined in (4). This problem, parametrized by L, is Non-Convex however in previously works the gradient descent was employed without be care full about the convexity of the problem [8,20]. Similar to [8,20], the gradient respect to L can be stated as

$$\nabla \mathcal{L}(L) = 2L \sum_{i=1}^{n} (\hat{y}_i - y_i) \frac{\sum_{j=1}^{n}(\hat{y}_i - y_j)K_{ij}\boldsymbol{x}_{ij}\boldsymbol{x}_{ij}^T}{\sum_{j=1}^{n} K_{ij}} \tag{10}$$

where for simplicity in the notation we use $K_{ij} = K(\boldsymbol{x}_i, \boldsymbol{x}_j)$ and $\boldsymbol{x}_{ij} = (\boldsymbol{x}_i - \boldsymbol{x}_j)$.

Let the proximal projection in the unitary ball of the regularization function $\mathcal{R}$ are:

$$L^{t+1} := \underset{s_t, \mathcal{R}}{\mathbf{prox}}(L^t - s_t \nabla \mathcal{L}(L)) \tag{11}$$

in the case of the regularization term, we could use different variants, however the nuclear norm as regularize will give an structure of low rank matrix and will help the distance metric learned. The expression for proximal operator of the regularization function in nuclear norm $\mathcal{R}(L) = \lambda \|L\|_*$ are denoted by:

$$(\underset{\lambda \mathcal{R}}{\mathbf{prox}}(L)) = U(\underset{\lambda, \mathcal{R}}{\mathbf{prox}}(\Sigma))_{ij} V^T \tag{12}$$

where the matrix are decomposed in singular value $L = U \Sigma V$. Here the proximal operator $(\underset{\lambda, \mathcal{R}}{\mathbf{prox}}(\Sigma))_{ij}$ refer to ℓ_1 projection.

In the following we will refer to the algorithms PG_MLKR. A detailed description of the algorithm PG_MLKR is shown in algorithm (1). As for the application of the Accelerated Proximal Gradient APG algorithm under the conditions of a non-convex problem, the strategy defined in [4,11] was followed. In this approach, the convergence in to local minimum are controlled by proximal function as we can see in the line 9 of the algorithm. In another hand, the accelerated strategy are based on the current and the previous iteration according to the heuristic described in the line 5. The condition (8) are used to stopping criterion in each iteration (Line 6 in the algorithm). As we can see, in this stopping condition we select the minimum objective value between the two proximal operators applied in lines 8 and 9.

4   Experiments

In this section, we describe the experimental setup and discuss the main results of the proposed PG_MLKR algorithm. In the first place, we present technical details related to the datasets, parameter setup and implementations.

Next, we present comparative results when using the learned distance in NW kernel estimator with low rank structure of the metric learning as a regularization methods. We compare our proposal with the classical NW kernel regression one and the original implementation of MLKR [20] algorithm over sixteen datasets available for regression problem. The standard regression data sets utilized in our experiments are from *Evaluating Learning in Valid Experiments* (Delve) [12]. They are Kin family of data sets and Pumadyn family of data sets available in Delve repository[1]. They are generated by two synthetic robot arms. Half of the sixteen datasets have 32 dimensions and the other half are of dimension 8. Each data set has already been randomly split into four disjoint training sets of size $n = 1024$ and four corresponding test sets of the same size. The final result is the

---

[1] http://www.cs.toronto.edu/delve/data/datasets.html.

Algorithm 1.1. Accelerated proximal gradient descent in metric learning for kernel regression PG_MLKR

Input : $X \in \mathbb{R}^{n \times p}, Y \in \mathbb{R}^n, \lambda$
Output : L
1 Initialize L
2 $L_0 = L$
3 **for** $t = 1 : Iters$ **do**
4   Update L
5      $L_y^t = L^t + \frac{t}{t+3}(L^t - L_0)$
6   **while**
     $\min(f(L_z^{t+1}), f(L_v^{t+1})) \leq f(L_y^t) + \langle \nabla f(L_y^t), L_z^{t+1} - L_y^t \rangle + \frac{1}{2s_t}\|L_z^{t+1} - L_y^t\|_F^2$
     do
7   Update $\nabla \mathcal{L}(L_y^t)$ see eq. (10)
8          $L_z^{t+1} := \mathbf{prox}_{s_t, \mathcal{R}}(L_y^t - s_t \nabla \mathcal{L}(L_y^t))$ see eq. (12)
9          $L_v^{t+1} := \mathbf{prox}_{s_t, \mathcal{R}}(L^t - s_t \nabla \mathcal{L}(L^t))$
10          $s_t = 0.5 s_t$
11      $L_0 = L^t$
12   **if** $f(L_z^{t+1}) < f(L_v^{t+1})$ **then**
13          $L = L_z^{t+1}$
14   **else**
15          $L = L_v^{t+1}$
16   **if** $|F(L^{t+1}) - F(L^t)| \leq \epsilon$ **then**
17   break

---

mean of the results of the four individual runs. In our proposal an internal cross validation procedure was executed to obtain the best value of the regularization parameter λ. All algorithms are initialized with PCA in the optimization solver.

As in other similar works in regression context, we use the Root Mean Square Error (RMSE) as a performance measure. Late, we use the Friedman procedure with finner post-hoc correction tests to compare algorithms over multiple datasets as recommended by Demsar [2] and its extensions [3].

The best results are shown in Table 1 for all datasets. In the first three columns we can find the state of the art algorithms MLKR, NW and KR_SML [8,20] respectively. The last column correspond to the results achieved by our proposal. The best performance for PG_MLKR can be found in six of the datasets while the rest of metric learning for kernel regression win in five datasets each one. The statistical significance Friedman test show that the proposal based on low rank structure in metric learning have competitive results respect to state of the art in our experimentation. The Fig. 1 show the Friedman test results in the numeric ranking ray. Its very important remark that the preliminary experimental results have significance difference between the metric learning for kernel regression than classical Nadayara Watson estimator. Finally, our solver solution

Table 1. RMSE obtained for PG_MLKR respect to KR_SML, MLKR and classical NW algorithms on each dataset. In bold text we remark the best result in each dataset.

Datasets	MLKR	KR_SML	NW	**PG_MLKR**
kin8fh	0.047	0.046	0.076	**0.043**
kin8fm	**0.015**	0.018	0.064	0.017
kin8nh	0.185	0.179	0.249	**0.176**
kin8nm	**0.106**	0.113	0.248	0.125
kin32fh	0.332	**0.267**	0.364	0.288
kin32fm	0.154	**0.121**	0.295	0.184
kin32nh	0.542	0.479	0.481	**0.468**
kin32nm	0.472	0.433	0.442	**0.424**
puma8fh	3.48	3.315	4.601	**3.191**
puma8fm	1.159	**1.114**	3.965	1.129
puma8nh	3.482	3.417	5.341	**3.241**
puma8nm	**1.151**	1.251	5.033	1.264
puma32fh	0.027	**0.021**	0.025	0.022
puma32fm	0.006	**0.005**	0.015	0.007
puma32nh	**0.031**	0.034	0.035	0.034
puma32nm	**0.012**	0.027	0.029	0.023

have better convergence rate $O(1/k^2)$ than gradient descent $O(1/k)$ witch are a good practical contribution in our paper.

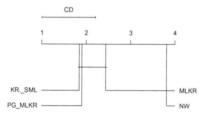

Fig. 1. Friedman ranking test results p-value $6.1e{-}07$ with significance difference respect to NW estimator

5 Concluding Remarks and Further Work

An attempt to improve kernel regression through metric learning has been done by introducing an specific regularization strategies that allow to learn sparse or low rank structures in metric learning. The mixing of these strategies has lead to very competitive results in the preliminary experimentation carried out.

Future work is being planned in several directions. On one hand, different optimization schemes, as it may be Stochastic Gradient Descent, can be adopted both to improve efficiency and performance. On the other hand, others machine learning task, like multi-target regression, can be extended in the context to kernel regression using metric learning approach.

References

1. Benedetti, J.K.: On the nonparametric estimation of regression functions. J. R. Stat. Soc. Ser. B (Methodological) **23**, 248–253 (1977)
2. Demšar, J.: Statistical comparisons of classifiers over multiple data sets. J. Mach. Learn. Res. **7**, 1–30 (2006)
3. García, S., Fernández, A., Luengo, J., Herrera, F.: A study of statistical techniques and performance measures for genetics-based machine learning: accuracy and interpretability. Soft Comput. **13**(10), 959–977 (2009)
4. Ghadimi, S., Lan, G.: Accelerated gradient methods for nonconvex nonlinear and stochastic programming. Math. Program. **156**(1–2), 59–99 (2016)
5. Härdle, W.K., Müller, M., Sperlich, S., Werwatz, A.: Nonparametric and Semiparametric Models. Springer, Heidelberg (2012). https://doi.org/10.1007/978-3-642-17146-8
6. Hu, J., Sun, C.S., Lam, K.M.: Semi-supervised metric learning for image classification. In: Qiu, G., Lam, K.M., Kiya, H., Xue, X.-Y., Kuo, C.-C.J., Lew, M.S. (eds.) PCM 2010. LNCS, vol. 6298, pp. 728–735. Springer, Heidelberg (2010). https://doi.org/10.1007/978-3-642-15696-0_67
7. Huang, K., Ying, Y., Campbell, C.: GSML: a unified framework for sparse metric learning. In: Ninth IEEE International Conference on Data Mining, ICDM 2009, pp. 189–198. IEEE (2009)
8. Huang, R., Sun, S.: Kernel regression with sparse metric learning. J. Intell. Fuzzy Syst. **24**(4), 775–787 (2013)
9. Kulis, B.: Metric learning: a survey. Found. Trends Mach. Learn. **5**(4), 287–364 (2012)
10. Kumar, S., Kolluru, P.K., Chowdary, E.D., Babu, J.B.: Image denoising using combined FFT, kernel regression and local content metrics. J. Adv. Res. Dyn. Control Syst. **2**, 1339–1347 (2017)
11. Li, H., Lin, Z.: Accelerated proximal gradient methods for nonconvex programming. In: Advances in Neural Information Processing Systems, pp. 379–387 (2015)
12. Neal, R.M.: Assessing relevance determination methods using DELVE. Nato Asi Ser. F Comput. Syst. Sci. **168**, 97–132 (1998)
13. Schultz, M., Joachims, T.: Learning a distance metric from relative comparisons. In: Advances in Neural Information Processing Systems (NIPS), p. 41 (2004)
14. Sun, S., Chen, Q.: Kernel regression with a mahalanobis metric for short-term traffic flow forecasting. In: Fyfe, C., Kim, D., Lee, S.-Y., Yin, H. (eds.) IDEAL 2008. LNCS, vol. 5326, pp. 9–16. Springer, Heidelberg (2008). https://doi.org/10.1007/978-3-540-88906-9_2
15. Tibshirani, R., Wainwright, M., Hastie, T.: Statistical Learning with Sparsity: The Lasso and Generalizations. Chapman and Hall/CRC, Boca Raton (2015)
16. Wang, Q., Wan, J., Yuan,Y.: Deep metric learning for crowdedness regression. IEEE Trans. Circuits Syst. Video Technol., 10 (2018). https://doi.org/10.1109/TCSVT.2017.2703920

17. Wang, Q., Wan, J., Yuan, Y.: Locality constraint distance metric learning for traffic congestion detection. Pattern Recognit. **75**, 272–281 (2018)
18. Weinberger, K., Blitzer, J., Saul, L.: Distance metric learning for large margin nearest neighbor classification. In: Advances in Neural Information Processing Systems, vol. 18, p. 1473 (2006)
19. Weinberger, K.Q., Saul, L.K.: Distance metric learning for large margin nearest neighbor classification. J. Mach. Learn. Res. **10**, 207–244 (2009)
20. Weinberger, K.Q., Tesauro, G.: Metric learning for kernel regression. In: Artificial Intelligence and Statistics, pp. 612–619 (2007)
21. Ying, Y., Huang, K., Campbell, C.: Sparse metric learning via smooth optimization. In: Advances in Neural Information Processing Systems, pp. 2214–2222 (2009)

A Reinforcement Learning Approach for the Report Scheduling Process Under Multiple Constraints

Beatriz M. Méndez-Hernández[1]([⊠]), Jessica Coto Palacio[2],
Yailen Martínez Jiménez[1], Ann Nowé[3],
and Erick D. Rodríguez Bazan[4]

[1] Universidad Central "Marta Abreu" de Las Villas,
Carretera a Camajuaní Km 5½, Santa Clara, Villa Clara, Cuba
{bmendez,yailenm}@uclv.edu.cu
[2] UEB Los Caneyes, Santa Clara, Villa Clara, Cuba
jcotopalacio@gmail.com
[3] Vrije Universiteit Brussel, Pleinlaan 2, 1050 Brussels, Belgium
ann.nowe@vub.ac.be
[4] Inria Sophia Antipolis-Mediterranee,
2004 Route des Lucioles, 06902 Valbonne, France
erick-david.rodriguez-bazan@inria.fr

Abstract. Scheduling problems appear on a regular basis in many real life situations, whenever it is necessary to allocate resources to perform tasks, optimizing one or more objective functions. Depending on the problem being solved, these tasks can take different forms, and the objectives can also vary. This research addresses scheduling in manufacturing environments, where the reports requested by the customers have to be scheduled in a set of machines with capacity constraints. Additionally, there is a set of limitations imposed by the company that must be taken into account when a feasible solution is built. To solve this problem, a general algorithm is proposed, which initially distributes the total capacity of the system among the existing resources, taking into account the capacity of each them, after that, each resource decides in which order it will process the reports assigned to it. The experimental study performed shows that the proposed approach allows to obtain feasible solutions for the report scheduling problem, improving the results obtained by other scheduling methods.

Keywords: Reports scheduling · Reinforcement learning · Parallel machines
Dispatching rules

1 Introduction

Scheduling problems are present in all those situations where a set of tasks has to be executed on a set of available resources in time intervals. In [1] scheduling is defined as the process of selecting alternative plans and assigning resources and times to a set of activities. Because of this, the assignments must obey certain constraints that reflect the

© Springer Nature Switzerland AG 2018
Y. Hernández Heredia et al. (Eds.): IWAIPR 2018, LNCS 11047, pp. 228–235, 2018.
https://doi.org/10.1007/978-3-030-01132-1_26

temporal relationships between activities and the limitations of shared resources. Most of the research in scheduling has been focused on the development of exact procedures for the generation of a base solution assuming there is all the necessary information and a deterministic environment [2, 3]. This approach is known in literature as scheduling in offline environments.

In online environments, on the other hand, a sequence of jobs $J = J_1, J_2, ..., J_n$ has to be processed in certain number of machines. The jobs arrive to the system one by one, and every time a new job arrives, it has to be immediately dispatched to one of the machines, without any knowledge about future jobs. The objective is to optimize certain objective function [4–6].

Scheduling problems can be classified taking into account the environment of the machines, the characteristics of the jobs and the objective function. This classification is commonly known as $(\alpha \mid \beta \mid \gamma)$ [3, 7–9], where α represents the environment of the machines, β the characteristics of the jobs and γ the criteria to be optimized. According to the environment of the machines, the simplest scenario contains only one resource, since the jobs have only one operation to be processed and there is only one machine that can execute it. When there are multiple machines the environment becomes more complicated, since they can be identical or they can differ in speed [10–12]. The possible environments with parallel machines are summarized as follows [13, 14]:

- Identical Parallel Machines: They process the jobs at the same speed.
- Different Parallel Machines: The processing time depends on the machine.
- Unrelated Parallel Machines: The processing time depends on the machine and the job.

This work focuses on solving a problem that corresponds to a parallel machines environment. This solution proposal has different machines to process the reports, each one has different characteristics, and only a specific machine or at most two of them can process each report. That is to say, when we construct a solution for this problem it must be taken into account that each machine has a number of jobs to be processed and the order to execute them must be determined according to the objective to be optimized. The remainder of this paper is organized as follows: Sect. 2 presents the description of the problem, Sect. 3 proposes a new approach to handle the reports scheduling problem using the Q-Learning algorithm and the experimental results are presented in Sect. 4. The paper finishes with conclusions and future work.

2 Problem Description

In real world scheduling problems, the jobs are processed following certain order, in such a way that the times in which they transit through the system can be optimized. The execution of the reports generated by the customers of the supermarkets through their purchases can be seen as a scheduling problem. Many of these reports must meet a series of conditions and the system must be able to prioritize its execution if necessary. In order to process the reports there are m types of machines, and each type has a specific number of resources. There are also n reports in lots, grouped by the type of report, and a specific type of machine must process them. These reports also have an

ID, an average processing time, certain number of orders and a total processing time that is given by the number of orders requested. The reports can be processed at the same time; they are independent, as long as there is space available. If the machines are busy, the reports should wait until one of them becomes available. There is a resource that has no capacity limit, only the limit that the system imposes to avoid overload. All the reports that do not need to be executed by a specific machine are sent to this resource. There is no relationship between the resources. Table 1 shows an example where it is possible to see the format of the data that needs to be processed.

Table 1. Data format

Job	Total time	Executions	Time per report	Machine	Priority
J_1	229455.709	103	2227.71562	7	1
J_2	90256.683	51	1769.71927	0	1
J_3	210295.147	119	1767.18611	0	3
J_4	233587.705	136	1717.54934	7–9	1
J_5	24852.869	17	1461.87476	1	4

3   The Proposed Approach

The assignment of n independent jobs to m parallel machines is a combinatorial problem. Therefore, the use of a metaheuristic is advisable in order to find a solution in an acceptable computational time. In the next figure, we show the pseudocode of the proposed solution. The algorithm input is an excel document with the format shown in Table 1. The reports are loaded into priority queues according to the resource that it needs to use; therefore, there is a priority queue per resource. Inside each priority queue, the criteria to order the reports is the priority (last column in Table 1), the reports with same priority are ordered using the total processing time because the objective to optimize is the final makespan (the time needed to process all the reports) (Fig. 1).

```
Input: PriorityQueue reports, PriorityQueue machines
Output: makespan
makespan = 0;
repeat
    int [] a = distribution(cant);
    for i = 1 to machines.size() do
        for j = 1 to a[i] do
            machines[i].pool[j] = reports[i].pop();
        end for
    end for
    Report report_exit = find_min();
    machines[report_exit].remove();
    makespan = max(makespan, report_exit.getFinalTime())
until reports.isEmpty()
return makespan
```

Fig. 1. Pseudocode of the proposed algorithm.

The proposed approach has two steps, it first distributes the capacity of the whole system among the machines, and afterwards each machine decides the order in which it will execute the reports received. To accomplish the first step, while there are reports waiting to be processed, the algorithm generates a combination of numbers (using the function "*distribution(cant)*"), which establishes the number of reports that each machine has to process. According to this number, the algorithm takes the first lot of reports from each priority queue. When the first lot of reports finishes its execution, the algorithm generates a new combination taking into account the number of reports that are being processed at the moment, because the availability of the system decreases. The reports distribution among the machines, regardless the technique used, must satisfy the following constraints:

- The sum of the numbers in the first combination generated, is the system capacity limit.
- The algorithm generates a number per machine, which is lower than the number of machines of that type and the number of reports that are waiting to be processed.
- For different combinations from the first one, the algorithm takes into account the number of reports being processed by the machines.
- The reports that need two machines must be sent to both machines at the same time and with the same number of lots.

3.1 Reinforcement Learning, the Q-Learning Algorithm

Reinforcement Learning is a machine learning technique that allows the agents to learn how to optimally behave in a stochastic environment [15]. At each time step, the agent is located in a particular state of the environment ($s \in S$, S represents the set of states) and needs to choose an action $a \in A$ (where A represents the set of actions). The agent actions will determine not only its intermediate reward, but also its next state. The objective of the agent is to optimize the reward received over time, therefore the agent should not only take into account the immediate reward received but also the delayed reward. Q-Learning is an important RL algorithm proposed in [16]. Its main idea is to learn, through an action-value update rule, how good a given action is in a given state.

Each state-action pair has a Q-value associated ($Q{:}S \times A \rightarrow R$). At each time step t, an action a is selected according to a policy [15]. The function $Q(s,a)$ is the estimated utility function and it tells us how good an action is for a given state. More formally, the Q-values update rule is:

$$Q(s, a) \leftarrow Q(s, a) + \alpha[r + \gamma \max Q(s', a') - Q(s, a)] \tag{1}$$

where α ($0 \le \alpha \le 1$) is the learning rate which determines to what extent the newly acquired information will update the Q-value, r is the immediate reward received after taking action a from state s. The discount factor γ ($0 \le \gamma \le 1$) represents the importance of future rewards. The state s' is the next state after the action a is applied. The action a' is the best action according to the current Q-values in the next state s'.

3.2   Q-Learning Applied to the Reports Scheduling Problem

When applying Q-Learning to the report scheduling problem there are different elements to be defined [4, 17].

States: The current state is composed by the set of machines previously chosen.

Actions: An action is to select the position where the next machine must be inserted into the current state (set of previously chosen machines).

Reward: The reward is associated to the makespan (r = 1/makespan).

Action Selection Strategy: ε-greedy is the action selection strategy used because it allows to balance the exploitation and the exploration ($\varepsilon = 0.1$).

The algorithm keeps an ordered list of machines, which is sorted in decreasing order according to their total processing time. We use only one agent, and its main task is to select the position to insert the next machine in the current state. The first machine is randomly selected, and the remaining machines are taken from the ordered list and inserted one by one following the e-greedy policy, which means that a percentage of the time they are placed in a position at random and the rest of the time in the position that will optimize the makespan. To improve the solution, it is advisable to execute several iterations, which implies a better learning process.

We find the partial makespan for each assignment and we compare it to the best previously found, in order to keep the minimum value. In each iteration, the Q-values are updated so that the agents keep an updated experience over the actions selection quality.

4   Experimental Results

In order to evaluate the performance of the algorithm, we use 10 different machines with the following capacities: {130, 15, 60, 10, 4, 2, 10, 6, 1, 20}. For the Q-Learning algorithm the parameters are defined as: $\alpha = 0.1$, $\gamma = 0.8$ and $\epsilon = 0.1$. We use 6 files with different number of reports, with the same format presented in Table 1:

- File 1: 1416   • File 3: 75   • File 5: 300
- File 2: 19   • File 4: 100   • File 6: 500

The number of iterations is not fixed. The algorithm stops when the makespan remains being the same for the last 100 iterations. The results show that the proposed algorithm converges over 1000 iterations.

The implemented algorithm is compared to other two techniques to distribute the number of reports per machine. The first alternative uses the Most Work Remaining (MWKR) dispatching rule, in this case, the priority to choose a machine is a proportion between the number of reports it has to process and its available capacity. The second technique is the NEH heuristic, a constructive heuristic which works by ordering the machines in descendent order, according to the total processing time. Then, it takes the first two machines and schedules them in order to minimize the partial makespan as if there were only these two machines. The rest of the machines are added afterwards using the same criteria. The following table shows the final makespan obtained by the three techniques using the six files or datasets.

Table 2. Comparison of the results obtained for the six datasets

File/alternative	NEH	MWKR	Q-learning
File 1	1507456.622	1446676.297	**1418194.8708**
File 2	218498.712	213132.546	**212954.391**
File 3	253717.145	**239754.938**	**239754.938**
File 4	386542.268	439143.066	**386238.711**
File 5	487930.899	462347.397	**462294.595**
File 6	577369.61	522730.409	**522724.8527**

The following tables show the results of the Friedman and Wilcoxon tests which were applied to the results obtained in the simulation (Table 2), in order to compare the performances of the alternatives.

Table 3. Statistical analysis of the results using the Friedman test

	Mean Rank
NEH	3.67
MWKR	2.33
Q-Learning	**1.08**

N	6
Chi-square	14.00
ql	3
Sig.	**.003**

Table 3 shows the results of the Friedman test, it is possible to see that the significance is 0.003, a value lower than 0.05, which means that the null hypothesis is rejected, therefore, there are significant differences between the alternatives, the mean ranks indicate that the Q-Learning algorithm yields better results, that is why in the following table we only show comparisons 2 by 2 between this algorithm and the other two alternatives (Table 4).

Table 4. Comparison of the results using the Wilcoxon test

	Q-learning - NEH	Q-learning - MWKR
Z	−2.201(a)	−2.201(a)
Sig. (bilateral)	.028	.028

According to the results of the Wilcoxon test, it is possible to conclude that the alternative using Q-Learning has significant differences compared to the other two, and according to the positive and negative ranks of this test, and the mean rank obtained using the Friedman test, it is possible to conclude that it yields the best results for the six datasets. We also use the Nemenyi test, executed in R using the *scmamp* package, which has the advantage of having an associated graph to represent the results of the comparison [18].

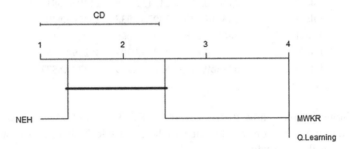

Fig. 2. Comparison of the results using the Nemenyi test.

Figure 2 shows the critical differences between the different techniques. Each alternative is located on an axis according to its average range. Those that do not show significant differences are grouped using a horizontal line. The figure also shows the size of the critical difference required to consider two alternatives as significantly different. It is possible to see that there are significant differences between the Q-Learning approach and the other two ones.

5   Conclusions and Future Work

In this work, a Reinforcement Learning approach has been proposed, in order to optimize the makespan in a report scheduling problem. The proposal uses a two-step procedure, it first decides the number of reports each machine will process and then each resource decides the order in which it will execute the reports that have been assigned to it. In order to evaluate the performance of the proposal we use six datasets or files with different number of reports, and the results are compared to other scheduling techniques. Each of them was executed 10 times and the results obtained were validated using statistical tests, concluding that the alternative using Q-Learning is able to obtain results that significantly improves those obtained by the dispatching rule and the NEH heuristic.

As future work it will be interesting to test other feedback functions in the Q-Learning update rule, to modify the algorithm and to optimize other objectives such as the tardiness, due to its importance in the manufacturing industry, and also to apply the proposed approach to data sets with higher number of reports in order to analyze its performance and scalability.

References

1. Zhang, W.: Reinforcement learning for job shop scheduling. Oregon State University, Ph.D. Thesis; p. 190 (1996)
2. Herroelen, W., Leus, R.: Project scheduling under uncertainty: survey and research potentials. Eur. J. Oper. Res. **165**(2), 289–306 (2005)
3. Graham, R.L., Lawler, E.L., Lenstra, J.K., Rinnooy Kan, A.H.G.: Optimization and approximation in deterministic sequencing and scheduling: a survey. Ann. Discrete Math. **5**, 287–326 (1979)
4. Martínez Jiménez, Y.: A generic multi-agent reinforcement learning approach for scheduling problems. Ph.D. thesis, Vrije Universiteit Brussel, p. 128 (2012)
5. Sivasankaran, P., Sornakumar, T., Panneerselvam, R.: Efficient heuristic to minimize makespan in single machine scheduling problem with unrelated parallel machines. Intell. Inf. Manag. **2**, 188–198 (2010)
6. Nhu Binh, H.O., Joc Cing, T.A.Y.: Evolving dispatching rules for solving the flexible job-shop problem. In: IEEE Congress on Evolutionary Computation, pp. 2848–2855 (2005)
7. Sourd, F.: Scheduling tasks on unrelated machines: large neighbourhood improvement procedures. J. Heuristics **7**, 519–531 (2001)
8. Alharkan, I.M.: Algorithms for Sequencing and Scheduling. Industrial Engineering Department King Saud University, Riyadh (2010)
9. Al-Turki, U., Andijani, A., Arifulsalam, S.: A new dispatching rule for the stochastic single-machine scheduling problem. SIMULATION Trans. Soc. Model. Simul. Int. **80**, 165–170 (2014)
10. Monien, B., Woclaw, A.: Scheduling unrelated parallel machines computational results. Exp. Algorithms **4007**, 195–206 (2006)
11. Hariri, A.M., Potts, C.N.: Heuristics for scheduling unrelated parallel machines. Comput. Oper. Res. **18**, 323–331 (1991)
12. Mokotoff, E., Jimeno, J.L.: Heuristics based on partial enumeration for the unrelated parallel processor scheduling problem. Ann. Oper. Res. **17**, 133–150 (2002)
13. Piersman, N., Van Dijk, W.: A local search heuristic for unrelated parallel machine scheduling with efficient neighbourhood search. Math. Comput. Model. **24**, 11–19 (1996)
14. Zahmani, M.H., Atmani, B., Bekrar, A.: Efficient dispatching rules based on data mining for the single machine scheduling problem. In: Computer Science and Information Technology, pp. 199–208 (2015)
15. Sutton, R.S., Barto, A.G.: Reinforcement Learning: An Introduction. The MIT Press, Cambridge (1998)
16. Watkins, C., Dayan, P.: Technical note: Q-learning. Mach. Learn. **8**, 279–292 (1992)
17. Gabel, T.: Multi-agent reinforcement learning approaches for distributed job-shop scheduling problems. Ph.D. thesis, Universität Osnabrück (2009)
18. Calvo, B., Santafé, G.: scmamp: statistical comparison of multiple algorithms in multiple problems. R J **8**, 248–256 (2016)

Pattern Recognition and Applications

A Restriction-Based Approach to Generalizations

Milton García-Borroto[(⊠)] [iD]

Universidad Tecnológica de la Habana José Antonio Echeverría, CUJAE,
114 No. 11901 e/ Ciclovía y Rotonda, Marianao, Cuba
`mgarciab@ceis.cujae.edu.cu`

Abstract. Generalizations, also known as contrast patterns, are in the core of many learning systems. A key component to automatically find generalizations is the predicate to select the most important ones. These predicates are usually formed by restrictions that every generalization must fulfill. Previous studies are mainly focused on the types of generalizations, each one associated to a particular predicate. In this paper, we shift the focus from predicates to restrictions. Restrictions are analyzed based on a set of intuitions that they materialize. Additionally, an analysis of the restrictions used in a large collection of existing generalizations suggests interesting conclusions.

Keywords: Generalizations · Emerging patterns · Contrast patterns
Subgroup discovery

1 Introduction

One capability associated to learning is the ability to *generalize*: to analyze a large number of specific observations to extract and retain the important common features that characterize classes of these observations [22]. Searching generalizations are the core of many tasks in machine learning, pattern recognition, and artificial intelligence.

Supervised classification is the task of labeling objects based on the knowledge contained in a collection of previously labeled objects. This task is frequently performed by finding generalizations in the object collection. The presence of a generalization in a query object can be taken as a signal of the object's label.

A key component to define a generalization is the predicate that selects the important ones [22]. This importance is expressed as a collection of *restrictions*. In this way, each generalization type contains a particular set of restrictions. Examples of generalization types are *subgroups* [28], *emerging patterns* [6], *contrast sets* [3], *supervised descriptive rule* [24], *contrast patterns* [5], and *discriminative patterns*[20].

The abundance of different generalizations poses some challenges to select the appropriate for a given problem. On the one hand, comparative studies evaluates

© Springer Nature Switzerland AG 2018
Y. Hernández Heredia et al. (Eds.): IWAIPR 2018, LNCS 11047, pp. 239–246, 2018.
https://doi.org/10.1007/978-3-030-01132-1_27

types of generalizations, obscuring the contribution of individual restrictions. On the other hand, some types of generalizations are introduced as novel although they are formed by already known restrictions or have minor changes with respect to previous types.

The main contribution of this paper is a theoretical study about generalizations from the perspective of their restrictions. For a better understanding, we grouped restrictions based on intuitions or insights about what a good generalization is. Additionally, analyzing the restrictions used in a large collection of existing generalizations leads to interesting conclusions.

2   Generalizations

In 1982, Mitchel [22] formally defines the problem of generalization (Definition 1).

Definition 1. Given:

1. *A language in which to describe instances*
2. *A language in which to describe generalizations*
3. *A matching predicate that matches generalizations to instances*
4. *A set of positive and negative training instances of the target generalization to be learned*
5. *A predicate to select the important generalizations*

We define the problem of generalization *as to determine the important generalizations within the provided language.*

In this section, the first four components are described. The fifth component, which is directly related to this paper, is analyzed in depth in the Sect. 3.

1. A Language in which to describe instances
Instances are usually described in two different languages: transactional and attribute-values. In a transactional language, every object is a subset of a global collection of transactions. In attribute-value languages, every object contains a value in a fixed collection of attributes. There are cases where these two languages can be transformed between them. In an attribute-value database, we can discretize numerical features and then convert every pair (*attribute*, *value*) into a transaction. On the other hand, transactional databases containing an small collection of transactions can be converted into an attribute-value database by defining a Boolean attribute per transaction.

More complex languages exists, but are less frequent. For example, [22] describe instances as an unordered collection of feature vectors, where every feature vector is similar to instances in the attribute-value databases. For example: *Instance*$_1$: (*large red square*) (*small yellow circle*).

2. A Language in which to describe generalizations
Each language to describe generalizations tries to capture different types of relations among the instances and the classes. Since mining generalizations is a

searching problem [22], the selection of the generalization language set a balance among two contradicting forces: language generality and searching time. In a more general language, more potentially useful generalizations can be found, but the search could be significantly slower. On the other hand, searching using a restricted language could be faster but important generalizations could be missed.

Generalizations are usually expressed as a set of items related by Boolean or fuzzy operators, but other variants exists. For example, [21] introduces Disjunctive Emerging Patterns (DEP), a restricted conjunctive normal form (CNF) where all generalizations are conjunctions of disjunctions of items. In this structure, every disjunction only contains items from a single feature. No negation is allowed and there must be at least one item per feature.

Items are commonly structured as $[Feature\#ValueOrSet]$, where $\#$ is a set, relational or membership operators. Transactional databases allow a constrained set of operators like $=$ and $\in$, but attribute-value databases allows a richer set including $=$, $\neq$, $\leq$, $\in$, and $\subset$. Other structures are also possible. In DeEPs [18], generalizations contain only a feature value, and an instance matches a generalization if the difference between the values is below a neighborhood factor α. In the case of fuzzy patterns [12], items contains a pair $[Attribute \text{ is } FuzzySet]$, where $FuzzySet$ can be a fuzzy set in the domain of the attribute or a set modified by hedges.

3. A matching predicate that matches generalizations to instances
The matching predicate is dependent on the language of the instances and generalizations. In transactional databases, a generalization matches an instance if it contains a subset of the transactions in the instance. In attribute-value databases, a generalization matches an instance if the instance values complies all the properties contained on it. For example, instance $(color = Red, size = 25, speed = 3.45)$ is matched by generalization $[color = Red] \wedge [size > 12]$ but not by generalization $[color = Black] \wedge [speed < 34.6]$.

4. A set of positive and negative training instances of the target generalization to be learned
This requirement differentiate generalizations from other important concepts like frequent sets. Each generalization must describe a significant collection of instances in a class and at most few instances in the remaining classes. Problem with many classes can be converted to problems with two classes using One-Versus-All or One-versus-One strategies.

3 Restrictions in Generalization

The predicate to select the important generalizations is usually composed by a set of restrictions, where each restriction imposes a limitation to the generalization. In this section, we present an extensive collection of restrictions used in most published papers. Because of space limitations, quality measures appearing in this paper are not fully references. Nevertheless, details can be found in [11].

Restrictions are used for three main purposes: speeding up the mining process, filtering noisy generalizations, and filtering redundant generalizations. In this section, restrictions are grouped based on the associated intuition they materialize. We identify particular restrictions per intuition by capital letters surrounded by parenthesis.

In this paper, we use the following notations. The probability of finding an object with a given generalization or pattern P is denoted by $p(P)$, while the probability of not finding an object with a given pattern is denoted as $p(\neg P)$. With respect to a given class C, probabilities of finding an object of a given class or from a different class are denoted as $p(C)$ and $p(\neg C)$, respectively. Joint probabilities are then denoted as $p(PC)$, $p(P\neg C)$, and so on.

Intuition 1. Each pattern must be frequent enough to guarantee it is not due to chance
This intuition is commonly measured using the pattern support $p(P) > \mu$ (**Rst.A**). In some extreme cases, even the support in the negative class must be greater than a threshold $p(P\neg C) > \mu$ (**Rst.B**).

Intuition 2. Each pattern must be distinctive of its representing class
This intuition is usually measured by the following heuristic restrictions:

- Evaluating the pattern confidence $p(C|P)$ (**Rst.A**), including using Laplace correction (**Rst.B**) or a fuzzy version (**Rst.C**) [12].
- Contrasting the probability of finding the pattern in both classes estimated by division in Emerging Patterns (**Rst.D**) $\frac{p(P|C)}{p(P|\neg C)}$ and Subgroups (**Rst.E**) $\frac{p(PC)}{p(P\neg C)+g}$ or by difference in Contrast Sets (**Rst.F**) $p(P|C) - p(P|\neg C)$.
- Restrict the appearance of the pattern in the negative class (**Rst.G**) $p(P\neg C) \leq \mu$ or even forbid it (**Rst.H**) $p(P\neg C) = 0$.
- Contrasting the probability of finding and not finding the pattern in the positive class, using for example (**Rst.I**) Relative Risk $\frac{p(C|P)}{p(C|\neg P)}$
- Testing for dependency between the pattern and the positive class, using (**Rst.J**) WRACC $p(CP) - p(P)p(C)$, (**Rst.K**) Lift $\frac{p(CP)}{p(P)p(C)}$, (**Rst.L**) χ^2, (**Rst.M**) Pearson correlation, (**Rst.N**) Odds Ratio, or (**Rst.O**) NetConf.

Intuition 3. Shortest more general patterns are preferred, because they contains the irreducible relations among attributes that determines the class
The simplest restriction based on this intuition is (**Rst.A**) to remove all non-minimal patterns (with respect to the item subset inclusion) fulfilling the remaining restrictions. A different set of restrictions allow for non-minimal patterns, but only when they are better than their subsets according to the following restrictions:

- (**Rst.B**) Positive growth rate (GR) improvement, where
  $rateimp(P) = \min_{P' \subset P}\{GR(P) - GR(P')\}$ [30]
- (**Rst.C**) Relative growth rate improvement greater than 1, where
  $relrateimp(P) = \min_{P' \subset P}\{GR(P)/GR(P')\}$ [30]

- (**Rst.D**) Positive coverage improvement, where $\forall P' \subset P : \text{Support}(P) > \text{Support}(P')$ [30]
- (**Rst.E**) Statistically different than sub-patterns.
  $(|P| = 1) \vee (|P| > 1 \wedge \forall P' \subset P, |P'| = |P| - 1 \Rightarrow chiTest(P, P') \geq \eta)$, where $\eta = 3.84$ is a minimum chi-value threshold
- (**Rst.F**) Positive strength improvement. $\forall P' \subset P, \text{Support}(P') \geq \mu \wedge \text{GR}(P') \geq \rho \Rightarrow \text{Streng}(P) > \text{Streng}(P')$
- (**Rst.G**) Productive restriction. For every pair of patterns P_1 and P_2 formed by a partition of the items in P, $p(P|C) > p(P_1|C)p(P_2|C)$ and $p(P|\neg C) > p(P_1|\neg C)p(P_2|\neg C)$.
- (**Rst.H**) Conditional discriminative, where $\min_{P' \subset P}\{\text{SupDif}(P')\} \geq \mu$ [30]
- (**Rst.I**) Correlation improvement, if $\forall P' \subset P : |\text{Pearson}(P) - \text{Pearson}(P')| \geq \gamma$

Intuition 4. Largest patterns are preferred, because they allow a condensed representation of the whole pattern collection and are less prone to over-training
The simplest restriction based on this intuition is (**Rst.A**) to remove all non-maximal patterns fulfilling the remaining restrictions. This restriction can be relaxed (**Rst.B**) by allowing non-maximal patterns but only if they cover more instances: $\forall P \subset P' : \text{Support}(P) > \text{Support}(P')$.

Table 1 presents a large collection of existing types of generalizations. Each table column is associated with a particular intuition, and each cell contains the restriction used in the particular case.

4 Discussion and Conclusions

There are some interesting results that can be extracted from Table 1. First, most types of generalizations were introduced in the period prom 1997 to 2007. After that period, papers are mainly focused on improving the mining algorithms, creating better classification algorithms based on the generalizations, or applying the generalizations to solve real problems.

Second, restrictions based on the second intuition, the pattern representativeness in its class, are present in all generalizations. This is expected, because the contrast among classes is explicitly set in the component 4 of the definition. Although there is a large collection of restrictions that materialize each intuition, the high correlations reported among them [11] deserves to be studied in depth.

Third, most generalizations restricted to minimal patterns includes a restriction forcing a minimal support. This is somewhat unexpected, because minimal patterns are usually those with larger pattern support.

Fourth, only half of the generalizations uses restriction based on support. The remaining generalizations only contains restrictions based on contrast. This can be explained by the fact that finding a good threshold for minimal support is hard, because it depends on database characteristics that cannot be accurately estimated a-priori. Interestingly, the same problem with thresholds appears on

Table 1. Restrictions used on different type of generalizations. Rightmost columns are associated to intuitions I1 .. I4

Year	Generalization type	I1	I2	I3	I4
1982	Consistent Generalization [22]		2H		
1997	Unusual subgroup [28]	1A	2J		
1998	CAR [19]	1A	2A		
1999	Emerging Pattern (EP) [6]		2D		
1999	Jumping EP (JEP) [6]		2H, 2D		
2000	Constrained EP (ConsEP) [30]		2H	3B or 3C, 3D	
2001	Contrast set(CS) [4]		2F, 2L		
2002	Interesting subgroup [10]		2E		
2002	Essential JEP (eJEP) [8]	1A	2H	3A	
2003	Constrained EP (CEP) [2]	1A	2G		
2003	Interesting EP [9]	1A	2D	3B, 3E	
2003	Predictive AR [29]	1A	2B		
2004	Interesting subgroup [16]		2J		
2004	Strong Frequent Pattern [26]	1A	2A	3D	
2004	Maximal EP (MaxEP) [27]	1A	2D		4A
2005	Chi EP (Chi-EP) [25]	1A	2D	3F, 3E	
2005	Relative Risk Pattern [17]		2I		
2005	Odds Ratio Pattern [17]		2N		
2006	Strong JEP [7]	1A	2H	3A	
2006	Noise tolerant EP (NEP) [7]	1A	2G	3A	
2007	Contrast set in CIGAR [15]	1A	2F, 2L, 2M	3I	
2009	Interesting subgroup [1]		2J,2K		
2011	Fuzzy EP [12]		2C		
2012	CAR-NF [14]	1A	2A,2O		
2015	Nofong EP [23]	1A, 1B	2D		
2015	Productive EP [23]	1A, 1B	2D	3G	
2017	Conditional Discrim. Pattern [13]		2F	3H	

the second intuitions, because measures of contrast are very sensible to noise. Nevertheless, in this last case, restrictions cannot be removed.

Fifth, the same restriction appears in different generalizations. For example, restriction 1A appears 15 times and 2D appears 7 times. Additionally, different generalizations contains almost identical subsets of restrictions, what makes harder to select the appropriate one for a given problem.

Finally, the use of minimal generalizations is more popular than using maximal generalizations. To explain this, we should note that although minimal generalizations are affected by over-training, maximal ones have a larger problem:

they are less prone to appear in query objects, so they increases the classifier abstention level.

Some limitations of this paper deserves to be studied in depth as future work. First, the close relationship among different restrictions materializing the same intuition should be measured and evaluated. As a result, maybe we can simplify the list and select an small group of significantly different restrictions. Secondly, some theories presented in the discussion are debatable and should be verified by experiments. Finally, this study can be enriched with restrictions applied to pattern sets, that cannot be included here for the limited space.

References

1. Atzmueller, M., Lemmerich, F.: Fast subgroup discovery for continuous target concepts. In: Rauch, J., Raś, Z.W., Berka, P., Elomaa, T. (eds.) ISMIS 2009. LNCS (LNAI), vol. 5722, pp. 35–44. Springer, Heidelberg (2009). https://doi.org/10.1007/978-3-642-04125-9_7

2. Bailey, J., Manoukian, T., Ramamohanarao, K.: Classification using constrained emerging patterns. In: Dong, G., Tang, C., Wang, W. (eds.) WAIM 2003. LNCS, vol. 2762, pp. 226–237. Springer, Heidelberg (2003). https://doi.org/10.1007/978-3-540-45160-0_22

3. Bay, S.D., Pazzani, M.J.: Detecting change in categorical data: mining contrast sets. In: Proceedings of the Fifth ACM SIGKDD International Conference on Knowledge Discovery and Data Mining, KDD 1999, pp. 302–306. ACM, New York (1999)

4. Bay, S.D., Pazzani, M.J.: Detecting group differences: mining contrast sets. Data Min. Knowl. Discov. 5(3), 213–246 (2001)

5. Dong, G., Bailey, J.: Contrast Data Minint. Concepts, Algorithms, and Applications. Taylor & Francis, Abingdon (2013)

6. Dong, G., Li, J.: Efficient mining of emerging patterns: discovering trends and differences. In: Proceedings of the Fifth ACM SIGKDD International Conference on Knowledge Discovery and Data Mining, KDD 1999, pp. 43–52. ACM, New York (1999)

7. Fan, H., Ramamohanarao, K.: Fast discovery and the generalization of strong jumping emerging patterns for building compact and accurate classifiers. IEEE Trans. Knowl. Data Eng. 18(6), 721–737 (2006)

8. Fan, H., Kotagiri, R.: An efficient single-scan algorithm for mining essential jumping emerging patterns for classification. In: Chen, M.-S., Yu, P.S., Liu, B. (eds.) PAKDD 2002. LNCS (LNAI), vol. 2336, pp. 456–462. Springer, Heidelberg (2002). https://doi.org/10.1007/3-540-47887-6_45

9. Fan, H., Ramamohanarao, K.: Efficiently mining interesting emerging patterns. In: Dong, G., Tang, C., Wang, W. (eds.) WAIM 2003. LNCS, vol. 2762, pp. 189–201. Springer, Heidelberg (2003). https://doi.org/10.1007/978-3-540-45160-0_19

10. Gamberger, D., Lavrač, N.: Expert-guided subgroups discovery: methodology and applications. J. Artif. Intell. Res. 17, 501–527 (2002)

11. Garca-Borroto, M., Loyola-Gonzlez, O., Martnez-Trinidad, J.F., Carrasco-Ochoa, J.A.: Evaluation of quality measures for contrast patterns by using unseen objects. Expert Syst. Appl. 83(C), 104–113 (2017)

12. Garcia-Borroto, M., Martínez-Trinidad, J.F., Carrasco-ochoa, J.A.: Fuzzy emerging patterns for classifying hard domains. Knowl. Inf. Syst. 28(1), 473–489 (2011)

13. He, Z., Gu, F., Zhao, C., Liu, X., Wu, J., Wang, J.: Conditional discriminative pattern mining: concepts and algorithms. Inf. Sci. **375**, 1–15 (2017)
14. Hernández-León, R., Carrasco-Ochoa, J., Martínez-Trinidad, J.F., Hernández-Palancar, J.: CAR-NF: a classifier based on specific rules with high netconf. Intell. Data Anal. **16**(1), 150–158 (2012)
15. Hilderman, R.J., Peckham, T.: Statistical methodologies for mining potentially interesting contrast sets. In: Guillet, F.J., Hamilton, H.J. (eds.) Quality Measures in Data Mining. SCI, vol. 43, pp. 153–177. Springer, Heidelberg (2007)
16. Lavrac, N., Flach, P.: Subgroup discovery with CN2-SD. J. Mach. Learn. Res. **5**, 153–188 (2004)
17. Li, H., Li, J., Wong, L., Feng, M., Tan, Y.-P.: Relative risk and odds ratio: a data mining perspective. In: PODS 2005, pp. 368–377 (2005)
18. Li, J., Dong, G., Ramamohanarao, K.: Instance-based classification by emerging patterns. In: Zighed, D.A., Komorowski, J., Żytkow, J. (eds.) PKDD 2000. LNCS (LNAI), vol. 1910, pp. 191–200. Springer, Heidelberg (2000). https://doi.org/10.1007/3-540-45372-5_19
19. Liu, B., Hsu, W., Ma, Y.: Integrating classification and association rule mining. In: KDD 1998 (1998)
20. Liu, X., Wu, J., Gu, F., Wang, J., He, Z.: Discriminative pattern mining and its applications in bioinformatics. Brief. Bioinform. **16**(16), 884–900 (2015)
21. Loekito, E., Bailey, J.: Fast mining of high dimensional expressive contrast patterns using zero-suppressed binary decision diagrams. In: KDD 2006, Philadelphia, Pennsylvania, USA (2006)
22. Mitchell, T.M.: Generalization as search. Artif. Intell. **18**(1982), 203–226 (1982)
23. Nofong, V.M.: Mining productive emerging patterns and their application in trend prediction. In: 13-th Australasian Data Mining Conference (AusDM 2015), pp. 109–117 (2015)
24. Novak, P.K., Lavrač, N., Webb, G.I.: Supervised descriptive rule discovery: a unifying survey of contrast set, emerging pattern and subgroup mining. J. Mach. Learn. Res. **10**, 377–403 (2009)
25. Ramamohanarao, K., Bailey, J., Fan, H.: Efficient mining of contrast patterns and their applications to classification, pp. 1–9 (2005)
26. Sucahyo, Y.G., Gopalan, R.P.: Building a more accurate classifier based on strong frequent patterns. In: Webb, G.I., Yu, X. (eds.) AI 2004. LNCS (LNAI), vol. 3339, pp. 1036–1042. Springer, Heidelberg (2004). https://doi.org/10.1007/978-3-540-30549-1_98
27. Wang, Z., Fan, H., Ramamohanarao, K.: Exploiting maximal emerging patterns for classification. In: Webb, G.I., Yu, X. (eds.) AI 2004. LNCS (LNAI), vol. 3339, pp. 1062–1068. Springer, Heidelberg (2004). https://doi.org/10.1007/978-3-540-30549-1_102
28. Wrobel, S.: An algorithm for multi-relational discovery of subgroups. In: Komorowski, J., Zytkow, J. (eds.) PKDD 1997. LNCS, vol. 1263, pp. 78–87. Springer, Heidelberg (1997). https://doi.org/10.1007/3-540-63223-9_108
29. Yin, X., Han, J.: CPAR: classification based on predictive association rules. In: Barbar, D., Kamath, C. (eds.) Proceedings of the SIAM International Conference on Data Mining, pp. 331–335. SIAM (2003)
30. Zhang, X.X., Dong, G., Ramamohanarao, K.: Exploring constraints to efficiently mine emerging patterns from large high-dimensional datasets. KDD 2000, pp. 310–314 (2000)

Expanding MLkNN Using Extended Rough Set Theory

Gabriela Pérez[1], Marilyn Bello[1,2(✉)], Gonzalo Nápoles[2],
María Matilde García[1], Rafael Bello[1], and Koen Vanhoof[2]

[1] Department of Computer Science,
Central University "Marta Abreu" of Las Villas, Santa Clara, Cuba
mbgarcia@uclv.cu
[2] Faculty of Business Economics, Hasselt University, Hasselt, Belgium

Abstract. Multi-label classification refers to the problem of associating an object with multiple labels. This problem has been successfully addressed from the perspective of problem transformation and adaptation of algorithms. *Multi-Label k-Nearest Neighbour* (MLkNN) is a lazy learner that has reported excellent results, still there is room for improvements. In this paper we propose a modification to the MLkNN algorithm for the solution to problems of multi-label classification based on the *Extended Rough Set Theory*. More explicitly, the key modifications are focused in obtaining the relevance of the attributes when computing the distance between two instances, which are obtained using a heuristic search method and a target function based on the quality of the similarity. Experimental results using synthetic datasets have shown promising prediction rates. It is worth mentioning the ability of our proposal to deal with inconsistent scenarios, a main shortcoming present in most state-of-the-art multi-label classification algorithms.

Keywords: Multi-label classification · k-Nearest Neighbour
Extended Rough Set Theory · Measure Quality of Similarity

1 Introduction

The pattern classification problem can be defined as the process of identifying the right category (among those in a predefined set) to which an observation belongs. It should be remarked that an observation can only be related with a single category (also known as decision class). In contrast, in the case of multi-label classification (MLC) problem, an observation may associated with more than one label [27].

In recent years, this problem has attracted the attention of the machine learning community as a result of its broad potentialities in modelling real-world applications, such as: text classification [4], the prediction of gene and protein functions [6], medical diagnosis [17], among others [2, 3, 22].

The MLC problem has been tackled from two main perspectives [11], namely: problem transformation methods and algorithm adaptation methods. *Problem*

© Springer Nature Switzerland AG 2018
Y. Hernández Heredia et al. (Eds.): IWAIPR 2018, LNCS 11047, pp. 247–254, 2018.
https://doi.org/10.1007/978-3-030-01132-1_28

transformation methods modify the multi-label problem into a classical classification problem. This approach may involve loss of information such as labels that are disregarded, loss in the correlation between labels, in some cases, it has an irreversible transformation and deletes multi-label information from the set, etc. Moreover, the transformation process often demands a high computational complexity [13]. In contrast, *algorithm adaptation methods* are devoted to framing classic classification models within the MLC problem. Representative models include: Neural Networks [14, 21], Decision Trees [1], k-Nearest Neighbour (k-NN) [19, 26]. In spite of their relative success, these algorithms are not well-equipped to deal with inconsistent problems.

Perhaps the most popular adaptation approaches are based lazy learners. The essence of instance-based learning is to compute the solution to a problem based on the solution to similar (previously solved) problems. The k-NN algorithm is a strong representative of this type of classifier. In the MLC context, the MLkNN model [26] has become a key procedure due to its simplicity and performance. Recall that this algorithm is highly dependent on the distance function to achieve high prediction rates. On the other hand, this method is not properly equipped to deal with problems involving inconsistency (i.e., there are observations that have equal or reasonably similar values according to the most important attributes, however, the classification differs between one and the other).

In this paper, we proposed an adaptation to the MLkNN algorithm that is based on extensions to the *Rough Set Theory* to solve multi-label classification problems in data sets where inconsistency appears. The proposal based on the *Extended Rough Set Theory* [18, 24] constitutes a tool very useful for the handling of information not complete or imprecise [5], thus enabling the solution of problems with inconsistency. This proposed method uses the Measure Quality of Similarity and a population-based search method to calculate features weights. This measure uses a binary fuzzy relation to quantify the strength of the similarity relationship in a range of [0,1]. The fuzzy relation is characterized by a membership function, which in this case is defined by a similarity function instead of being characterized by an equivalence relation.

The remainder of this paper is structured as follows. In Sect. 2 it is proposed one modifications to MLkNN and the main steps of this improvement are explained. Section 3 evaluates the proposal starting from international datasets and the use of measures that have been used arbitrarily in multi-label classification experiments. Conclusions and pointers to future work are given in Sect. 4.

2 Expanding MLkNN Using Extended Rough Set Theory

The MLkNN algorithm uses the *maximum a posteriori* principle to determine the set of labels associated with a new observation. This principle is based on the *priori* and *posteriori probabilities* defined in [26], which is used to compute the frequency of each label in the k neighbors. *Heterogeneous Euclidean-Overlap Metric* (HEOM) [23] is the distance function used by this method, which reduces the effects of arbitrary ordering of nominal values. However, this function only considers the surface difference between the objects being compared. This approach is excessively shallow due to it does not use additional information comprised into the nominal attributes that can help obtain better prediction rates.

2.1   The Proposed Algorithm

In this section, we present a new model called *Multi-Label k-Nearest Neighbour based on Extended Rough Set Theory* (MLkNN_ERST) which reduces the problems of MLkNN when using the HEOM distance to compute the neighbours. The new algorithm modifies MLkNN in the following aspects: the distance to be used when computing the nearest k neighbors and the weights assigned to the attributes.

MLkNN_ERST uses a metaheuristic that allows to make a ranking of the attributes, for example in [10] *Particle Swarm Optimization* (PSO), defined in [12], is suggested, for the kindness that it offers. This method assigns weights to attributes based on measures defined within the *Rough Set Theory* to deal with inconsistent scenarios. More precisely, for the purpose of this research we select the *Measure Quality of Similarity* [8] as it suits well the semantics of MLC problems.

The selection of attributes appears as a problem machine learning [16, 25]. The attribute selection problem can be defined as the process of finding the (often minimal) subset of attributes describing the problem domain. The result of the selection can be binary $\{0,1\}$, in the sense that each attribute is selected or not, or it can result in the degree of relevance of the attribute (weight), usually in the interval $[0,1]$. Therefore, the calculation of the weight of attributes consists of finding the set of weights $\Gamma = \{w(1), w(2), \ldots, w(N)\}$, where N is the number of features. As mentioned, to find the set Γ we rely on the PSO metaheuristic, but other search method can be used as well.

The quality of candidate solutions (particles) is calculated using the *Measure Quality of Similarity*, which uses a binary fuzzy relationship, which quantifies the strength of the similarity relationship between two objects in a range of $[0,1]$. The fuzzy relationship is characterized by a membership function that is defined by a similarity function based on the *Extended Rough Set Theory* [15].

This measure represents the degree of similarity between the objects of a heterogeneous decision system and constitutes an important tool for the intelligent analysis of the data. Equation (1) formalizes the degree to which the similarity between objects in the decision system (DS)-using the features in A-is equivalent to the similarity obtained according to the decision feature $d \notin A$,

$$\theta(\text{DS}) = \sum\nolimits_{i=1}^{N} \varphi(x)/N \tag{1}$$

where

$$\varphi(x) = \left(\sum_{i=1}^{N} [1 - |\mu R_1(x_i) - \mu R_2(x_i)|] \right) / N. \tag{2}$$

The fuzzy relations R_1 and R_2 are adopted to define the fuzzy sets $N_1(x)$ and $N_2(x)$ as defined in Eqs. (3) and (4), where $N_1(x)$ and $N_2(x)$ are the fuzzy sets of similar objects x according to the relationships R_1 and R_2. In these equations, U is the universe of discourse while $\mu(.,.)$ denotes a membership function.

$$N_1(x) = \{(y, \mu R_1(x, y)), \forall y \in U\} \tag{3}$$

$$N_2(x) = \{(y, \mu R_2(x, y)), \forall y \in U\} \tag{4}$$

The problem of finding an adequate resemblance relation is to find R_1 and R_2 leading to the highest similarity between the fuzzy sets $N_1(x)$ and $N_2(x)$. As mentioned, R_1 and R_2 are binary fuzzy relations used to find the degree of similarity with respect to the degrees of condition and the decision features, respectively, between the instances x and y. The relations R_1 and R_2 in Eqs. (5) and (6) are defined upon the similarity functions F_1 and F_2, such that F_1 considers the attributes while F_2 considers the labels. These functions can be designed using the Euclidean distance and the Jaccard or Hamming distances [9] respectively.

$$xR_1y = F_1(x, y) \tag{5}$$

$$xR_2y = F_2(x, y) \tag{6}$$

The weighted Euclidean distance is used as the dissimilarity functional defined in Eq. (7),

$$d(x, y) = \sum_{j=1}^{M} w_j * \partial(a_j(x), a_j(y)) \tag{7}$$

where

$$\partial(a_j(x), a_j(y)) = \begin{cases} 1 - \frac{|a_j(x) - a_j(y)|}{Max(a_j) - Min(a_j)} & if \quad a_j \text{ is continuous} \\ 1 & if \quad a_j \text{ is discrete and } a_j(x) = a_j(y) \\ 0 & if \quad a_j \text{ is discrete and } a_j(x) \neq a_j(y) \end{cases} . \tag{8}$$

The following pseudocode formalizes our proposal.

MLkNN_ERST Algorithm

`Input`: dataset, new instance, iterations and particles
`Output`: set of labels for the instance

`P1`: Determine the importance of attributes.
   `P11`: Initialize PSO parameters (iterations; particles; $w = \{w(1), w(2), ..., w(N)\}$: random generation of particles, taking into account position and speed).
   `P12`: Determine the best particle
     `FOR` i=1 `UNTIL` iterations
       `FOR` j=1 `UNTIL` particles
       Update speed and position.
       Calculate local optimum using measure of the quality of the similarity defined in Equation (1).
       `ENDFOR`
     `ENDFOR`
`P2`: Calculate the probabilities idem to steps MLkNN [14].
   `P21`: Compute the probability a priori.
   `P22`: Compute the probability a posteriori.
`P3`: Select the k nearest instances using Equation (7).
`P4`: Compute the set of labels for the instance using its k nearest instances.

3   Evaluation of the Proposal

To evaluate our proposal, we selected the following datasets: *emotions*, *scene*, *flags*, *yeast*, *cal500*, *enron*, *medical*, *foodtruck*, *stackex_coffe* and *stackex_chess* from international datasets [20] and we used measures that have been used arbitrarily in multi-label classification experiments [27].

The parameters associated with the PSO metaheuristic are fixed as follows: the number of iterations ranges from 10 to 100, the number of particles ranges from 5 to 20, the cognitive acceleration coefficient (c_1) and cognitive acceleration coefficient (c_2) are set to 2.05 as suggested [7]. It should be highlighted that increasing the number of particles and generations in the PSO metaheuristic may lead to better results at expenses of increasing the computational complexity.

Table 1 shows the results achieved by the MLkNN and MLkNN_ERST algorithms with *Hamming Loss* metric (see also Fig. 1). This table contains four rows; the second column shows the result reached by MLkNN algorithm, the third column shows the result achieved by MLkNN_ERST algorithm, and the last column shows the consistency value for each datasets.

Table 1. Results achieved by the MLkNN and MLkNN_ERST algorithms.

Dataset	Results achieved by the MLkNN algorithm	Results achieved by the MLkNN_ERST algorithm	Consistency
emotions	0.1951	0.1887	0.983
scene	0.0862	0.08	0.025
flags	0.2536	0.2502	0.994
yeast	0.1933	0.1928	0.0
cal500	0.1388	0.1382	0.38
foodtruck	0.1561	0.1517	1.0
stackex_coffee	0.0165	0.0162	0.072
stackex_chess	0.0105	0.0104	0.357

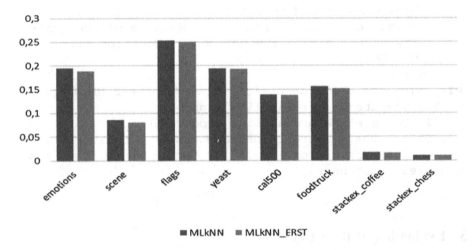

Fig. 1. Results achieved by the MLkNN and MLkNN_ERST algorithms with Hamming Loss metric.

In order to examine the existence of statistically significant differences in performance, the next step is to determine whether the superiority for each metrics used of the MLkNN_ERST regarding to MLkNN is statistically significant or not. By doing so, we resorted to the Wilcoxon signed rank test [22].

The *p*-value obtained for *Hamming Loss* metric is 0.011719. For this metric, the Wilcoxon suggests rejecting the null hypothesis using a confidence level of 95%, hence confirming that there are significant differences between the algorithms across the selected datasets. The statistical analysis supports that MLkNN_ERST is the best-ranked algorithm.

4 Conclusions

In this paper, a modification to the MLkNN algorithm based on extensions to the *Rough Set Theory* is proposed to solve multi-label classification problems in data sets where inconsistency appears. This modification introduces values for the features in the similarity function used in retrieving the instances. These weights are computing by using the *Measure Quality of Similarity*.

The effectiveness of the proposed method is demonstrated from experiments, comparing it with the original method. In all cases, the experimental results showed the proposed method obtained better results.

In future work, the behaviour of the method must be analysed with other distances such as, *Heterogeneous Manhattan-Overlap Metric* (HMOM) and *Heterogeneous Value Difference Metric* (HVDM). In addition, we will assess the parallelization of the algorithm in such a way as to improve the temporal complexity of the proposal.

References

1. Bi, W., Kwok, J.T.: Multi-label classification on tree-and dag-structured hierarchies. In: Proceedings of the 28th International Conference on Machine Learning (ICML-11), pp. 17–24 (2011)
2. Briggs, F., et al.: Acoustic classification of multiple simultaneous bird species: a multi-instance multi-label approach. J. Acoust. Soc. Am. **131**(6), 4640–4650 (2012)
3. Cakir, E., Heittola, T., Huttunen, H., Virtanen, T.: Polyphonic sound event detection using multi label deep neural networks. In: 2015 International Joint Conference on Neural Networks (IJCNN), pp. 1–7. IEEE (2015)
4. Charte, F., Rivera, A.J., del Jesus, M.J., Herrera, F.: Quinta: a question tagging assistant to improve the answering ratio in electronic forums. In: EUROCON 2015-International Conference on Computer as a Tool (EUROCON), IEEE, pp. 1–6. IEEE (2015)
5. Chin, K.S., Liang, J., Dang, C.: Rough set data analysis algorithms for incomplete information systems. In: Wang, G., Liu, Q., Yao, Y., Skowron, A. (eds.) RSFDGrC 2003. LNCS (LNAI), vol. 2639, pp. 264–268. Springer, Heidelberg (2003). https://doi.org/10.1007/3-540-39205-X_35
6. Chou, K.C., Wu, Z.C., Xiao, X.: iLoc-Euk: a multi-label classifier for predicting the subcellular localization of singleplex and multiplex eukaryotic proteins. PLoS ONE **6**(3), e18258 (2011)
7. Clerc, M., Kennedy, J.: The particle swarm-explosion, stability, and convergence in a multidimensional complex space. IEEE Trans. Evol. Comput. **6**(1), 58–73 (2002)
8. Coello, L., Frías, M., Fernández, Y., Filiberto, Y., Bello, R., Caballero, Y.: Construcción de relaciones de similaridad borrosa basada en la medida calidad de la similaridad. Investig. Oper. **38**(2), 132–140 (2018)
9. Deza, M.M., Deza, E.: Encyclopedia of Distances, pp. 1–583. Springer, Berlin (2009). https://doi.org/10.1007/978-3-642-00234-2
10. Filiberto, Y.: Métodos de aprendizaje para dominios con datos mezclados basados en la teoría de los conjuntos aproximados extendida. Universidad Central de Las Villas (2012)
11. Gibaja, E., Ventura, S.: Multi-label learning: a review of the state of the art and ongoing research. Wiley Interdiscip. Rev. Data Min. Knowl. Discov. **4**(6), 411–444 (2014)

12. Kennedy, J.: Particle swarm optimization. In: Sammut, C., Webb, G.I. (eds.) Encyclopedia of Machine Learning, pp. 760–766. Springer, Heidelberg (2011). https://doi.org/10.1007/978-0-387-30164-8

13. Madjarov, G., Kocev, D., Gjorgjevikj, D., Džeroski, S.: An extensive experimental comparison of methods for multi-label learning. Pattern Recognit. **45**(9), 3084–3104 (2012)

14. Calders, T., Esposito, F., Hüllermeier, E., Meo, R. (eds.): ECML PKDD 2014. LNCS (LNAI), vol. 8725. Springer, Heidelberg (2014). https://doi.org/10.1007/978-3-662-44851-9

15. Pawlak, Z., Skowron, A.: Rough sets: some extensions. Inf. Sci. **177**(1), 28–40 (2007)

16. Ruiz, R., Aguilar–Ruiz, Jesús S., Riquelme, José C., Díaz–Díaz, N.: Analysis of Feature Rankings for Classification. In: Famili, A.Fazel, Kok, Joost N., Peña, José M., Siebes, A., Feelders, A. (eds.) IDA 2005. LNCS, vol. 3646, pp. 362–372. Springer, Heidelberg (2005). https://doi.org/10.1007/11552253_33

17. Shao, H., Li, G., Liu, G., Wang, Y.: Symptom selection for multi-label data of inquiry diagnosis in traditional chinese medicine. Sci. China Inf. Sci. **56**(5), 1–13 (2013)

18. Slowinski, R., Vanderpooten, D.: A generalized definition of rough approximations based on similarity. IEEE Trans. Knowl. Data Eng. **12**(2), 331–336 (2000)

19. Spyromitros, E., Tsoumakas, G., Vlahavas, I.: An Empirical Study of Lazy Multilabel Classification Algorithms. In: Darzentas, J., Vouros, George A., Vosinakis, S., Arnellos, A. (eds.) SETN 2008. LNCS (LNAI), vol. 5138, pp. 401–406. Springer, Heidelberg (2008). https://doi.org/10.1007/978-3-540-87881-0_40

20. Tsoumakas, G., Xioufis, E., Vilcek, J., Vlahavas, I.: Mulan multi-label dataset repository (2014). http://mulan.sourceforge.net/datasets.html

21. Wang, J., Yang, Y., Mao, J., Huang, Z., Huang, C., Xu, W.: CNN-RNN: a unified framework for multi-label image classification. In: Proceedings of the IEEE conference on computer vision and pattern recognition, pp. 2285–2294 (2016)

22. Wilcoxon, F.: Individual comparisons by ranking methods. In: Kotz, S., Johnson, N.L. (eds.) Breakthroughs in Statistics, pp. 196–202. Springer, New York (1992). https://doi.org/10.1007/978-1-4612-4380-9_16

23. Wilson, D.R., Martinez, T.R.: Improved heterogeneous distance functions. J. Artif. Intell. Res. **6**, 1–34 (1997)

24. Yao, Y.Y.: On generalizing rough set theory. In: Wang, G., Liu, Q., Yao, Y., Skowron, A. (eds.) RSFDGrC 2003. LNCS (LNAI), vol. 2639, pp. 44–51. Springer, Heidelberg (2003). https://doi.org/10.1007/3-540-39205-X_6

25. Yu, L., Liu, H.: Efficient feature selection via analysis of relevance and redundancy. J. Mach. Learn. Res. **5**, 1205–1224 (2004)

26. Zhang, M.L., Zhou, Z.H.: ML-KNN: a lazy learning approach to multi-label learning. Pattern Recognit. **40**(7), 2038–2048 (2007)

27. Zhang, M.L., Zhou, Z.H.: A review on multi-label learning algorithms. IEEE Trans. Knowl. Data Eng. **26**(8), 1819–1837 (2014)

Proactive Forest for Supervised Classification

Nayma Cepero-Pérez⬤, Luis Alberto Denis-Miranda⬤,
Rafael Hernández-Palacio⬤, Mailyn Moreno-Espino⬤,
and Milton García-Borroto$^{(\boxtimes)}$⬤

Universidad Tecnológica de la Habana José Antonio Echeverría, CUJAE,
114 No. 11901, e/ Ciclovía y Rotonda, Marianao, Cuba
{ncepero,ldenis,rhernandezpe,my,mgarciab}@ceis.cujae.edu.cu

Abstract. Random Forest is one of the most used and accurate ensemble methods based on decision trees. Since diversity is a necessary condition to build a good ensemble, Random Forest selects a random feature subset for building decision nodes. This generation procedure could cause important features to be selected in multiple trees in the ensemble, decreasing the diversity of the entire collection. In this paper, we introduce Proactive Forest, an improvement of Random Forest that uses the information of the already generated trees to induce the remaining trees. Proactive Forest calculates the importance of each feature for the constructed ensemble in order to modify the probabilities of selecting those features in the remaining trees. In the conducted experiments, Proactive Forest increases the diversity of the obtained ensembles with a significant impact in the classifier accuracy.

Keywords: Decision forests · Random Forest · Diversity

1 Introduction

The digital revolution provided relatively inexpensive and accessible means of data collection and storage. This caused the current world to evolve significantly around data. This unlimited data growth has made the process of extracting knowledge from them very difficult. Data mining aims to solve this problem by focusing on the process of extracting patterns from data and transforming them into useful knowledge [11].

Supervised learning is one of the most commonly used data mining tasks today. It is defined as the process of finding a model (or function) that describes the relations among some important properties of the objects with the class. This model can then be used to predict the class of new objects. Decision trees are very popular learners because they are accurate, easy to interpret, nonparametric, robust to outliers, and with few parameters to tune. On the other hand, decision trees have some disadvantages, mainly because the greedy strategies followed by most inducting procedures. This strategy could impact the generalization ability of the tree.

© Springer Nature Switzerland AG 2018
Y. Hernández Heredia et al. (Eds.): IWAIPR 2018, LNCS 11047, pp. 255–262, 2018.
https://doi.org/10.1007/978-3-030-01132-1_29

Ensembles of decision trees, known as decision forests, are an effective solution to the generalizing limitations of decision trees by combining the predictive power of individual members. Like most ensemble methods, to achieve a high accuracy, the forest must be formed by a diverse collection of accurate trees [7]. To generate diverse trees, the tree inductor must be changed either by modifying parameters, or by selecting a subset of the training instances or features.

One of the most popular and accurate ensembles of decision trees is Random Forest [6]. Random Forest uses a random feature subset for building each decision node of the tree, selecting the best split. This generation procedure could cause important features to be selected in several trees, decreasing the diversity of the entire collection. This decreasing in the diversity of the ensemble members usually has a negative impact in its accuracy.

In this paper, we introduce Proactive Forest, an improvement of Random Forest that uses the information of the already generated trees in order to induce each new tree. Proactive Forest has a proactive behavior, a property usually found in intelligent agents. A proactive behavior refers to the ability of a component to sense the environment and take actions toward a predefined goal [1]. Proactive Forest considers as changing environment the decision trees already built, and uses an evaluation of the importance of the features to set the selection probabilities of features in the remaining trees.

2   Decision Forest Induction

Ensemble learning refers to the generation and the combination of multiple models to solve a particular learning task. This methodology imitates the human beings nature to seek various opinions before making a crucial decision, such as choosing a particular medical treatment [7]. The fundamental principle is to give a weight to each of the individual opinions and combine them all in order to obtain a decision that is better than those obtained by each one of them separately.

Ensemble methods usually improve the predictive power of individual models. These methods work particularly well when used with decision trees as base models, which is known as a decision forest. As with other ensemble methods, two principles must be followed to build an accurate forest [7]:

- Diversity: each individual decision tree must be sufficiently different from the others.
- Predictive power: the predictive power of individual trees should be the best possible or at least better than a random prediction model.

To design a method based on these principles is challenging for two reasons. First, the principles are contradictory because accurate models tend to be similar to each other and the highest diversity can be achieved among models that are not related with the problem. Second, an increase in diversity does not necessarily imply an increase in the accuracy of the ensemble [4]. To find a good tradeoff, it is theoretically and empirically proved that the accuracy of the decision forest is positively correlated with the degree to which the errors committed by the trees are not correlated [12].

Tree diversity can be achieved by modifying the tree induction procedure. Since most methods for tree induction follow a top-down greedy procedure, the modifications are aimed to explore different feature relations that might appear as non-optimal in the short term. The classical tree induction algorithm can be summarized in the following steps. For a given set of instances I described according to a set of features F and belonging to a set of classes C:

1. Check stop conditions. The induction procedure ends if all the objects in I belong to the same class.
2. Generate split candidates. Split candidates are generated taking into account the type and values of the features in I.
3. Evaluate split candidates, usually by evaluating the lose in impurity of the splitting.
4. Select the split candidate to generate the node based on the split evaluation.
5. Split the objects based on the selected candidate, and recursively execute the same set of steps.

To generate the best decision tree, single-tree methods usually select the top evaluated split, using all available features and using all the available objects. In this way, to generate diversity, the forest inductor can: (1) use a subset of the available objects, (2) use a subset of the available features, (3) select one of the non-optimal splits, or (4) modify other parameters in the inductor, like the equation to evaluate the split. Some examples of existing algorithms following these ideas are the following:

– Bagging [5] randomly chooses the instances that are part of the training set with which each tree is built.
– Random Subspaces [10] builds each tree using a random sample of the features in the original training set.
– Boosting [13] considers the information contained in previous trees to build the remaining decision trees. After building each tree, Boosting adjust the weight of the objects according to how good they are classified by the forest. Due to this, the quality of individual trees deteriorates on each iteration and Boosting depends of a particular weighting scheme to achieve higher accuracies.
– Delete Best Feature [9]. This method deletes the feature appearing in the root node from the available features to build the remaining decision trees.
– Delete Best Property and Delete Best Property by Level [9] forbid used properties (pair feature - value) from appearing in the remaining decision trees. Together with Delete Best Feature, these methods are deterministic.

Random Forest [6] is probably the most cited and accurate decision forest builder. Random Forest uses unpruned decision trees, whose outputs are combined using unweighted votes. To induce each random tree, randomness is injected into the construction algorithm at two different points. First, each decision tree is trained using a sample of instances taken with replacement of the original training set (like Bagging). Second, candidate splits are generated based on a random feature subset instead of using all available features, and the best split is selected.

3   Proactive Forest

Random Forest takes the best candidate split from the selected features. This could cause the most relevant features to be selected in many different trees in the ensemble, decreasing the diversity of the entire collection. Frequently, many trees in the forest have the same features appearing in different levels of the tree. This decrease in the diversity of the ensemble members usually has a negative impact in the ensemble accuracy.

To increase the diversity of Random Forest inductor while maintaining the quality of the individual trees we introduce Proactive Forest. Proactive Forest uses the information of previously induced trees to modify the selection probability of features in the remaining trees. When some features are very important in the collection of already induced trees, their selection probability is decreased. On the other hand, features that have not being considered in the induction process have a higher chance to be selected in the remaining trees. Individual tree quality is guaranteed by selecting the best candidate split among selected features.

To calculate the feature importance, we use Mean Decrease Impurity metric (1) [6]. This metric evaluates the importance of a variable X_m for predicting Y by adding up the weighted impurity decreases $p(t)\Delta i(s_t, t)$ for all nodes t where X_m is used, averaged over all N_T trees in the forest. In this equation, $p(t)$ is the proportion N_t/N of samples reaching t, $v(s_t)$ is the variable used in split s_t, and $\Delta i(s_t, t) = i(t) - p_L i(t_L) - p_R i(t_R)$ is the impurity gain of node t.

$$ImpX_m = \frac{1}{N_T} \sum_T \sum_{t \in T : v(s_t) = X_m} p(t)\Delta i(s_t, t) \tag{1}$$

For building each decision node in the tree, Proactive Forest takes the best split from a feature subset selected from a roulette. In this roulette, each feature has a probability of selection $p(Feat)$. The larger the value of $p(F')$ is, the higher the probability of feature F' to be selected. The value of $p(Feat)$, which is initially set to $\frac{1}{FeatCount}$, is modified after building each tree using the following procedure.

Step 1. Calculate the importance of each feature $Imp(Feat)$ using (1).
Step 2. Update the feature selection probability by

$$p(Feat) \leftarrow p(Feat) * (1 - Imp(Feat) * \alpha * (tree\_idx/tree\_count))$$

where α is a diversity factor, $tree\_idx$ is the current tree index, and $tree\_count$ is the total number of trees. We performed an experiment for tuning the

α value, that was finally set to 0.1. Details about this experiment are not presented in this paper due to space limitations.

Step 3. Since $p(Feat)$ are probabilities, change their values to sum one by $p(Feat) \leftarrow \frac{p(Feat)}{\sum_{F \in AllFeats} p(F)}$.

4 Experimental Results

4.1 Experimental Setup

Experiments were performed in 32 databases of the UCI Repository for Machine Learning [2]. Databases, shown in Table 1, contain from 3 to 64 features, from 2 to 26 classes and from 106 to 20000 instances. All decision forests were composed of 100 unpruned trees.

Since methods to compare are not deterministic, we use a 5-times 10-fold cross-validation, averaging the results. For statistical comparisons, we use the Wilcoxon Signed-Ranks Test, as suggested by [8]. The Wilcoxon Signed Ranks Test is a non-parametric alternative to the paired t-test, which ranks the differences in performance of two classifiers for each data set, ignoring the signs, and compares the ranks for the positive and the negative differences.

4.2 Measuring Ensemble Diversity

In this section, we compare Random Forest with Proactive Forest in terms of generated diversity. Diversity is evaluated using the Percentage of Correct Diversity (PCD) [3]. PCD is defined as the proportion of instances classified correctly by between 10% and 90% of the ensemble members. In this way, the examples for which there is a general consensus are not considered useful to determine the diversity of the ensemble. On the contrary, if the classification of the example is ambiguous, then the classifiers, for at least that example, are said to be diverse.

Figure 1 shows the differences in PCD between Random Forest and Proactive Forest. In this way, positive values appear on those cases where Proactive Forest obtains higher values. This figure reveals that Proactive Forest obtains higher levels of diversity in most databases. In those databases where Random Forest generates more diversity, the magnitude of differences is smaller.

4.3 Measuring Classifier Accuracy

In this section, we compare the accuracy of Random Forest and Proactive Forest. Accuracy, which is the ratio of good objects correctly classified, is the most popular measure of classifier behavior.

Figure 2 shows the differences in the average accuracy between Random Forest and Proactive Forest, so positive values are obtained for database where Proactive Forest behave better. As the figure shows, Proactive Forest obtains higher accuracies in most databases. In those databases where the difference is negative, its absolute value is smaller than in the positive differences.

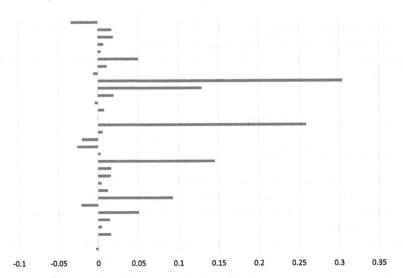

Fig. 1. Difference of diversity values between Proactive Forest and Random Forest per database (Rows)

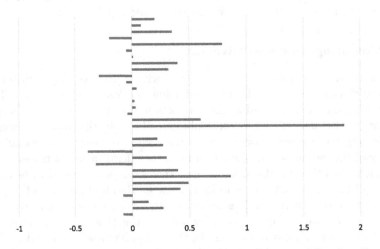

Fig. 2. Difference of accuracy values between Proactive Forest and Random Forest per database (Rows)

In the statistical comparison, Wilcoxon test determines that there is a significant increase in accuracy (0.1579) when using Proactive Forest compared to Random Forest, $W = 402.0$, p-value $= 0.010$ (p-value ≤ 0.05). Then, the hypothesis that both classifiers have equal accuracy can be rejected.

Table 1. Description of the databases used.

Database	Instances	Features	Classes
balance scale	625	4	3
car	1728	6	4
cmc	1473	9	3
credit-g	1000	20	2
diabetes	768	8	2
ecoli	336	7	8
flags religion	194	29	8
glass	214	9	6
haberman	306	3	2
heart-statlog	270	13	2
ionosphere	351	34	2
iris	150	4	3
kr-vs-kp	3196	36	2
letter	20000	16	26
liver	345	6	2
lymph	148	18	4
molecular	106	58	2
nursery	12960	8	5
optdigits	5620	64	10
page blocks	5473	10	5
pendigits	10992	16	10
segment	2310	19	7
solar flare 1	323	12	6
solar flare 2	1066	12	6
sonar	208	60	2
spambase	4601	57	2
splice	3190	61	3
tae	151	5	3
vehicle	846	18	4
vowel	990	13	11
wdbc	569	30	2
wine	178	13	3

5   Conclusions and Future Work

In this paper, we introduce Proactive Forest, a new method for generating ensembles of decision trees. Proactive Forest modifies the feature selection procedure of the classical Random Forest algorithm in order to increase the tree diversity without sacrificing the individual tree quality. The new feature selection procedure uses the information contained in the already built decision trees in order to bias the selection toward the less explored features in the ensemble. Experiments on a collection of repository databases show that the trees generated by Proactive Forest are more diverse. This has a clear impact in the ensemble accuracy.

Proactive Forest has some limitations that need to be explored in future works. First, it is slower than the original classifier because of the computation of the feature selection probability and its use in the induction procedure. Second, because of the dependence among the tree builder with previous trees, Proactive Forest is harder to parallelize. Finally, accuracy and diversity results are dependent of the α parameter, and this dependency must be explored in depth.

References

1. Agrawal, P., Varakantham, P.: Proactive and reactive coordination of non-dedicated agent teams operating in uncertain environments. In: Proceedings of the 26th International Joint Conference on Artificial Intelligence, IJCAI 2017, pp. 28–34. AAAI Press (2017)
2. Bache, K., Lichman, M.: UCI machine learning repository (2013). http://archive.ics.uci.edu/ml
3. Banfield, R.E., Hall, L.O., Bowyer, K.W., Kegelmeyer, W.P.: A new ensemble diversity measure applied to thinning ensembles. In: Windeatt, T., Roli, F. (eds.) MCS 2003. LNCS, vol. 2709, pp. 306–316. Springer, Heidelberg (2003). https://doi.org/10.1007/3-540-44938-8_31
4. Bi, Y.: The impact of diversity on the accuracy of evidential classifier ensembles. Int. J. Approx. Reason. 53(4), 584–607 (2012)
5. Breiman, L.: Bagging predictors. Mach. Learn. 24(2), 123–140 (1996)
6. Breiman, L.: Random forests. Mach. Learn. 45(1), 5–32 (2001)
7. Dai, Q., Ye, R., Liu, Z.: Considering diversity and accuracy simultaneously for ensemble pruning. Appl. Soft Comput. 58, 75–91 (2017)
8. Derrac, J., Garca, S., Molina, D., Herrera, F.: A practical tutorial on the use of nonparametric statistical tests as a methodology for comparing evolutionary and swarm intelligence algorithms. Swarm Evol. Comput. 1(1), 3–18 (2011)
9. García-Borroto, M., Martínez-Trinidad, J., Carrasco-Ochoa, J.: Finding the best diversity generation procedures for mining contrast patterns. Expert Syst. Appl. 42(11), 4859–4866 (2015)
10. Ho, T.K.: The random subspace method for constructing decision forests. IEEE Trans. Pattern Anal. Mach. Intell. 20(8), 832–844 (1998)
11. Moghadam, A.N., Ravanmehr, R.: Multi-agent distributed data mining approach for classifying meteorology data: case study on Iran's synoptic weather stations. Int. J. Environ. Sci. Technol. 15(1), 149–158 (2018)
12. Sheng, W., Shan, P., Chen, S., Liu, Y., Alsaadi, F.E.: A niching evolutionary algorithm with adaptive negative correlation learning for neural network ensemble. Neurocomputing 247, 173–182 (2017)
13. Sun, Y., Wong, A.: Boosting an associative classifier. IEEE Trans. Knowl. Data Eng. 18, 988–992 (2006)

Student Desertion Prediction Using Kernel Relevance Analysis

Jorge Fernández[1]([✉]), Angelica Rojas[2,3], Genaro Daza[2], Diana Gómez[2], Andrés Álvarez[1], and Álvaro Orozco[1]

[1] Automatics Research Group, Pereira, Colombia
jorgeferram17@utp.edu.co
[2] Vicerrectoria de Responsabilidad Social y Bienestar Universitario, Universidad Tecnológica de Pereira, Pereira, Colombia
angelica.rojas@utp.edu.co
[3] Maestria en Administracion del Desarrollo Humano y Organizacional, Universidad Tecnológica de Pereira, Pereira, Colombia

Abstract. This paper presents a kernel-based relevance analysis to support student desertion prediction. Our approach, termed KRA-SD, is twofold: (i) A feature ranking based on centered kernel alignment to match demographic, academic, and biopsychosocial measures with the output labels (deserter/not deserter), and (ii) classification stage based on k-nearest neighbors and support vector machines to predict the desertion. For concrete testing, the student desertion database of the Universidad Tecnologica de Pereira is employed to assess the KRA-SD under a training, validation, and testing scheme. Attained results show that the proposed approach can recognize the main features related to the student desertion achieving an 85.64% of accuracy. Therefore, the proposed system aims to serve as a handy tool for planning strategies to prevent students from leaving the university without finishing their studies.

Keywords: Student desertion · Relevance analysis
Feature selection · Kernel methods

1 Introduction

The university desertion is the disruption of the formal higher education, that is, the students do not finish their studies leaving the university before graduation. In a strict sense, in Colombia, a student is considered a university deserter when the semestral university enrolment process is not completed for two consecutive periods. Thereby, the university desertion is a significant issue that affects the students, their family, the educational institute, and the whole society. As a personal matter, desertion cause frustration in students and families, as they fail to achieve one crucial part of their initial life project. For the institution, the desertion represents a reduction of the academic performance and the failure of institutional objectives. In the society, with student desertion the inequality

© Springer Nature Switzerland AG 2018
Y. Hernández Heredia et al. (Eds.): IWAIPR 2018, LNCS 11047, pp. 263–270, 2018.
https://doi.org/10.1007/978-3-030-01132-1_30

grows, as the job opportunities for students without a bachelor degree are limited. Furthermore, most of the students of public universities in Colombia are subsidized; therefore, desertion implies an economic loss for the state.

In Colombia, the Ministry of Education identified that 52% of the students that start a professional career do not finish it [4]. Additionally, the same institution reports that the university desertion rate during 2015 was 9.3%. Research about desertion considers four main analysis topics: socio-economic development, personal behavior, academic performance and institutional conditions. Individually, economic difficulties represent the primary issue for the desertion from around 39.52% university students in 2016 [2]. Particularly, in the Universidad Tecnológica de Pereira (UTP), there is significant interest to recognize the main variables related to the student desertion, and subsequently, develop a system to perform the desertion prediction. This system will enable the required attention to be delivered efficiently to those students with desertion risk.

Regarding the state-of-the-art methods devoted to the student desertion analysis, some data mining and machine learning-based approaches have been proposed to extract relevant information related to the desertion risk, e.g., decision trees, neural networks, Bayesian learning [2,6–8]. Nevertheless, most of the approaches require a vast number of features and complex models to achieve reliable results, not mentioning the lack of interpretability concerning the relationships between the prediction results and demographic, social, and biopsychological elements. It is worth noting that such relations can benefit the university to plan suitable strategies oriented to prevent student desertion. In [5] the authors analyze and weight the factors related to student desertion and graduation; therefore, an automatic feature selection for desertion and graduation prediction was developed, concerning the usage of the well-known sequential forward selection algorithm and decision trees learning. The validation was made using a private database from the Catholic University of Temuco, containing 15183 students and 76 variables; notwithstanding, such an approach does not consider a strict assessment.

Here, we introduce a new student desertion prediction system based on kernel-based feature relevance analysis; aiming to obtain an automatic classification system to separate students into deserter and not deserter classes. Namely, the method includes a centered kernel alignment (CKA) technique to recognize relevant variables related to student desertion. So, we match demographic, academic, and biopsychosocial measures with the output labels (deserter/not deserter) through non-linear representations [1]. Besides, our proposal benefits the computational efficiency, the numerical stabilization, and denoising capabilities. In turn, we perform a selection analysis based on the classification accuracy and the CKA-based feature ranking. In particular, a k-nearest neighbors and a support vector machine classifiers are used to predict the desertion. Attained results on a UTP database demonstrate that the approach proposed favors the identification of the main features related to the student desertion.

The rest of the paper is organized as follows: Sect. 2 presents the main theoretical background, Sect. 3 describes the experimental set-up, Sect. 4 the results and discussion, and finally, Sect. 5 shows the conclusions.

2   Kernel-Based Feature Relevance Analysis

Let $\{\boldsymbol{X} \in \mathbb{R}^{N \times D}, \boldsymbol{y} \in \{-1, 1\}^N\}$ be an input-output pair set holding N samples and D features. Here, the samples are related to a set of university students meanwhile the features correspond to qualitative and quantitative student desertion measures, e.g., demographic, social, academic, and psychological properties. Likewise, an output label $y_n = -1$ denotes a not deserter student, and $y_n = +1$ represents a deserter one ($n \in \{1, 2, \ldots N\}$). From $\boldsymbol{X}$, we aim to select $M < D$ relevant features according to their discrimination capability. Therefore, a *Centered Kernel Alignment* (CKA) approach is performed to determine the relevance weight from each student desertion feature, as follows [1]:

Let $\kappa_X : \mathbb{R}^D \times \mathbb{R}^D \to \mathbb{R}$ be a positive definite kernel function, which reflects an implicit mapping $\phi : \mathbb{R}^D \to \mathcal{H}_X$, associating an element $\boldsymbol{x}_n \in \mathbb{R}^D$ with the element $\phi(\boldsymbol{x}_n) \in \mathcal{H}_X$, that belongs to the Reproducing Kernel Hilbert Space (RKHS), $\mathcal{H}_X$. In particular, the Gaussian kernel is preferred since it seeks an RKHS with universal approximation capability, as follows [3,9]:

$$\kappa_X(\boldsymbol{x}_n, \boldsymbol{x}_{n'}; \sigma) = \exp\left(-v^2(\boldsymbol{x}_n, \boldsymbol{x}_{n'})/2\sigma^2\right); \; n, n' \in \{1, 2, \ldots, N\}, \qquad (1)$$

where $v(\cdot, \cdot) : \mathbb{R}^D \times \mathbb{R}^D \to \mathbb{R}$ is a distance function in the input space, and $\sigma \in \mathbb{R}^+$ is the kernel bandwidth that rules the observation window within the assessed similarity metric. Likewise, for the output labels space $\mathcal{L} = \{-1, 1\}$, we also set a positive definite kernel $\kappa_L : \mathcal{L} \times \mathcal{L} \to \mathcal{H}_L$. In this case, the pairwise similarity distance between samples is defined as $\kappa_L(y_n, y_{n'}) = \delta(y_n - y_{n'})$, being $\delta(\cdot)$ the delta function. Each of the above defined kernels reflects a different notion of similarity and represents the elements of the matrices $\mathbf{K}_X, \mathbf{K}_L \in \mathbb{R}^{N \times N}$, respectively. In turn, to evaluate how well the kernel matrix $\mathbf{K}_X$ matches the target $\mathbf{K}_L$, we use the statistical alignment between those two kernel matrices as [1]:

$$\hat{\rho}(\mathbf{K}_X, \mathbf{K}_L) = \frac{\langle \bar{\mathbf{K}}_X, \bar{\mathbf{K}}_L \rangle_{\mathrm{F}}}{\sqrt{\langle \bar{\mathbf{K}}_X \bar{\mathbf{K}}_X \rangle_{\mathrm{F}} \langle \bar{\mathbf{K}}_L \bar{\mathbf{K}}_L \rangle_{\mathrm{F}}}}, \qquad (2)$$

where the notation $\bar{\mathbf{K}}$ stands for the centered kernel matrix calculated as $\bar{\mathbf{K}} = \tilde{\boldsymbol{I}} \mathbf{K} \tilde{\boldsymbol{I}}$, being $\tilde{\boldsymbol{I}} = \boldsymbol{I} - \mathbf{1}^\top \mathbf{1}/N$ the empirical centering matrix, $\boldsymbol{I} \in \mathbb{R}^{N \times N}$ is the identity matrix, and $\mathbf{1} \in \mathbb{R}^N$ is an all-ones vector. The notation $\langle \cdot, \cdot \rangle_{\mathrm{F}}$ represents the matrix-based Frobenius norm. Hence, Eq. (2) is a data driven estimator that allows to quantify the similarity between the input feature space and the output label space [1]. In particular, for the Gaussian kernel κ_X, the Mahalanobis distance is selected to perform the pairwise comparison between samples:

$$v_{\boldsymbol{A}}^2(\boldsymbol{x}_n, \boldsymbol{x}_{n'}) = (\boldsymbol{x}_n - \boldsymbol{x}_{n'})\boldsymbol{A}\boldsymbol{A}^\top(\boldsymbol{x}_n - \boldsymbol{x}_{n'})^\top, \; n, n' \in \{1, 2, \ldots, N\}, \qquad (3)$$

where the matrix $A \in \mathbb{R}^{D \times P}$ holds the linear projection in the form $w_n = x_n A$, with $w_n \in \mathbb{R}^P$, and being $AA^\top$ the corresponding inverse covariance matrix in Eq. (3), assuming $P \leq D$. Therefore, intending to compute the projection matrix A, the formulation of a CKA-based optimizing function can be integrated into the following kernel-based learning algorithm:

$$\hat{A} = \arg \max_A \log \left(\hat{\rho}(\mathbf{K}_X(A; \sigma), \mathbf{K}_L) \right), \qquad (4)$$

where the logarithm function is employed for mathematical convenience. The optimization problem from Eq. (4) is solved using a recursive solution based on the well-known gradient descent approach. After the estimation of the projection matrix $\hat{A}$, we assess the relevance of the D input features extracted from X. To this end, the most contributing features are assumed to have the higher values of similarity relationship with the provided output labels. Specifically, the CKA-based relevance analysis calculates the feature relevance vector index $\varrho \in \mathbb{R}^D$, holding elements $\varrho_d \in \mathbb{R}^+$ that allow to measure the contribution from each of the d-th input feature in building the projection matrix $\hat{A}$. Hence, to calculate those elements, a stochastic measure of variability is utilized as follows: $\varrho_d = \mathbb{E}_P \{|a_{d,p}|\}$; where $p \in \{1, 2, \ldots P\}$, $d \in \{1, 2, \ldots D\}$, and $a_{d,p} \in \hat{A}$.

The next step is to sort the features according to their relevance value ϱ_d, and generate a performance curve by iteratively classifying the dataset while adding in succession the features ranked. Consequently, the input matrix is now $\hat{X} \in \mathbb{R}^{N \times M}$, where $M < D$ is the number of relevant features concerning the classification performance.

3   Experimental Set-Up

Database. To test our *kernel-based relevance analysis approach to support desertion prediction* (KRA-SD), we employ the student desertion dataset of the Universidad Tecnologica de Pereira (SD-UTP), which belongs to the Vicerrectoria de Responsabilidad Social y Bienestar Universitario from the same institution. For concrete testing, we use the information of the first semester in 2016, yielding an input-output set of $N = 16826$ students, 1382 labeled as deserter and 15444 as not deserter. The labels were fixed according to the SPADIES system of the National Minister of Education of Colombia. Moreover, $D = 20$ features are considered, which include: gender, age, career's program, career's faculty, shift work, student's high school, student's city, student's department; the following binary measures: the student's city is a capital or not, the student was attended by Programa de Atencion Integral (PAI-UTP) or not, the student received bio-psychosocial attention (BPS) or not, the student received academic support or not, the student received social-economic attention or not; number of PAI attentions, student's social stratum, current semester, number of available credits, number of periods completed, and average grade.

KRA-SD Training. A k-means based down-sampling is used to balance the input data. So, we select $N' = 3104$ samples, 2001 holding not deserter labels and the remaining 1103 with deserter outputs. Next, we compute the feature relevance vector index $\varrho \in \mathbb{R}^D$ as explained in section Sect. 2, fixing $P = 5$ as the required number of dimensions to preserve the 90% of the input data variability. Afterwards, we estimate a performance curve by adding one-by-one the features ranked regarding their relevance value in ϱ. For concrete testing, a k-nearest neighbor classifier (k-NN) is trained for each feature subset towards a training, validation, and testing partition. In particular, training and validation sets are built under a nested 10-fold cross-validation strategy, to search the number of neighbors from the set $\{1, 3, 5, 7, 9, 11\}$. Next, the best subset of features $\hat{X} \in \mathbb{R}^{N' \times M}$ concerning the validation accuracy is used to train a Gaussian kernel-based support vector machine classifier (SVM), varying the kernel bandwidth between the range $[0.1\sigma_o, \sigma_o]$, being $\sigma_o \in \mathbb{R}^+$ the median of the input space Euclidean distances; and searching the regularization parameter within the set $\{0.1, 1, 100, 500, 1000\}$. Finally, the best SVM-based classification model is evaluated in the testing set with $N - N'$ samples. Figure 1 summarizes the KRA-SD training pipeline. It is worth noting that all experiments are performed using the Matlab software on a Lenovo Y50-70 notebook equipped with a graphics core NVIDIA GEFORCE GTX 960M and an Intel processor Core i7-4710HQ. The CKA code was developed by Alvarez-Meza et al. in [1] and is publicly available[1].

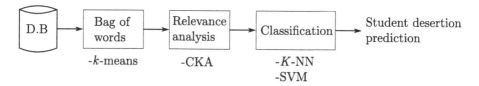

Fig. 1. Sketch of the proposed kernel-based relevance analysis to support student desertion prediction (KRA-SD).

4   Results and Discussions

Figure 2(a) shows the normalized relevance value of the provided demographic, social, academic, and biopsychological features on the SD-UTP database. As seen, social features exhibit a remarkable relevance regarding our KRA-SD-based criteria; especially, measures related to the PAI program of the Vicerrectoria de Responsabilidad Social y Bienestar Universitario, present the highest relevance. Hence, university programs related to the analysis and prevention of desertion risk, match the desertion labels concerning the CKA-based analysis presented in Sect. 2. Alike, demographic information such as gender and student's city and department, show a considerable influence. Now, as seen in Fig. 2(b), the provided subset of samples after the bag of words-based down-sampling, provides an insight into the data overlapping. Remarkably, the relevance values in Fig. 2(a) mainly depend on the discrimination capability of the Gaussian kernel

---

[1] https://github.com/andresmarino07utp/EKRA-ES.

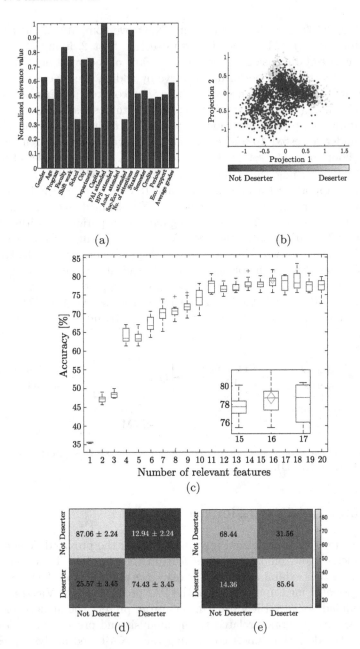

Fig. 2. Student desertion prediction results on the SD-UTP data. (a) Feature relevance values. (b) 2D input data projection using CKA. (c) Performance curve for a k-NN classifier by adding one-by-one the features ranked based on KRA-SD (green diamond represents the best subset of relevant features). (d) Confusion matrix for the validation set in $\hat{X}$ ($M = 16$) under a nested 10-fold cross-validation scheme using a SVM classifier. (e) Confusion matrix for the testing set using a SVM classifier. (Color figure online)

in Eq. (1). Also, the overlapping of the studied classes (deserter vs. not deserter), can also be attributed to the different feature domains, e.g., binary and continuous measures, and to the imbalance issues of the SD-UTP database. Nonetheless, the k-NN's performance curve in Fig. 2(c) that is computed using the relevance ranking in Fig. 2(a), demonstrates that our KRA-SD approach extracts discriminative features, including binary and continuous measures, which facilitate the desertion prediction. In this sense, a reliable result (high classification accuracy and precision), can be obtained with the first $M = 16$ relevant features.

Furthermore, as is evidenced by the confusion matrix of the validation sets in Fig. 2(d), an SVM classifier over the first 16 most relevant features, is able to obtain $87.06 \pm 2.24\%$ and $74.43 \pm 3.45\%$ accuracies for the not deserter and deserter classes, respectively. As expected, the SVM can achieve a more reliable prediction than the k-NN because of its generalization capability. Finally, Fig. 2(e) shows the student prediction results for the testing set, that is, we predicted the output label for the remaining $N - N' = 13722$ samples students that were not employed during the KRA-SD training. Achieved results display a 68.44% and an 85.64% of accuracy for the not deserter and deserter classes, respectively (70.05% average). In particular, our approach can infer better the desertion risk than the not deserter label, which is more useful for the university programs aiming to avoid a reduction of the academic performance. Remarkably, the results obtained agree with the ones presented in [5], which attain an average accuracy of 86.1% from an input set of 76 variables. However, our approach measures only 20 input variables and employs a more strict assessment scheme.

5   Conclusions

A kernel-based relevance analysis is introduced to support student desertion prediction (KRA-SD). Our approach highlights the primary features to predict between the deserter and not deserter students. Therefore, KRA-SD quantifies the relevance of demographic, academic, and biopsychological parameters towards a CKA-based algorithm that matches the input space with the output labels, to support further prediction stages. Attained results on the SD-UTP database demonstrate that our proposal correctly predicts the 85.64% of deserter students using 16 features; under a strict training, validation, and testing assessment scheme. In particular, according to the performed relevance analysis, the best subset of relevant features include measures related to the PAI program of the Vicerrectoria de Responsabilidad Social y Bienestar Universitario, and demographic information such as gender and student's city and department. Remarkably, KRA-SD is comparable to state-of-the-art results concerning the trade-off between the accuracy achieved and the required number of features, with a database obtained from students in other country [5]. As future work, authors plan to extend the relevance analysis by using information theoretic measures and graph theory. Also, a KRA-SD enhancement based on an SVM classifier devoted to imbalance issues could be an exciting research line.

Acknowledgments. Under grants provided by the Colciencias project: "ATTENDO" - code: FP44842-424-2017. Also, we would like to thank the support of the UTP's Vicerrectoria de Responsabilidad Social y Bienestar Universitario.

References

1. Alvarez-Meza, A.M., Orozco-Gutierrez, A., Castellanos-Dominguez, G.: Kernel-based relevance analysis with enhanced interpretability for detection of brain activity patterns. Front. Neurosci. **11**, 550 (2017)
2. Argote, I., Jimenez, R.: Detección de patrones de deserción en los programas de pregrado de la universidad mariana de san juan de pasto, aplicando el proceso de descubrimiento de conocimiento sobre base de datos (kdd) y su implementación en modelos matemáticos de predicción. In: Congresos CLABES (2016)
3. Brockmeier, A.J., et al.: Information-theoretic metric learning: 2-D linear projections of neural data for visualization. In: EMBC, pp. 5586–5589. IEEE (2013)
4. Gartner Isaza, M.L., Gallego Giraldo, C.: La deserción estudiantil en la universidad de caldas: sus características, factores determinantes y el impacto de las estrategias institucionales de prevención. In: Conferência latino-americana sobre o abandono, V, Talca, Peru (2015)
5. Peralta, B., Poblete, T., Caro, L.: Automatic feature selection for desertion and graduation prediction: a chilean case. In: SCCC, pp. 1–8. IEEE (2016)
6. Pereira, R.T., Romero, A.C., Toledo, J.J.: Aplicación de la minería de datos en la extracción de perfiles de deserción estudiantil [application of data mining in extracting student dropout profiles]. Ventana Informática (28), 31–47 (2013)
7. Spositto, O., Etcheverry, M., Ryckeboer, H., Bossero, J.: Aplicación de técnicas de minería de datos para la evaluación del rendimiento académico y la deserción estudiantil. In: Novena Conferencia Iberoamericana en Sistemas, Cibernética e Informática, CISCI, vol. 29, p. 6 (2010)
8. Torres, C.Z., Ramos, C.A., Moraga, J.L.: Estudio de variables que influyen en la deserción de estudiantes universitarios de primer año, mediante minería de datos. Ciencia Amazónica:(Iquitos) **6**(1), 73–84 (2016)
9. Wang, Y.: Tracking neural modulation depth by dual sequential monte carlo estimation on point processes for brain-machine interfaces. IEEE Trans. Biomed. Eng. **63**(8), 1728–1741 (2016)

Medical Equipment Replacement Prioritization Indicator Using Multi-criteria Decision Analysis

Tlazohtzin Mora-García[1], Fernanda Piña-Quintero[2],
and Martha Ortiz-Posadas[1($\boxtimes$)]

[1] Electrical Engineering, Universidad Autónoma Metropolitana-Iztapalapa,
Av. San Rafael Atlixco 186, Col. Vicentina, 09340, Mexico City, Mexico
tlazohtzin@live.com, posa@xanum.uam.mx
[2] Service of Electro-Medicine, National Institute of Pediatrics,
Mexico City, Mexico
ing.ferpina@gmail.com

Abstract. The objective of this work was to develop an evaluation tool based on Multi-criteria decision analysis, for the replacement of older medical equipment installed at the National Institute of Pediatrics from Mexico, considering technical and economic aspects. The result of such tool was an indicator that provides the functionality condition of the medical equipment and determines its replacement priority. The indicator was applied to a sample of medical equipment located at the critical care units from the Institute.

Keywords: Medical equipment replacement · Medical equipment assessment
Replacement priority indicator · Multi-criteria decision analysis

1 Introduction

In developing countries, as Mexico, decision-makers in the healthcare sector face a global challenge of developing evidence-based methods for making decisions about medical equipment (ME) available in hospitals. The objective of this work was to develop an indicator for prioritize the replacement of older medical equipment installed at the National Institute of Pediatrics from Mexico, considering two aspects: technical and economic. The evaluation tool was based on the Multi-criteria decision analysis (MCDA) approach, and the result was an indicator called Medical Equipment Replacement Prioritization Indicator (MERUPI), which provides information about the ME functionality and determines its replacement priority. The indicator was applied to a sample of ME located at two intensive care units from the Institute.

2 Technological Problem

The National Institute of Pediatrics from Mexico is a tertiary public hospital with 243 beds. It has a total of 6165 medical equipment, 3699 are located in clinical and research laboratories and 2466 in healthcare areas. About 1603 equipment is less than or equal

© Springer Nature Switzerland AG 2018
Y. Hernández Heredia et al. (Eds.): IWAIPR 2018, LNCS 11047, pp. 271–279, 2018.
https://doi.org/10.1007/978-3-030-01132-1_31

to 10 years old, 1356 is between 11 and 20 years old and, 3206 is more than 20 years old [1]. Obsolescence is a characteristic related to the medical equipment antiquity. It implies the increasingly difficult to obtain spare parts, accessories and consumables for its correct operation, with the consequence that the equipment will stop working so, it will be necessary to acquire a new one to continue providing healthcare services to patients. The evaluation tool developed in this work provides an auxiliary criterion for making decisions about the replacement priority of the ME, the rational investment of the financial resource and, where appropriate, the acquisition of new medical equipment.

3   Mathematical Model

In order to realize the mathematical model we selected the Multi-criteria decision analysis (MCDA) which is usually an *ex ante* evaluation tool, and is particularly used for the examination of the intervention's strategic choices. This assessment can take place to collect the opinions of decision-makers and beneficiaries about the effectiveness of the activities in order to reach the given objective [2].

The mathematical modeling involved the process of variable selection, which yields a description of the objects under study (medical equipment), and the knowledge of their relative importance (the one such variables have in this case). We defined the variables and their domains, as well as their weights to define, for each variable, the relative valuations of a shift between the top and bottom of a defined domain. Afterwards, we generated two partial indicators for each aspect (technical and economic), and with both of these we generated a global one, the Medical Equipment Replacement Prioritization Indicator (MERUPI).

3.1   Variables

In total twelve variables (x_i) were defined: eight for technical aspect and four for the economic aspect. Each variable has a qualitative domain (Q_i) used by the technical staff of the Service of Electro-medicine (SE) for evaluating the medical equipment. However, for mathematical modelling it was necessary to assign a quantitative domain (M_i) into [0, 1], where 1 represents the worst condition of the medical equipment and zero the best. Each variable and each aspect has different importance, and a weighting was defined for each of them, jointly with the technical staff of the SE (Table 1). The relevance for the technical aspect was $\omega_T = 0.90$, and for the economic aspect was $\omega_E = 0.40$.

Technical Variables. Eight variables were defined for evaluating technical aspect of medical equipment (Table 1). Their qualitative and quantitative domains are shown in Table 2. Observe that the variable "Equipment function" (x_5) defines the application and environment in which the equipment item will operate and it considers 10 functions [3]. "Physical risk" (x_7) defines the worst-case scenario in the event of equipment malfunction [3]. "Maintenance requirement" (x_8) describes the level and frequency of maintenance according to the manufacturer's indications or accumulated experience [3].

Table 1. Variables and weighting defined for technical and economic aspects

Technical aspect ($\omega_T = 0.90$)			Economic aspect ($\omega_E = 0.40$)	
x_i	(ρ_i)	Variable name	x_i	Variable name
x_1	0.9	Consumables available next 5 years	x_9	Purchase cost
x_2	0.8	Spare parts available next 5 years	x_{10}	Maintenance cost
x_3	0.7	Equipment age	x_{11}	Consumables cost
x_4	0.6	Days of the equipment out of service	x_{12}	Useful lifetime
x_5	0.5	Equipment function		
x_6	0.4	Equipment failure frequency		
x_7	0.3	Physical risk		
x_8	0.2	Maintenance requirement		

Table 2. Variables (x_i) and quantitative (M_i) and qualitative domains (Q_i) for technical aspect

x_i	M_i	Q_i	x_i	M_i	Q_i
x_1	(0, 1)	Yes/no			
x_2	(0, 1)	Yes/no	x_6	0.0	[0, 1]
x_3	0.0	[1, 5]		0.4	[2, 4]
	0.4	[6, 10]		0.6	[5, 7]
	0.6	[11, 15]		0.8	[8, 10]
	0.8	[16, 20]		1.0	>10
					(failures/period evaluated)
	1.0	[20, ∞]			
x_4	0.0	[0, 1]	x_7	0.0	No significant risk (NSR)
	0.4	[2, 3]		0.4	Patient discomfort (PD)
	0.6	[4, 5]		0.6	Inappropriate therapy or
	0.8	[6, 7]			misdiagnosis (ITM)
	1.0	[8, 10]		0.8	Patient or operator injury (POI)
		>10		1.0	Patient or operator death (POD)
x_5	0.0	Non patient (NP)			
	0.2	Patient related and other (PR)	x_8	0.0	Minimum (M)
	0.3	Computer and related (CR),		0.4	Less than the average (LA)
	0.4	Laboratory accessories (LR)		0.6	Average (A)
	0.5	Analytical laboratory (AL)		0.8	More than the average (MA)
	0.6	Additional monitoring and diagnostic (AMD)		1.0	Importants (I)
	0.7	Surgical and intensive care monitoring (SICM)			
	0.8	Physical therapy and treatment (PTT)			
	0.9	Surgical and intensive care (SIC)			
	1.0	Life support (LS)			

Economic Variables. Four variables were defined for evaluating economic aspect of medical equipment (Table 1), and their qualitative and quantitative domains are shown in Table 3. Note that Q_i is expressed in thousands of dollars (KUSD) and the variables have no weight because they generate four partial indicators (I_j) and, these were weighting (γ_j) later, jointly with technical staff of the SE (Table 4).

Once variables for both aspects were defined, we proceed to generate de partial indicators (technical and economic) as well as the global indicator called Medical Equipment Substitution Prioritization Indicator (MERUPI), as follows.

Table 3. Variables (x_i) and quantitative (M_i) and qualitative (Q_i) domains for economic aspect

x_i	M_i	Q_i (KUSD)	x_i	M_i	Q_i (KUSD)	x_i	M_i	Q_i (KUSD)
x_9	0.0	0,	x_{10}	0.0	{0	x_{11}	0.0	{0
	0.1	[0–4)		0.2	(0–0.15)		0.2	(0–0.1)
	0.2	[0.4–10)		0.3	[0.15–0.45)		0.3	[0.1–0.25)
	0.3	[10–12.5)		0.4	[0.45–4)		0.4	[0.25–1)
	0.4	[12.5–17.5)		0.5	[4–10)		0.5	[1–3.5)
	0.5	[17.5–25)		0.6	[10–30)		0.6	[3.5–10)
	0.6	[25–37.5)		0.7	[30–50)		0.7	[10–30)
	0.7	[37.5–50)		0.8	[50–125)		0.8	[30–50)
	0.8	[50–75)		0.9	[125–150]		0.9	[50–75]
	0.9	[75–110]		1.0	>150}		1.0	>75}
	1.0	>110						

3.2 Partial Indicators

Technical Indicator (I_T). A mathematical function (1) was developed by incorporating the eight variables and its relevance factor (Table 1).

$$I_T = \frac{\sum_{i=1}^{n} \rho_i x_i}{N_T} \tag{1}$$

where x_i is the variable, i = {1, ..., 8}, ρ_i is the relevance factor for x_i, and N_T is the normalization factor for obtaining the I_T result into [0, 1]. N_T is calculated by (2).

$$N_T = \sum_{i=1}^{n} \rho_i M_{imáx} \tag{2}$$

where $M_{imáx}$ is the maximum value of M_i for each variable x_i. Then, $N_T = 4.4$.

Economic Indicator (I_E). First, four partial indicators (I_j) with their respective weighting (γ_j) were defined (Table 4). Indicators I_1 and I_4 were normalized. In the case of I_1, because of the use of the 2017 Mexico inflation rate ($i_R = 6.77$) [4] and, substituting the maximum value (1) of the variables, we may obtain $I_1 = 7.77$ therefore, to get the result into [0, 1], it was necessary to divide by 7.77. In the case of I_3, we use the years of the variables "Equipment age" (x_3) and "useful lifetime" (x_{12}), and it was divided by 3 (the result of dividing the maximum value of $x_3 = 24$ and the minimum value of $x_{12} = 8$).

Table 4. Economic partial indicators and their relevance

I_i	Indicator name	Mathematical function	γ_i
I_1	Purchase cost at present	$I_1 = (x_9(1 + x_3 i_R))/7.77$	0.2
I_2	Maintenance cost	$I_2 = x_{10}$	0.8
I_3	Consumables cost	$I_3 = x_{11}$	0.4
I_4	Depreciation %	$I_4 = (x_3/x_{12})/3$	0.6

Then, we defined a global economic indicator (I_E) involving all partial indicators described above:

$$I_E = \frac{\sum_{j=1}^{4} \gamma_j I_j}{N} \tag{3}$$

where I_j is the indicator j, $j = \{1, ..., 4\}$; γ_j is the relevance for each indicator, and N_E is the normalization factor. N_E is calculated by (4):

$$N_E = \sum_{j=1}^{4} \gamma_j M_{jm\acute{a}x} \tag{4}$$

where $M_{jm\acute{a}x}$ is the maximum value of M_j for each variable I_j, $j = \{1, ...,4\}$. Given the maximum value for each $I_j = 1$ then, $N_E = 2$.

Medical Equipment Replacement Prioritization Indicator. The Medical Equipment Replacement Prioritization Indicator (MERUPI) is a mathematical function (5) that incorporates the two partial indicators and its relevance explained before:

$$MERUPI = \frac{\sum_{j=1}^{2} \omega_j I_j}{N_{MERUPI}} = \omega_E I_E + \omega_T I_T \tag{5}$$

$$N_{MERUPI} = \sum_{j=1}^{2} \omega_j I_{jm\acute{a}x} = 1.3 \tag{6}$$

3.3 Application of the Medical Equipment Replacement Prioritization Indicator

The Medical Equipment Replacement Prioritization Indicator (MERUPI) was applied to ten medical equipment located at the intensive care unit (ICU) and the neonatal intensive care unit (NICU) from the Institute: two vital signs monitor (VSM), two radiant heat cradles (RHC), two ventilators (V), two defibrillators (D), one electro-cardiograph (ECG) and one ultra-sonographer (US). It was considered the data from 2017 available in the records of the SE. In order to illustrate the application of the partial indicators as well as the MERUPI, we chose the vital sign monitor (SVM$_1$) located at ICU.

Application of the Technical Indicator (IT). To evaluate the technical aspect of VSM_1, we substitute in (1) the quantitative values of each variable and its weighting (Table 5).

$$I_{T_{MSV1}} = \frac{\begin{matrix} 0.9(1) + 0.8(1) + 0.7(1) + 0.6(0) + 0.5(0.6) + 0.4(0.4) \\ + 0.3(0.6) + 0.2(0.6) \end{matrix}}{4.4} = 0.72$$

This result means that MVS_1 has a deficient functionality (remember that the zero value is the best condition of the medical equipment and 1 the worst). This is consistent with its 24 years old and, the condition about the market no longer offers the consumables or spare parts necessary for its correct operation.

Application of the Economic Indicator (IE). To evaluate the economic aspect of the VSM_1, first we applied the four partial indicators. We substituted the quantitative values of each variable and its weighting from its economic description (Table 6) in the given expression for each partial indicator (Table 4):

$$I_{1_{MSV_1}} = \frac{x_{12}(1 + x_3 i_R)}{7.77} = \frac{0.1(1 + 1(6.77))}{7.77} = 0.10$$

$$I_{2_{MSV_1}} = x_{13} = 0.20, \quad I_{3_{MSV_1}} = x_{14} = 0.30, \quad I_{4_{MSV_1}} = \frac{x_3/x_{15}}{3} = \frac{24/10}{3} = 0.80$$

In order to calculate the global economic indicator I_{EMVS1} we substituted these four results in expression (3):

$$I_{E_{MSV_1}} = \frac{(0.2)(0.10) + (0.8)(0.20) + (0.4)(0.30) + (0.6)(0.80)}{2} = 0.39$$

This result means that the operating expenses of the monitor, from its acquisition to the present, represent almost 40%. Note that depreciation obtained the highest value $(I_{4_{MSV_1}} = 0.80)$ due to its 24 years old and considering its relevance (0.6), it has an important contribution to the result of I_E. On the other hand, although the maintenance result $(I_{2_{MSV_1}} = 0.20)$ was moderate, it has the highest relevance (0.8) so, its contribution into the I_E result is also important.

The results of the economic partial indicators as well as the global one (I_E) for all medical equipment are shown in Table 7. Note that defibrillator D_1 required the least expense for its operation, because it is 3 years old (Table 5). RHC_2 and MSV_1 obtained the highest value of I_E (0.43 and 0.39 respectively), because both are 24 years old (Table 5).

Table 5. Technical description of medical equipment in qualitative and quantitative terms

		Qualitative description					Quantitative description				
ICU	x_i	VSM_1	RHC_1	V_1	D_1	ECG	VSM_1	RHC_1	V_1	D_1	ECG
	x_1	no	yes	yes	yes	no	1	0	0	0	1
	x_2	no	yes	yes	yes	no	1	0	0	0	1
	x_3	24	10	12	3	15	1	0.4	0.6	0	0.8
	x_4	0	0	0	0	0	0	0	0	0	0
	x_5	AMD	SIC	LS	LS	AMD	0.6	0.9	1	1	0.6
	x_6	2	0	1	0	1	0.4	0	0	0	0
	x_7	ITM	POI	POD	POD	ITM	0.6	0.8	1	1	0.6
	x_8	A	A	A	MA	A	0.6	0.6	0.6	0.8	0.6
NICU	x_i	VSM_2	RHC_2	V_2	D_2	US	VSM_2	RHC_2	V_2	D_2	US
	x_1	Si	Si	Si	Si	Si	0	0	0	0	0
	x_2	Si	Si	Si	Si	Si	0	0	0	0	0
	x_3	5	24	9	7	5	0	1	0.4	0.4	0.5
	x_4	0	0	0	0	0	0	0	0.4	0	0
	x_5	AMD	SIC	LS	LS	AMD	0.6	0.9	1	1	0.6
	x_6	0	6	3	2	1	0	0.6	0.4	0.4	0
	x_7	ITM	POI	POD	POD	ITM	0.6	0.8	1	1	0.6
	x_8	A	A	A	MA	A	0.6	0.6	0.6	0.8	0.6

Table 6. Economic description of medical equipment in qualitative and quantitative terms

		x_i	MSV_1	CCR_1	V_1	D_1	ECG
Qualitative description	ICU	x_{12}	3777 (USD)	10668 (USD)	18397 (USD)	11310 (USD)	606 (USD)
		x_3	24	10	12	3	15
		x_{13}	13 (USD)	13 (USD)	2165 (USD)	0 (USD)	7 (USD)
		x_{14}	123 (USD)	19 (USD)	0 (USD)	78 (USD)	400 (USD)
	NICU	x_i	MSV_2	CCR_2	V_2	D_2	US
		x_{12}	8364 (USD)	1250 (USD)	33524 (USD)	11020 (USD)	55579 (USD)
		x_3	5	24	9	7	5
		x_{13}	13 (USD)	33 (USD)	2165 (USD)	26 (USD)	3953 (USD)
		x_{14}	425 (USD)	26 (USD)	0 (USD)	78 (USD)	7950 (USD)
Quantitative description		x_i	MSV_1	CCR_1	V_1	D_1	ECG
	ICU	x_{12}	0.1	0.3	0.5	0.3	0.1
		x_3	1	0.4	0.6	0	0.8
		x_{13}	0.2	0.3	0.2	0	0.2
		x_{14}	0.3	0.2	0	0.2	0.4
		x_i	MSV_2	CCR_2	V_2	D_2	US
	NICU	x_{12}	0.2	0.1	0.6	0.3	0.8
		x_3	0	1	0.4	0.4	0
		x_{13}	0.2	0.2	0.4	0.2	0.4
		x_{14}	0.4	0.2	0	0.2	0.4

Application of the Medical Equipment Replacement Prioritization Indicator. In order to do the final evaluation of the SVM_1 we applied the given expression (5) for MERUPI and substituting the I_T and I_E results and its weighting (0.90 and 0.40 respectively):

$$MERUPI_{VSM1} = \sum_{j=1}^{2} \omega_j I_j = \omega_T I_T + \omega_E I_E = (0.90)(0.72) + (0.40)(0.39) \cong 0.62$$

For the interpretation of the quantitative result of MERUPI, a qualitative scale was determined. There are 3 intervals that indicate where the equipment should be replaced: [0, 0.3) in long-term (10 years); [0.3, 0.6) in medium-term (6 years); and [0.6, 1] in short-term (3 years). These intervals were defined in conjunction with the technical staff of the SE and also, considering the purchase process at the Institute which takes about 2 years. According to the qualitative interpretation scale, the result $MERUPI_{VSM1} \cong 0.62$ indicates that the monitor VSM_1 must be replaced in the short term (3 years), because the equipment is 24 years old, it does not have consumables or spare parts available, and its depreciation (I_4) is 80%, therefore it is an obsolete equipment. The result of MERUPI for all medical equipment is shown in Table 8. Note that 6 of the 10 equipment require their replacement in the long-term (10 years). In the case of the ECG, the RHC_2 and the V_2 must be replaced in the medium term (6 years).

Table 7. Partials and global economic indicators results

ICU	I_i	VSM_1	RHC_1	V_1	D_1	ECG
	I_1	0.10	0.14	0.33	0.04	0.08
	I_2	0.20	0.30	0.20	0.00	0.20
	I_3	0.30	0.20	0.00	0.20	0.40
	I_4	0.80	0.42	0.50	0.10	0.50
	I_E	**0.39**	**0.30**	**0.26**	**0.07**	**0.32**
NICU	I_i	VSM_2	RHC_2	V_2	D_2	US
	I_1	0.03	0.10	0.29	0.14	0.10
	I_2	0.20	0.20	0.40	0.20	0.40
	I_3	0.40	0.20	0.00	0.20	0.40
	I_4	0.17	1.00	0.38	0.23	0.21
	I_E	**0.21**	**0.43**	**0.30**	**0.20**	**0.31**

Table 8. Technical, economic and MERUPI indicators results

Clinical area	Medical equipment	I_T	I_E	MERUPI	Replacement priority
ICU	VSM_1	0.72	0.39	0.62	3 years
	RHC_1	0.26	0.30	0.27	10 years
	V_1	0.30	0.26	0.29	10 years
	D_1	0.22	0.07	0.17	10 years
	ECG	0.65	0.32	0.55	6 years
NICU	VSM_2	0.14	0.21	0.16	10 years
	RHC_2	0.40	0.43	0.41	6 years
	V_2	0.27	0.30	0.31	6 years
	D_2	0.32	0.20	0.28	10 years
	US	0.19	0.31	0.23	10 years

4 Conclusions

The MERUPI indicator was a very useful tool to know the status of the functionality and the expenses of the operation of the medical equipment. This information provides an auxiliary criterion for making decisions about the medical equipment that should be replaced, and planning the purchase of the new equipment. Now we are currently working on the development of a clinical indicator that considers the impact of the medical equipment in the diagnosis and treatment of patients.

Later, a computational tool based on this model (MERUPI) will be developed with the objective to do the automatic evaluation of all the medical equipment available at the Institute and promoting a program of substitution of medical technology that allows to plan the acquisition for those equipment that require replacement in the short term (3 years).

References

1. Piña Quintero, M.F.: Technical report from the Service of Electro-medicine. National Institute of Pediatrics, Mexico City (2017). (in Spanish)
2. Department for Communities and Local Government: Multi-criteria analysis: a manual. Eland House Bressenden Place, London (2009)
3. World Health Organization: Medical equipment maintenance programme overview. Geneve: WHO (2011). World Health Organization. http://apps.who.int/iris/bitstream/handle/10665/44587/9789241501538_eng.pdf?sequence=1. Accessed 3 May 2018
4. Central Bank of Mexico: "Inflation rate". Banxico. http://www.banxico.org.mx/portal-inflacion/index.html. Accessed 4 May 2018

Imbalanced Data Classification Using a Relevant Information-Based Sampling Approach

Keider Hoyos[1]([✉]), Jorge Fernández[1], Beatriz Martinez[1], Óscar Henao[1], Álvaro Orozco[1], and Genaro Daza[2]

[1] Automatic Researh Group, Universidad Tecnológica de Pereira, Pereira, Colombia
jkhoyos@utp.edu.co
[2] Instituto de Epilepsia y Parkinson del Eje Cafetero, Pereira, Colombia

Abstract. The imbalanced data refer to datasets where the number of samples in one class (majority class) is much higher than the other (minority class) causing biased classifiers in favor of the majority class. Currently, it is difficult to develop an effective model using machine learning algorithms without considering data preprocessing to balance the imbalanced data sets. In this paper, we propose a Relevant Information-based under-sampling (RIS) approach to improve the classification performance for the minority class by selecting the most relevant samples from the majority class as training data. Our RIS approach is based on a self-organizing principle of relevant information, which allows extracting the underlying structure of the majority class preserving different levels of detail of the original data with a smaller number of samples. Additionally, the RIS captures the data structure beyond second order statistics by estimating information theoretic measures which quantify the statistical structure of the majority class accurately, decreasing the consequences of the imbalanced classes distribution problem. We test our methodology on synthetic and real-world imbalanced datasets. Finally, we use a cross-validation scheme to quantify the classifier performance by evaluating the geometric mean. Results show that our proposal outperforms the state of the art methods for imbalanced class distributions regarding classification geometric mean, especially in highly imbalanced datasets.

1 Introduction

Commonly, in binary classification tasks, a classifier assumes that the number of samples in both classes are equal. Nevertheless, many datasets in real applications (mechanical engineering, financial systems, information and medical science, among others) involve imbalanced classes distribution problems [1]. The class imbalance occurs when one class (i.e. the minority class) contains a small number of data points and the other (i.e. the majority class) contains a large number of data points. Without consideration of the class imbalance problem,

© Springer Nature Switzerland AG 2018
Y. Hernández Heredia et al. (Eds.): IWAIPR 2018, LNCS 11047, pp. 280–287, 2018.
https://doi.org/10.1007/978-3-030-01132-1_32

the classification algorithms can be overwhelmed by the majority class and can ignore the minority class [2]. However, in some applications the minority class is the most important. A classic example is an industrial production process, where the occurrence of defective pieces is much lower than the normal ones. In this context, it is a priority to identify a defective sample, unfortunately, the high amount of samples from majority class causes biased decision boundaries in the classification system [3].

Due to the great importance of the imbalanced data distribution problem in different application fields, several methods have been proposed in the literature for dealing with this issue. These methods try to solve the class distribution problem by modifying the learning algorithms or the dataset. At the algorithmic level, the developed methods are divided into two branches: cost-sensitive learning [4] and recognition-based learning [5]. A cost-sensitive classifier learns more features of samples from minority class in comparison to the majority class. This is done by setting a high cost to the misclassification of a minority class sample. Nonetheless, misclassification costs are often unknown, and a cost-sensitive classifier may result in overfitting [6]. On the other hand, recognition-based learning is focused on one-class learning, which is more suitable than two-class approaches under certain conditions such as highly imbalanced data [7]. At data level, there are several approaches to deal with the imbalance problem, which are divided into two groups: ensemble-based and sampling-based approaches. The ensemble of classifiers is a useful technique for improving prediction accuracy by combining several base classifiers [8]. Each classifier is trained separately, and the final decision is made by majority vote. The sampling approaches are preprocessing techniques, where the data distribution is rebalanced to reduce the effect of the imbalanced class distribution in the learning process [9]. The sampling methods split into oversampling and under-sampling approaches. The over-sampling approach increases the number of minority class samples to reduce the imbalance effects, however, the over-sampling techniques may increase the likelihood of overfitting in the model construction process [10]. On the contrary, the under-sampling approaches reduce the number of samples from the majority class. A simple method known as random-under-sampling (RUS) [11] randomly selects samples from the majority class, generating a new training set. Nonetheless, some useful data present in the majority class might be eliminated. More recent sampling strategies have been developed in the last years. Remarkably, the clustering-based under-sampling (CBUS) technique which performs the sub-sampling by partitioning the dataset in several clusters by using K-means algorithm [10], then, the original data in the same groups are replaced by the cluster centers, thereby reducing the size of the majority class. Nevertheless, the K-means clustering procedure is usually affected by outliers, and it is not robust to complex data distributions, because CBUS codes the majority class structure by dividing it according to distances and minimizing a cost function that only considers second-order statistics (means and variances).

In this work, we propose a new under-sampling strategy based on the principle of relevant information (RIS). We want to represent the distribution and internal structure of the majority class in an imbalanced dataset for improving the classification results. The RIS approach captures the structure of data beyond second order statistics by computing information theoretic measures. This measures quantify accurately the statistical micro-structure of the majority class, reducing the effects of the imbalanced classes distribution problem. We asses our methodology on 6 synthetic and 15 real-world imbalanced datasets. In addition, we compare our results with two common sampling techniques: random under-sampling (RUS) and cluster-based under-sampling (CBUS). The experiments show that our proposal achieves the highest results, especially for highly imbalanced datasets, outperforming the comparison methods concerning geometric mean. This measure takes into account the relative balance of the classifier's performance on both the positive and the negative classes.

Our paper contains: a mathematical description of Relevant Information-based sampling approach (Sect. 2), the experimental setup (Sect. 3), results and discussion (Sect. 4) and conclusions (Sect. 5).

2   Relevant Information-Based Sampling

Let $X \in \mathbb{R}^{N \times P}$ be an imbalanced input training set, where the samples belonging to minority and majority classes are represented by matrices $X_- \in \mathbb{R}^{N_- \times P}$ and $X_+ \in \mathbb{R}^{N_+ \times P}$, where P, N, N_-, N_+, are the dimensionality, number of samples, number of minority and majority class samples, respectively. We aim to reveal the M most representatives samples from majority class such that $M < N_+$ to avoid biased classification results. Therefore, we use a self-organizing principle of relevant information to capture the underlying structure of data by minimizing the entropy while preserving different levels of detail about the original data [12]. Specifically, we are looking for the subset $\tilde{X} \in \mathbb{R}^{M \times P}$ by solving the following optimization problem:

$$\tilde{X} = \arg\min_{\tilde{X}} \left[H_2(\tilde{X}) + \lambda D_{CS}(\tilde{X} \| X_+) \right] \tag{1}$$

where $\lambda \in \mathbb{R}^+$ is a trade off parameter which controls the level of distortion in the sub-sampled data (the modes of the data, the principal curves, and vector-quantized approximations), $H_2(\tilde{X}) : \mathbb{R}^{M \times P} \to \mathbb{R}$ is the Renyi's quadratic entropy, and $D_{CS}(\tilde{X} \| X_+) : \mathbb{R}^{M \times P} \times \mathbb{R}^{N_+ \times P} \to \mathbb{R}$ is the Cauchy - Schwarz Probability Density Function (PDF) divergence. In particular, using a Parzen-based approximation of the PDF, $\hat{H}_2(\tilde{X})$ is estimated as $\hat{H}_2(\tilde{X}) = -\log\left(\frac{1}{M^2} \sum_{i=1}^{M} \sum_{j=1}^{M} G_\sigma(\tilde{x}_i, \tilde{x}_j)\right)$, where $\tilde{x}_i, \tilde{x}_j \in \tilde{X}$ and $G_\sigma(x, y) = \exp\left(-0.5\|x - y^2\|/\sigma^2\right)$ is the Gaussian kernel with bandwidth σ. Similarly, the $D_{CS}(\tilde{X} \| X_+)$ can be estimated in terms of Renyi's quadratic entropy as $\hat{D}_{CS}(\tilde{X} \| X_+) = 2\hat{H}_2(\tilde{X}, X_+) - \hat{H}_2(\tilde{X}) - \hat{H}_2(X_+)$, where $\hat{H}_2(\tilde{X}, X_+) = -\log \hat{V}(\tilde{X}, X_+)$ is the logarithm of the cross-information potential. This measure corresponds to an inner product between probability density functions, with $\hat{V}(\tilde{X}, X_+) = \frac{1}{MN_+} \sum_{i=1}^{M} \sum_{j=1}^{N_+} G_\sigma(\tilde{x}_i, x_j)$ where $x_j \in X_+$.

Then, the optimization problem in Eq. (1) can be solved through an information theoretic learning-based framework using a fixed point estimation, yielding:

$$\tilde{x}_k^{(n+1)} = c\frac{(1-\lambda)}{\lambda}\frac{\sum_{j=1}^{M} G_\sigma(\tilde{x}_k^n, x_j)x_j}{\sum_{j=1}^{N_+} G_\sigma(\tilde{x}_k^n, x_j)} + \frac{\sum_{j=1}^{N_+} G_\sigma(\tilde{x}_k^n, x_j)x_j}{\sum_{j=1}^{N_+} G_\sigma(\tilde{x}_k^n, x_j)}$$
$$- c\frac{(1-\lambda)}{\lambda}\frac{\sum_{j=1}^{M} G_\sigma(\tilde{x}_k^n, \tilde{x}_j^n)}{\sum_{j=1}^{N_+} G_\sigma(\tilde{x}_k^n, x_j)}\tilde{x}_k^n, \tag{2}$$

where $c = \frac{\hat{V}(\tilde{X}, X_+)}{\hat{V}(\tilde{X})}\frac{N_+}{M}$.

3   Experimental Setup

Databases: First, to evaluate the RIS approach, we test it on a synthetic imbalanced dataset. The database consists of 2D points distributed in two concentric circles, that have been distorted with six different levels of Gaussian noise with the following variances: $\gamma^2 \in \{0.3, 0.4, 0.5, 0.6, 0.7, 0.8\}$. The points belonging to the inner circle are the minority class $X_- \in \mathbb{R}^{60 \times 2}$ and those belonging to the outer circle are the majority class $X_+ \in \mathbb{R}^{300 \times 2}$. We also evaluate the RIS in several benchmark imbalanced datasets available in the public UCI repository. In particular, we employ 15 real-world databases (including pathologies, vehicle engineering, biological information, financial, among others areas) used by authors in [13,14].

RIS Training: To perform the RIS algorithm, first, we normalize the input features for all datasets between zero and one. Then, we take the majority class X_+ of each dataset, and we place $M = N_-$ samples belonging to $\tilde{X}$ at random locations within the unit square. The parameter λ is empirically set as $\lambda = 1000$ minimizing the Cauchy - Schwarz PDF divergence, yielding a vector-quantization approximation of the data. During the training stage, initially, we set a large kernel-bandwidth, which we adjust progressively for ensuring convergence of the method. In this experiment, the initial kernel size for the processing elements was empirically set to $\sigma_0 = 5$ and it decays after every iteration according to $\sigma_n = \frac{\sigma_0}{1+n}$ [12]. Using Eq. (2), the samples from $\tilde{X}$ reveal the structure of the majority class. Our Matlab implementation of the Relevant Information-based sampling was uploaded in a Github repository[1].

Baseline: We compare the RIS against the RUS [11] and CBUS [15] approaches. For all methods, we train the 1-Nearest Neighbor classifier using the samples selected by each one. Finally, we employ a 10-fold cross-validation strategy. To quantify the performance of comparison methods, we evaluate the G-mean measure which describes the trade-off between sensitivity and specificity measures.

---

[1] https://github.com/keider95/Relevant-Information-Sampling/.

4   Results and Discussion

A visual inspection of Fig. 1 shows the samples selected by each method and how the RIS approach reveals the most relevant samples from the majority class X_+. It can be observed that samples selected by RIS are better distributed than those selected by the baseline methods, regarding the original structure of the majority class. This is explained because our method minimizes the Cauchy-Schwarz divergence, particularly, the cost function used captures the structure of data beyond second order statistics. In other words, the samples belonging to $\tilde{X}$, selected by the RIS, follow a PDF with a reduced entropy, achieving a similar behavior to the original PDF of X_+. Also, the RIS does not select near or agglomerated samples, because it minimizes redundancy between samples. Furthermore, unlike the comparison methods, the RIS sub-sampling technique

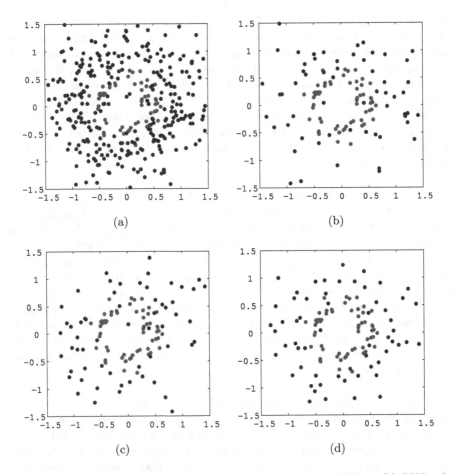

Fig. 1. (a) Original synthetic dataset with the sixth degree of Noise (b) RUS sub-sampled version (c) CBUS sub-sampled version (d) RIS sub-sampled version. Blue points are the majority class and the red ones are the minority one (Color figure online)

Table 1. The testing G-mean of sub-sampling approaches on synthetic datasets with different noise levels.

γ^2	RUS	CBUS	RIS
0.3	97.8150 ± 3.5887	98.0730 ± 4.0857	**98.5568 ± 3.1233**
0.4	93.0482 ± 8.8321	92.2593 ± 6.3106	**94.1460 ± 4.2548**
0.5	85.9379 ± 10.6190	81.8731 ± 13.3784	**88.2284 ± 13.0630**
0.6	82.5058 ± 14.5694	81.9665 ± 8.9428	**89.5026 ± 5.9296**
0.7	84.8676 ± 8.3843	86.1116 ± 12.8588	**86.5697 ± 11.8888**
0.8	81.9994 ± 11.9478	79.0232 ± 7.4884	**83.9502 ± 8.7513**
Mean	87.6956 ± 6.3485	86.5111 ± 7.2815	**90.1590 ± 5.3293**

Table 2. The testing G-mean of sub-sampling approaches on some benchmark datasets

Dataset	Imbalance ratio	Features	RUS [11]	CBUS [15]	RIS
Balance	0.0851	4	63.6421 ± 27.9535	61.1776 ± 24.6974	**73.3974 ± 17.7094**
BankNote	0.8005	4	96.1554 ± 1.5180	95.8052 ± 0.8980	**96.8710 ± 1.1497**
biodeg	0.5093	41	82.4067 ± 4.3624	82.0224 ± 3.8002	**82.5728 ± 5.1013**
cmc	0.2921	9	65.7800 ± 6.1526	**67.0590 ± 7.5556**	65.1131 ± 5.6620
HaberMan	0.3600	4	**61.4086 ± 11.8589**	57.0977 ± 14.2602	57.3636 ± 13.6922
Housing	0.0743	13	35.9092 ± 34.5960	64.5300 ± 14.3714	**67.7452 ± 15.2967**
Ionosphere	0.5600	34	**81.4631 ± 10.5201**	77.3791 ± 8.7177	77.8651 ± 14.8479
Iris	0.5000	4	100.0000 ± 0.0000	100.0000 ± 0.0000	100.0000 ± 0.0000
page-blocks	0.1021	10	94.0222 ± 2.9364	94.5748 ± 2.5347	**96.6757 ± 1.4727**
Prima-Indians	0.5360	8	70.8515 ± 7.1288	**78.9377 ± 6.4901**	70.5229 ± 4.9085
Transfusion	0.3123	4	64.8746 ± 7.3003	62.9896 ± 7.3648	**68.5679 ± 7.6168**
Vehicle	0.3076	18	92.3689 ± 3.1124	**98.7074 ± 1.3996**	90.3310 ± 5.4136
Wine	0.3315	13	96.0535 ± 6.6991	97.3312 ± 4.3611	**98.6603 ± 4.2366**
Wisconsin	0.5938	30	95.4910 ± 4.1410	94.8280 ± 2.8510	**96.3145 ± 3.0648**
Yeast	0.1098	8	82.9708 ± 14.1938	87.1955 ± 8.9412	**89.6586 ± 6.7575**
Mean			78.8931 ± 18.0842	81.3091 ± 15.4585	**82.1106 ± 14.3172**

is not affected by the outliers. Although our algorithm does not consider the minority class to perform the sub-sampling, visually, there is less overlapping with the minority class than the other two sampling approaches.

Table 1 shows the classification G-mean of RUS, CBUS and RIS for the synthetic data. As it is shown in Table 1, the proposed RIS obtains the best G-mean measure for all different degrees of noise. Numerical results confirm that our methodology preserves the internal structure from majority class achieving the maximum trade-off between sensitivity and specificity (G-mean).

Table 2 summarizes the information of the real-world imbalanced datasets and the classification results of the compared sub-sampling methods. Here, the imbalance ratio is defined as $I_r = N_-/N_+$; in this sense, the lower the rate, the higher the imbalance degree. Concerning classification results, for the most of cases, the RIS algorithm surpasses the other approaches. A global analysis (average results of Table 2) shows that our method obtains the best G-mean. Note the case of the most imbalanced datasets, those with the lowest imbalance ratio such as *Balance, Housing, Page-blocks* and *Yeast* datasets. In these extreme cases, our approach outperforms the comparison sub-sampling methods. The above highlight is because the RIS extracts the inherent properties of the majority class regardless of the imbalance ratio. Conversely, RUS and CBUS methods lose the structure of the data by randomly selecting few samples. Further, for the rest of datasets, our method achieves statistically comparable results with the other approaches, except in the *Prima-Indians* dataset where the imbalance ratio is high, precisely equal to 0.536. However, that is a case where the imbalance effect is not as problematic. Overall, the RIS method is an alternative to the current sampling methods for improving the performance of a classifier in highly imbalanced databases. Also, note the simplicity of this formulation which is described by only two parameters: the weighting parameter λ and the resolution parameter σ in the kernel of the Parzen estimation. The resolution parameter controls the scale of the analysis, whereas the weighting parameter combines the regularization and similarity terms in an appropriate proportion for capturing different aspects of the structure of data.

5   Conclusions

In this paper, we introduced a novel strategy to address the class imbalance problem using a Relevant Information-based Sampling approach (RIS). Following this notion, our RIS methodology employs a principle of relevant information. This principle formulates the sub-sampling issue as a trade-off between the Renyi's quadratic entropy of the sub-sampled version of the majority class in terms of their Cauchy-Schwarz divergence. In other words, RIS approach seeks the minimization of redundancy with the distortion between the original data and a compressed version of itself. Also, the RIS approach is an interesting alternative to capture the structure of data beyond second order statistics, which makes the method robust to complex data distributions. Moreover, the RIS technique computes information of theoretic features which make a suitable quantification of the statistical microstructure of majority class. Our method was tested on synthetic and real-world datasets for imbalanced data classification. The results show a G-mean average of 90.1590 ± 5.3293 and 82.1106 ± 14.3172 for synthetic and real datasets respectively, outperforming state of the art methods that address the class imbalance problem through a sub-sampling approach. Thereby, the Relevant Information-based sampling is presented as an alternative to deal with imbalanced datasets where it is necessary to capture the underlying structure from majority class, improving the classification results.

As future work, we want to formulate a sub-sampling approach that considers the minority class. We, also pretend to change the Kernel type and to scale the method for large datasets by using GPU techniques for decreasing the computation time.

Acknowledgments. Under grants provided by the project 1110-744-55958 funded by COLCIENCIAS. Also, K. Hoyos is partially funded by the project E6-18-5 (VIIE) and by the Maestría en Ingeniería Eléctrica both from Universidad Tecnológica de Pereira.

References

1. Thammasiri, D., Delen, D., Meesad, P., Kasap, N.: A critical assessment of imbalanced class distribution problem: the case of predicting freshmen student attrition. Expert Syst. Appl. **41**(2), 321–330 (2014)
2. He, H., Garcia, E.A.: Learning from imbalanced data. IEEE Trans. Knowl. Data Eng. **21**(9), 1263–1284 (2009)
3. Liu, Y., Yu, X., Huang, J.X., An, A.: Combining integrated sampling with SVM ensembles for learning from imbalanced datasets. Inf. Process. Manag. **47**(4), 617–631 (2011)
4. López, V., del Río, S., Benítez, J.M., Herrera, F.: Cost-sensitive linguistic fuzzy rule based classification systems under the mapreduce framework for imbalanced big data. Fuzzy Sets Syst. **258**, 5–38 (2015)
5. Ganganwar, V.: An overview of classification algorithms for imbalanced datasets. Int. J. Emerg. Technol. Adv. Eng. **2**(4), 42–47 (2012)
6. Yen, S.-J., Lee, Y.-S.: Cluster-based under-sampling approaches for imbalanced data distributions. Expert Syst. Appl. **36**(3), 5718–5727 (2009)
7. Elkan, C.: The foundations of cost-sensitive learning. In: International Joint Conference on Artificial Intelligence, vol. 17, pp. 973–978. Lawrence Erlbaum Associates Ltd. (2001)
8. López, V., Fernández, A., García, S., Palade, V., Herrera, F.: An insight into classification with imbalanced data: empirical results and current trends on using data intrinsic characteristics. Inf. Sci. **250**, 113–141 (2013)
9. Galar, M., Fernandez, A., Barrenechea, E., Bustince, H., Herrera, F.: A review on ensembles for the class imbalance problem: bagging-, boosting-, and hybrid-based approaches. IEEE Trans. Syst. Man Cybern. Part C (Appl. Rev.) **42**(4), 463–484 (2012)
10. Lin, W.-C., Tsai, C.-F., Ya-Han, H., Jhang, J.-S.: Clustering-based undersampling in class-imbalanced data. Inf. Sci. **409**, 17–26 (2017)
11. Prusa, J., Khoshgoftaar, T.M., Dittman, D.J., Napolitano, A.: Using random undersampling to alleviate class imbalance on tweet sentiment data. In: 2015 IEEE International Conference on Information Reuse and Integration (IRI), pp. 197–202. IEEE (2015)
12. Principe, J.C., Xu, D., Fisher, J.: Information theoretic learning. Unsupervised Adaptive Filtering, vol. 1, pp. 265–319 (2000)
13. Liu, X.-Y., Wu, J., Zhou, Z.-H.: Exploratory undersampling for class-imbalance learning. IEEE Trans. Syst. Man Cybern. Part B (Cybern.) **39**(2), 539–550 (2009)
14. Tang, Y., Zhang, Y.-Q., Chawla, N.V., Krasser, S.: SVMs modeling for highly imbalanced classification. IEEE Trans. Syst. Man Cybern. Part B (Cybern.) **39**(1), 281–288 (2009)
15. Rayhan, F., Ahmed, S., Mahbub, A., Jani, M., Shatabda, S., Farid, D.M., et al.: Cusboost: cluster-based under-sampling with boosting for imbalanced classification. arXiv preprint arXiv:1712.04356 (2017)

Economic Feasibility of Projects Using Triangular Fuzzy Numbers

Marieta Peña Abreu[1]([✉]) [ID], Carlos R. Rodríguez Rodríguez[1,2] [ID],
Roberto García Vacacela[3] [ID], and Pedro Y. Piñero Pérez[1]

[1] University of Informatics Sciences, Havana, Cuba
mpabreu@uci.cu
[2] Federal University of Kazan, Tatarstan, Russia
[3] Santiago de Guayaquil Catholic University, Guayaquil, Ecuador

Abstract. The feasibility analysis of projects is an indispensable process for software development organizations. The intangible nature of software and the multiple criteria considered, introduce uncertainty in this process. This article proposes a method that uses triangular fuzzy numbers to evaluate traditional economic criteria Net Present Value, Internal Rate of Return, and Period of Recovery of Investment; which provides higher flexibility and certainty in the prediction. The article also presents the definitions of fuzzy economic criteria and discusses some variants for different cash flows. The proposal allows treating the variations that may occur during the life cycle of the project. The final value of the criteria is obtained by considering three possible scenarios: pessimistic, more accurate and optimistic. The proposal was applied experimentally, in 30 finished software projects. The target was to determine if there were significant differences in the order of feasibility of the projects, comparing the results obtained by the fuzzy economic criteria with those obtained by the traditional economic criteria. Significant differences were found in favor of the fuzzy economic criteria Net Present Value and Internal Rate of Return. Better results were achieved by fuzzy Period of Recovery of Investment, but, the difference was not statistically significant.

Keywords: Economic evaluation of projects · Feasibility analysis
Triangular fuzzy numbers · Uncertainty

1 Introduction

The feasibility analysis of projects is carried out with the objective of determining the profitability of the project. The concept of feasibility analysis had been mainly focused on analysis of economic criteria since its origin [1]. These criteria help in the correct arrangement and systematization of the monetary information in the project [2].

Schneider' investment theory [3], was an important reference for the analysis of economic criteria. Since experts started using the feasibility analyzes, uncertainty facts began to be seen as something that affected decision making. However, statistics has been an important element in helping to solve this problem. The Cash Flow (CF), the Net Present Value (NPV), the Internal Rate of Return (IRR) and the Period of Recovery

© Springer Nature Switzerland AG 2018
Y. Hernández Heredia et al. (Eds.): IWAIPR 2018, LNCS 11047, pp. 288–298, 2018.
https://doi.org/10.1007/978-3-030-01132-1_33

of Investment (PRI), well-known traditional economic methods, do not include the uncertainty in their conception [4, 5]. These deterministic methods are calculated from classical mathematic with limitations associated with lack of flexibility [6].

The CF method does not consider the chronology of cash flows, nor the value of money over time. CF is based on perfect markets [7, 8]. On the other hand, NPV depends a great deal on the previous calculation of CF. If income and expenses are calculated without considering the uncertainty, the calculation of this criterion is also affected in the sense that they do not provide a completely reliable result. NPV has limitations to calculate accurate update rates [9].

The main limitation of the IIR, is the number of consecutive approximations that are made using exact numbers, which produces inconsistencies [8]. Finally, the PRI as the previous criteria does not consider the changes in the costs of the assets on the market and the changes that could arise with the income.

Traditional economic criteria are uncertain [10]. Seeking for optimum solutions to the deficiencies of traditional methods, some probability –based methods such as the real option models [11] have been applied. For applying these models, markets must be perfect. Therefore, an alternative of using fuzzy sets in real option models as an additional approach [9, 11] in contexts other than software development [6].

Among the classifications developed in this context we have: the continuous fuzzy model (MCF) [12], the fuzzy pay-off method (FPOM) [13] and discrete fuzzy time models (MDF) [14]. To apply those methods, it is necessary to calculate the volatility of the project, which requires successive simulations that causes an expensive from the computational point of view [11].

An alternative to solve some of those deficiencies is the treatment of uncertainty from fuzzy logics. The calculation of costs to evaluate economic criteria must consider uncertainty in contexts of imperfect markets [15].

A fuzzy number is an excellent instrument which has fuzzy logics to represent amounts estimated or observed diffusely, its core is a confidence interval [16]. In [17] proposed the use of triangular fuzzy numbers (TFN) to operate on the uncertain. The TFN are a more simplified version of the general concept of fuzzy number [18].

Among the investigations that relate the TFN to the analysis of economic and financial criteria [8, 19–24] are highlighted. However, the NPV, IIR y PRI with TFN are not formally defined. This is a disadvantage for applying them in the economic evaluation of software projects.

Taking into account specific applications shown as advantages of using fuzzy numbers, they consider all possible values taken by a variable and they work with them to reach the final result [25].

Additionally, a fuzzy number associates two concepts: the confidence interval and the level of presumption [18]. Performing operations with this principle allows working with information based on perception, which is adjustable for economic criteria [23]. The confidence intervals indicate the certainty of the information.

This article proposes the modification of traditional economic criteria using TFN. It aims to gain the flexibility of its calculation, as well as better precision in uncertainty environments.

2 Fuzzy Economic Criteria

In this section, new definitions of traditional economic criteria are presented: CF, NPV, IRR and PRI. The classical definitions of these criteria are expanded through TFN. The extension includes equations for calculating these criteria and all its variables with TFN considering uncertainty. In the literature review carried out, no contribution combining the definition and the formulation for the four criteria for the fuzzy case was found.

2.1   Fuzzy Cash Flows

Definition 1. The fuzzy cash flow is the succession of t triangular fuzzy numbers that express the difference between the collections and payments generated by the project in each of its t periods of operation, since the first investment expense is made ($t = 0$) until it is liquidated or replaced at the end of its useful life ($t = n$), considering three possible scenarios (pessimistic, more accurate and optimistic), and defined as (1).

$$CF\widetilde{(p,c,o)} = \left\{ CF\widetilde{(p,c,o)}_0, CF\widetilde{(p,c,o)}_1, \ldots, CF\widetilde{(p,c,o)}_n \right\} \tag{1}$$

For a period of operation t, the fuzzy cash flow is obtained according to Eq. (2), from calculating the fuzzy balance $\tilde{S}$ (Eq. 3) and the fuzzy tax $\tilde{I}_n$ (Eq. 4).

$$CF\widetilde{(p,c,o)}_t = -\tilde{A} + \left(\tilde{S} - \tilde{P}\right) + \tilde{V}_r + \tilde{D} \tag{2}$$

$$\tilde{S} = \tilde{I}_n + \widetilde{B_e} - \tilde{E} - \tilde{D} \tag{3}$$

$$\tilde{P} = \tilde{S} \times \widetilde{f_{imp}} \tag{4}$$

Where:

$\tilde{A}$: Estimated investment expenses for period t, $\tilde{A} = (a_p, a_c, a_o)$.

$\tilde{S}$: Estimated balance for period t, $\tilde{B} = (b_p, b_c, b_o)$.

$\tilde{I}_n$: Estimated income for period t, $\tilde{I}_n = (i_p, i_c, i_o)$.

$\widetilde{B_e}$: Extraordinary benefits estimated for period t, $\widetilde{B_e} = (b_p, b_c, b_o)$.

$\tilde{E}$: Expenses estimated for period t, $\tilde{E} = (e_p, e_c, e_o)$.

$\tilde{D}$: Estimated depreciation for period t, $\tilde{D} = (d_p, d_c, d_o)$.

$\tilde{P}$: Estimated income tax for period t, $\tilde{P} = (p_p, p_c, p_o)$.

$\widetilde{f_{imp}}$: Estimated factor for period t, $\widetilde{f_{imp}} = (f_p, f_c, f_o)$.

$\tilde{V}_r$: Residual value of the investment estimated for period t, $\tilde{V}_r = (v_p, v_c, v_o)$.

Generally, for the case of $t = 0$ (project 0 period) only the initial investment $\tilde{A}$, and to have to $\tilde{S} = \tilde{I}_p = \tilde{V}_r = \tilde{D} = 0$, so for $t = 0$, $CF\widetilde{(p,c,o)}_0 = -\tilde{A}$.

It is appropriate to treat all cash flow variables as a TFN due to two reasons:

(1) represent estimated values and therefore have a certain degree of uncertainty
(2) the relationship of dependence between them causes that, if one is inaccurate, those obtained from it are also imprecise.

A TFN $\tilde{X} = (x_1, x_2, x_3)$ can be expressed by its level sets (α-cuts) using the extension principle according to (5).

$$\tilde{X}_\alpha = [x_{1\alpha}, x_{3\alpha}] = [x_1 + (x_2 - x_1)\alpha, x_3 - (x_3 - x_2)\alpha] \tag{5}$$

Where: for $\alpha = 0$, $\tilde{X}_{\alpha=0} = [x_{1\alpha=0}, x_{3\alpha=0}] = [x_1, x_3]$, while
for $\alpha = 1$, $\tilde{X}_{\alpha=1} = [x_{1\alpha=1}, x_{3\alpha=1}] = [x_2, x_2]$.

Operations defined for TFN are used to operate on the Eqs. (2–4) and obtain the Eqs. (6–8).

$$\widetilde{CF(p,c,o)}_\alpha = \left[fc_{p_\alpha}, fc_{o_\alpha}\right] = \left[\begin{array}{l} -a_{p_\alpha} + \left(s_{p_\alpha} - p_{o_\alpha}\right) + v_{p_\alpha} + d_{p_\alpha}, \\ -a_{o_\alpha} + \left(s_{o_\alpha} - p_{p_\alpha}\right) + v_{o_\alpha} + d_{o_\alpha} \end{array}\right] \tag{6}$$

$$\tilde{S}_\alpha = \left[s_{p_\alpha}, s_{o_\alpha}\right] = \left[\left(i_{p_\alpha} + b_{p_\alpha} - e_{o_\alpha} - d_{o_\alpha}\right), \left(i_{o_\alpha} + b_{o_\alpha} - e_{p_\alpha} - d_{p_\alpha}\right)\right] \tag{7}$$

$$\tilde{P} = \left[p_{p_\alpha}, p_{o_\alpha}\right] = \left[\begin{array}{l} min\left(s_{p_\alpha} \times f_{p_\alpha}; s_{p_\alpha} \times f_{o_\alpha}; s_{o\alpha} \times f_{p_\alpha}; s_{o_\alpha} \times f_{o_\alpha}\right), \\ max\left(s_{p_\alpha} \times f_{p_\alpha}; s_{p_\alpha} \times f_{o_\alpha}; s_{o_\alpha} \times f_{p_\alpha}; s_{o_\alpha} \times f_{o_\alpha}\right) \end{array}\right] \tag{8}$$

2.2 Fuzzy Net Present Value

Definition 2: The fuzzy net present value $\widetilde{NPV(p,c,o)}$ is the triangular fuzzy number that expresses the updated value of the fuzzy cash flows $\widetilde{CF(p,c,o)}_t$ generated for a project during its useful life n. Consider three possible scenarios (pessimistic, more accurate and optimistic) in which a fuzzy discount rate $\tilde{k}$ is handled, its defined as (9).

$$\widetilde{NPV(p,c,o)} = \sum_{t=0}^{n} \frac{\widetilde{CF(p,c,o)}_t}{(1+\tilde{k})^t} \tag{9}$$

Where:

$\widetilde{CF(p,c,o)}_t$: Fuzzy cash flow for the period of operation t.
$\tilde{k}$: Fuzzy discount rate $(k_o < k_c < k_p)$.

According to nature of fuzzy cash flows and fuzzy discount rate, the procedure to obtain the $\widetilde{NPV}$(p,c,o) has four cases. Then we discuss each one and formalize its calculation method. For this, α-cuts are used as expressed in Eq. (5).

In the basic case, $\widetilde{CF(p,c,o)}_t$ is conventional (it has only one change of sign), and

$\tilde{k}$ is constant for the useful life of the project n. In that way, $\forall t |\ 0 \le t \le n$, $\widetilde{NPV}(p,c,o)$ is monotonically decreasing respect to $\tilde{k}$ and is calculated according to (10).

$$\widetilde{NPV}(p,c,o) = \left[NPV_{p_\alpha}; NPV_{o_\alpha} \right] = \left[\sum_{t=0}^{n} \frac{\left(cf_{p_t}\right)_\alpha}{\left(1+k_{p_\alpha}\right)^t}; \sum_{t=0}^{n} \frac{\left(cf_{o_t}\right)_\alpha}{\left(1+k_{o_\alpha}\right)^t} \right] \tag{10}$$

However, for the case where the $\widetilde{CF}(p,c,o)_t$ is not conventional, although $\tilde{k}$ is constant for the useful life of the project n, cannot be sure the relationship monotone decreasing between $\widetilde{NPV}(p,c,o)$ and $\tilde{k}$. This is because some values of $\widetilde{CF}(p,c,o)_t$ can produce inflection points. In this case, NPV_{p_α} and NPV_{o_α} are obtained by (11) and (12).

$$\widetilde{NPV}_{p_\alpha} = Min \left\{ \sum_{t=0}^{n} \frac{\left(cf_{p_t}\right)_\alpha}{\left(1+k_{o_\alpha}\right)^t}, \sum_{t=0}^{n} \frac{\left(cf_{p_t}\right)_\alpha}{\left(1+k_{p_\alpha}\right)^t} \right\} \tag{11}$$

$$\widetilde{NPV}_{o_\alpha} = Max \left\{ \sum_{t=0}^{n} \frac{\left(cf_{o_t}\right)_\alpha}{\left(1+k_{o_\alpha}\right)^t}, \sum_{t=0}^{n} \frac{\left(cf_{o_t}\right)_\alpha}{\left(1+k_{p_\alpha}\right)^t} \right\} \tag{12}$$

In third case $\widetilde{CF}(p,c,o)_t$ is conventional, but $\tilde{k}$ is variable for each period t of project's useful life n. In this case, we proceed as in the first case but considering the variability of $\tilde{k}$. The NPV_{p_α} and NPV_{o_α} are obtained by means of (13) and (14).

$$\widetilde{NPV_p^{k_p}}_\alpha = \left(cf_{p_0}\right)_\alpha + \frac{\left(cf_{p_1}\right)_\alpha}{1+k_{p_\alpha}^1} + \frac{\left(cf_{p_2}\right)_\alpha}{\left(1+k_{p_\alpha}^1\right)\left(1+k_{p_\alpha}^2\right)} + \cdots + \frac{\left(cf_{p_n}\right)_\alpha}{\left(1+k_{p_\alpha}^1\right)\left(1+k_{p_\alpha}^2\right)\left(1+k_{p_\alpha}^n\right)} \tag{13}$$

$$\widetilde{NPV_o^{k_o}}_\alpha = \left(cf_{o_0}\right)_\alpha + \frac{\left(cf_{o_1}\right)_\alpha}{1+k_{o_\alpha}^1} + \frac{\left(cf_{o_2}\right)_\alpha}{\left(1+k_{o_\alpha}^1\right)\left(1+k_{o_\alpha}^2\right)} + \cdots + \frac{\left(cf_{o_n}\right)_\alpha}{\left(1+k_{o_\alpha}^1\right)\left(1+k_{o_\alpha}^2\right)\left(1+k_{o_\alpha}^n\right)} \tag{14}$$

Finally, we analyze the case in which $\widetilde{CF}(p,c,o)_t$ is not conventional and $\tilde{k}$ is considered variable for each period t of the project's useful life n. In this, the extremes of the interval of $\widetilde{NPV}(p,c,o)$ are obtained by determining the minimum between Eqs. (13) and (15) and the maximum between Eqs. (14) and (16).

$$\widetilde{NPV_p^{k_o}}_\alpha = \left(cf_{p_0}\right)_\alpha + \frac{\left(cf_{p_1}\right)_\alpha}{1+k_{o_\alpha}^1} + \frac{\left(cf_{p_2}\right)_\alpha}{\left(1+k_{o_\alpha}^1\right)\left(1+k_{o_\alpha}^2\right)} + \cdots + \frac{\left(cf_{p_n}\right)_\alpha}{\left(1+k_{o_\alpha}^1\right)\left(1+k_{o_\alpha}^2\right)\left(1+k_{o_\alpha}^n\right)} \tag{15}$$

$$NPV_{o}^{\widetilde{k_p}}{}_{\alpha} = (cf_{0_0})_{\alpha} + \frac{(cf_{0_1})_{\alpha}}{1+k_{p_{\alpha}}^{1}} + \frac{(cf_{0_2})_{\alpha}}{\left(1+k_{p_{\alpha}}^{1}\right)\left(1+k_{p_{\alpha}}^{2}\right)} + \cdots + \frac{(cf_2)_{\alpha}}{\left(1+k_{p_{\alpha}}^{1}\right)\left(1+k_{p_{\alpha}}^{2}\right)\left(1+k_{p_{\alpha}}^{n}\right)} \quad (16)$$

2.3   Fuzzy Internal Rate of Return

Definition 3: The internal rate of return fuzzy $\widetilde{IIR}(p,c,o)$ is the triangular fuzzy number that expresses the fuzzy discount rate that equals the current value of the collection stream with the current value of the current payments. Consider three possible scenarios (pessimistic, more accurate and optimistic) and defined as (17).

$$\widetilde{IIR}(p,c,o) = \left[IIR_{p_{\alpha}}; IIR_{o_{\alpha}} \right]$$

$$= \left[r_1^{p} + \frac{\left(NPV_p^{p}\right)_{\alpha}\left(r_2^{p}-r_1^{p}\right)}{\left(NPV_p^{p}\right)_{\alpha} + \left|\left(NPV_n^{p}\right)_{\alpha}\right|}; r_2^{o} + \frac{\left(NPV_p^{o}\right)_{\alpha}\left(r_2^{o}-r_1^{o}\right)}{\left(NPV_p^{o}\right)_{\alpha} + \left|\left(NPV_n^{o}\right)_{\alpha}\right|} \right] \quad (17)$$

Where:

r_1^{p}: Update rate in which the NPV^p is positive (NPV_p^{p}) and approaches zero.
r_2^{p}: Update rate in which the NPV^p is negative (NPV_n^{p}) and approaches zero.
r_1^{o}: Update rate in which the NPV^o is positive (NPV_p^{o}) and approaches zero.
r_2^{o}: Update rate in which the NPV^o is negative (NPV_n^{o}) and approaches zero.
NPV_p^{p}: the positive value of the NPV^p closer to zero, updated with r_1^{p}.
NPV_n^{p}: the negative value of the NPV^p closer to zero, updated with r_2^{p}.
NPV_p^{o}: the positive value of the NPV^o closer to zero, updated with r_1^{o}.
NPV_n^{o}: the negative value of the NPV^o closer to zero, updated with r_2^{o}.

To calculate the $\widetilde{IIR}(p,c,o)$ by means of its α-cuts, it's calculated discount rates (r_1^{x} and r_2^{x}). These rates are the ones that closest to zero each extreme of the $\widetilde{NPV}(p,c,o)$ until they take their last positive value and their first negative value. It's taken the last positive value and the first negative value. The value of the IIR for extremes is obtained by interpolating between both rates (r_1^{x} and r_2^{x}) by means of Eq. (17).

In accordance with this criterion the project with the highest $\widetilde{IIR}(p,c,o)$ must be selected. However, this condition is not sufficient to affirm the feasibility of the project. It must be verified that the $\widetilde{IIR}(p,c,o)$ is higher than the $\tilde{k}$ with which the $\widetilde{NPV}(p,c,o)$ was obtained. The difference between $\widetilde{IIR}(p,c,o)$ and $\tilde{k}$ represent the fuzzy net profitability $\widetilde{R_n}$ for each monetary unit invested in the project. $\widetilde{R_n}$ obtained by Eq. (18).

$$\widetilde{R_n} = \left[(r_{n_p})_\alpha; (r_{n_o})_\alpha \right] = \left[IIR_{p_\alpha} - k_{p_\alpha}; IIR_{o_\alpha} - k_{o_\alpha} \right] \tag{18}$$

In case of projects where $\tilde{k}$ varies for each of its execution periods, a single $\tilde{k}$ must be considered to compare the $\widetilde{IIR}(p, c, o)$. Two variants are proposed: calculate the average $\tilde{k}$ using operations for TFN or calculate a fixed $\tilde{k}$ with which, it obtains the same value of $\widetilde{NPV}(p, c, o)$ that was obtained using the $\tilde{k}$ variables for each period of time.

2.4   Fuzzy Period of Recovery of Investment

Definition 4: The fuzzy discounted recovery period of the investment $\widetilde{PRI^d}(o, c, p)$, is the triangular fuzzy number that expresses the period of time in which, through the discounted cash flows from the project, the investment made is recovered. Consider three possible scenarios (optimistic, more accurate and pessimistic), see (19).

$$\widetilde{PRI^d}(o, c, p) = \left[PRI^d_{o_\alpha}; PRI^d_{p_\alpha} \right]$$
$$= \left[u_o + \frac{|(NAB_o)_\alpha|}{|(NAB_o)_\alpha| + (PAB_o)_\alpha}; u_p + \frac{|(NAB_p)_\alpha|}{|(NAB_p)_\alpha| + (PAB_p)_\alpha} \right] \tag{19}$$

$$NAB_{x_\alpha} = \left(\sum_{t=0}^{u_x} \frac{(cf_{x_t})_\alpha}{(1 + k_{x_\alpha})^t} \right) < 0 \tag{20}$$

$$PAB_{x_\alpha} = -NAB_x + \frac{(cf_{x_{u+1}})_\alpha}{(1 + k_{x_\alpha})^{u+1}} \tag{21}$$

Where:

  u: Periods of time with a negative balance accumulated since the project starts.
  NAB: Value of last period of time with a negative effect on the accumulated balance.
  PAB: Value of first period of time with a positive effect on the accumulated balance.
  $\tilde{k}$: Fuzzy discount rate $(k_o < k_c < k_p)$.

Equation (19) model the $\widetilde{PRI^d}(o, c, p)$ calculation of the updated (discounted) value of the $\widetilde{CF}(p, c, o)_t$ according to the fuzzy discount rate $\tilde{k}$. $\widetilde{PRI^d}(o, c, p)$ resolves one of the limitations indicated to the traditional PRI: not consider the value of money over time. In addition, since the discount rate is modeled as an TFN, it allows working with all the possible values of $\tilde{k}$ in the interval $[k_o; k_p]$.

To obtain the interval represented by the $\widetilde{PRI^d}(o, c, p)$ in the form of α-cuts, in (20) and (21) the subscript x it replaced by o or p according to the extreme of the interval. The lower extreme of the interval (PRI^d_o) is obtained operating with the upper extreme of the fuzzy cash flow (cf_o) and the lower extreme of the fuzzy discount rate (k_o). The upper extreme of the interval (PRI_p^d) is obtained operating with the lower extreme of the fuzzy cash flow (cf_p) and the upper extreme of the fuzzy discount rate (k_p).

In accordance with this criterion, the project with the minor $\widetilde{PRI^d}(o,c,p)$ is more feasible. However, when either extreme of the $\widetilde{NPV}(p,c,o)$ is negative, the corresponding extreme of the $\widetilde{PRI^d}(o,c,p)$ will be higher than the lifetime of the project. In those cases, the investment does not recover and therefore the project is not feasible.

When the rate $\tilde{k}$ varies for each period t of the useful life n of the project, the $\widetilde{PRI^d}(o,c,p)$ is obtained according to (19) but it considering the variability of the rate $\tilde{k}$ in Eqs. (20) and (21), similar to how it is done to calculate the $\widetilde{NPV}(p,c,o)$.

3   Experiment

We experimented with a database of finished projects (Feasility_Dataset) published by the Project Management Research Laboratory of the University of Informatics Sciences. It is composed of 30 software projects, these vary in their scope and size.

3.1   Design of Quasi-Experiment

Objective: To determine if there are significant differences in the order of feasibility of the projects, between the results obtained with the fuzzy econometric criteria and those obtained with the traditional economic criteria.

Procedure: There is a "master" list of the 30 projects, which shows the real feasibility order according to each criterion. Fuzzy and traditional economic criteria are applied. Two different lists of the projects are obtained according to the feasibility order. Both lists are compared with the pattern. The distance between the real position and the value obtained in each listing is calculated. These distances are represented as related samples and compared with the Wilcoxon statistical test. The Monte Carlo method with a 99% reliance interval is used. For $p \leq 0.05$ the difference is considered to be significant.

3.2   Results of Quasi-Experiment

The comparison between the results of fuzzy and traditional economic criteria showed that the fuzzy economic criteria better in all cases. The values of the mean square error (MSE) in the prediction of each applied criteria given in Table 1. These results indicate that the fuzzy criteria were better in pretending the real values. That is, the values obtained with fuzzy criteria were closer to the real values.

Table 1. Values of the MSE for the criteria $NPV\widetilde{(p,c,o)}$, $IRR\widetilde{(p,c,o)}$ and $PRI^d\widetilde{(o,c,p)}$.

Criteria	Fuzzy vs real	Traditional vs real
NPV	0.2	31.2
IIR	0.73	3.73
PRI	0.47	0.87

The results of the Wilcoxon test for the NPV and IIR criterion founded significant differences. For the NPV, Z rate gave a value of -3.491. In the case of the IRR, Z rate gave a value of -3.907. For both criteria, the asymptotic significance and the one with the Monte Carlo Method was 0.00 for all cases. These values are smaller than the decision rule established ($p \leq 0.05$) and they show significant differences. Those values permit affirming that for analyzed sample the NPV and IIR criterion offer better results.

In the case of the PRI, the Wilcoxon test did not find significant differences. The reason Z rate gave a value of -2.309 and the asymptotic significant values (0.021) and with the Monte Carlo Method unilateral (0.018) and bilateral (0.037) were greater than the decision rule established ($p \leq 0.05$). However, in the descriptive statistics, lower values of mean and standard deviation are observed for the case of the diffuse criterion.

Figure 1 shows a summary of the experiment. The line that covers a smaller area indicates a better result. As noted, the fuzzy criteria cover an area smaller than the area covered by traditional criteria. The fuzzy NPV and PRI did not give false negative and positive results. While the fuzzy IRR only gave a false negative. On the other hand, the values of the MSE, the mean and the standard deviation are lower.

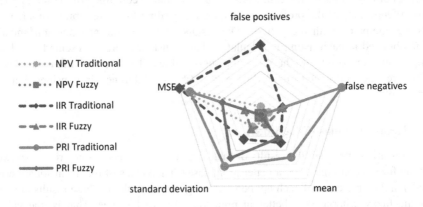

Fig. 1. Summary of the results of the experiment.

4   Conclusions

The traditional economic criteria of feasibility analysis do not consider the uncertainty of the environment, which affects its predictive capacity. The redefinition of traditional criteria using soft computing techniques enabled experts to obtain a better interpretation of the feasibility analysis results to make decisions in the economic feasibility studies. The use of TFN provides the representation of: pessimistic, more accurate and optimistic scenarios. This provides a confidence interval for the decision maker. Proper projection of cash flows influences the estimation of the other criteria. For this reason, the definition of income and expenses in three scenarios helps the assessment of risks occurrence on the impact of the execution of the project, which facilitates taking actions. The representation of the α-cuts of each criterion permits handling different intervals from the level of presumption.

The experiment found significant differences in favor of the NPV and IRR fuzzy criteria. For diffuse PRI the results were better but, the difference was not statistically significant. The values of the mean, standard deviation and MSE, as well as the number of false positive and false negative cases, were better for the fuzzy criteria.

As a line of future research, the investigators should work to solve the limitation of classical IRR that remains in fuzzy IRR for not conventional cash flow.

Acknowledgments. We thank Dr. Lilliana Casar for her valuable contribution in the revision of the language when writing the article.

References

1. Cruz, A.D., Hidalgo, K.M.E., Medina, M.Q.: Evaluación de factibilidad de proyectos de inversión. Rev. Caribeña Cienc. Soc. **2014**(10), 10–15 (2014)
2. Miranda, J.J.: Gestión de proyectos: identificación, formulación, evaluación: financiera, económica, social, ambiental. MM Editores (2005)
3. Schneider, E.: Teoría de la Inversión. El Ateneo, Buenos Aires (1956)
4. Dubs de Moya, R.: El proyecto factible: una modalidad de investigación. Sapiens. Revista Universitaria de Investigación **3**(2), 45–62 (2002)
5. Rodríguez Mesa, G.: La evaluación financiera y social de proyectos de inversión. Tercera Edición. Universidad de La Habana, La Habana (2006)
6. Tanaka, Á.T., Montero, C.M.: Valorización de opciones reales: modelo Ornstein-Uhlenbeck. J. Econ. Finance Adm. Sci. **21**(41), 56–62 (2016)
7. Florez-Ríos, L.S.: Evolución de la Teoría Financiera en el Siglo XX. Revista Ecos de Economía **27**, 145–168 (2008)
8. Milanesi, G.S.: La tasa interna de retorno promedio borrosa: desarrollos y aplicaciones. J. Econ. Finance Adm. Sci. **21**(40), 39–47 (2016)
9. Vedovoto, G.L., Prior, D.: Opciones reales: una propuesta para valorar proyectos de I + D en centros públicos de investigación agraria. Revista Contaduría y administración **60**(1), 145–179 (2015)
10. Mullor, J., Sansalvador, M.E., Trigueros, J.A.: Lógica borrosa y su aplicación en la contabilidad. Revista española de financiación y contabilidad XXIX **103**, 83–106 (2000)

11. Milanesi, G.S.: Modelo binomial para la valoración de empresas y los efectos de la deuda: escudo fiscal y liquidación de la firma. J. Econ. Finance Adm. Sci. **19**(36), 2–10 (2014)
12. Carlsson, C., Fullér, R., Heikkila, M., Majlender, P.: A fuzzy approach to R&D project portfolio selection. Int. J. Approx. Reason. **44**(2), 93–105 (2007)
13. Collan, M., Fullér, R., Mezei, J.: Fuzzy pay-off method for real option valuation. J. Appl. Math. Decis. Syst. **1**, 1–14 (2009)
14. Zdnek, Z.: Generalised soft binomial American real option pricing model. Eur. J. Oper. Res. **207**, 1096–1103 (2010)
15. Haugen, R.A.: Finance from a new perspective. Financ. Manage. **25**(1), 86–97 (1996)
16. De Andrés-Sánchez, J.: Estimación de la estructura temporal de los tipos de interés mediante números borrosos. Aplicación a la valoración financiero-actuarial y análisis de la solvencia del asegurador de vida. Universitat Rovira i Virgili (2000)
17. Kaufmann, A., Gil-Aluja, J.: Introducción a la teoría de los subconjuntos borrosos a la gestión de las empresas. Milladoiro (1986)
18. Gil-Lafuente, A.M., Santoyo, F.G., Romero, B.F.: Presupuesto base cero, gestión de la tesorería en contexto de incertidumbre (fuzzy logic): técnica y aplicación. Rev. Nicolaita Estud. Económicos **10**(1), 39–52 (2017)
19. Milanesi, G.S.: Valoración probabilística versus borrosa, opciones reales y el modelo binomial. Aplicación para proyectos de inversión en condiciones de ambigüedad. Estudios gerenciales **30**(36), 211–219 (2014)
20. Magni, C.: The internal rate of return approach and the AIRR paradigm: a refutation and a corroboration. Eng. Econ. **58**(2), 73–111 (2012)
21. Guerra, M.C., Stefanini, L.: Interval and fuzzy average internal rate of return for investment appraisal. Fuzzy Sets Syst. **257**, 217–241 (2014)
22. Hazen, G.: An extension of internal rate of returns to stochastic cash flow. Manage. Sci. **55**(6), 1030–1034 (2009)
23. Gutiérrez, J.C.: Aplicación de los conjuntos borrosos a las decisiones de inversión. AD-MINISTER Universidad EAFIT Medellín **9**(jul–dic), 62–85 (2006)
24. Ramos, F., Gómez, J., González, E., López, N.: Metodología para la evaluación integral de proyectos de reconversión azucarera en el concepto de biorrefinería con enfoque difuso. ICIDCA. Sobre los Derivados de la Caña de Azúcar **48**(3), 3–10 (2014)
25. Abreu, M.: Modelo para el análisis de factibilidad de proyectos de software en entornos de incertidumbre. Universidad de las Ciencias Informáticas, La Habana (2017)

Variable Selection for Journal Bearing Faults Diagnostic Through Logical Combinatorial Pattern Recognition

Joel Pino Gómez[1(✉)], Fidel E. Hernández Montero[1],
and Julio C. Gómez Mancilla[2]

[1] Technological University of Havana, 19390 Havana, Cuba
joelpinogomez@gmail.com
[2] National Polytechnic Institute, 07738 Mexico City, Mexico

Abstract. Experts in industrial diagnostics can provide essential information, expressed in mixed variables (quantitative and qualitative) about journal bearing faults. However, researches on feature selection for fault diagnostic applications discard the important qualitative expertise. This work focuses on the identification of the most important features, quantitative and also qualitative, for fault identification in a steam turbine journal bearings through the application of logical combinatorial pattern recognition. The value sets that support this research come from diagnostics and maintenance reports from an active thermoelectric power plant. Mixed data processing was accomplished by means of logical combinatorial pattern recognition tools. Confusion of raw features set was obtained by employing different comparison criterion. Subsequently, testors and typical testors were identified and the informational weight of features in typical testors was also computed. The high importance of the mixed features that came from the expert knowledge was revealed by the obtained achievements.

Keywords: Mixed features · Confusion · Journal bearing · Feature selection
Testor

1 Introduction

In order to keep high availability of rotatory machines and to improve maintenance results, the implementation of right diagnostic techniques is required [1–3]. Journal bearings are great useful in rotating machines of heavy industry, where besides may cause significant breakdowns [4]. In practice, an adequate dynamical stability of journal bearing can be assured by the analysis of many factors, some of them often expressed by diagnostic expert in a non-formalized mathematical language due to the intangible nature of such features [5–8]. The identification of the main variables, given all available features (quantitative and qualitative) to describe the faults, is essential for a successful diagnostic.

The journal bearing fault diagnostic has been carried out using only quantitative variables [9–13]. Although the application of powerful novel techniques (such as artificial neuronal networks (*ANN*), support vector machines (*SVM*), Fisher

© Springer Nature Switzerland AG 2018
Y. Hernández Heredia et al. (Eds.): IWAIPR 2018, LNCS 11047, pp. 299–306, 2018.
https://doi.org/10.1007/978-3-030-01132-1_34

discriminant analysis (*FDA*) and K-nearest neighbor (*KNN*) for diagnostics implementation has exhibited good outcomes, im proved results could be obtained by the inclusion of the qualitative expertise in the analysis. The pattern recognition combinatorial logical approach (*PRCLA*) provides many useful tools for mixed (quantitative and qualitative) features processing. This research proposes the application of such an approach on the selection of the main features (quantitative and qualitative) involved on journal bearing fault diagnostics [14]. Data supporting this research came from three journal bearings of turbines installed in an active thermoelectric power plant.

2   Theoretical Foundations

2.1   Logical Combinatorial Patter Recognition Approach

PRCLA involves techniques for variable selection and classification. Descriptions of the objects can be carried out by using a feature set of different natures, which could be processed by numerical functions [14]. The present research work is focused on variable selection, where the set of features is reduced to the essential ones in order to describe the faults. The comparison criterion is a fundamental concept of this approach.

2.2   On the Comparison Criterion

The comparison criterion (*CC*) concept is a mathematical formulation that computes the similarity between two values of a same feature of two different objects. There are different ways of defining *CC* [15], for example:

- A *CC* can state that if two values of a feature are equals then such values are similar (this *CC* will be denoted as *CC*1 in this work). This *CC* involves only variables defined by a discrete and finite set of values.
- A *CC* can state that if two values of a feature belong to the same interval then they are similar (this *CC* will be denoted as *CC*2 in this work).
- A *CC* can state that if the difference between two values of a feature does not exceed a predefined threshold then they are similar (this *CC* will be denoted as *CC*3 in this work).
- A *CC* can be defined in such a way that it represents a number between zero and one according to how close a value of a feature is with respect to another (this *CC* will be denoted as *CC*4 in this work).
- A *CC* can state that if two values of a feature belong to the same set then they are similar (this *CC* will be denoted as *CC*2c in this work). This *CC* involves both quantitative and qualitative variables.

2.3   Confusion

The Confusion or error related to a feature (or feature set) is defined as the number of pair of values stated as similar, according to some comparison criterion implemented on features belonging to different classes. The lower the confusion is, the more significant the feature is for being used in order to differentiate the classes [15].

2.4   Testor and Typical Testor. Extended Definition

Given a table T with descriptions of objects from classes $T0$ and $T1$ and a set of columns of T denoted as τ, if as consequence of removing every column from T, except for those belonging to τ, no row in $T0$ is considered as similar with respect to any row in $T1$, then τ is defined as testor of classes $T0$ and $T1$. A testor is called as *typical testor* if it stops of being a testor as consequence of removing any of its columns [15]. Accordingly, if table T contains objects considered as similar and belonging to different classes, then testors could not be obtained.

In general, it's not usual to find descriptions of classes without overlapping between objects from different classes (disjoint classes). That is why an extended definition of testor states that if as consequence of removing every column from T, except for those belonging to τ, no new pairs of similar rows in $T0$ and $T1$ appear, then τ is defined as testor of table T [15].

2.5   Features Importance

Features involved in classification tasks exhibit different degrees of importance. There are different feature importance criteria. Feature importance can be determined by the following criteria [15]:

- As the proportion between the number of typical testors that contain the feature and the total number of typical testors ($I1$). Accordingly, a feature is more important as its presence in typical testors is higher.
- As the proportion between the inverse of the length of each typical testor that contains the feature and the number of typical testors that contain the feature ($I2$).

A more effective choice is to determine feature importance by the combination of these both definitions [15].

3   Applied Methodology and Available Data

As explained above, this research is focused on the application of pattern recognition combinatorial logical tools on the selection of the main features (quantitative and qualitative) involved on journal bearing fault diagnostics. To do that, data (vibration) from three journal bearings ($JB1$, $JB2$ and $JB3$) of turbines installed in an active thermal power plant were gathered for 10 years. During the monitoring time, 4 fault conditions were given: babbitt damage in the bottom half of JB (B), excessive clearance (C), babbitt damage in the bottom half of JB and excessive clearance (BC), and babbitt damage in the bottom half of JB, babbitt damage in the top half of JB and excessive clearance (BTC). Vibration data acquired from vertical and horizontal directions was processed independently, taking into account that the effect of a fault over the vibration from one of such directions can be quite different with respect to the other one (expert's criteria). Data sets of fault class B, fault class C, fault class BC and fault class BTC were comprised by 215, 354, 553 and 553 objects, respectively. The set of features built in order to describe each object was obtained from expert knowledge about vibration measures and journal bearings. A group of 18 numerical variables was created, comprising the amplitudes of the eight harmonics (*1X* to *8X*), the amplitudes of the seven inter-harmonics and the amplitudes of the three sub-synchronous frequencies. Besides, a group of 18 qualitative variables was created, comprising the name of the predominant spectral component (*Pred*) and 17 expert's opinion about the ratio between the amplitudes of each numerical variable and the synchronal component (*O2* to *O18*). *Pred* is a nominal variable and the rest of the qualitative features are ordinal variables.

In order to assess the effectiveness of the application of different criteria, the confusion between classes and the confusion of a feature for the same class were determined. The confusion between classes was computed by means of definitions given in Sect. 2.2. However, for the computation of the confusion of a feature for the same class, a new definition was proposed in this work. In this case, the confusion was determined by the number of time a feature (or features) did not result in similar. Features yielding confusions below 35% was the practical condition used in order to select the best comparison criterion. In addition to the simplification of the testors search, as an important result of this procedure, a first reduction of the feature set was achieved.

Comparison criteria *CC2*, *CC3* and *CC4* involve only quantitative variables. *CC1* and *CC2c* involve both quantitative and qualitative variables, however in this work such criteria involve only qualitative variables because the involved quantitative variables belong to the real number domain.

In order to measure how close two ordinal qualitative data are, a new comparison criterion, denoted as *CCm1*, was proposed to be applied for a qualitative feature *Xs*:

$$CCm1(Xs(Oi), Xs(Oj)) = 1 - \frac{|n(Xs(Oi)) - n(Xs(Oj))|}{k - 1} \qquad (1)$$

where k is the size of the alphabet of possible values of feature *Xs*, *Oi* and *Oj* are the objects to compare, and $n(Xs(Oi))$ and $n(Xs(Oj))$ are the positions of values taken by $Xs(Oi)$ and $Xs(Oj)$, respectively, in the entirely ordered alphabet.

Based upon the expert criteria, 5 sets of intervals were defined for working with *CC2*, 7 thresholds were defined for working with *CC3* and 5 groups of data sets were defined for working with *CC2c*. Since the output of criteria *CC4* and *CCm1* are both real, 8 and 5 thresholds, respectively, were also defined in order to measure similarity.

Results obtained by the confusion calculation were used in order to reduce the feature set, to select the best comparison criterion and to provide required information for typical testor identification. Typical Testors were computed based upon definitions presented in Sect. 2.4. The informational importance of features in typical testors is determined by using both definitions from Sect. 2.5 and the mean of them (*I3*). Computations were done by means of MATLAB, version R2015.

4   Results

The best results obtained from the computation of confusion for horizontal and vertical vibrations are shown in Tables 1 and 2, respectively. The terms between parentheses in these tables indicate the comparison criteria by means of which the best results were accomplished. Features $1X$, $2X$, $3X$, $4X$, $5X$ and $8X$ were the numerical data features that exhibited the best confusion results. For such features, $CC3$ was the most effective comparison criterion since the best confusion results are majority obtained by using this comparison criterion. Features $O2$, $O3$, $O4$, $O5$, $O7$, $O8$, $O16$ and $Pred$ were the qualitative data features that exhibited the best confusion results.

Table 1. Better confusion results. horizontal vibration

Feature	$JB1$ (%)	$JB2$ (%)			$JB3$ (%)	
	B-BC	B-C	C-BC	B-BC	C-BTC	
$1X$	–	–	–	29.49($CC2$)	–
$2X$	17.74($CC3$)	–	–	–	18.95($CC3$)
$3X$	–	4.47($CC3$)	24.12($CC4$)	29.94($CC3$)	–
$4X$	–	9.13($CC3$)	15.38($CC3$)	–	–
$5X$	–	–	15.98($CC3$)	27.95($CC4$)	–
$O2$	–	–	–	–	1.58($CCm1$)
$O3$	–	6.2($CC2c$)	4.5($CC2c$)	7.1($CC2c$)	–
$O4$	–	18.58($CC2$)	6.98($CC2c$)	32.54($CC1$)	–
$O5$	–	–	–	34.63($CC1$)	–
$O7$	–	–	6.12($CC2c$)	–	–
$O8$	–	–	25.37($CC2c$)	–	–
$O16$	3.88($CC2c$)	30.03($CC1$)	17.47($CC1$)	–	–
$Pred$	–	–	16.48($CC1$)	27.47($CC1$)	–

Table 2. Better confusion results. Vertical vibration

Feature	$JB1$ (%)	$JB2$ (%)			$JB3$ (%)	
	B-BC	B-C	C-BC	B-BC	C-BTC	
$1X$	–	–	–	–	$8.56_{(CC3)}$
$2X$	–	–	–	$17.96_{(CC3)}$	–
$3X$	$13.61_{(CC3)}$	$11.3_{(CC3)}$	$24.82_{(CC3)}$	–	$1.40_{(CC3)}$
$4X$	–	$3.24_{(CC3)}$	$16.25_{(CC3)}$	$13.97_{(CC3)}$	$1.69_{(CC3)}$
$8X$	–	$12.07_{(CC3)}$	$15.21_{(CC3)}$	–	$12.65_{(CC5)}$
$O4$	–	–	$26.05_{(CC1)}$	–	$6.10_{(CC1)}$
$O5$	–	$17.89_{(CC1)}$	–	–	–
$O8$	–	$13.28_{(CC1)}$	$15.11_{(CC1)}$	–	–
$O16$	$26.06_{(CC2c)}$	–	–	–	–
$Pred$	–	–	$30.01_{(CC2c)}$	$32.67_{(CC1)}$	–

The best confusion results were achieved by the work with *CC2c* and the processing of horizontal vibration acquired from journal bearings *JB*1 and *JB*2, and by the work with *CCm*1 and the processing of horizontal vibration acquired from journal bearing *JB*3 (Table 1). In case of vertical vibration, the best results were achieved in general by the work with *CC*3. Particularly in cases of faults *C* and *BC*, the best results were achieved by the work with *CC*1 (Table 2).

Typical testors obtained in order to differentiate classes are shown in Tables 3 and 4. In case of horizontal vibration, qualitative features play an important role in classes differentiation, since 8 of 12 features comprising typical testors are qualitative (*O*2, *O*3, *O*4, *O*5, *O*7, *O*8, *O*16 and *Pred*); the rest of features are quantitative.

Table 3 reveals that the pair of classes *B-BC*, related to *JB*2, can be differentiated by 9 typical testors; the pair of classes *B-C*, related to *JB*2, can be differentiated by 4 typical testors; the pair of classes *C-BC*, related to *JB*2, can be differentiated by 2 typical testors: the pair of classes *C-BTC*, related to *JB*3, can be differentiated by 2 typical testors; and the pair of classes *B-BC*, related to *JB*1, can be differentiated by only 1 typical testor. Table 4 shows that the pair of classes *C-BTC*, related to *JB*3, can be differentiated by 3 typical testors as the rest of the class pairs can be differentiated by only 1 typical testor. It is expected that the subsequent classification procedure performs better, for the pair of classes differentiated by the larger number of typical testors, once the testor concept is applied.

Table 3. Typical Testor. Horizontal vibration

JB#	JB1	JB2															JB3	
Fault	B-BC	B-C				B-BC									C-BC		C-BTC	
Testor	1X	1X	1X	1X	1X	2X	2X	1X	1X	1X	1X	1X	1X	1X	O3	3X	2X	1X
	2X	2X	2X	2X	2X	3X	3X	3X	3X	3X	2X	2X	2X	2X			3X	2X
	4X	O3	4X	3X	3X	4X	4X	4X	4X	4X	3X	3X	3X	3X			O2	3X
	O4	O4	O3	O3	O3	O3	O2	O4	O2	O2	4X	4X	4X	4X			O16	4X
	O8	O5	O5	O5	O5	O4	O4	O5	O4	O4	O7	O5	O3	O2				O16
	O16	O16	O16	O8	O7	O5	O5	O7	O7	O5	O8	O7	O7	O7				
	Pred			O16	O16	O7	O7	Pred	Pred	O7								
						O8	Pred			O8								
						Pred												

Table 4. Typical Testor. Vertical vibration

JB#	JB1	JB2			JB3		
Fault	B-BC	B-C	B-BC	C-BC	C-BTC		
Testor	Pred	Pred	Pred	Pred	Pred	1X	1X
						O4	2X
						O5	O4

The informational weights computed for each feature in some typical testor are shown in Tables 5 and 6. Here, features are ordered from the one with higher informational weight to the less significant feature.

Table 5. Features importance. Horizontal vibration

Feature	3X	2X	1X	4X	O7	O3	O5	O16	O4	O2	O8	Pred	5X
I1	0.78	0.72	0.72	0.67	0.56	0.39	0.50	0.39	0.39	0.28	0.28	0.28	0.0
I2	0.218	0.162	0.157	0.152	0.146	0.271	0.143	0.173	0.137	0.162	0.138	0.133	0.0
I3	0.499	0.441	0.438	0.411	0.353	0.331	0.322	0.282	0.264	0.221	0.209	0.207	0.0

For the case of horizontal vibration, Table 5 reveals that the 4 quantitative features are more significant than the qualitative ones, and that the feature $5X$ can be removed since its importance index is equal to 0.

For the case of vertical vibration, Table 6 reveals that the nominal feature *Pred* is clearly higher than the rest of the features, and that 5 features can be removed since their importance index is equal to 0. It can be also realized that a number of quantitative features larger than the number of qualitative features, which do not form part of any typical testor, can be removed without a significant loss of effectiveness of the fault class differentiation.

Table 6. Features importance. Vertical vibration

Feature	Pred	O4	1X	O5	2X	3X	4X	8X	O8	O16
I1	0.714	0.286	0.286	0.143	0.143	0.0	0.0	0.0	0.0	0.0
I2	1	0.33	0.33	0.33	0.33	0.0	0.0	0.0	0.0	0.0
I3	0.857	0.31	0.31	0.238	0.238	0.0	0.0	0.0	0.0	0.0

5   Conclusions

This research work represents an application of logical combinatorial pattern recognition on the identification of the important features employed to describe journal bearing faults. This is a first step oriented to perform journal bearing diagnosis and the first time that true data, coming from journal bearings of turbines installed in an active thermal power plant, is used in this kind of research.

This work also proposes the novelty of to include qualitative knowledge of experts about journal bearings diagnosis, in addition to quantitative information, onto the selection of the most important features for journal bearing fault diagnosis.

Through the applied methodology, the most important features involved on the description of the faults under study were identified. Indeed, a feature reduction was achieved when a starting data set comprising 36 features was reduced to 17 features.

The obtained results revealed the importance of qualitative data for journal bearing fault description.

References

1. El-Thalji, I., Jantunen, E.: A summary of fault modelling and predictive health monitoring of rolling element bearings. Mech. Syst. Signal Process. **60–61**, 252–272 (2015). ISSN 0888-3270
2. Khelf, I., Laouar, L., Bouchelaghem, A.M., Rémond, D., Saad, S.: Adaptive fault diagnosis in rotating machines using indicators selection. Mech. Syst. Signal Process. **40**(2), 452–468 (2013). ISSN 0888-3270
3. Lei, Y., Lin, J., He, Z., Zuo, M.J.: A review on empirical mode decomposition in fault diagnosis of rotating machinery. Mech. Syst. Signal Process. **35**(1–2), 108–126 (2013). ISSN 0888-3270
4. Pino Gómez, J., Hernández Montero, F.E., Montesinos Otero, M.E., Tellez, M.A., Gonzalez Martínez, J., Cruz Gúzman, Y., Arce Miranda, J.C.: Importancia para el mantenimiento de elementos mecánicos y fallos en turbinas de vapor. Análisis de históricos. Revista de Ingeniería Energética **XXXVIII**(2), 106–114 (2017). ISSN 1815-5901
5. Bilošová, A., Biloš, J.: Vibrations diagnostics. European Social Fund (ESF), Ostrava (2012). Project no. CZ.1.07/2.2.00/15.0132
6. Branagan, L.A.: Survey of damage investigation of babbitted industrial bearings. Lubricants **3**, 91–112 (2015)
7. Gómez-Mancilla, J., Castillo-Ginori, M.A., Marín-Herrera, A.: A turbo compressor operating with severe misaligned bearing problems. In: Proceedings of ASME-France, Workshop: Bearings under Severe Operating Conditions, EDF/LMS Poitiers, Francia (2002)
8. Gomez-Mancilla, J.C., Nosov, V., Silva-Navarro, G.: Rotor-bearing system stability performance comparing hybrid versus conventional bearings. Int. J. Rotating Mach. **1**, 16–22 (2005)
9. Saridakis, K.M., Nikolakopoulos, P.G., Papadopoulos, C.A., Dentsoras, A.J.: Fault diagnosis of journal bearings based on artificial neural networks and measurements of bearing performance characteristics. In: Proceedings of the Ninth International Conference on Computational Structures Technology, Stirlingshire, UK (2008). https://doi.org/10.4203/ccp.88.118
10. Byungchul, J.: Statistical approach to diagnostic rules for various malfunctions of journal bearing system using fisher discriminant analysis. In: European Conference of the Prognostics and Health Management Society (2014). http://www.phmsociety.org
11. Babu, T.N., Raj, T.M., Lakshmanan, T.: High frequency acceleration envelope power spectrum for fault diagnosis on journal bearing using DEWESOFT. Res. J. Appl. Sci. Eng. Technol. **8**(10), 1225–1238 (2014). https://doi.org/10.19026/rjaset.8.1088
12. Moosavian, A.: Comparison of two classifiers; K-nearest neighbor and artificial neural network, for fault diagnosis on a main engine journal-bearing. Shock Vib **20**(2), 263–272 (2013). https://doi.org/10.1155/2013/360236
13. Saridakis, K.M., Nikolakopoulos, P.G., Papadopoulos, C.A., Dentsoras, A.J.: Identification of wear and misalignment on journal bearings using artificial neural networks. J. Eng. Tribol. **226**(1), 46–56 (2012)
14. Ruiz-Shulcloper, J.: Pattern recognition with mixed and incomplete data. Pattern Recognit. Image Anal. **18**(4), 563–576 (2008)
15. Ruiz-Shulcloper, J., Abidi, M.A.: Logical combinatorial pattern recognition: a review. In: Recent Research Developments in Pattern Recognition, vol. 3, pp. 133–176 (2002). ISBN: 81-7895-050-2

Signals Analysis and Processing

Electroencephalographic Signals and Emotional States for Tactile Pleasantness Classification

Miguel A. Becerra[1]([✉]), Edwin Londoño-Delgado[3], Sonia M. Pelaez-Becerra[3], Andrés Eduardo Castro-Ospina[2], Cristian Mejia-Arboleda[2], Julián Durango[3], and Diego H. Peluffo-Ordóñez[4]

[1] Institución Universitaria Pascual Bravo, Medellín, Colombia
migb2b@gmail.com
[2] Instituto Tecnológico Metropolitano, Medellín, Colombia
[3] Institución Universitaria Salazar y Herrera, Medellín, Colombia
[4] SDAS Research Group, Yachay Tech, Urcuquí, Ecuador
http://www.sdas-group.com/

Abstract. Haptic textures are alterations of any surface that are perceived and identified using the sense of touch, and such perception affects individuals. Therefore, it has high interest in different applications such as multimedia, medicine, marketing, systems based on human-computer interface among others. Some studies have been carried out using electroencephalographic signals; nevertheless, this can be considered few. Therefore this is an open research field. In this study, an analysis of tactile stimuli and emotion effects was performed from EEG signals to identify pleasantness and unpleasantness sensations using classifier systems. The EEG signals were acquired using Emotiv Epoc+ of 14 channels following a protocol for presenting ten different tactile stimuli two times. Besides, three surveys (Becks depression, emotion test, and tactile stimuli pleasant level) were applied to three volunteers for establishing their emotional state, depression, anxiety and the pleasantness level to characterize each subject. Then, the results of the surveys were computed and the signals preprocessed. Besides, the registers were labeled as pleasant and unpleasant. Feature extraction was applied from Short Time Fourier Transform and discrete wavelet transform calculated to each sub-bands (δ, θ, α, β, and γ) of EEG signals. Then, Rough Set algorithm was applied to identify the most relevant features. Also, this technique was employed to establish relations among stimuli and emotional states. Finally, five classifiers based on the support vector machine were tested using 10-fold cross-validation achieving results upper to 99% of accuracy. Also, dependences among emotions and pleasant and unpleasant tactile stimuli were identified.

Keywords: Electroencephalographic signal · Sensorial stimulus
Signal processing · Tactile pleasantness

© Springer Nature Switzerland AG 2018
Y. Hernández Heredia et al. (Eds.): IWAIPR 2018, LNCS 11047, pp. 309–316, 2018.
https://doi.org/10.1007/978-3-030-01132-1_35

1   Introduction

The multisensorial (touch, taste, hearing, eyesight, smell) systems are very relevant for human-computer interfaces [1,12]. Most investigations are focused on eyesight and hearing senses, while, for touch, taste, and smell senses are reported few studies, and they are an open research field. The somatosensation is associated with the largest organ of the human body named skin, it has innumerable receptors and perceives and identify alterations of the surface (textures). This perception is crucial for relations among individuals and their context [14].

In [12] was proposed a method based on EEG signals, alongside Fast Fourier transform, principal component analysis, and artificial neural networks alongside particle swarm optimization for evaluating feeling of subjects when touching objects using 12 categories. This method achieved 67% of accuracy. In [14] is analyzed the sensation inducted by tactile caressing textile fabric of different textures on forearm in order to generate pleasant and unpleasant stimuli. They demonstrated the relation between affective valence and tactile perception. Besides, predicted pleasant and unpleasant tactile sensations from sub-band β of right hemispheric EEG signals achieving accuracy around of 70% using Bayesian logistic classifier. 13 volunteers participated in the experiments. In [7] a study from EEG signals using SVM and adaptive Auto-Regressive parameters for object shapes recognition from responses tactile, visual-tactile and audio-tactile stimuli achieved an accuracy of 88.02%. Ten rigid objects were used, and the signals were acquired from 10 subjects using Emotiv Headset of 14 channels. In [15] a tactile location prediction study based on linear support vector machine and features obtained from EEG signals is presented achieving an accuracy of 96.76%, which allow establishing the capability of the subjects for detecting the location of stimuli applied on their right forearm in 4 different locations. In [11] the effects of periodical sliding of natural textures (silk, wood, denim, and baking paper) against fingertip were analyzed from EEG signals and steady state evoked potential (SSEP) for tagging cortical activity, demonstrating the effectivity of the proposed approach and direct relation with the EEG amplitude at 3 Hz. Others studies have been focused on applications to BCI systems taking into account the tactile force and applications of somatosensory multimedia [10], visual and tactile feedback in HMI from EEG signals [3], wheelchair driving based on vibration somatosensory SSPE [8].

Based on state of the art, we considered that studies of tactile stimuli from EEG signals are limited yet, which was suggested by [11] in their review stating that there are no studies of the brain activity when stroking natural textures in humans.

In this work, is presented a study on three subjects for predicting pleasant and unpleasant of tactile stimuli from EEG signals and classifiers based on support vector machine. Four main stages were performed: Acquisition of signals (the subjects were exposed to ten different somatosensorial stimuli twice), then, signals were preprocessed. Feature extraction stage was carried out using wavelet transform, statistical measures and other features as area, energy, and entropy calculated from EEG sub-bands. Finally, SVM classifiers were tested with five different Kernels using 10-fold cross-validation. The best result 100% was achieved using polynomial, linear, custom kernel and all sub-bands. Finally, emotions states were analyzed, and their relationships regarding the ten stimuli were identified using Rough Set algorithms.

2 Experimental Setup

Figure 1 shows the procedure carried out in this study. First, a paradigm for EEG acquisition was applied, then, the preprocessing was performed for removing artifacts from the signals, standardization, and decomposition in 5 sub-bands. Then, multiples features were extracted from each sub-band obtained using discrete wavelet transform (DWT) and the Short Time Fourier Transform (STFT), follow by the feature selection for establishing relations and dependences, and finally, in the classification stage was used support vector machine algorithm with 5 different kernels, which were tested using 10 cross-fold validation.

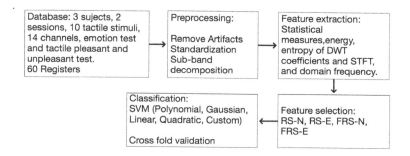

Fig. 1. Experimental procedure

2.1 Signal Acquisition Process

Three volunteers (one woman and two men) signed a consent form before the data acquisition. Besides, they filled out an anxiety survey [5], and a Beck's Depression Inventory [2]. The characterization of each subject is shown in Table 1. The participants had no diseases that affected the experiments such as skin allergies, chronic, or mental diseases. All subjects have normal ups and downs of depression levels and low anxiety (see Table 1). After the experiment, the participant filled out a questionnaire about identification and pleasantness level of tactile stimulus. Additionally, emotion survey was fulfilled before and after of the tactile stimuli using manikins showed to subjects to establish valence and arousal levels (b-valence: valence before the stimulus, b-arousal: arousal before the stimulus, a-valence: valence after the stimulus, and a-arousal:arousal after the stimulus) following the methodology depicted in [9]. Twenty registers were acquired per subject, and each recording has 14 EEG signals per stimulus.

Table 1. Depression and anxiety level, and age of subjects

Survey	Subject 1	Subject 2	Subject 3
Beck's depression	8 (Normal)	7 (Normal)	0 (Normal)
Anxiety level	Low	Low	Low
Age (years)	52	43	30

Fig. 2. Tactile stimuli

Table 2. Label of tactile stimuli - pleasant and unpleasant

Tactile stimulus	Contact paper	Feathers	Silicone	Wool	Wrikled aluminum foil
Label	Pleasant	Pleasant	Pleasant	Pleasant	Unpleasant
Tactile stimulus	Stones	Sand	Push pins	Sandpaper	Scratched cardboard
Label	Unpleasant	Unpleasant	Unpleasant	Unpleasant	Unpleasant

In Fig. 2 are shown the tactile stimuli, which are silicone, push pins, sandpaper, sand, stones, contact paper, wool, feathers, wrinkled aluminum foil, and scratched cardboard textures were used as tactile stimuli. The stimuli were labeled as pleasant and unpleasant based on the tactile stimuli pleasant level survey; it is shown in Table 2.

The acquisition of EEG signals was carried out in a controlled environment with low sound and low light. It is shown in the photo of Fig. 3. The participants had their shaved head. They seated on a comfortable chair, and Emotiv Epoc+ device was placed on their head. Then, the test was explained, and the participant was asked to keep their eyes closed. During the trial, ten tactile stimuli were presented in random order, but trying to alternate pleasant and unpleasant tactile stimulus following the paradigm shown in Fig. 3. The register was carried out in twenty seconds, from which 13 s were recorded as a baseline without the stimulus and between the seconds thirteen and twenty, cardboard was rubbed on the hand. The participant rested for twenty seconds, and his/her hand was cleaned using a handkerchief. Then, the subject took a rest for 20 s more before applying a new tactile stimulus. This trial was repeated two times with each subject.

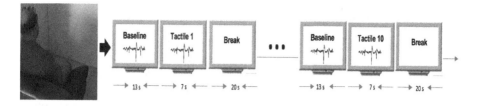

Fig. 3. Paradigm for EEG signals acquisition

2.2 Preprocessing

The EEGLAB software were used for removing artifacts manually and the EEG signals were standardized between -1 and 1. Besides, these were decomposed into 5 sub-bands δ ($0.5\,\text{Hz} - 4\,\text{Hz}$), θ ($4\,\text{Hz} - 7.5\,\text{Hz}$), α ($8\,\text{Hz} - 13\,\text{Hz}$), β ($13\,\text{Hz} - 30\,\text{Hz}$), and γ ($>30\,\text{Hz}$) using a 10th order Butterworth band-pass FIR filter.

2.3 Feature Extraction

Linear and non-linear statistical measures (mean, standard deviation, kurtosis, log energy entropy, Shannon entropy) were calculated alongside energy measures to coefficients obtained from the decomposition of EEG signals by discrete wavelet transform [6] using the Mother Wavelet Daubechies 10 ($Db10$). The same measures together with domain frequency were calculated to results obtained from applying STFT to EEG Signals. Forty five features were obtained from each sub-band (δ, θ, α, β, and γ) of EEG signals.

2.4 Feature Selection

We follow the methodology depicted in [13] for tuning the parameters of Rough Set Neighbor RS-N, Rough Set Entropy RS-E, Fuzzy Rough Set Neighbor FRS-N, and Fuzzy Rough Set Entropy FRS-E algorithm to establish the relationship among emotions (b-valence, b-arousal, a-valence and a-arousal), EEG signals, and tactile stimuli.

2.5 Classification

Support vector machine (SVM) [4] with five different kernels (Gaussian, Polynomial, Custom, Linear, and Quadratic) was tested for classifying the tactile stimuli as pleasantness and unpleasantness. The accuracy measure was calculated for establishing the performance of classifiers using 10-fold cross-validation. The classifiers were tested using features of each sub-band and features obtained calculated from all sub-bands for each subject and all subjects.

3   Results and Discussion

In Tables 3, 4, 5, and 6 are shown the results obtained for subject 1, subject 2, subject 3 and all subjects respectively, using SVM classifiers with 5 different kernels for each sub-band (δ, θ, α, β, and γ) and with all sub-bands. The best result for subject 1 was 99.49% of accuracy and was obtained for the sub-band α. Nevertheless, the best global result 99.86% was achieved using the polynomial kernel and all sub-bands. For subject 2, the best mean result of accuracy 97.44% was obtained using all sub-bands. The best global result 100% was achieved by three different kernels (polynomial, linear and custom) using all sub-bands. An accuracy of 95.9% was achieved using the sub-band β for subject 3 and the best global result 99.74% was obtained using custom kernel using the sub-band β. For all subjects the best mean result of accuracy 99.49% was obtained using the sub-band α and the best global result 99.86% was achieved using polynomial kernel using all sub-bands.

The relevance analysis results obtained from FRS-N, RS-E, FRS-N, and FRS-E algorithms demonstrated the relationship among EEG signals, tactile stimuli emotions expressed by valence and arousal measures. Besides, the results determined that for the domain frequency of the signal, Shannon Entropy of DWT and Energy of DWT as the most relevant features for all sub-bands.

Table 3. Percentage of accuracy performance - Subject 1

Kernel	δ	θ	α	β	γ	All
Gaussian	97.29 ± 1.68	99.22 ± 0.54	99.41 ± 0.58	99.09 ± 0.57	99.37 ± 0.65	99.43 ± 0.53
Polynomial	96.77 ± 2.52	99.41 ± 0.48	99.79 ± 0.37	99.18 ± 0.53	99.31 ± 0.6	$\mathbf{99.86 \pm 0.24}$
Linear	97.03 ± 2.6	99.43 ± 0.42	99.71 ± 0.44	99.28 ± 0.47	99.50 ± 0.48	99.75 ± 0.28
Quadratic	95.00 ± 2.22	$98.8 + 0.87$	98.76 ± 0.66	99.28 ± 0.57	98.99 ± 0.78	94.5 ± 1.95
Custom	99.46 ± 0.44	99.46 ± 0.51	99.77 ± 0.46	99.26 ± 0.52	99.43 ± 0.44	99.82 ± 0.26
Mean	99.11	99.26	$\mathbf{99.49}$	99.22	99.32	98.67

Table 4. Percentage of accuracy performance - Subject 2

Kernel	δ	θ	α	β	γ	All
Gaussian	98.61 ± 1.26	98.26 ± 1.64	97.85 ± 2.08	97.29 ± 2.05	96.32 ± 2.3	98.47 ± 1.63
Polynomial	97.36 ± 2.11	96.94 ± 2.72	97.85 ± 1.77	96.60 ± 1.93	97.36 ± 2.04	$\mathbf{100}$
Linear	97.08 ± 1.78	97.99 ± 1.77	97.64 ± 1.52	97.22 ± 1.57	96.53 ± 1.67	$\mathbf{100}$
Quadratic	91.80 ± 3.18	91.53 ± 5.3	85.14 ± 4.76	93.82 ± 3.88	93.06 ± 3.01	88.75 ± 4.75
Custom	97.22 ± 1.92	97.57 ± 2.32	97.57 ± 2.12	96.81 ± 2.17	97.29 ± 2.26	$\mathbf{100}$
Mean	96.42	96.46	95.21	96.35	96.11	$\mathbf{97.44}$

This work is compared in Table 7 with other studies based on the prediction of pleasant and unpleasant of tactile stimuli. This work presents the best result.

Table 5. Percentage of accuracy performance - Subject 3

Kernel	δ	θ	α	β	γ	All
Gaussian	78.91 ± 6.53	75.68 ± 4.83	81.72 ± 4.9	89.95 ± 3.42	84.9 ± 3.98	93.07 ± 3.4
Polynomial	99.43 ± 0.96	94.17 ± 3.01	96.93 ± 2.26	99.64 ± 0.67	98.07 ± 1.13	99.27 ± 1.21
Linear	99.53 ± 0.93	94.11 ± 2.83	96.82 ± 2.03	99.53 ± 1.3	97.97 ± 1.43	99.32 ± 1.46
Quadratic	86.25 ± 4.72	73.70 ± 6.16	80.78 ± 4.04	90.63 ± 3.48	84.32 ± 4.45	80.89 ± 6.39
Custom	99.43 ± 1.26	94.74 ± 2.82	96.98 ± 2.16	$\mathbf{99.74 \pm 1.17}$	98.13 ± 1.61	99.48 ± 1.18
Mean	92.71	86.48	90.65	$\mathbf{95.9}$	92.68	94.41

Table 6. Percentage of accuracy performance - All Subjects.

Kernel	δ	θ	α	β	γ	All
Gaussian	98.84 ± 0.69	99.22 ± 0.54	99.41 ± 0.58	99.09 ± 0.57	99.37 ± 0.65	99.43 ± 0.53
Polynomial	99.73 ± 0.32	99.41 ± 0.48	99.79 ± 0.37	$99.18 + 0.53$	99.31 ± 0.6	$\mathbf{99.86 \pm 0.24}$
Linear	99.48 ± 0.56	99.43 ± 0.42	99.71 ± 0.44	99.28 ± 0.47	99.50 ± 0.48	99.75 ± 0.28
Quadratic	98.04 ± 1.06	98.8 ± 0.87	98.76 ± 0.66	99.28 ± 0.57	98.99 ± 0.78	94.5 ± 1.95
Custom	99.46 ± 0.44	99.46 ± 0.51	99.77 ± 0.46	99.26 ± 0.52	99.43 ± 0.44	99.82 ± 0.26
Mean	99.11	99.26	$\mathbf{99.49}$	99.22	99.32	98.67

However, each study considered some different variables that can make them not comparable. Therefore, they should be analyzed in detail.

Table 7. Comparison with other approaches

Approach	Bayesian logistic classifier [14]	Artificial neural networks [12]	SVM (This work)
Accuracy	70%	67%	**99.86%**

4   Conclusions

In this paper, a study of pleasant and unpleasant tactile stimuli was presented. Support vector machine with polynomial kernel demonstrated a high performance using features extracted of all sub-bands (δ, θ, α, β, and γ) of EEG signals. We demonstrated the direct relationships among emotions, pleasant and unpleasant stimuli from EEG signals. As future work, we propose to widen the number of stimuli, number of subjects and make a multiclass classification analysis for improving the proposed system regarding discernibility and generality. In addition, a study of time traceability of tactile stimuli must be made for establishing if there exists a fingerprint of these or if these EEG responses are constructed based on the experience of the subject.

References

1. Becerra, M.A., Alvarez-Uribe, K.C., Peluffo-Ordoñez, D.H.: Low data fusion framework oriented to information quality for BCI systems. In: Rojas, I., Ortuño, F. (eds.) IWBBIO 2018. LNCS, vol. 10814, pp. 289–300. Springer, Cham (2018). https://doi.org/10.1007/978-3-319-78759-6_27
2. Beck, A.T., Steer, R.A., Brown, G.K.: BDI-II, Beck Depression Inventory: Manual, 2nd edn. (1996)
3. Chavarriaga, R., Perrin, X., Siegwart, R., Millan, J.D.R.: Anticipation- and error-related EEG signals during realistic human-machine interaction: a study on visual and tactile feedback. In: 2012 Annual International Conference of the IEEE Engineering in Medicine and Biology Society, vol. 2012, pp. 6723–6726. IEEE (2012). https://doi.org/10.1109/EMBC.2012.6347537
4. Cortes, C., Vapnik, V.: Support-vector networks. Mach. Learn. **20**(3), 273–297 (1995). https://doi.org/10.1023/A:1022627411411
5. Julian, L.J.: Measures of anxiety: state-trait anxiety inventory (STAI), beck anxiety inventory (BAI), and hospital anxiety and depression scale-anxiety (HADS-A). Arthritis Care Res. **63**(Suppl. 11), 467–472 (2011). https://doi.org/10.1002/acr.20561
6. Khalid, M.B., Rao, N.I., Rizwan-i Haque, I., Munir, S., Tahir, F.: Towards a brain computer interface using wavelet transform with averaged and time segmented adapted wavelets. In: 2009 2nd International Conference on Computer, Control and Communication, pp. 1–4. IEEE (2009). https://doi.org/10.1109/IC4.2009.4909189
7. Khasnobish, A., Datta, S., Konar, A., Tibarewala, D., Janarthanan, R.: Object shape recognition from EEG signals with tactile, visuo-tactile and audio-tactile stimuli. In: 2014 International Conference on Communication and Signal Processing, pp. 122–126. IEEE (2014). https://doi.org/10.1109/ICCSP.2014.6949812, http://ieeexplore.ieee.org/document/6949812/
8. Kim, K.T., Lee, S.W.: Towards an EEG-based intelligent wheelchair driving system with vibro-tactile stimuli. In: 2016 IEEE International Conference on Systems, Man, and Cybernetics (SMC), pp. 002382–002385. IEEE (2016). https://doi.org/10.1109/SMC.2016.7844595
9. Koelstra, S., et al.: DEAP: A Database for Emotion Analysis; Using Physiological Signals (2012). https://doi.org/10.1109/T-AFFC.2011.15
10. Kono, S., Rutkowski, T.M.: Tactile-force brain-computer interface paradigm. Multimed. Tools Appl. **74**(19), 8655–8667 (2015). https://doi.org/10.1007/s11042-014-2351-1
11. Moungou, A., Thonnard, J.L., Mouraux, A.: EEG frequency tagging to explore the cortical activity related to the tactile exploration of natural textures. Sci. Rep. **6**(1), 20738 (2016). https://doi.org/10.1038/srep20738
12. Nakamura, T., Tomita, Y., Ito, S.i., Mitsukura, Y.: A method of obtaining sense of touch by using EEG. In: 2010 IEEE RO-MAN, pp. 276–281. IEEE (2010)
13. Orrego, D., Becerra, M., Delgado-Trejos, E.: Dimensionality reduction based on fuzzy rough sets oriented to ischemia detection. In: Proceedings of the Annual International Conference of the IEEE Engineering in Medicine and Biology Society, EMBS (2012). https://doi.org/10.1109/EMBC.2012.6347186
14. Singh, H.: The brainâs response to pleasant touch: an EEG investigation of tactile caressing. Front. Human Neurosci. **8**, 893 (2014)
15. Wang, D., Liu, Y., Hu, D., Blohm, G.: EEG-based perceived tactile location prediction. IEEE Trans. Auton. Mental Dev. **7**(4), 342–348 (2015). https://doi.org/10.1109/TAMD.2015.2427581. http://ieeexplore.ieee.org/document/7097691/

Multi-horizon Scalable Wind Power Forecast System

Camilo Valenzuela[1]([✉]), Héctor Allende[1], and Carlos Valle[2]

[1] Departamento de Informática, Universidad Técnica Federico Santa María,
Valparaso, Chile
{camilo.valenzuela,hector.allende}@usm.cl
[2] Departamento de Computación e Informática, Universidad de Playa Ancha,
Valparaso, Chile
carlos.valle@upla.cl

Abstract. Wind power is the Non-Conventional Renewable Energy that
has become more relevant in recent years. Given the stochastic behavior of wind speed it is necessary to have efficient prediction models at
different horizons. Several kind of models have been used to forecast
wind power, but using the same kind of model to forecast at different
horizons is not recommendable, therefore a multi-model system needs to
be implemented. We propose an scalable wind power forecasting system
for multiple horizons using open source software, focusing on the forecast model selection, validated with Chilean wind farms data. Showing
that RNN models can make significantly better forecasts than traditional
models and can scale easily.

Keywords: Wind power forecast · Distributed system
Recurrent neural network · Long-short term memory
Echo state network · ARIMA

1 Introduction

Non-renewable sources of energy, such as oil, coal and natural gas, have been
used to generate energy, however this kind of energy source damages the environment and its use is related to climate change [11]. Given the above, new ways
of generating electricity have been developed with non-conventional renewable
sources such as photo-voltaic cells, wind turbines, reservoirs, etc.

Among the Non-Conventional Renewable Energies (NCREs), wind energy
has showed an important development due to its lower cost and faster returns
[8]. In spite of the above, its integration in electrical systems presents numerous
challenges due to the stochastic nature of the wind. For example, in the power
distribution schedule is very important to know how much power will generate
each power plant. An accurate forecast model is critical to know how much power
a wind farm will generate. Some countries impose by law generate wind power

Y. Hernández Heredia et al. (Eds.): IWAIPR 2018, LNCS 11047, pp. 317–325, 2018.
https://doi.org/10.1007/978-3-030-01132-1_36

forecasts at different time horizons. In Chile the agency in charge of the energy distribution schedule is the Economic Dispatch of Power Center (EDPC).

According to the Technical Standard of Safety and Service Quality delivered by the EDPC [1], the coordinator of a wind farm has to inform to the EDPC, the following information on the wind power forecast of the plant:

1. Short Term Forecast: Estimated hourly generation for the next twelve (12) hours, with hourly update.
2. Forecast of the Next Day: Estimated generation for the next forty-eight (48) hours, updated every six (6) hours.
3. Weekly Forecast: Estimated generation for the next week (next 168 h), updated every twenty-four (24) hours.

Therefore a multi-horizon forecast system is necessary to address the forecast required by law. Due the big amount of data generated by the different wind farms, the forecast system has to be able to scale easily.

In this paper, we propose an scalable wind power forecast system architecture using open-source software to make multi-horizon forecast. We detail each component of the system giving emphasis to the model selection.

This paper is structured as follows. In Sect. 2 we explain the wind power forecast problem. Section 3 has a system overview with the details of each component, emphasizing the models used and how they was selected. Finally, Sect. 4 is devoted to conclusions.

2   Wind Power Forecast

The models used to make wind power forecast can be divided in Physical models, Statistical models and Machine Learning models.

Physical models use numerical approximations to perform a phenomenological modeling that takes into account all physical factors and laws that affect wind speed. To use these models it is necessary to know the orography of the place, which can be expensive.

Statistical models seek to model the underlying stochastic process of the time series using historical data. The most used statistical models are those of the ARIMA family [4]. ARIMA models, model the underlying stationary stochastic process in terms of its past values and the aggregation of random innovations. Given a time series $\{x_t\}_{t \in T}$ indexed by the time T, the $ARIMA(p, d, q)$ model is defined as:

$$\Phi_p(B)(1 - B^d)x_t = \Theta_q(B)w_t, \tag{1}$$

where B is the back-shift operator $Bx_t = x_{t-1}$, $\Phi_p(B) = (1 - \phi_1 B - \phi_2 B^2 \cdots - \phi_p B^p)$ is the autoregressive operator, $\Theta_q(B) = (1 + \theta_1 B + \theta_2 B^2 \cdots + \theta_q B^q)$ is the moving average operator and w_t is a white noise process.

For a seasonal stochastic process, like the wind speed behavior, a Seasonal ARIMA (SARIMA) model can be used. It models the time series as a stationary and a seasonal component separately, and then are integrated in a new model.

Machine learning models consider wind power forecast as a regression problem. In a regression problem the model learns a mapping function (f) from a feature vector (x) to a continuous output vector (y).

One of the most used model for wind power forecast are the Artificial Neural Networks (ANN) [10]. ANN models are highly non-linear connectivist models inspired by the by the biological neural networks.

A time series can be seen as a sequence of numbers, so it is possible to use a Recurrent Neural Network (RNN). RNN are a family of ANN that specialize in sequential data processing.

An RNN can be seen as a dynamic system [3] of the form

$$y^{(t)}, s^{(t)} = g(x^{(t)}, s^{(t-1)}),\tag{2}$$

where $x^{(t)} = (x_1^{(t)}, x_2^{(t)}, \ldots, x_I^{(t)})$ is the input vector of the sequence at time t, $y^{(t)} = (y_1^{(t)}, y_2^{(t)}, \ldots, y_O^{(t)},)^T$ is the output vector of the sequence at time t, $s^{(t)}$ is the internal state of the network at time t and $g(\cdot)$ is the transition function that maps the input vector and the state at time $t-1$ to the output vector and the state at time t.

Depending on the RNN architecture of the network, the flow of information to the internal state may vary.

A popular RNN in wind power forecast is the Echo State Network [2]. The Echo-State Network (ESN) proposed by [6] uses fixed random weights between the input and the hidden layer and a big reservoir of neurons with random sparse recurrent connections (Fig. 1).

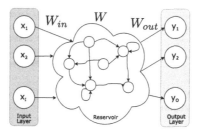

Fig. 1. Representation of a echo state network

In a ESN only the output weights W_{out} are trained. The training of an ESN start generating the input weights W_{in} and the sparse recurrent weights W with a random uniform distribution. Then the data is driven through the ESN. Given M sequences $\{x_i^{(0)}, x_i^{(1)}, \ldots, x_i^{(t)}\}_{1\ldots M}$ the output state of the sequence is updated by the following equation:

$$s_i^{(t)} = (1-a)s^{(t-1)} + a \cdot f(W^{in}x_i^{(t)} + Ws_i^{(t-1)}) \quad, i = 1 \ldots M,\tag{3}$$

where $s_i^{(t)}$ is the state at the time t from the $i - th$ sequence, f is an activation function usually tanh or sigmoid and a is a value between $[0, 1]$ called leaking rate that determine the flow of information to the new state.

After all the sequences are driven through the ESN, the final state of each state $S \in \mathbb{R}^{M \times N}$ is concatenated with the input vector $X^{(t)} \in \mathbb{R}^{M \times I}$ and the output weights W_{out} are the ones that minimize the equation:

$$[X; S] \cdot W_{out} = Y, \tag{4}$$

where Y is the output vector for each sequence. The minimization can be solved using least squares or a regularized version as *Lasso* or *Ridge regression*.

Other RNN architecture used for Wind Power Forecast is the Long-Short Term Memory [7], this RNN is designed to learn long term dependencies. The LSTM proposed by [5] replace the traditional neurons to a *memory cell*. A *memory cell* has traditional neurons in a specific connection pattern (Fig. 2).

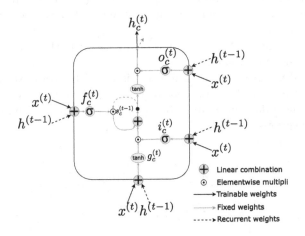

Fig. 2. A LSTM's memory cell representation, the sub-index c indicates the value of the cureent memory cell, without the sub-index notation refers to the layer output.

The components of a *memory cell* are the following: (1) Input Node (g_c): this node gives new information to the cell, (2) Input Gate (i_c): controls the flow of information that enters the cell, (3) Internal State (s_c): stores the internal state of the cell and has a fixed recurrent weight, (4) Forget Gate (f_c): it restrict the information that is maintained in the internal state of the cell, (5) Output Gate (o_c): controls the information output flow of the cell.

Given an input sequence $\{x^{(0)}, x^{(1)}, \ldots, x^{(t)}\}$, the *forward-propagation* of an LSTM is defined with the following equations

$$g^{(t)} = tanh(W^{gx}x^{(t)} + W^{gh}h^{(t-1)} + b_g) \tag{5}$$

$$i^{(t)} = \sigma(W^{ix}x^{(t)} + W^{ih}h^{(t-1)} + b_i) \tag{6}$$

$$f^{(t)} = \sigma(W^{if}x^{(t)} + W^{if}h^{(t-1)} + b_f) \tag{7}$$

$$o^{(t)} = \sigma(W^{io}x^{(t)} + W^{io}h^{(t-1)} + b_f) \tag{8}$$

$$s^{(t)} = g^{(t)} \odot i^{(t)} + f^{(t)} \odot s^{(t-1)} \tag{9}$$

$$h^{(t)} = tanh(s^{(t)}) \odot o^{(t)}, \tag{10}$$

where $h^{(t)}$ is the output of the *memory cell* at time t, W are the weights of a gate or node, σ is the sigmoid function and $\odot$ is an elementwise multiplication.

Each wind power forecast model type is better for different forecast horizons, physical models are better for long term forecast, on the other hand, statistical and machine learning models are useful for short and very-short term forecast [9], for that reason a multi-model system is a better option for a multi-horizon forecast.

3 System Overview

The design of the Multi-Horizon Scalable Wind Power Forecast System was guided with a self-imposed goal: Has to be easily replicated by other organizations, universities or companies.

To ensure this goal and have a industrial grade system, the software selected has to fulfill the following:

- **Open Source:** The system has to be constructed using Open Source Software, or community versions of commercial products, due their big community.
- **Hardware Independent:** It has to be able to work in a wide range of possible hardware, including Cloud and Virtual Machines (VMs).
- **High-Availability (HA):** The system must operate even when some of the components fails, and should continue working while it is maintained, updated or upgraded.
- **Secure:** Each component of the software must follow the basic security standards and practices.

The System Design (Fig. 3) is divided in two layers, the Database and Services Layers. The first one consist of a Time Series Database that store both the wind farm data and the forecast of each model, the forecast data then can be used to further improve the forecast model.

The second layer contains all the services needed for the system. To ensure that each component inside the service layer is isolated and secure we use Docker Containers[1], these containers recreate a system environment, similar to a virtual machine but lighter.

---

[1] https://www.docker.com.

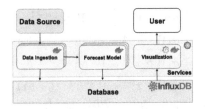

Fig. 3. System overview design

To have HA with Docker Container an orchestrator is needed. A Docker Container Orchestrator is used to deploy Docker Containers in a distributed environment, it handles the resource administration, fault tolerance in the event of a machine failure and works as a load balancer.

There are two main Docker Container Orchestator, Docker Swarm comes integrated with the Docker environment. The other one is Kubernetes[2]. Kubernetes was developed for a production environment instead of a developer one. The Docker Container Orchestator for this works will be Kubernetes.

The components inside the service layer are divided in three types: Data Ingestion, Visualization and Forecast Models.

Data Ingestion components will depend on the Data Source, there are generic data collection software, for example Logstash and Collectd, however, for this work we used a custom web scrapper to download and parse the Real Operation Power from the EDPC. The data is then sended to the Database to be stored, and is used by the Forecast Models to generate a new forecasts. On the other side the visualization component is used to monitor the new data and forecasts, the tool selected for this component is Grafana[3]. Grafana is a time series monitoring tool used to create interactive dashboards, its main feature is the simplicity to connect with time series databases.

More details about the Database Layer and Forecast Model Component are in Subsects. 3.1 and 3.2 respectively.

3.1 Database

The Database used for the Multi-Horizon Scalable Wind Power Forecast System is a Time Series Database (TSDB). This type of databases are optimized to handle time series data.

Now a days there are many powerful open source TSDBs. Most of them uses a Metric/Value schema to store the data. InfluxDB[4] is one of the most popular TSDB because it has a good performance and a simple configuration, but its community version doesn't have a distributed deployment.

Some alternative TSDB are services that uses powerful NO-SQL databases as backend, for example KairosDB uses a Cassandra cluster as backend or

---

[2] https://kubernetes.io.

[3] https://grafana.com/grafana.

[4] https://www.influxdata.com.

OpenTSDB uses the Hadoop's HBase database to store the data. Any of the alternatives above has an HTTP API to query the database with an scripting language to connect with Grafana.

In this work we use an InfluxDB Database in a single node, but for a distributed environment a KairosDB or OpenTSDB database can be used.

3.2   Forecast Model

To select the Forecast Model we need to look into its efficiency and effectiveness. The efficiency of the model is measured by the time used to make a new forecast, in other hand the effectiveness of a model is measured with an error metric in our experiments we used the Root Mean Squared Error (RMSE) defined as:

$$RMSE^{(h)} = \sqrt{\sum_{i=1}^{N}(\hat{y}_i^{(h)} - y_i^{(h)})^2}, \tag{11}$$

where $\hat{y}^{(h)}$ is the forecast of the model in the horizon h.

To validate the model forecast effectiveness two data sets from Chileans wind farms were used, Canela (Lat: -31.28699, Long: -71.599407) and Monte Redondo (Lat: -31.061664, Long: -71.613067) both in the Region of Coquimbo. Each data set has 7 years of hourly data, and each dataset is divided with 80% for training and 20% to test, and a further division of the training set for a 20% validation set to select the model hyper-parameters.

The models tested were the ARIMA, SARIMA, ESN and LSTM, as reference we use a naive model defined as

$$y^{(t+h)} = y^{(t)}. \tag{12}$$

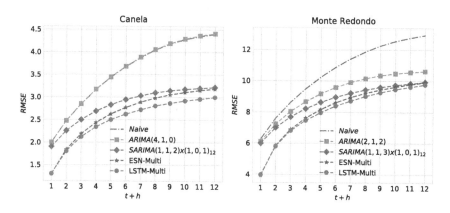

Fig. 4. RMSE for each horizon for the best models.

The results showed that for the short term horizon (12 h) the RNN models are better than the traditional stochastic models (Fig. 4), the latest make assumptions over the time series that limits the series that can be modelled. For a higher forecast horizon the forecast with all models are statistically the same, using another model is more appropriate.

In terms of efficiency, both the statistical and RNN models made the forecast in a short amount of time compared with the update time given by law. But the RNN models are implemented or can be implemented with high performance machine learning frameworks like Tensorflow or PyTorch, that scales to a cluster environment and GPU computation without any development.

4   Conclusions

Due to the multiple horizons that is required in some countries by law, a multiple model solution is needed to achieve the best results.

With the use of open source software, a replicable and scalable architecture can be built to support the multiple model system, and the development can be focused on the selection and implementation of the model.

Given the behavior of the wind power time series, complex models are required, traditional SARIMA models deal with the seasonal component of the wind speed giving better results compared to a naive and ARIMA model. On the other hand RNN models given their non-linearity can obtain better results, also this type of models are implemented in highly scalable frameworks that can be deployed in a multi node and GPU environment.

Acknowledgments. This work was supported in part by Fondecyt Grant 1170123, in part by Basal Project FB0821.

References

1. CDEC: Norma Tcnica de Seguridad y Calidad de Servicio. Gobierno de Chile (2016)
2. Chitsazan, M.A., Fadali, M.S., Nelson, A.K., Trzynadlowski, A.M.: Wind speed forecasting using an echo state network with nonlinear output functions. In: American Control Conference (ACC), pp. 5306–5311. IEEE (2017)
3. Goodfellow, I., Bengio, Y., Courville, A., Bengio, Y.: Deep learning, vol. 1. MIT Press, Cambridge (2016)
4. Grigonyte, E., Butkeviciute, E.: Short-term wind speed forecasting using arima model. Energetika **62**(1–2) (2016)
5. Hochreiter, S., Schmidhuber, J.: Long short-term memory. Neural Comput. **9**(8), 1735–1780 (1997)
6. Jaeger, H.: Echo state network. Scholarpedia **2**(9), 2330 (2007)
7. López, E., Valle, C., Allende, H., Gil, E., Madsen, H.: Wind power forecasting based on echo state networks and long short-term memory. Energies **11**(3), 526 (2018)
8. Schmidt, T.S., Born, R., Schneider, M.: Assessing the costs of photovoltaic and wind power in six developing countries. Nat. Clim. Change **2**(7), 548 (2012)

9. Soman, S.S., Zareipour, H., Malik, O., Mandal, P.: A review of wind power and wind speed forecasting methods with different time horizons. In: North American Power Symposium (NAPS), pp. 1–8. IEEE (2010)
10. Syed, M.S., Sivanagaraju, S.: Short term wind speed forecasting using hybrid elm approach. Indian J. Sci. Technol. **10**(8) (2017)
11. Team, C.W., Pachauri, R.K., Reisinger, A.: Climate change 2007: synthesis report, 104 p. IPCC, Geneva, Switzerland (2007)

Multiple Instance Learning Selecting Time-Frequency Features for Brain Computing Interfaces

Julian Caicedo-Acosta[✉], Luisa Velasquez-Martinez, David Cárdenas-Peña, and Germán Castellanos-Dominguez

Signal Processing and Recognition Group, Universidad Nacional de Colombia, Km 9 Vía al Aeropuerto la Nubia, Manizales, Colombia
{juccaicedoac,lfvelasquezm,dcardenasp,cgcastellanosd}@unal.edu.co

Abstract. Brain-Computer Interface is a technology which uses measures of brain activity to help people with motor disabilities. BCI applications based on Electroencephalography commonly rely on Motor Imagery paradigm. However, the estimation of motor brain patterns is affected by both variations in the signal properties over time (i.e. non-stationarity) and differences between frequency bands activations. Generally, Common Spatial Patterns is used as feature extraction. Nevertheless, its performance depends on the filter band selection and the time when the brain activity is associated with the task. A new method of time-frequency segmentation based on multi-instance learning is proposed. The spatial filters are built taking to account the obtained frequency-temporal segments where an instance selection based on Sparse Representation Classification method is developed together with a feature selection stage. The experiments are developed using a well-known dataset BCI competition IV dataset IIa that contains EEG records of nine subjects recorded from 22-electrodes mesh. The results evidencing that significant features appear at the end of MI interval and the found spatial patterns are consistent with MI neurophysiology. Furthermore, the proposed method outperforms the average classification accuracy of both CSP and SFTOFCRC for 8.21% and 1.23% respectively without deteriorating classification accuracy with statistical significance for subjects that present high accuracy with the compared methods.

Keywords: Electroencephalography · Motor Imagery
Multi-instance learning · Feature selection · Instance selection

1 Introduction

Nowadays, Brain-Computer Interface (BCI) is an important technology which uses measures of brain activity to help people with motor disabilities allowing them to an efficient communication with the world. Usually, BCI applications are based on electroencephalography (EEG) due to its non-invasive brain signal measurement method. A common EEG-based BCI system relies on Motor

© Springer Nature Switzerland AG 2018
Y. Hernández Heredia et al. (Eds.): IWAIPR 2018, LNCS 11047, pp. 326–333, 2018.
https://doi.org/10.1007/978-3-030-01132-1_37

Imagery (MI) paradigm that is the imagination of a given motor action without executing it. Decoding MI activity can be checked by the changes in the power bands [14]. However, estimating these changes are affected by (i) Variations in the signal properties over time known as non-stationarity due to the natural variability of neural responses even for the same condition. Additionally, these variations are associated to artifacts like loose electrodes, muscle movements, blinking, sudden shifts of attention, and effects of tiredness [7]. (ii) Differences between subjects brain activations, i.e. differences in frequency bands which are related to developed brain network for MI activations [1].

Consequently, the discrimination of MI activations requires a feature representation, feature extraction, and classification methodologies that must be suitably developed to reveal the main brain patterns from EEG. Common Spatial Pattern (CSP) is an algorithm proposed in [8] as a strategy of MI feature extraction. It searches optimal spatial filters to maximize variance for a class while minimizing variance for another class. However, CSP performance depends on the filter band selection [5]. In this regard, several methods are proposed as in [18] Optimum Spatio-Spectral Filtering Network (OSSFN) and in [19] Sparse Filter Band Common Spatial Pattern (SFBCSP). OSSFN proposed a CSP feature selection from multiple frequency bands. Similarly, SFBCSP method introduced by exploiting sparse regression for automatic frequency band selection. Nevertheless, the time during which the subject performs the MI task is known, the time when the brain activity is associated with the task is unknown. Despite, the significance of temporal features is exposed in [6,14] the extracted temporal features are ponderated without taking into account the variability between trials of the neural response.

A new method of time-frequency segmentation based on multi-instance learning defined as MILCSP is proposed. Our proposal build the spatial filters taking to account the obtained frequency-temporal segments. Each time-frequency segment CSP features is considered as an instance belonging to a bag. A relevance analysis allows analyzing of each time-frequency segment depending on the form of cerebral activation presented in each trial, without being tied to the search for a time window or a general frequency band for each subject. Multi-Instance Learning (MIL) framework used in [9,11,13] proposes an instance selection in order to choose the most relevant information for the classification stage. In summary, MILCSP in order to use only the significant time-frequency information, the instance selection is developed based on Sparse Representation Classification (SRC) [16] method which is proposed together with a feature selection stage as in [14].

2   Materials and Methods

2.1   Instance Selection

A multiple-instance learning problem holds a set of samples (bags) formed by several feature vectors (instances) [10]. For binary discrimination of MI tasks, we define the i-th EEG trial as a bag $\boldsymbol{B}_i \in \mathbb{R}^{M \times p}$ with M feature vectors extracted from time windows sliding along frequency bands, termed time-frequency instances, $x_{ij} \in \mathbb{R}^p$, and a label $l_i \in \{-1, +1\}$. Based on the sparse representation classifier (SRC) [16], bag instances are ranked according to their results for regressing instances of the same class as follows: $\beta_i = \arg\min_{\beta_i} \left(\frac{1}{2}\|A_i\beta_i - x_{ij}\| + \lambda_1\|\beta_n\|_1 \right)$, where $\|.\|_1$ and $\|.\|$ denote the L1 and euclidean norm, respectively, $\beta_i \in \mathbb{R}^M$ represents the vector of scalar coefficients for the linear regression, λ_1 is a positive regularization parameter which controls the sparsity of β_i, and the dictionary A_i holds the instances of other bags belonging to the class of B_i, i.e., $A_i = \{x_{kj}\forall l_k = l_k; k \neq i\}$. As a result, an instance of the i-th bag is sparsely reconstructed as the linear combination of the elements within the i-th dictionary $y_{ij} = A_i\beta_i$. Further, the residual criterion selects the instances with reconstruction error smaller than a threshold as $\widetilde{B}_i = \{\widetilde{x}_{ij}| \quad \|x_{ij} - y_{ij}\| < \mathbb{E}\{\|x_{ik} - y_{ik}\|\}; k = 1, \cdots, M\}$ [17].

2.2 Supervised Discriminant Representation

Under the assumption that discriminant time-frequency instances vary for each trial, a sparse regression of the labels allows selecting the instances better classifying a bag in a supervised framework: $z = \arg\min_z \left(\frac{1}{2}\|Sz - l\| + \lambda_2\|z\|_1 \right)$. Where the vector $l \in \{-1, +1\}^N$ contains the labels of the N training bags, $z \in \mathbb{R}^q$ is the sparse vector to be learned, $\lambda_2 \in \mathbb{R}^+$ is the regularization parameter. Matrix $S \in \mathbb{R}^{q \times N}$ contains the dissimilarity representation of the training bags:

$$
S = \begin{bmatrix} s(\widetilde{x}_1, B_1) & \cdots & s(\widetilde{x}_1, B_N) \\ s(\widetilde{x}_2, B_1) & \cdots & s(\widetilde{x}_2, B_N) \\ \vdots & \ddots & \vdots \\ s(\widetilde{x}_q, B_1) & \cdots & s(\widetilde{x}_q, B_N) \end{bmatrix}.
\tag{1}
$$

being $s(\widetilde{x}_q, B_i)$ the dissimilarity function between the bag B_i and the selected instance $\widetilde{x}_q$ [9]: $s(\widetilde{x}, B_i) = \max_j \exp\left(-\frac{\|x_{ij} - \widetilde{x}\|^2}{\sigma^2} \right)$. With $\sigma \in \mathbb{R}^+$ is the bandwidth of a radial basis function. As a result, the instances with $|z_q| > 0$ compose a set of the most discriminant features that correspond to the time-windows and frequency-bands that better reflect the MI task, so that the performance of classification machines is improved.

3 Experimental Set-Up

3.1 BCI Competition IV Dataset IIa

This database contains EEG records of nine subjects recorded from 22-electrodes mesh[1]. The subjects are instructed to perform four types of MI classes (left, hand, right hand, both feet, and tongue) in two sessions. Each session comprehends 6 runs with 48 trials (i.e., 12 trials per class and 288 trials per session). At the

---

[1] http://www.bbci.de/competition/iv/.

beginning of each trial, a cross of fixation is shown on black screen. After 2 s a cue in the form of an arrow pointing to the left, right, down or up (corresponding to the four classes respectively) appears by 1.25 s, where the subjects are asked to carry out the MI task until the fixation cross disappeared from the screen after 4 s. Finally, a short break is made where the screen is black. The EEG signals are sampled at $F_s = 250\,\text{Hz}$ and bandpass-filtered between 0.5 Hz and 100 Hz. In this analysis, all the trials marked with artifact are excluded and the EEG signals between 0.5 and 2.5 s after the visual cue onset are extracted for training as in [2].

In order to compare the proposed MILCSP method with the other state-of-the-art approaches, the first two classes are selected.

3.2   Parameter Tuning

CSP method is applied to a set of 48 frequency-temporal segments obtained from both frequency filter bands and time windows for each trial. To obtain the frequency-temporal segments, each trial is filtered using 16 sliding filters of 4 Hz between 6–40 Hz with 2 Hz overlap. Then, each slide filtered trial is segmented using sliding one-second time windows with 50% overlap [14]. Thereafter, a bag of instances is generated, which contains all the frequency-temporal components of each trial. Additionally, a dictionary is created for each bag and the instances are selected using a sparse regression that uses the regularization parameter λ_1. After the instance-based feature mapping to the dissimilarity space, a sparse regression (with regularization parameter λ_2) is performed in order to select features. The parameters λ_1 and λ_2 are tuned according to the maximum classification accuracy for each subject through a thorough search. Finally, the classification stage is developed using a KSVM through 5-fold cross-validation scheme. A Gaussian kernel is employed to estimate the similarity between s_i and s_t as $K(s_i, s_t) = exp\left(-\|s_i - s_t\|_2^2/2\theta^2\right)$ where the kernel bandwidth parameter θ is tuned as proposed in [4]. Figure 1 presents chosen parameters λ_1 and λ_2 for the maximum accuracy value (represented by the red dot). For illustrative purposes, these results are presented for the subjects 2, 3, and 5.

4   Results and Discussion

This paper proposes a new approach to the analysis of EEG mainly based on both instance and feature selection in a multiple instance learning framework. The importance of the two mentioned stages can be highlighted by analyzing the behavior of the subjects shown in the Figs. 1 and 2. Accordingly, for the subject 2 (Fig. 1-a), as is shown for the selected parameters values $\lambda_1 = 0.89$ and $\lambda_2 = 0.27$, the regularization generates a smaller instance selection matrix U. On the other hand, the subject 5 (Fig. 1-c) presents values $\lambda_1 = 0.18$ and $\lambda_2 = 0.56$, i.e., that not all the selected instances serve as discriminating features for this subject, so, the greatest contribution of the algorithm in this particular case is in the feature selection. This finding is in accordance to [3], who reported that

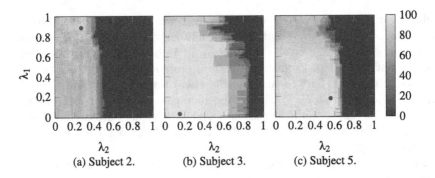

(a) Subject 2.   (b) Subject 3.   (c) Subject 5.

Fig. 1. Parameter tuning of features and instances selection.

subjects with the lower performance show fewer prominent features(or instances in our case) than those who perform better. Finally, subject 3 (Fig. 1-b) shows little regularization in the two stages($\lambda_1 = 0.03$ and $\lambda_2 = 0.15$), which shows that the proposed approach select effectively the most relevant regularization for each subject.

The instance selection and the feature selection with and without the instance selection are presented in Fig. 2 for the subjects 3 (a, b, c) and 5 (d, e, f) respectively. The analysis shows a grid of 16 frequency bands for 3 time windows where the lighter colors represent the most often selected components in both instance selection and feature selection stages. The subject 5 (d, e, f) shows activity during the two final segments of time in frequencies corresponding to high β band that is present in some subjects as is presented in [1]. These results evidencing that significant features appear at the end of MI interval and the importance of the time-frequency segmentation and instance-features selection presented. According to the subject 3 (a, b, c), while the obtained classification accuracy by CSP, SFTOFSRC and the proposed MILCSP method (see Fig. 4) is high, the selected features shows activity in the mu(μ) which is mainly linked to the motor cortex activity.

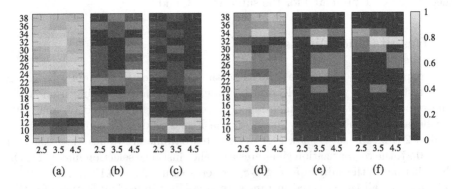

        (a)   (b)   (c)   (d)   (e)   (f)

Fig. 2. Relative frequency of the time-frequency components for instance selection (a, d), feature selection without (b, e) and with (c, f) instance selection. (Color figure online)

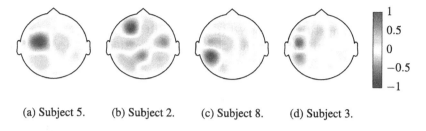

(a) Subject 5.   (b) Subject 2.   (c) Subject 8.   (d) Subject 3.

Fig. 3. spatial pattern during MI of left and right hand using the proposed MILCSP.

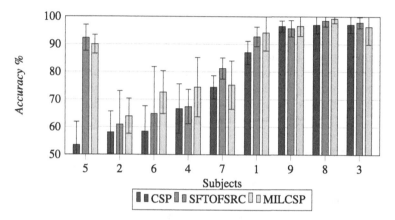

Fig. 4. Comparison of classification accuracies obtained by CSP, SFTOFSRC and the proposed method, MILCSP.

Figure 3 shows the computed spatial filters using the proposed MILCSP for both the two subjects with the worst and the two subjects with the best classification performing (i.e. the subjects 5, 2, 8, and 3). The found CSP spatial patterns include the discriminative information between all time-frequency extracted windows. For all the subjects the proposed method MILCSP found spatial patterns over the primary motor cortex (M1) and others secondary motor cortices as the posterior parietal cortex (PP) and supplementary motor area (SMA) which is consistent with MI neurophysiology [12,15]. Movement preparation links the M1 region which is important in sensory processing, the PP that translate visual information into motor commands and generating mental movement representations, and SMA which is important for planning and coordinating tasks. However, for the subjects 5 and 2 also show spatial patterns in frontal and prefrontal regions. This activation is related to higher mental functions as concentration or emotional expressions, that as is shown in [1], psychological and physiological states generate a low performance, as well as, reported the MI illiteracy having a less-developed brain network that is incapable of motor imagery.

Figure 4 contains classification accuracies for the nine subjects using CSP [8], SFTOFSRC [14], and the proposed MILCSP. The average classification accuracy of MILCSP improvements are 8.21% and 1.23% over CSP and SFTOFCRC respectively. The results of the proposed method are both significantly better than CSP and competitive compared to SFTOFSRC improving accuracy especially in subjects 2, 6 and 7 without deteriorate classification accuracy with statistical significance for other subjects.

5   Conclusions and Future Work

This work proposed a new method of time-frequency segmentation based on multi-instance learning. The multiple-instance learning techniques together with the selection of instances and features allow an effective selection of the frequency-temporal segments where the cognitive task is carried out, allowing to use the relevant information in each domain. The results evidencing that significant features appear at the end of MI interval and the found spatial patterns are consistent with MI neurophysiology. Furthermore, the proposed method outperforms the average classification accuracy of both CSP and SFTOFCRC for 8.21% and 1.23% respectively without deteriorating classification accuracy with statistical significance for subjects that present high accuracy with the compared methods.

From the attained findings of the work, we propose two future research directions for MIL: Firstly, we plan to improve the dictionary construction using multiple bags aiming to reduce the computational cost. Secondly, we intend to combine multiple similarity measures and features extraction procedures, highlighting discriminant properties of trials from subjects with low performance.

Acknowledgments. This work is developed within the framework of the research project 111077757982, funded by COLCIENCIAS.

References

1. Ahn, M., Jun, S.C.: Performance variation in motor imagery brain-computer interface: a brief review. J. Neurosci. Methods **243**, 103–110 (2015)
2. Alimardani, F., Boostani, R., Blankertz, B.: Weighted spatial based geometric scheme as an efficient algorithm for analyzing single-trial EEGS to improve cuebased BCI classification. Neural Netw. **92**, 69–76 (2017). https://doi.org/10.1016/j.neunet.2017.02.014
3. Allison, B.Z., Neuper, C.: Could anyone use a BCI? In: Tan, D., Nijholt, A. (eds.) Brain-computer Interfaces, pp. 35–54. Springer, London (2010). https://doi.org/10.1007/978-1-84996-272-8_3
4. Álvarez-Meza, A.M., Cárdenas-Peña, D., Castellanos-Dominguez, G.: Unsupervised Kernel function building using maximization of information potential variability. In: Bayro-Corrochano, E., Hancock, E. (eds.) Progress in Pattern Recognition, Image Analysis, Computer Vision, and Applications, pp. 335–342. Springer International Publishing, Cham (2014). https://doi.org/10.1007/978-3-319-12568-8_41
5. Ang, K.K., Chin, Z.Y., Wang, C., Guan, C., Zhang, H.: Filter bank common spatial pattern algorithm on BCI competition IV datasets 2a and 2b. Frontiers Neurosci. **6**, 39 (2012)

6. Balzi, A., Yger, F., Sugiyama, M.: Importance-weighted covariance estimation for robust common spatial pattern. Pattern Recognit. Lett. **68**, 139–145 (2015)
7. Bian, Y., Qi, H., Zhao, L., Ming, D., Guo, T., Fu, X.: Improvements in event-related desynchronization and classification performance of motor imagery using instructive dynamic guidance and complex tasks. Comput. Biol. Med. **96**, 266–273 (2018). https://doi.org/10.1016/j.compbiomed.2018.03.018. http://www.sciencedirect.com/science/article/pii/S0010482518300751
8. Blankertz, B., Tomioka, R., Lemm, S., Kawanabe, M., Müller, K.R.: Optimizing spatial filters for robust EEG single-trial analysis. IEEE Signal Process. Mag. **25**(1), 41–56 (2008). https://doi.org/10.1109/MSP.2008.4408441
9. Chen, Y., Bi, J., Wang, J.Z., Member, S.: MILES: multiple-instance learning via embedded instance selection. IEEE Trans. Pattern Anal. Mach. Intell. **28**(12), 1–17 (2006)
10. Dietterich, T.G., Lathrop, R.H., Lozano-Pérez, T.: Solving the multiple instance problem with axis-parallel rectangles. Artif. Intell. **89**(1–2), 31–71 (1997). https://doi.org/10.1016/S0004-3702(96)00034-3. http://linkinghub.elsevier.com/retrieve/pii/S0004370296000343
11. Fu, Z., Robles-Kelly, A., Zhou, J.: MILIS: multiple instance learning with instance selection. IEEE Trans. Pattern Anal. Mach. Intell. **33**(5), 958–977 (2011). https://doi.org/10.1109/TPAMI.2010.155
12. Hanakawa, T., Immisch, I., Toma, K., Dimyan, M.A., Van Gelderen, P., Hallett, M.: Functional properties of brain areas associated with motor execution and imagery. J. Neurophysiol. **89**(2), 989–1002 (2003)
13. Li, W.J., Yeung, D.Y.: MILD: multiple-instance learning via disambiguation. IEEE Trans. Knowl. Data Eng. **22**(1), 76–89 (2010). https://doi.org/10.1109/TKDE.2009.58
14. Miao, M., Wang, A., Liu, F.: A spatial-frequency-temporal optimized feature sparse representation-based classification method for motor imagery EEG pattern recognition. Med. Biol. Eng. Comput. **55**(9), 1589–1603 (2017). https://doi.org/10.1007/s11517-017-1622-1
15. Saiote, C., et al.: Resting-state functional connectivity and motor imagery brain activation. Hum. Brain Mapp. **37**(11), 3847–3857 (2016)
16. Shin, Y., Lee, S., Lee, J., Lee, H.N.: Sparse representation-based classification scheme for motor imagery-based brain-computer interface systems. J. Neural Eng. **9**(5), 056002 (2012). https://doi.org/10.1088/1741-2560/9/5/056002
17. Wright, J., Yang, A.Y., Ganesh, A., Sastry, S.S., Ma, Y.: Robust face recognition via sparse representation. IEEE Trans. Pattern Anal. Mach. Intell. **31**(2), 210–227 (2009). https://doi.org/10.1109/TPAMI.2008.79. http://www.ncbi.nlm.nih.gov/pubmed/21646680
18. Zhang, H., Chin, Z.Y., Ang, K.K., Guan, C., Wang, C.: Optimum spatio-spectral filtering network for brain-computer interface. IEEE Trans. Neural Netw. **22**(1), 52–63 (2011)
19. Zhang, Y., Zhou, G., Jin, J., Wang, X., Cichocki, A.: Optimizing spatial patterns with sparse filter bands for motor-imagery based brain-computer interface. J. Neurosci. Methods **255**, 85–91 (2015)

Sub Band CSP Using Spatial Entropy-Based Relevance in MI Tasks

Camilo López-Montes[(✉)], David Cárdenas-Peña,
and Germán Castellanos-Dominguez

Signal Proccesing and Recognition Group, Universidad Nacional de Colombia,
Manizales, Colombia
{julopezm,dcardenasp,cgcastellanosd}@unal.edu.co

Abstract. In motor imagery-based Brain-Computer Interfaces (BCI), discriminative patterns are extracted from the electroencephalogram (EEG) using the Common Spatial Pattern (CSP) algorithm. However, successful application of CSP heavily depends on the filter band and channel selection for each subject. To solve this issue, this work introduces a new supervised spatio-spectral relevance analysis (named HFB) from EEG. The proposal parameters allow controlling the number of selected spatio-spectral components and CSP features. The experimental results evidence an improved accuracy in comparison with CSP, FB and SFB assessed in the BCI competition IV dataset IIa. As a conclusion, focusing on the discriminative channels and sub-bands enhances the MI classification with a neurophysiological interpretation of the components.

Keywords: Spatio-spectral relevance · Renyi entropy
Brain-computer interface

1 Introduction

Current challenges in rehabilitation demand the development of viable and effective paths of communication between the brain and the exterior environment. Brain-computer interfaces (BCI) provide such a path with a particular attractive for re-establishing the capabilities of severely disable people to control the environment. Conventional BCI translates the brain activity encoded in the measured electroencephalogram (EEG), due to its easiness of use and noninvasivity [7]. Since the EEG amplitude is very weak and likely to be contaminated by artifacts as the muscular and eye movements, common spatial patterns (CSP) feature extraction reduces the influence of the common noise present along the recordings and highlights differences between mental imagination tasks [12].

Due to extracted CSP features depend on the frequency bands selected on each channel where it operates, wrongly filtered EEG yields poor performances [10]. Hence, setting a broad frequency range or manually selecting a subject-specific frequency ranges are joined to the CSP algorithm. To address the problem of manually selecting the operational subject-specific frequency band for

© Springer Nature Switzerland AG 2018
Y. Hernández Heredia et al. (Eds.): IWAIPR 2018, LNCS 11047, pp. 334–341, 2018.
https://doi.org/10.1007/978-3-030-01132-1_38

the CSP algorithm, filter band selection approaches either optimize the spectral filters [4,6] before applying CSP or selecting significant features from multiple frequency bands [2,11]. Nonetheless, both cases compute CSP from the full channel set that contains task-irrelevant and redundant information, yielding to overtrained systems [8].

For overcoming the above issues, this work proposes a spatio-spectral relevance analysis simultaneously selecting channels and bands in a supervised scheme. The approach, termed HFB, characterizes each channel within the set of bandpass-filtered EEG recordings trough the Renyi entropy. Then, we test whether trials from two classes have the same mean entropy, so that resulting p-values rank the spatio-spectral. According to a subject-dependent significance level, spatio-spectral components (channels in a frequency band) are selected to feed the CSP feature extraction and LDA classifier. Attained results prove that the introduced relevance analysis improves the classifier performance and enhances the representation of the motor imagery paradigm.

2   Materials and Methods

2.1   MI Dataset and Preprocessing

The proposed spatio-spectral analysis is evaluated on the publicly available BCI competition IV dataset IIa[1]. A collection of EEG signals recorded using a 22-electrode montage from nine subjects that compose the dataset. Each subject performs two sessions on different days with four motor imagery tasks, namely left hand, right hand, both feet, and tongue on two sessions. The session includes six runs with twelve trials per task, obtaining 144 trials for each class. Being the most used MI paradigm in the literature, this work considers the binary classification of left and right movement, for which Common Spatial Patterns (CSP) [3] and Linear Discriminant Analysis (LDA) perform the feature extraction and classification stages, respectively.

2.2   Sub-band Common Spatial Patterns

Let $\{x_n^c \subset X \in \mathbb{R}^T : n \in N, c \in C\}$ be a set of N acquired EEG recordings of length T and C the number of channels to be further bandpass filtered, adjusting two main parameters for each subject: elemental bandwidth $B \subset F$ and their band overlapping $\delta_B \subset B$. Therefore, the following set of bandpass-filtered EEG data is obtained: $\{\tilde{x}_{n,b}^c \subset \tilde{X} : b \in B\}$. For the above-described MI database, as carried out in [11], we use 17 band-pass filters with a bandwidth of $B = 4\,Hz$ as to cover the whole frequency EEG band $F \in \mathbb{R}^+$, ranging from 4 to 40 Hz and fixing the overlap between each other at $\delta_B = 2\,Hz$.

In binary classification tasks, conventional CSP finds a spatial filter matrix $W_b \in \mathbb{R}^{C \times 2K}$ to linearly map the bandpass-filtered EEG data $\tilde{X}_b \in \mathbb{R}^{N \times C}$ onto a space $\tilde{\tilde{X}}_b = W_b \tilde{X}_b$, so that variance of the mapped signal is maximized

---

[1] http://www.bbci.de/competition/iv/.

for one class while the variance of another class is minimized. The spatial filters $\boldsymbol{w}_b^* \in \mathbb{R}^C$ are the solution of maximizing the Rayleigh quotient:

$$\boldsymbol{w}_b^* = \max_{\boldsymbol{w}_b} \frac{\boldsymbol{w}_b^\top \boldsymbol{\Sigma}_b^- \boldsymbol{w}_b}{\boldsymbol{w}_b^\top \boldsymbol{\Sigma}_b^+ \boldsymbol{w}_b}, \text{ s.t.: } \|\boldsymbol{w}_b\|_2 = \boldsymbol{I}_C \tag{1}$$

where $\boldsymbol{I}_C$ is the identity matrix size $C \times C$, and the spatial covariance matrix of the class $l \in \{-, +\}$ is estimated as $\widehat{\boldsymbol{\Sigma}}_b = \mathbb{E}\left\{ \tilde{\boldsymbol{X}}_b^r \tilde{\boldsymbol{X}}_b^{r\top} : \forall r \in N_l \right\}$, being N_l the number of trials in class l. Notations $\| \cdot \|_2$ and $\mathbb{E}\{\cdot\}$ stand for ℓ_2-norm and expectation operator, respectively.

In practice, the optimization framework in Eq. (1) is equivalently transformed into the generalized eigenvalue problem $\widehat{\boldsymbol{\Sigma}}_b^- \boldsymbol{w}_b^* = \lambda \widehat{\boldsymbol{\Sigma}}_b^+ \boldsymbol{w}_b^*$ with $\lambda \in \mathbb{R}^+$. Thus, a set of spatial filters $\boldsymbol{W}_b^* = [\boldsymbol{w}_{b,1}^* \ldots \boldsymbol{w}_{b,2K}^*]$ are obtained by collecting eigenvectors that correspond to the K largest and smallest eigenvalues of the generalized eigenvalue problem. Therefore, the CSP feature vector that accounts for the bandpass filtered components (termed sub-band CSP – SBCSP) is formed as $\boldsymbol{\xi}_b = [\xi_{b,k} : k \in 2K]$ with $\boldsymbol{\xi}_b \in \mathbb{R}^{2K}$, where $\boldsymbol{\xi}_b$ in all trial that defined as follows

$$\boldsymbol{\xi}_b(\boldsymbol{X}) = \ln(\text{var}\{ \boldsymbol{W}_b^{*\top} \tilde{\boldsymbol{X}}_b \}) \tag{2}$$

where $\text{var}\{\cdot\}$ stands for the variance operator.

2.3 Improved Data-Driven Sub-band Spatial Relevance

Mainly, the plain SBCSP method in Eq. (2) does not reflect the contribution of $2K$ selected eigenvalues to discriminative spatial filter designing, encouraging the use of data-driven approaches to enhance the relevance estimation of each bandwidth. Besides, the CSP-based feature extraction methods poorly behave for the nonstationarity of EEG signals arises (not mentioning its degradation because of outlier and artifacts). In this regard, Entropy accounts better for time-variant structural information and is not sensitive to multiple modes.

Here, to select the most discriminative spatio-spectral components, we propose to compute the dissimilarity between different classes through the positive-semidefinite entropy metrics $H(\cdot) \in \mathbb{R}^+$, instead of further using variance-based methods as a measure of uncertainty. Provided a couple of class labels l, therefore, we define an entropy-based relevance criterion for enhancing the discriminative power of CSP features, extracted from b-th temporal-frequency component, as follows:

$$\rho_b^c(\tilde{\boldsymbol{x}}_{n,b}^c | l) = \text{d}\{\mathbb{E}\left\{ H(\tilde{\boldsymbol{x}}_{r,b}^c) : \forall r \in N_- \right\} - \mathbb{E}\left\{ H(\tilde{\boldsymbol{x}}_{r,b}^c) : \forall r \in N_+ \right\}\} \tag{3a}$$

$$\text{s.t.: } \rho_b^c(\tilde{\boldsymbol{x}}_{n,b}^c | l) \leq \varepsilon \in \mathbb{R}^+; \forall b \in B, c \in C \tag{3b}$$

where $\text{d}\{\cdot\} \in \mathbb{R}^+$ is a certain distance between class-related measures of entropy. Note that the smaller the value $\rho_b^c(\cdot)$, the more significative the component.

For purposes of implementation, the supervised distance $\text{d}\{\cdot\}$ is estimated as the significance of statistical t-test value, being ε a minimal threshold of accepted relevance computed for any bandpass filtered component that is fixed empirically. As regards computation of the measure of uncertainty in Eq. (3a), we use the Renyi entropy estimated below:

$$H_\alpha(\tilde{x}_b^c) = \frac{1}{1-\alpha} \log \sum_{t \in T} p^\alpha(\tilde{x}_b^c(t)) \tag{4}$$

where $p(\nu) \in \mathbb{R}[0,1]$ is the probability of ν, $\alpha \in \mathbb{R}^+$ is the entropy order and $t \in T$ are the time samples. Therefore, the feature set in Eq. (2) can be computed from the subset of channels and bands that agree the relevance criterion, $X_\varepsilon = \{\tilde{x}_{n,b}^c : \rho_b^c(\tilde{x}_{n,b}^c|l) \leq \varepsilon\}$, as $\xi_b(X_\varepsilon)$, enhancing the class discrimination in the new feature space.

2.4   Performed Classifier Accuracy

The introduced approach for sub-band CSP using relevance based on the spatial entropy (noted as HFB) is validated in an example of MI tasks, employing the LDA classifier accuracy a_c as a measure of the provided system performance. For the sake of comparison, HFB is contrasted towards similar approaches: Mutual-information Filter-bank (MFB) CSP [2] and Sparse Filter-bank (SFB) CSP [13] that accomplish the CSP feature selection stage using the mutual information and the Lasso regression, respectively. However, the latter approach includes a dimension reduction procedure additionally through a Lasso regularization algorithm. Likewise, an expanded version of HFB that incorporates the Lasso regression is also considered (noted as $H_\lambda FB$).

Therefore, three parameters are to be tuned: the entropy order α that means the considered degrees of freedom or complexity of computational burden, the Lasso regularization term, $\lambda \in \mathbb{R}^+$ that regularizes the bias-variance tradeoff of prediction error for each feature extracted from the sub-bands, and the significance threshold for the t-test $\varepsilon \in (0,1]$ that bounds the amount of spatio-spectral components to be selected. Thus, the entropy order is empirically fixed to 10, while ε, λ are set up based on a grid search for the best-reached accuracy as shown in Fig. 1, depicting by a dashed line the best-adjusted parameters for each subject.

As seen, the accuracy of subjects S3, S8, and S9 increases fast by fixing $\lambda = 0.4, 0.6, 0.6$, respectively. Hence, small and more restrictive significance thresholds are required to achieve a suitable performance, resulting in a few selected components. Nevertheless, for subjects S1, S5, and S7, a_c increases not so fast to achieve their best accuracy with less restrictive significance thresholds demanding a more substantial number of components to learn the common spatial patterns. Note that the parameter tuning allows selecting a small subset of channels and sub-bands that achieves an optimal performance for each subject.

For all subjects, Table 1 summarizes the accuracy performed by each contrasted approach, showing HFB outperforms FB, and therefore the use of the Renyi Entropy as a measure of relevance allows improving the band and channel selection method. This advantage remains even after including the Lasso regularization algorithm since $H_\lambda FB$ reaches a better accuracy than SFB.

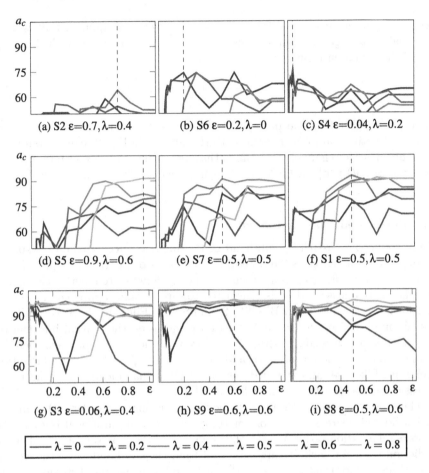

Fig. 1. Tuning curves for ε and λ. Subjects are sorted from the worst to the best performing in terms of the maximum achieved accuracy.

For visual inspection of the performed spatio-spectral relevance analysis, Fig. 2 illustrates the selected channels and sub-bands that have been selected for Subject #4 (with the least number of spatio-spectral components) and Subjects #5 (with most of the channels and bands). For the former subject, the approach selects only three sub-bands along the frontal and motor channels. Therefore, the representation space is reduced from 374 to just 19 features, increasing the achieved accuracy in 6% (SFB) and 10% (CSP) points. In the latter subject, all channels and most of the sub-bands are required to maximize discrimination between the two classes, either approach, HFB or SFB, performs similarly.

For the Subject #4, Fig. 3 depicts the spatial filters learned by CSP when EEG trials are band-pass filtered within 8–30 Hz and the ones for the selected channels and sub-bands. The channels with positive values (red) mean an additive term to build the spatial component, while negative values (blue) correspond

Table 1. Classification accuracy for the considered approaches. Mean and standard deviation for five-fold cross-validation is computed. Subjects are sorted according the performed accuracy, note that CSP is the baseline approach.

Subject	CSP	FB	HFB	SFB	$H_\lambda FB$
2	55.1 ± 8.1	46.9 ± 14.4	58.8 ± 5.2	58.0 ± 8.0	64.0 ± 8.8
6	56.6 ± 7.7	63.6 ± 6.3	74.3 ± 3.5	66.4 ± 3.5	74.3 ± 3.5
4	66.6 ± 12.4	69.0 ± 5.8	74.4 ± 7.4	69.8 ± 12.5	76.0 ± 8.8
5	67.4 ± 2.5	83.7 ± 2.1	76.9 ± 11.1	91.4 ± 8.9	91.5 ± 5.0
7	78.9 ± 4.2	84.9 ± 6.1	85.8 ± 10.4	94.8 ± 4.2	91.0 ± 7.3
1	89.1 ± 4.6	92.0 ± 1.7	84.1 ± 5.9	92.0 ± 4.1	92.8 ± 5.8
3	96.3 ± 4.5	96.4 ± 3.6	97.1 ± 3.1	98.5 ± 2.0	98.6 ± 2.0
9	96.5 ± 1.9	96.6 ± 1.9	97.4 ± 3.9	96.5 ± 1.9	99.1 ± 1.9
8	97.8 ± 3.3	97.8 ± 3.3	94.7 ± 2.0	97.7 ± 3.4	98.5 ± 2.1
Avg.	78.3 ± 5.5	81.2 ± 5.0	82.6 ± 5.8	85.0 ± 5.4	87.3 ± 5.0

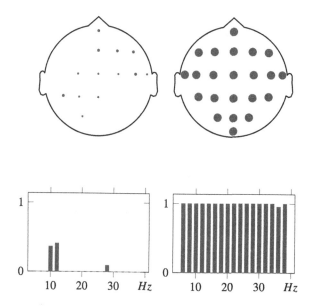

Fig. 2. Selected channels (top) and sub-bands (bottom) for Subjects #4 (left) and #5 (right).

to subtractive channels. White values implies that the channel lacks contribution in components selected. The 8–30 analysis (Fig. 3a) distributes the spatial filters all over the head without discriminating noninformative brain areas. On the other hand, the spatio-spectral relevance analysis (Figs. 3b to d) finds spatial filters that are consistent with MI neurophysiology as the inclusion of the primary motor cortex, the posterior parietal cortex, and supplementary motor area [5,9]. Additionally, HFB present frontal and prefrontal spatial filters at the frequencies of 10–14 Hz Fig. 3c and 8–2 Hz Fig. 3c that are related to higher

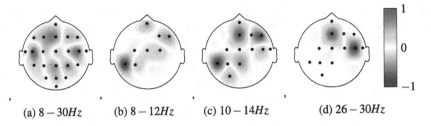

    (a) $8-30Hz$ (b) $8-12Hz$ (c) $10-14Hz$ (d) $26-30Hz$

Fig. 3. Spatial filters for the baseline band-pass filtered EEG and for the selected sub-bands of subject #4. (Color figure online)

mental functions (i.e. concentration or emotional expressions) [1]. The proposed method improves the classification accuracy by selecting the brain areas related to the MI activity.

3   Concluding Remarks

This work proposes a spatio-spectral relevance analysis to select the most discriminative spatial bandpass filtered components of EEG recordings, termed HFB. As the accuracy results prove supervised information to the relevance criterion enhances the discriminative power of the extracted CSP features. Besides, selected channels and frequency bands are neurophysiologically related to the cognition task of MI as the literature reports.

As a future work, the authors plan to construct sub-bands that can be adapted to each subject aiming to tackle the computational burden. Also, optimization of free parameters has to be studied using more elaborated strategies like particle swarm optimization (PSO) to avoid the exhaustive search of the tuning parameters λ and ε.

Acknowledgements. This work is supported by the project 111974454838 funded by COLCIENCIAS.

References

1. Ahn, M., Jun, S.C.: Performance variation in motor imagery brain-computer interface: a brief review. J. Neurosci. Methods **243**, 103–110 (2015)
2. Ang, K.K., Chin, Z.Y., Zhang, H., Guan, C.: Filter bank common spatial pattern (FBCSP) in brain-computer interface. In: 2008 IEEE International Joint Conference on Neural Networks. IEEE World Congress on Computational Intelligence, pp. 2390–2397, June 2008. https://doi.org/10.1109/IJCNN.2008.4634130
3. Blankertz, B., Tomioka, R., Lemm, S., Kawanabe, M., Muller, K.R.: Optimizing spatial filters for robust EEG single-trial analysis. IEEE Signal Process. Mag. **25**(1), 41–56 (2008). https://doi.org/10.1109/MSP.2008.4408441

4. Dornhege, G., Blankertz, B., Krauledat, M., Losch, F., Curio, G., Muller, K.R.: Combined optimization of spatial and temporal filters for improving brain-computer interfacing. IEEE Trans. Biomed. Eng. **53**(11), 2274–2281 (2006). https://doi.org/10.1109/TBME.2006.883649

5. Hanakawa, T., Immisch, I., Toma, K., Dimyan, M.A., Van Gelderen, P., Hallett, M.: Functional properties of brain areas associated with motor execution and imagery. J. Neurophysiol. **89**(2), 989–1002 (2003)

6. Higashi, H., Tanaka, T.: Simultaneous design of fir filter banks and spatial patterns for EEG signal classification. IEEE Trans. Biomed. Eng. **60**(4), 1100–1110 (2013). https://doi.org/10.1109/TBME.2012.2215960

7. Ortiz-Rosario, A., Adeli, H.: Brain-computer interface technologies: from signal to action. Rev. Neurosci. **24**(5), 537–552 (2013)

8. Qiu, H., Lee, J., Lin, J., Yu, G.: Wavelet filter-based weak signature detection method and its application on rolling element bearing prognostics. J. Sound Vib. **289**(4), 1066–1090 (2006). https://doi.org/10.1016/j.jsv.2005.03.007

9. Saiote, C., et al.: Resting-state functional connectivity and motor imagery brain activation. Hum. Brain Mapp. **37**(11), 3847–3857 (2016)

10. Sun, G., Hu, J., Wu, G.: A novel frequency band selection method for common spatial pattern in motor imagery based brain computer interface. In: The 2010 International Joint Conference on Neural Networks (IJCNN), pp. 1–6, July 2010. https://doi.org/10.1109/IJCNN.2010.5596474

11. Thomas, K.P., Guan, C., Lau, C.T., Vinod, A.P., Ang, K.K.: A new discriminative common spatial pattern method for motor imagery brain-computer interfaces. IEEE Trans. Biomed. Eng. **56**(11), 2730–2733 (2009). https://doi.org/10.1109/TBME.2009.2026181

12. Zhang, Y., Wang, Y., Jin, J., Wang, X.: Sparse bayesian learning for obtaining sparsity of EEG frequency bands based feature vectors in motor imagery classification. Int. J. Neural Syst. **27**(02), 1650032 (2017). https://doi.org/10.1142/S0129065716500325. pMID: 27377661

13. Zhang, Y., Zhou, G., Jin, J., Wang, X., Cichocki, A.: Optimizing spatial patterns with sparse filter bands for motor-imagery based brain-computer interface. J. Neurosci. Methods **255**, 85–91 (2015). https://doi.org/10.1016/j.jneumeth.2015.08.004

A New Approach for Fault Diagnosis of Industrial Processes During Transitions

Danyer L. Acevedo-Galán, Marcos Quiñones-Grueiro[✉],
Alberto Prieto-Moreno, and Orestes Llanes-Santiago

Departamento de Automática y Computación,
Universidad Tecnológica de la Habana, Havana, Cuba
marcosqg@automatica.cujae.edu.cu

Abstract. This paper presents a new approach for fault diagnosis of industrial processes during transitions. The proposed diagnosis strategy is based on the combination of the nearest-neighbor classification rule and the multivariate Dynamic Time Warping time series similarity measure. The proposal is compared with four different classification methods: Bayes Classifier, Multi-Layer Perceptron Neural Network, Support Vector Machines and Long Short-Term Memory Network which have high performance in the specialized scientific bibliography. The continuous stirred tank heater benchmark is used under scenarios of faults occurring at different moments of a transition and scarce fault data. The proposed approach achieves a classification performance approximately 20% superior compared to the best results of the four instance-based classifiers.

Keywords: Fault diagnosis · Transition process
Dynamic time warping

1 Introduction

Industrial processes are multivariable dynamic systems usually featuring multiple operating modes. The existence of multiple modes is caused by different factors such as the modification of the controller's set-point according to the desired manufacturing conditions (raw materials, product volume and desired quality) or environmental changes (variability in the climatic conditions of the production process) [4,10,15]. When a mode change occurs a process is considered to be in a transitional mode or transition. Some common transitions are startups, shutdowns, and changes of the controllers specifications.

Given that the widespread use of SCADAs in the industry guarantees the availability of historical data of the process, the use of data-based fault detection and identification (FDI) methods is appropriate. Data-driven fault diagnosis approaches develop pattern recognition and statistic-based models by using labeled data describing the process behavior [2]. A common strategy for fault diagnosis consists of using fault data for training a classification method offline.

© Springer Nature Switzerland AG 2018
Y. Hernández Heredia et al. (Eds.): IWAIPR 2018, LNCS 11047, pp. 342–350, 2018.
https://doi.org/10.1007/978-3-030-01132-1_39

Afterwards in the online stage, once a fault is detected, new unlabeled data are used for determining which fault occurs. Then, the process operator can make a decision for taking actions that prevent accidents and/or avoid process disruptions. Therefore, the accuracy in the fault diagnosis stage is of fundamental concern.

Data-driven FDI of processes under steady operating conditions has been tackled in several papers. Nonetheless, the fault diagnosis of industrial processes under transitional modes has not been completely addressed yet. Some previous papers have proposed an enhanced trend analysis approach or the Dynamic Locus Analysis method [11,12]. Those proposals, however, involve a large number of parameters to be set which makes unfeasible the practical implementation. Thus, the main contribution of this paper is a new approach to fault diagnosis of industrial processes during transitions. The proposal consists of a diagnosis scheme based on Multivariate Dynamic Time Warping (M-DTW). The fault diagnosis during transitions by using conventional instance-based classifiers may fail because they do not consider the time evolution of the signals. Since DTW is a similarity measure for time series, the application of a multivariate DTW is proposed for the diagnosis task in this article. The proposal is compared with the instance-based classifiers Bayes Classifier (BC), Multi-Layer Perceptron Neural Networks (ANN), Support Vector Machines (SVM) and Long Short-Term Memory Networks (LSTM). These methods were selected by considering their different working principles, good performance shown in the FDI literature and application advantages. The structure of this paper is the following. In Sect. 2 the classic approach to fault diagnosis is described together with the classification methods. The proposed approach is presented in Sect. 3. Section 4 introduces the Continuous Stirred Tank Heater as the case study and the fault scenarios considered. The results and discussion are presented in Sect. 5. Finally, conclusions are drawn.

2   Fault Diagnosis

The notion behind data-driven fault diagnosis is to make a decision respect to the fault affecting the industrial process under consideration by using the measured variables and a data-based classification tool. The classification process can be defined as the task of mapping the measurement space $(\mathbf{r} \in \Re^p)$ onto a set of z faults by using a decision function: $g(\mathbf{r}): \Re^p \rightarrow \Omega$ [5]. The decision function which guarantees the perfect identification of the faults is unknown. Thus, the parameters of $g(\mathbf{r})$ are estimated by using some examples (observations) of the faults data. If the classes to which the examples belong are known, the process of using data to determine the parameters of the decision function is known as supervised learning or training the classifier. The training process is developed offline, and the resulting classifier is used afterwards in the online stage for estimating the current fault. The descriptions of the four classification tools can be found in [3,5,6,9,13].

3   Proposed Fault Diagnosis Approach

The classification tools described in the above section map the input measurement space to the fault class space by considering a single observation. Thus, those methods are called instance-based. When a fault occurs in different moments of a transition the system's response is not always necessarily the same. For instance, if the transition is starting and a fault appears the control system may not be capable of completing the transition successfully. On the other hand, if the transition is finishing and the same fault appears the control system may be capable of compensating the fault effect. Therefore, since the process signals are time series, the time information must be considered when designing fault diagnosis methods for transitional modes. Hence, classification tools for time series can be used.

The most popular time series similarity measure is the Euclidean distance. When the time series to compare have different length the use of Euclidean distance is not appropriate given the known weakness of sensitivity to distortion in time axis [1]. Thus, given that fault training data may not necessarily have the same length of online data, the use of another similarity measure named Dynamic Time Warping is considered in this paper.

DTW is an elastic measure of similarity which allows the comparison of signals with different duration. Given two temporal sequences $T = \{t_1, t_2, \ldots, t_m\}, m \in \mathbb{N}$ and $R = \{r_1, r_2, \ldots, r_n\}, n \in \mathbb{N}$, an alignment path is defined as $C = \{c(1), c(2), \ldots, c(K)\}$ with $\{K \in \mathbb{N} | max(m,n) \leq K \leq m+n\}$ such that each element of $C(k) = (i_k, j_k)$ with $k = \{1, 2, \ldots, K\}$. Given any path the similarity between T and R can be calculated as $Distance(R, T) = \sum_{k=1}^{K} d(C(k))$. The Euclidean norm $d(C(k)) = ||t_{i_k} - r_{j_k}||$ is considered the measure of similarity between two observations. Thus, the DTW similarity is computed by finding an optimal alignment path

$$DTW(R, T) = \min_C \{\sum_{k=1}^{K} d(C(k))\} \tag{1}$$

The calculation of DTW is achieved by using recursive dynamic programming. In addition, the computational complexity is reduced by restricting the valid alignment path with monotonic and continuity constraints. Also, the Sakoe-Chiba Band as a global constraint is considered with a 10% width because a greater band does not guarantees necessarily a greater accuracy. There are myths regarding the impossibility of using DTW in a real time framework because of the time and space complexity. Nonetheless, those myths have been dispelled in previous papers by considering more complex constraints and comparison rules [16]. There are two main approaches for calculating the DTW similarity between two multivariate time series (M-DTW): the independent and the dependent way [8]. The independent consist of computing the individual DTW for each pair of variables independently and sum up all the distances. The dependent way formulates the distance d as a multivariate distance. The latter approach was

selected because it takes into account the similarity of all variables simultaneously and the former can be influenced by the signal scales. Finally, the decision
rule for fault classification is based on the 1-nearest neighbor rule:

$$g(M) = f_i \; with \; i = \min_{i=1,2,...,z} \{DTW(M, f_i)\} \tag{2}$$

where M is a multivariate time segment formed by the measured variables of a
process under faulty conditions. For determining the fault, a minimum length of
3 observations is considered for M. The segment size increases until a predefined
threshold such that a moving window approach should be defined. In this paper,
the threshold is set to the number of observations of the testing data set for
comparison purposes.

4   Continuous Stirred Tank Heater

The continuous stirred tank heater (CSTH) is a non linear benchmark problem
developed for assessing the performance of control and FDI schemes [14]. The
function of the CSTH is to distribute heated water for different processes. The
simulator is based on a real pilot process located at the University of Alberta [14].
Multiple operating modes are defined by the desired temperature and amount
of output water for consumption. Non gaussian noise is added to the outputs by
using real experimental signals [14]. Figure 1a shows the technological scheme of
the system. Hot and cold water are mixed within a tank continuously agitated.
The mixture is heated by using steam introduced by a heating coil. Input variables are the control signals of the valves for cold and hot water, as well as the
steam. The only measured variables considered are output temperature, level of
the tank and cold water flow with a sampling time of 1 s. All measurements
are in 4–20 mA format. The process simulation is performed with the Simulink
platform from $MATLAB^{©}$. Two operating modes defined in this paper are
[mA]:

1. {Level = 12, Output Temperature = 10.5, Hot-Water Valve position = 0}
2. {Level = 12, Output Temperature = 11, Hot-Water Valve position = 5.5}

   The mode change is given by an increase in the desired temperature of the
output water that provokes the opening of the hot water valve for achieving
quickly the desired temperature. The behavior of the variables is shown in
Fig. 1b. A transition occurs between mode 1 and mode 2 which lasts around
120 s.

4.1   Fault Scenarios

Four faults are considered to be diagnosed in this paper. A bias of the cold water
flow (f1), the level (f2) or the output temperature (f3) sensor, and the sticking
of the cold water flow valve at the 85% of the valve rod (f4). The faults type

(a)   **(b)**

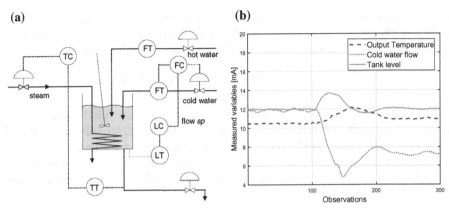

Continuous stirred tank heater.   Behavior of the measured variables
                                         when there is a mode change.

Fig. 1. (a) Continuous stirred tank heater. (b) Behavior of the measured variables
when there is a mode change.

is abrupt with a magnitude of -2.5 mA. Such large magnitude is simulated to
guarantee the fault detection given that the purpose of this paper is to assess
the fault diagnosis performance. Therefore, a detection delay of 10 observations
is considered after every fault is introduced. Each fault scenario is characterized
by the two conditions explained next. First, the moment of appearance of the
fault during the transition. The fault effect at different stages of the transition
may provoke different data features. Thus, the generalization power of the classification tool must be assessed for each fault independently of the occurrence
moment during the transition. Three different instances are then considered for
introducing the fault: 25%, 50% and 75% of the total length of transition which
correspond to observations 30, 60 and 90 after the transition starts respectively.
Second, the time of simulation for the fault. Although there is usually an abundance of normal data, the fault data is generally scarce. The performance of
classifiers must be assessed under a scenario when fault data is limited. Thus,
each fault is simulated over half the total duration of the transition after it is
detected (50 observations) for the training data sets. There are three fault scenarios: (1) occurring at 25% of transition, (2) occurring at 50% of transition, and
(3) occurring at 75% of transition. For all scenarios a training set of 50 observations and testing set of 100 observations were considered. Note that for the
testing data set the fault is simulated over twice the length of the training data
set for determining the performance achieved by the classification tools. The
results shown in the next section for each fault are obtained from the average
performance of the three experiments.

5 Results and Discussion

5.1 Classifiers' Performance and Parameter Selection

The performance of the classifiers is calculated by analyzing the correct identification of each fault. Thus, the confusion matrix $A = [A(i, j)]$ is used for defining performance measures. The element (i, j) of A represents the number of samples with the true class label i which are classified as class j [13]. From A, the overall accuracy and classification error can be estimated. The percentage of data that has been correctly classified determines the overall accuracy (Ac). Given z faults, Ac can be computed from the confusion matrix according to $Ac = \frac{1}{m} \sum_{i=1}^{z} A(i, i)$ where m is the number of observations. Hence, the overall percentage error is $Err = 100 - Ac$.

The parameters of each classifier should be adjusted for achieving the maximum possible accuracy. The procedure for setting the parameters is based on the ten-fold cross validation method to prevent the classifiers from overfitting and the loss of generalization capacity [3]. Then, the classifiers' overall accuracy is estimated by using the test data which has not been used for adjusting the parameters. For the Bayes classifier discriminant functions (minimum-error-rate classification) among the classes are used. The multivariate Gaussian is the (class-conditional) probability density function used [3]. In addition, different covariance matrices are assumed for each class and a priori probabilities are considered equal.

The multilayer feedforward neural network is selected in this paper because it is commonly used in pattern recognition tasks. The weights of the neural networks are adjusted according to the back-propagation error principle by using the scaled conjugate gradient method. A single hidden layer is selected given the Universal Approximation Theorem for ANNs [3]. The soft-max transfer function is used for the output layer such that normalized output vectors sum to 1.0, and that can be interpreted as the fault probabilities. The training set was split in this case. Part of the data (2/3) were used to optimize the layers' weights, and the other part (1/3) was used to decide the number of hidden neurons such that the maximum accuracy is achieved. The number of neurons estimated for the hidden layer equals 10. For the SVM classifier, the parameters $\{C, \sigma\}$ were optimized by using the error-correcting output codes approach included in the $MATLAB^{©}$ software. Three kernel functions were tested: Gaussian, linear and polynomial with order 5. The one-against-one strategy is selected in this work based on previous comparisons [7]. LSTM is a special type of Recurrent Neural Network (RNN) that eases the "vanishing gradient" problem [6]. RNNs employ recurrence, which consists of using information from a previous forward pass over the network, to make predictions where the data is in the form of a sequence (series of observations where order is important). LSTM networks are capable of accurately modeling complex multivariate sequences because of their ability to learn long term correlations in a sequence. The LSTM used in this study consists of a sequence of 4 layers: an input layer, 1 LSTM hidden layer, a dense hidden layer and an output layer with soft-max activation. The number of neurons obtained in the LSTM layer is 45 by using the sigmoid activation function. Achieving the minimum of the loss function known as categorical cross Entropy is considered for setting the number of epochs (1000).

5.2   Fault Diagnosis Results

The average overall train and test accuracy of each classification tool can be observed in Table 1. The instance-based classifiers with best generalization performance for each fault are highlighted in bold letter. The training accuracy of the LSTM networks is omitted because the maximum is always obtained in the experiments. The overall test accuracy of the Multivariate Dynamic Time-Warping approach is the best for the first three fault scenarios. The performance of the instance-based classifiers does not overcomes the 80% overall test accuracy. The valve sticking fault (f4) presents a distinctive pattern with respect to the other three faults which are the same type (a bias on a sensor). Thus, the fourth fault is classified with a satisfactory performance independently of the approach.

Table 1. Performance for the fault scenarios

Fault	Ac_{train}/Ac_{test} [%]						
	$LSTM$	BC	ANN	SVM_{Gauss}	SVM_{Poly5}	SVM_{Lin}	1-NN+M-DTW
f1	-/77.2	99.3/42.6	100/**78.06**	99.3/71.3	81.7/73.93	100/78	-/**91.4**
f2	-/47.8	100/37.96	98.03/39.1	100/**55.93**	89.5/45.86	88/53	-/**98.13**
f3	-/65.4	98.66/61.06	98.03/48.53	100/33.16	94.76/**78.4**	96.6/57.28	-/**93.93**
f4	-/100	100/**100**	100/**100**	99.33/99.3	99.33/99.3	100/99.3	-/100
Total	-/72.45	99.5/60.4	99/66.43	99.8/60.63	91.33/**74.43**	96.16/72	-/**95.9**

The loss of generalization power provokes a performance degradation between 10% and up to 60% for the instance-based classifiers. This result is motivated by two causes. First, the fault data for training is scarce (only the first 50 observations). Such scenario is not advantageous for the LSTM networks which demand more data for capturing the variables' relationships. Second, the time series patterns are different depending on the time of appearance of the fault. For instance, the patterns of faults occurring at 25% of the duration of the transition are different from the patterns of the same faults occurring at 75%. Therefore, the classification tool should be capable of determining which fault occurs independently of its moment of appearance during a transition. Hence, the proposed approach of using 1-nearest-neighbor M-DTW is appropriate because it considers the similarity of time-series for classification. Finally, the Dynamic Locus Analysis (DLA) method proposed in [11] without considering the fault separability constraint. If such constraint would be considered some observations might not be diagnosed preventing the process operator from making a decision. The overall test accuracy obtained was 91.13%. This result reinforces the motivation of this paper because DLA is also a time series similarity measure. The performance obtained, however, is not superior compared to the proposed method because the approach of searching similar segments followed in DLA introduces an error for the diagnosis process.

6   Conclusions

A new approach to fault diagnosis of industrial processes during transitions is presented. The proposal is based on the nearest-neighbor classification rule combined with the time series similarity measure Dynamic Time Warping in its multivariate form. The advantage of the proposed strategy is compared with four different classifiers: LSTM, BC, ANN and SVM. Their performance was tested under different fault scenarios during a transition in the CSTH benchmark. Among the classification tools the SVM variants outperform the rest. Nonetheless, the proposed approach achieves a superior performance.

References

1. Berndt, D., Clifford, J.: Using dynamic time warping to find patterns in time series. In: AAAI Workshop on Knowledge Discovery in Databases, pp. 229–248 (1994)
2. Chiang, L.H., Russell, E.L., Braatz, R.D.: Fault Detection and Diagnosis in Industrial Systems. Springer, London (2001). https://doi.org/10.1007/978-1-4471-0347-9
3. Dougherty, G.: Pattern Recognition and Classification. Springer, New York (2013). https://doi.org/10.1007/978-1-4614-5323-9
4. He, Y., Zhou, L., Ge, Z., Song, Z.: Distributed model projection based transition processes recognition and quality-related fault detection. Chemom. Intell. Lab. Syst. **159**, 69–79 (2016)
5. Heijden, F.V.D., Duin, R., Ridder, D.D., Tax, D.: Classification, Parameter Estimation and State Estimation. Wiley, Hoboken (2004)
6. Hochreiter, S., Schmidhuber, J.: Long short term memory networks. Neural Comput. **9**(8), 1735–1780 (1997)
7. Hsu, C., Lin, C.: A comparison of methods for multiclass support vector machines. IEEE Trans. Neural Netw. **13**(2), 415–425 (2002)
8. Mueen, A., Keogh, E.: Extracting optimal performance from dynamic time warping. In: KDD, pp. 2129–2130 (2016)
9. Scholkopf, B., Smola, A.: Learning with Kernels: Support Vector Machines, Regularization, Optimization, and Beyond. MIT Press, Cambridge (2002)
10. Song, B., Tan, S., Shi, H.: Key principal components with recursive local outlier factor for multimode chemical process monitoring. J. Process Control **47**, 136–149 (2016)
11. Srinivasan, R., Qian, M.S.: Online fault diagnosis and state identification during process transitions using dynamic locus analysis. Chem. Eng. Sci. **61**, 6109–6132 (2006)
12. Sundarraman, A., Srini, R.: Monitoring transitions in chemical plants using enhanced trend analysis. Comput. Chem. Eng. **27**, 1455–1472 (2003)
13. Theodoridis, S., Koutroumbas, K.: Pattern Recognition. Elsevier (2009)

14. Thornhill, N.F., Patwardhan, S.C., Shah, S.L.: A continuous stirred tank heater simulation model with applications. J. Process Control **18**, 347–360 (2008)
15. Wang, L., Yang, C., Sun, Y.: Multi-mode process monitoring approach based on moving window hidden Markov model. Ind. Eng. Chem. Res. **57**(1), 292–301 (2017)
16. Wang, X., Mueen, A., Ding, H., Trajcevski, G., Scheuermann, P., Keogh, E.: Experimental comparison of representation methods and distance measures for time series data. Data Min. Knowl. Discov. **26**, 275–309 (2013)

Detecting EEG Dynamic Changes Using Supervised Temporal Patterns

Luisa F. Velasquez-Martinez$^{(\boxtimes)}$, F. Y. Zapata-Castaño, David Cárdenas-Peña, and Germán Castellanos-Dominguez

Signal Processing and Recognition Group, Universidad Nacional de Colombia, Manizales, Colombia
lfvelasquezma@unal.edu.co

Abstract. The electroencephalogram signal records the neural activation at electrodes placed over the scalp. Brain-Computer Interfaces decode brain activity measured by EEG to send commands to external devices. The most well-known BCI systems are based on Motor Imagery paradigm that corresponds to the imagination of a motor action without execution. Event-Related Desynchronization and Synchronization shows the channel-wise temporal dynamics related to the motor activity. However, ERD/S demands the application of a large bank of narrowband filters to find dynamic changes and the assumption of temporal alignment ignores the between-trial temporal variations of neuronal activity. Taking to account the temporal variations, this work introduces a signal filtering analysis based on the estimation of Supervised Temporal Patterns that decode brain dynamics in MI paradigm which result from the solution of a generalized eigenvalues problem. The signal filtering analysis detects temporal dynamics related to MI tasks within each trial. The method highlights MI activity along channels and trials and shows differences between subjects performing these kinds of tasks.

Keywords: Supervised Temporal Patterns · EEG signal
Motor Imagery · Temporal dynamics

1 Introduction

The human brain is a complex network containing billions of neurons and trillions of connections that activate differently for mental conditions [12]. Although neural data is both observed and registered by several noninvasive neuroimage techniques, the high temporal resolution and low cost of the electroencephalogram (EEG) signal make it widely used to study brain dynamics in several applications as evoked potentials, investigating epilepsy and locating seizure origin [10,17]. EEG records the neural activation at electrodes placed over the scalp. Moreover, Brain-Computer Interfaces (BCI) decode the mental intentions from the EEG to send commands to external devices. Nowadays, BCI systems range from applications to improve the live quality of physically-disabled people

© Springer Nature Switzerland AG 2018
Y. Hernández Heredia et al. (Eds.): IWAIPR 2018, LNCS 11047, pp. 351–358, 2018.
https://doi.org/10.1007/978-3-030-01132-1_40

to applications enhancing the experience of games and education [18]. The most known BCI systems follow the Motor Imagery (MI) paradigm that corresponds to the imagination of a motor action without execution because of the similarities between imagined and executed actions at the neural level. So that particular frequencies, known as sensorimotor rhythms, arise on the EEG recording [9].

To identify the response of an MI intention, Event-Related Desynchronization (ERD) and Synchronization (ERS) show the channel-wise temporal dynamics within an EEG channel as the average energy relative to a reference time segment [4]. Despite highlighting changes in the excitation at the cortical motor regions and rhythms μ ([8, 13] Hz) and β ([13, 30] Hz), ERD/S demands the application of a large bank of narrowband filters to find dynamic changes [19]. Moreover, the MI neural patterns depend on complex brain activations including visual stimuli, selection and generation of the appropriate MI. The above activations generate a non-time-locked response, which indicates that the MI responses vary over trials [8, 16]. To solve such an issue, the spatial and temporal design of filters from data highlights the EEG time dynamics [7]. However, the assumption of temporal alignment neglects the between-trial temporal variations of neuronal activity [5].

Aiming to overcome the within-trial variations, this work proposes a signal filtering analysis based on the estimation of Supervised Temporal Patterns that decode brain dynamics in MI paradigm. The initial time embedding of EEG channels tackles the temporal variability. Then, the Supervised Temporal Patterns result from the solution of a generalized eigenvalues problem as the impulse response of a linear filter. Finally, the signal filtering analysis allows detecting dynamics related to MI tasks within each trial. Evaluation of the proposed methodology on two subjects from well-known BCI dataset indicates the highlighting of MI activity along channels and trials. Further, the patterns estimated from EEG data decode differences between subjects performing these kinds of tasks. The remainder of this work is organized as follows: Sect. 2 contains the theoretical background of Supervised Temporal Patterns estimation. Section 3 describes the performed experiments. Section 4 discusses the attained results. Finally, Sect. 5 presents the conclusions and future work.

2   Supervised Temporal Patterns

Let $\{\boldsymbol{x}_r^c \in \mathbb{R}^T : r \in [1, R], c \in [1, C]\}$ and $\{\boldsymbol{y}_s^c \in \mathbb{R}^T : s \in [1, S], c \in [1, C]\}$ be two sets of EEG trials that last T time instants, and belong to two different conditions. c, r, s index the channel, trials from condition X, and from Y, respectively. For each trial and channel, the temporal embedding produces matrices $\boldsymbol{X}_r^c \in \mathbb{R}^{M \times N}$ and $\boldsymbol{Y}_s^c \in \mathbb{R}^{M \times N}$ by stacking the N time-lagged windows of size M that fit in the trial duration [7]. Then, the condition-wise temporal covariances are given by $\boldsymbol{\Sigma}_X = \mathbb{E}\left\{\boldsymbol{X}_r^c \boldsymbol{X}_r^{c\top} : r\right\}$ and $\boldsymbol{\Sigma}_Y = \mathbb{E}\left\{\boldsymbol{Y}_s^c \boldsymbol{Y}_s^{c\top} : s\right\}$, both sizing $M \times M$.

Aiming to discriminate X and Y from their embeddings, the simultaneous diagonalization of covariances matrices solves the optimization problem

$$\max_{\boldsymbol{W}} \boldsymbol{W}^\top \boldsymbol{\Sigma}_X \boldsymbol{W}, \quad \text{s.t. } \boldsymbol{W}^\top \left(\boldsymbol{\Sigma}_X + \boldsymbol{\Sigma}_Y\right) \boldsymbol{W} = \boldsymbol{I}, \tag{1}$$

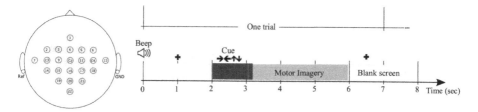

Fig. 1. Left: dataset EEG electrode positions. **Right**: trial timing of the MI (Cue MI: left hand, right hand, feet, and tongue.)

being $W \in \mathbb{R}^{M \times M}$ the diagonalization matrix. Stating the simultaneous diagonalization as a generalized eigenvalues problem allows to find M orthogonal projections of covariance matrices. Combination of the cost function and the constraint encodes most of the variance of Σ_X in the first eigenvectors, while the last eigenvectors accounts most of the variance of Σ_Y. As a result, directly deriving the generalized eigenvectors from data defines the impulse responses of linear filters, termed Supervised Temporal Patterns, that are optimally suited for distinguishing between the two conditions at the channel level.

3 Experimental Set-Up

3.1 EEG Dataset

Dataset 2a, provided by the Institute for Knowledge Discovery at the Graz University of Technology, contains EEG signals measured from 9 subjects with 22 channels sampled at $F_s = 250\,\text{Hz}$ and bandpass-filtered between 0.5 and $100\,\text{Hz}$[1]. The dataset consists of trials belonging to one of four MI tasks (left hand, right hand, both feet, and tongue). The experiment included recordings from two days and six runs separated by short breaks. Each run holds 48 trials lasting of 7 s and distributed as depicted by Fig. 1. First, a beep indicates the trial beginning. Then, a fixation cross appears on the black screen for the first 2 s, followed by the task cue as an arrow to the left, the right, up or down for 1.25 s that indicate to imagine a left hand, right hand, both feet or tongue movement, respectively. During seconds 3 to 6, the subjects carry out the MI task while the cross reappears. Finally, the dataset marks trials with artifacts, that we further remove.

3.2 Parameter Set-Up

Figure 2 illustrates the proposed five-step procedure to compute the supervised temporal patterns: (i) For all the experimental trials, we conduct a channel-wise analysis. (ii) We define the two EEG conditions as MI task (X) and reference (Y). The latter results from extracting the 0–2 s when the subject is seeing the

---

[1] www.bbci.de/competition/iv/.

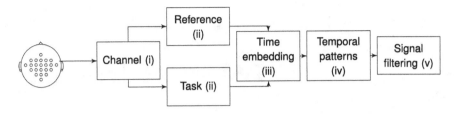

Fig. 2. Proposed pipeline to compute the supervised temporal patterns and the signal filtering by each channel.

fixation cross. The former includes the cue presentation and MI, that is, 2–4 s from trials belonging to left and right-hand tasks. (iii) The time embedding, performed over each extracted segment with an empirically-fixed window size $M = 350$, yields to $N = 500$ time windows. (iv) Solving the generalized eigenvalue problem for MI task and reference conditions estimates the supervised temporal patterns. (v) The last eigenvector filters each trial-channel by their convolution.

We contrast the supervised temporal patterns against two well-known filtering methods concentrated in the μ (8–13 Hz) and β (13–30 Hz) brain rhythms that explain the MI activity [4]. The first one corresponds to a five-order band-pass Butterworth filter between 8–30 Hz. The second filter relies on the Discrete Wavelet Transform using the Symlet (Sym-5) wavelet that is closely associated with the electrical brain activity [2]. We compute up to the second level detail coefficients to include both μ and β rhythms.

4   Results and Discussion

This work presents the results of signal filtering analysis for subjects $S3$ and $S2$, that generally attain the best and worst classification accuracies, respectively [13]. Figure 3 illustrates the obtained temporal patterns along their spectral analysis for channels C_3 and C_4 that detect the MI activity over the motor brain cortex [11]. For both subjects, $S3$ and $S2$, the power spectrum from the obtained supervised temporal patterns exhibit peaks of activation at frequencies lower than 8 Hz that arise when performing attention cognitive tasks (θ brain rhythm) as recognizing the instructed task during the MI trial execution [6]. On the one hand, the supervised temporal pattern of $S3$ exhibits a high power band between 10–20 Hz, due to the activation of α and β rhythms that contribute the most in MI tasks [3]. On the other hand, the pattern of $S2$ holds most of its energy under the 8 Hz and lacks components above 10 Hz, which is the behavior of BCI-illiterate subjects [1]. Therefore, the proposed estimation of supervised temporal patterns decodes the differences between subjects when performing MI tasks that are related to variations in brain activity [7].

Based on the performed MI paradigm during the EEG recording, different brain dynamics compose each trial. To highlight such dynamics, Fig. 4 presents the normalized short-time energy of each channel from all processed EEG trials

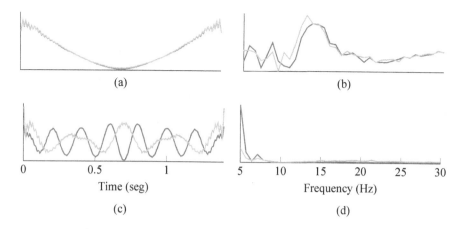

Fig. 3. Obtained supervised temporal patterns (a)–(c) and spectral analysis (b)–(d) by channels $-C_3 - C_4$. Subject $S3$ (a)–(b) and subject $S2$ (c)–(d).

using the three considered filtering approaches. As seen, the filtering performed by Butterworth and Wavelet neglects any dynamic change along the channels and trials. By contrast, the performed supervised temporal filtering identifies four changing dynamics in frontal, central and parietal brain regions of subject $S3$. These regions include the primary motor cortex, the supplementary motor area, and the posterior parietal cortex, that contain neurophysiological information of MI [15]. In this sense, the similar amount of energy within the intervals $[0, 2]$ s and $[6, 7]$ s explains the absence of MI task, which agrees with the trial timing. Then, the energy slowly decreases within $[2, 3]$ s implying a dynamic transition associated with the time that takes the brain to interpret the cue and execute the task. Further, such response latency varies among trials depending on memory, concentration, and tiredness inherent to each subject [14]. Regarding the filtering for $S2$, the supervised temporal pattern highlights dynamic changes only in frontal channels, without significant differences in the remaining ones, which also explains a BCI illiterateness. As a result, the proposed supervised temporal patterns allow decoding the dynamic changes related to cognitive tasks as interpretation and response to stimuli.

However, as is mentioned the window analysis for the time embedding was empirically-fixed additional analysis are required to automatically select.

5 Conclusions and Future Work

This work proposes an EEG signal filtering based on the estimation of Supervised Temporal Patterns that decode brain dynamics in MI paradigm. The considered time embedding and the estimation of generalized eigenvectors from data yield linear filters suited to discriminate two EEG conditions at the channel level. Results proved that supervised temporal patterns highlight both the MI activity and the subject-wise differences. Taking into account the attained results, we

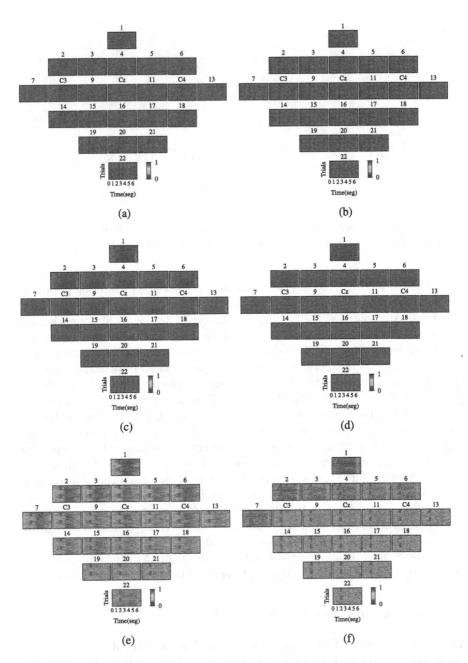

Fig. 4. Short-time energy analysis of each channel for all EEG trials on subjects $S3$ (4a, 4a y 4a) and $S2$ (right). Top: using a Butterworth filter between 8–30 Hz. Middle: applying Discrete Wavelet analysis. Bottom: using the estimated temporal patterns.

propose two future research directions. First, we need an automatic selection of temporal patterns that best discriminate EEG conditions. Secondly, we plan to restrict the temporal patterns according to the length of the window and the expected spectral components to improve MI discrimination.

Acknowledgement. Thanks to under grants provided by a Ph.D. scholarship code 727 and project code 111974454838 both financed by COLCIENCIAS.

References

1. Ahn, M., Cho, H., Ahn, S., Jun, S.C.: High theta and low alpha powers may be indicative of BCI-illiteracy in motor imagery. PloS One **8**(11), 1–11 (2013)
2. Alomari, M.H., Awada, E.A., Samaha, A., Alkamha, K.: Wavelet-based feature extraction for the analysis of EEG signals associated with imagined fists and feet movements. Comput. Inf. Sci. **7**(2), 17 (2014)
3. Álvarez-Meza, A.M., Velásquez-Martínez, L.F., Castellanos-Dominguez, G.: Time-series discrimination using feature relevance analysis in motor imagery classification. Neurocomputing **151**, 122–129 (2015)
4. Bian, Y., Qi, H., Zhao, L., Ming, D., Guo, T., Fu, X.: Improvements in event-related desynchronization and classification performance of motor imagery using instructive dynamic guidance and complex tasks. Comput. Biol. Med. **96**, 266–273 (2018). https://doi.org/10.1016/j.compbiomed.2018.03.018
5. Brockmeier, A.J.: Learning and exploiting recurrent patterns in neural data. Ph.D. thesis, University of Florida (2014)
6. Chacko, R.V., et al.: Distinct phase-amplitude couplings distinguish cognitive processes in human attention. NeuroImage **175**, 111–121 (2018). https://doi.org/10.1016/j.neuroimage.2018.03.003
7. Cohen, M.X.: Using spatiotemporal source separation to identify prominent features in multichannel data without sinusoidal filters. Eur. J. Neurosci. (2017)
8. Cohen, M.X.: Analyzing Neural Time Series Data: Theory and Practice. MIT Press, Cambridge (2014)
9. Emami, Z., Chau, T.: Investigating the effects of visual distractors on the performance of a motor imagery brain-computer interface. Clin. Neurophysiol. **129**(6), 1268–1275 (2018)
10. Guerrero-Mosquera, C., Navia-Vázquez, A.: Automatic removal of ocular artefacts using adaptive filtering and independent component analysis for electroencephalogram data. IET Signal Process. **6**(2), 99–106 (2012)
11. Kevric, J., Subasi, A.: Comparison of signal decomposition methods in classification of EEG signals for motor-imagery BCI system. Biomed. Signal Process. Control **31**, 398–406 (2017). https://doi.org/10.1016/j.bspc.2016.09.007
12. Mathalon, D.H., Sohal, V.S.: Neural oscillations and synchrony in brain dysfunction and neuropsychiatric disorders: it's about time. JAMA Psychiatry **72**(8), 840–844 (2015)
13. Miao, M., Zeng, H., Wang, A., Zhao, C., Liu, F.: Discriminative spatial-frequency-temporal feature extraction and classification of motor imagery EEG: an sparse regression and weighted naïve Bayesian classifier-based approach. J. Neurosci. Methods **278**, 13–24 (2017)
14. Yeung, N., Bogacz, R., Holroyd, C.B., Nieuwenhuis, S., Cohen, J.D.: Theta phase resetting and the error-related negativity. Psychophysiology **44**(1), 39–49 (2006). https://doi.org/10.1111/j.1469-8986.2006.00482.x

15. Saiote, C., et al.: Resting-state functional connectivity and motor imagery brain activation. Hum. Brain Mapp. **37**(11), 3847–3857 (2016)
16. Samek, W., Nakajima, S., Kawanabe, M., Müller, K.R.: On robust parameter estimation in brain-computer interfacing. J. Neural Eng. **14**(6), 061001 (2017)
17. Sanei, S., Chambers, J.A.: EEG Signal Processing. Wiley, Hoboken (2013)
18. Yang, Y., Chevallier, S., Wiart, J., Bloch, I.: Subject-specific time-frequency selection for multi-class motor imagery-based BCIs using few Laplacian EEG channels. Biomed. Signal Process. Control **38**, 302–311 (2017). https://doi.org/10.1016/j.bspc.2017.06.016
19. Yuan, H., He, B.: Brain-computer interfaces using sensorimotor rhythms: current state and future perspectives. IEEE Trans. Biomed. Eng. **61**(5), 1425–1435 (2014)

Entropy-Based Relevance Selection of Independent Components Supporting Motor Imagery Tasks

David Luna-Naranjo, David Cárdenas-Peña[✉],
and Germán Castellanos-Dominguez

Signal Processing and Recognition Group, Universidad Nacional de Colombia,
Km 9 Vía al Aeropuerto la Nubia, Manizales, Colombia
{dflunan,dcardenasp,cgcastellanosd}@unal.edu.co

Abstract. Brain-Computer Interfaces provide an alternative control of devices through the human brain activity. This paper proposes a trial-wise channel filtering by selecting the subset of independent components with the largest entropy. The proposal holds two free parameters: The order for the Renyi entropy weighs the component quantization according to its probability, and the percentage of retained entropy that rules the number of independent components to reconstruct the spatially filtered EEG channels. Both free parameters are tuned using a subject-dependent grid search for the best classification accuracy. The proposed approach outperforms against heuristic channels selection in a binary classification task using the dataset IIa of the BCI competition IV. Attained results prove that using ICA as a spatial filtering allows the feature extraction stage to build more discriminative spaces, reducing the influence of non-informative components. As an advantage, the resulting spatial filtering maintains the physiological interpretation of the EEG channels.

Keywords: Component selection · Renyi entropy
Brain Computer Interface

1 Introduction

Brain-Computer Interfaces (BCI) provide alternative control of devices through the human brain activity aiming to improve life quality of people suffering from severe disabilities. Typical BCI systems require the subjects to perform specific mental tasks to produce particular electroencephalographic (EEG) characteristics, that are generated voluntarily (slow cortical potentials and sensorimotor rhythms) or by stimulation (event-related potentials and steady-state evoked potential). However, the noise, task-unrelated, and redundant information hamper the performance of BCI systems for practical applications [3]. Further, commercial EEG devices with low spatial resolution cannot guarantee a near-optimal channel number and location [2].

© Springer Nature Switzerland AG 2018
Y. Hernández Heredia et al. (Eds.): IWAIPR 2018, LNCS 11047, pp. 359–367, 2018.
https://doi.org/10.1007/978-3-030-01132-1_41

Aiming to solve the above issues, heuristic algorithms select an optimal subset channel more related to the task with a higher signal-to-noise ratio. Some of the recent proposals are Glow Swarm Optimization algorithm followed by a naïve Bayes classifier [6], Sequential Floating Forward Selection by locally grouping EEG channels [10], Non-dominated Sorting Genetic Algorithm II for multi-objective optimization [7], and the backtracking search optimization algorithm by the binary encoding the selected channels [5]. Despite increasing the accuracy rates in comparison to the full channel set, heuristic and evolutionary algorithms heavily depend on the initialization of the algorithm due to the large set of hyperparameters to be tuned. Besides, the high computational cost in the training stage constraints their use in practical applications.

On the contrary, information measures provide less costly and more accessible to optimize approaches for selecting channels. For instance, the mutual information between the Laplacian derivation of the average channel power and the task labels significantly enhances the performance of the feature extraction by common spatial patterns (CSP) [13]. The wavelet-based maximum entropy criterion in the spatio-temporal domain selects channels considerably decreases the number of channels with a minimum accuracy loss. This kind of selection approaches uses Shannon or quadratic entropy as the fundamental information measures, which correspond to the particular case of Renyi's entropy of order 1 and 2, respectively. Then, neglecting the influence of the entropy order reduces the flexibility and intensifies the biasing of the estimator [9]. Further, channel selection reduces the discriminative information that is hidden in a surrogate channel combination [2].

To overcome the channel selection shortcomings, this paper proposes to select a subset of independent components based on a Renyi entropy relevance analysis. The independent components are estimated using the WASOBI algorithm that takes advantage of the temporal data structure. Therefore, reconstruction of the EEG signal using the most informative components is expected to reduce the noise influence and improve the discrimination performance of the feature extraction and classification stages using CSP and Linear Discriminant Analysis.

2   Methods

2.1   Independent Component Analysis for MI Tasks

In MI tasks, Independent Component Analysis (ICA) separates spatial components from their measured mixture of scalp EEG signals, without accessing the activity sources themselves or knowing the mixing system. The linear ICA model is given by $x(t) = As(t) + \eta(t)$, where $s(t) \in \mathbb{R}^D$ are D independent components that vary along time $t \in \mathbb{R}$, $x(t) \in \mathbb{R}^C$ are C mixed measured EEG channels, and $A \in \mathbb{R}^{C \times D}$ is the mixing matrix. Mainly, the ICA model assumes second-order stationarity, mutually uncorrelated components, and additive Gaussian noise, $\eta(t) \in \mathbb{R}^D$.

Estimation of mixing matrix can be reformulated within a weighted least-squares problem, so that instead of computing A from D vectors, a small number of the time-lagged sample correlation matrices are used. This algorithm, known as WASOBI, exploits the time structure of the components as follows:

$$\Sigma_{\bar{x}}(\tau) = \frac{1}{T-\tau} \sum_{t=1}^{T-\tau} \bar{x}(t)\bar{x}(t-\tau)^{\top}$$

$$= Q\Sigma_x(\tau)Q^{\top}, \ \tau \in [0, M-1] \tag{1}$$

where $Q \in \mathbb{R}^{C \times C}$ is an orthogonalization matrix, M is the number of time windows, and T is the time series length. In order estimate the spatially independent components $\hat{s}(t)$, the WASOBI algorithm jointly diagonalizes the matrices $\Sigma_x(\tau)$ by non-linear weighted least squares, resulting in an asymptotically optimal weighting matrix for Auto-Regressive Gaussian sources that improve the ICA stability and reduces the computational cost [4].

2.2 Entropy-Based Relevance Analysis

Given an estimate of the independent components $\hat{s}(t)$ for an EEG signal $x(t)$, the Renyi entropy H_α of the d-th independent component $\hat{s}_d(t)$ is defined as:

$$H_\alpha(\hat{s}_d) = \frac{1}{1-\alpha} \log \int p^\alpha(\hat{s}_d)d\hat{s}_d \tag{2a}$$

$$\approx \frac{1}{1-\alpha} \log \sum_{b \in B} p_{db}^\alpha \tag{2b}$$

where $\alpha \neq 1, \alpha \geq 0$ stands for the entropy order. The probability distribution $p(\hat{s}_d) \in [0,1]$ is computed by quantization of the estimated components [8]:

$$p_{db} = \mathbb{E}\left\{\kappa(s_b, q(\hat{s}_d(t); \theta)) : \forall t \in T\right\} \tag{3}$$

being $\kappa(\cdot, \cdot) \in \mathbb{R}^+$ a kernel function, and $q{:}\mathbb{R} \mapsto \mathbb{R}_\theta$ with parameter set θ a given quantization or projection function mapping $\hat{s}_d(t)$ to the nearest event in the subset of B bins $\{s_b \in \mathbb{R} : b \in [1, B]\}$. Notation $\mathbb{E}\{\cdot : \xi\}$ stands for the expectation operator across ξ.

Therefore, the entropy order allows weighting the events according to their probability [12]: H_0 only accounts the number of events with $p_{db} > 0$, whereas H_∞ only accounts the largest probability of p_d.

Upon the assumption of independence between components, the total amount of information held by the EEG signal can be computed as the summation of component entropies, that is, $\hat{H}_\alpha(x) = \sum_{d \in D} \hat{H}_\alpha(p_d)$. As a result, a relevance measure $\rho_d \in [0\%, 100\%]$ is introduced that ranks each component according as:

$$\rho_d = 100\hat{H}_\alpha(p_d)/\hat{H}_\alpha(x) \tag{4}$$

Consequently the relevance measure allows reconstructing the EEG channels with a subset of components as:

$$\tilde{x}(t) = \hat{A}W_\gamma\hat{s}(t)$$

where $\tilde{x}(t) \in \mathbb{R}^C$ is the reconstructed version of $x(t)$, and $W_\gamma \in \{0,1\}^{D \times D}$ is a diagonal matrix, indicating whether or not a component is selected to build $\tilde{x}(t)$. The selection rule is as follows: $w_\gamma(d,d) = \{1 : \rho_d \geq \gamma; 0 : \rho_d < \gamma\}$. As a result, reconstruction of the signal channels, using a subset of the most relevant components, tends to regret the non-informative electrodes, enhancing further processing stages.

3 Experimental Set-Up

EEG Dataset and Preprocessing

The proposed approach of relevance-based component selection is evaluated on the BCI competition IV dataset IIa[1], holding EEG data recorded by 22-electrode montage. Nine subjects were instructed to perform four MI tasks ("left hand", "right hand", "both feet", and "tongue"). On different days, each subject performed two sessions, each one including six runs to perform 48 trials (i.e., 12 trials per class) and resulting in 288 trials per sitting. Here, we consider just the bi-class classification task: left versus right hand.

In the preprocessing stage, all EEG recordings are band-pass filtered between [0.5–100] Hz and sampled at 250 Hz, followed by a fifth order Butterworth band-pass filter to remove noises over 30 Hz and slow baseline signal under 8 Hz. To focus on the learning part of the MI task, each trial recording is temporarily segmented, extracting for analysis the interval that ranges from 0.5 s to 4.5 s after the instructed MI task.

Lastly, feature extraction is achieved from the preprocessed recordings using Common Spatial Patterns that are referred as one of the most efficient algorithms for extracting discriminative patterns from motor imagery (MI) tasks, by projecting the EEG data into space where the discrimination between the classes is maximized. Thus, a CSP-based vector is computed per trial.

Parameter Tuning

Since the proposed component selection approach relies on an ICA model, we consider the WASOBI algorithm that takes advantage of the temporal structure of EEG data, for which the parameters are fixed to the default values. Namely, order of the autoregressive model, $o=1$, stabilization value ($r_{max}=0.99$), and condition number ($\varepsilon=0.99$).

Besides, for the Renyi entropy, the following parameters are settled as the free parameters: (*i*) Order $\alpha \in \mathbb{R}^+$ that weighs the bin probability, in such a way, that large values ($\alpha>1$) make the most probable bins contribute more to the entropy computation than the least probable ones. (*ii*) percentage of retained entropy $\gamma \in (0\%, 100\%])$ that rules the number of independent components to reconstruct the spatially filtered EEG channels so that the smaller the γ value - the fewer components are retained. Both free parameters are tuned using a subject-dependent grid search for the best classification accuracy.

---

[1] Available at http://www.bbci.de/competition/iv/.

For each subject, Fig. 1 displays the resulting tuning matrices. Note that the asymptotic effect, at $\alpha=1$, evenly distributes the entropy along the components so that larger γ values are required to select any reconstructing spatial component. Moreover, the best performing subjects according CSP baseline (S1, S3, S8, and S9) present a slowly growing accuracy w.r.t. γ, implying that most of the components contribute to discriminate the MI tasks. For these subjects, the optimal γ exceeds the 90% value. On the contrary, the percentage of retained entropy rejects more components for the subjects S2, and S5, aiming to attain the best performance. We hypothesize that this situation arises in the cases of worst-performing subjects when the criterion Eq. (4) tends to wrongly select some weak components, which may hold no discriminant information. As a result of the parameter tuning, EEG trials are reconstructed using only the most discriminant independent components for each subject as shown in Fig. 1.

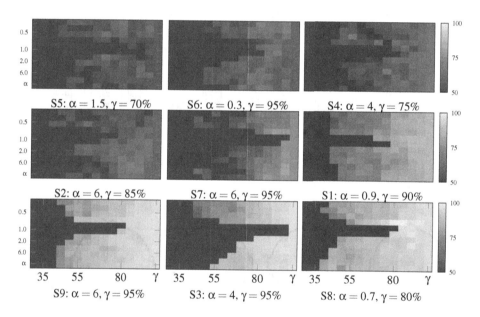

Fig. 1. Parameter tuning for each subject. Five-fold averaged accuracy is depicted along the percentage of retained entropy and entropy orders.

Performance Assessment

Performance of the proposed relevance analysis is assessed in terms of the classification accuracy for the left/right MI discrimination task. For the sake of comparision, we also evaluate the performance of two baseline approaches, namely, standard Common Spatial Patterns (CSP) and sequential floating forward selection (SFFS). The former consists in the widely accepted feature extraction approach for MI tasks, that is carried out over the whole set of channels with no component filtering, i.e. $\gamma=100\%$. The latter corresponds to an incremental heuristical search for the best classification accuracy with respect to a subset of EEG channels [10]. The Fig. 2 presents the classification performance attained by each considered approach for each subject. Aiming to gain interpretability on the peformance improvement, subjects are ascending-ordered according the CSP accuracy. Results evidence that filtering independent components for each trial outperforms CSP and SFFS for most of the subjects. In comparison to CSP, the proposed approach largely improves subjects S2, and S5, for which a smaller number of components are retained; while no significant difference is attained for subjects S9, S8, and S1, that hold most of their components. Regarding SFFS, despite improving CSP, the heuristic channel selection underperforms the component relevance, as it achieves a lower average accuracy with a larger standard deviation. Therefore, the entropy-based space filtering enhances the discrimination of mental tasks.

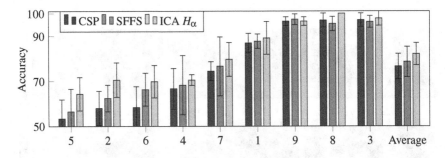

Fig. 2. Classification results attained by the considered approaches for each subject.

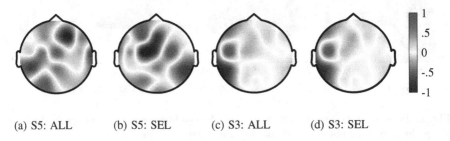

(a) S5: ALL   (b) S5: SEL   (c) S3: ALL   (d) S3: SEL

Fig. 3. Spatial patterns for the worst (S5) and best (S3) performing subjects according CSP baseline using all (ALL) and selected (SEL) components.

For illustrating the influence of entropy-based relevance on the CSP feature extraction, Fig. 3 depicts the spatial pattern distribution for the cases of the best and worst performing subjects, before and after performing the procedure of independent component selection. As seen, distribution of relevance varies across subjects. Thus, in the case of subject labeled as S3, the resulting topoplots show that the CSP feature set has no effect upon the proposed approach of relevance selection. This result can be explained because the optimal γ reaches to 95%, retaining most of the components to reconstruct each EEG trial. In turn, for S5, the component selection redistributes all spatial patterns over the head due to the more restrictive γ value (70%) that filters out components, hindering the task at hand. As a result, the optimal percentage of retained entropy allows the CSP-based feature set to better fit the discriminating patterns with no loss of relevant information.

4   Discussion

We introduce an approach for selection of independent components spatially separated in MI tasks, relying on the Renyi's entropy as the relevance measure. After validation of real-world EEG data, the following findings are worth to be mentioned:

The entropy order allows ranking the components following their measured probability. As seen in Fig. 1, the highest accuracy for the subjects with the worst performance (top row) is attained at low entropy orders. Hence, the least common bins contribute more to the relevance measure, implying that discriminant information concentrates on a few time instants. On the contrary, the best performing subjects (bottom row) achieve the highest accuracy at high entropy orders. It means that the entropy depends on the most common bins, showing that the discriminant information holds within a longer time interval.

Regarding the component selection criterion, the independence principle allows estimating the percentage of information that each of them holds. Therefore, one can define a subset of components to reconstruct the EEG channels by thresholding the computed entropy. Figure 1 shows that, at least, 40% of the information is required to build a suitable reconstructing subset. Mainly, $\alpha \rightarrow 1$ uniformly distributes the component relevance. Then, a larger threshold is required to reconstruct any trial. Also, the directly proportional relationship, between the performance and the threshold for subjects S1, S3, S7, S8, and S9, implies that each of their components holds information contributing to the EEG discrimination. For the remaining subjects, the optimal performance is attained at a lower γ, meaning that there exist a large number of components hindering the task at hand. Therefore, selecting components based on the percentage of information will always outperform the classification without component selection as the Fig. 2 further illustrates.

Finally, our proposal takes advantage of the space of independent components so that the spatial filtering accounts for the discriminant information on each channel. As seen in Fig. 2, component selection outperforms channel selection since discarding channels lead to suboptimal accuracy when the discriminative information varies among them. Further, the approach will never underperform the baseline CSP, as the spatial filters in Fig. 3 evidence. On the one hand, subjects with low accuracy (top) redistribute their spatial filters to improve the MI performance. They show spatial patterns in frontal and prefrontal regions that are related to higher mental functions as concentration or emotional expressions associated with low MI perfomance [1]. On the other hand, subjects with high accuracy (bottom) maintain its spatial filters since all the components are relevant. MI tasks link several brain regions (i.e., the primary motor, the posterior parietal cortices, and the supplementary motor area) in charge of sensory processing, translate visual information into motor commands, generating mental movement representations, as well as, planning and coordinating motor tasks [11]. Then, using ICA as a spatial filtering stage allows CSP to find the more discriminating filters by reducing the influence of non-informative components.

5   Conclusion

This work introduces a component selection approach using a relevance analysis based on the Renyi entropy. To accomplish the task, the WASOBI algorithm exploits the temporal data structure to compute the independent components, and the entropy order and percentage of retained information are tuned subject-wise to improve MI discrimination. As an advantage, the resulting spatial filtering maintains the physiological interpretation of the EEG channels.

From the attained findings of the work, two future research directions are proposed: Optimization of free parameters using more elaborated strategies to reduce the training times without compromising the performance. Incorporation of prior information about the labels in the component selection stage to improve accuracy rates for low performing subjects.

Acknowledgements. This work is supported by the project 111974454838 funded by COLCIENCIAS.

References

1. Ahn, M., Jun, S.C.: Performance variation in motor imagery brain-computer interface: a brief review. J. Neurosci. Methods **243**, 103–110 (2015)
2. Al-Ani, A., Al-Sukker, A.: Effect of feature and channel selection on EEG classification. In: 2006 International Conference of the IEEE Engineering in Medicine and Biology Society, pp. 2171–2174, August 2006. https://doi.org/10.1109/IEMBS.2006.259833
3. Arvaneh, M., Guan, C., Ang, K.K., Quek, C.: Optimizing the channel selection and classification accuracy in EEG-based BCI. IEEE Trans. Biomed. Eng. **58**(6), 1865–1873 (2011). https://doi.org/10.1109/TBME.2011.2131142
4. Bridwell, D.A., Rachakonda, S., Silva, R.F., Pearlson, G.D., Calhoun, V.D.: Spatiospectral decomposition of multi-subject EEG: evaluating blind source separation algorithms on real and realistic simulated data. Brain Topogr. **31**(1), 47–61 (2018). https://doi.org/10.1007/s10548-016-0479-1
5. Dai, S., Wei, Q.: Electrode channel selection based on backtracking search optimization in motor imagery brain-computer interfaces. J. Integr. Neurosci. **16**(3), 241–254 (2017). https://doi.org/10.3233/JIN-170017
6. Joseph, A.F.A., Govindaraju, C.: Channel selection using glow swarm optimization and its application in line of sight secure communication. Clust. Comput. 1–8 (2017). https://doi.org/10.1007/s10586-017-1177-9

7. Kee, C.Y., Ponnambalam, S.G., Loo, C.K.: Multi-objective genetic algorithm as channel selection method for P300 and motor imagery data set. Neurocomputing **161**, 120–131 (2015). https://doi.org/10.1016/j.neucom.2015.02.057

8. Meinicke, P., Ritter, H.: Quantizing density estimators. In: Advances in Neural Information Processing Systems, pp. 825–832 (2002)

9. Principe, J.C.: Information Theoretic Learning: Renyi's Entropy and Kernel Perspectives. Springer, Heidelberg (2010). https://doi.org/10.1007/978-1-4419-1570-2

10. Qiu, Z., Jin, J., Lam, H.K., Zhang, Y., Wang, X., Cichocki, A.: Improved SFFS method for channel selection in motor imagery based BCI. Neurocomputing **207**, 519–527 (2016). https://doi.org/10.1016/j.neucom.2016.05.035

11. Saiote, C., et al.: Resting-state functional connectivity and motor imagery brain activation. Human brain mapping **37**(11), 3847–3857 (2016)

12. Wood, A.J., Blythe, R.A., Evans, M.R.: Rényi entropy of the totally asymmetric exclusion process. J. Phys. A: Math. Theor. **50**(47), 475005 (2017)

13. Yang, H., Guan, C., Wang, C.C., Ang, K.K.: Maximum dependency and minimum redundancy-based channel selection for motor imagery of walking EEG signal detection. In: Proceedings of IEEE International Conference on Acoustics, Speech and Signal Processing, ICASSP, pp. 1187–1191. IEEE, May 2013. https://doi.org/10.1109/ICASSP.2013.6637838

Movement Identification in EMG Signals Using Machine Learning: A Comparative Study

Laura Lasso-Arciniegas[1(✉)], Andres Viveros-Melo[1], José A. Salazar-Castro[1,2],
Miguel A. Becerra[3], Andrés Eduardo Castro-Ospina[3],
E. Javier Revelo-Fuelagán[1], and Diego H. Peluffo-Ordóñez[2,4]

[1] Universidad de Nariño, Pasto, Colombia
laurad.lasso.a@gmail.com
[2] Corporación Universitaria Autónoma de Nariño, Pasto, Colombia
[3] Instituto Tecnológico Metropolitano (ITM), Medellín, Colombia
[4] Yachay Tech, Urcuqui, Ecuador

Abstract. The analysis of electromyographic (EMG) signals enables the development of important technologies for industry and medical environments, due mainly to the design of EMG-based human-computer interfaces. There exists a wide range of applications encompassing: Wireless-computer controlling, rehabilitation, wheelchair guiding, and among others. The semantic interpretation of EMG analysis is typically conducted by machine learning algorithms, and mainly involves stages for signal characterization and classification. This work presents a methodology for comparing a set of state-of-the-art approaches of EMG signal characterization and classification within a movement identification framework. We compare the performance of three classifiers (KNN, Parzen-density-based classifier and ANN) using spectral (Wavelets) and time-domain-based (statistical and morphological descriptors) features. Also, a methodology for movement selection is proposed. Results are comparable with those reported in literature, reaching classification performance of $(90.89 \pm 1.12)\%$ (KNN), $(93.92 \pm 0.34)\%$ (ANN) and 91.09 ± 0.93 (Parzen-density-based classifier) with 12 movements.

Keywords: ANN · EMG signals · Feature extraction · KNN · Parzen

1 Introduction

Nowadays, technologies for human-computer interfaces (HCIs) are being widely used, as they are becoming indispensable for people life's activities. Thanks to the development of fields such as pattern identification, signal processing, among others, there have been proposed different tools and systems to control a machine through the use of signals, as it is the case of Electromyographic (EMG) signals. Some outstanding applications of EMG-based HCI are: Wireless-computer

© Springer Nature Switzerland AG 2018
Y. Hernández Heredia et al. (Eds.): IWAIPR 2018, LNCS 11047, pp. 368–375, 2018.
https://doi.org/10.1007/978-3-030-01132-1_42

controlling through hand movement, wheelchair directing/guiding with finger motions, and rehabilitation [1,2].

Once acquired and digitalized, and since being electrical-unidimensional-type signals, the ECG signals are analyzed within a process mostly involving stages for preprocessing, characterization, data representation, and classification [3]: Firstly, preprocessing is aimed at filtering (removing artifacts and noisy information) as well as adjusting the signal for subsequent tasks (some processing procedures are sensitive to length or amplitude). Secondly, a characterization task is performed for extracting descriptive features or attributes (especially is required when using directly the amplitude values is unfeasible for length, informative, or computational cost reasons). Thirdly, to select or best represent the afore obtained features in terms of separability, a data representation may be used. Finally, the automatic classification process is applied over the data to assign to relate the EMG signal with an instruction (for instance, a movement in a HCI-based device). All these stages have addressed for some studies [4–6], but a highly accurate system for EMG semantic interpretation is still a problem to be solved.

Based on state-of-the-art techniques, this work proposes a methodology for EMG signal characterization and classification techniques to identify movements. In particular, the spectral features (wavelet coefficients, average frequency, peak frequency, Curtosis, Shanon, Fischer asymmetry coefficient), temporal features and statistics are used (Area under the curve, absolute mean value, effective value, standard deviation, variance, median,Willison amplitude, Histogram, simple square integral entropy) [1,4,7–12]. The characterization of the signal, leaves a matrix of large dimensions so it is necessary to make a dimension reduction. Two processes are performed to achieve a good reduction in size, the first is the selection of movements, proposed methodology of comparison between movements, seeking for which have a greater differentiability and present a lower error in their classification. The second process, is a selection of features, consists of the calculation of contribution of each feature to the classification, is carried out through the WEKA program and its RELIEF algorithm [13,14]. Finally, the performance comparison of three machine learning techniques, k-nearest neighbors (KNN), Artificial neural network (ANN) and classifier based on Parzen density. Each of the stages is developed and explained in depth in the text.

The rest of this paper is structured as follows: Sect. 2 describes the stages of the EMG signal classification procedure for movement identification purposes. Section 3 presents the proposed experimental setup. Results and discussion are gathered in Sect. 4. Finally, Conclusions and future work in Sect. 5.

2   Materials and Methods

This section describes the methodology used to carry out the comparative study and identify a group of features that allows get a high performance of classifiers.

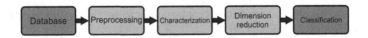

Fig. 1. Block diagram of the proposed methodology

In general, our research contains the following stages: preprocessing, segmentation, characterization, dimension reduction and finally classifiers as shown in the explaining block diagram from Fig. 1.

2.1 Database

For this research, we considered the database that is available *Ninaweb* repository from *Ninapro* project [7]. The Ninapro project describes the acquisition protocol and the subjects involved in the data acquisition. The muscle activity is recorded by 10 double differential electrodes, 8 electrodes are located uniformly around the forearm using an elastic band, at a constant distance, just below the elbow. In turn, two additional electrodes are placed in the long flexor and extensor of the forearm. The hand position is taken by a Dataglove and an inclinometer. The sample rate used is for 100 Hz and amplification factor is for 14000.

The Ninapro database include the electromyographic activity of upper-limb of 27 healthy people executing 52 movements, which are divided as: 12 movements of fingers, 8 isometric and isotonic configurations of the hand, 9 wrist movements and 23 functional grip movements [4].

2.2 Stages of System

Pre-processing. EMG signals can be affected by several factors, like Extrinsic and Intrinsic factors and others [15]. For the above, amplitude and frequency features are also affected, so it is necessary to compensate the effect of these factors with some procedure, in this research we applied a normalization and segmentation procedure. The normalization was applied to each electrode, we toke an electrode and found the maximum value of the signal of this electrode, finally the whole signal is divided with this maximum value. The Ninapro database contains a tag vector, which we used for segmentation procedure. The tag vector lets identify when the patient was doing a movement, in addition what kind of movement. So this vector facilitating the trimming of the signals.

Characterization. The matrix of features is organized in the following way: In each row, the data corresponding to patient n is placed, which is performing a movement w and a repetition k and so on. For columns, a bibliographic review is made, obtaining 45 different features for the EMG signals, which are applied to each of the 10 electrodes. As mentioned above, the feature matrix has a size of 14040 per 450. This matrix is organized as shown forward in the next matrix.

$$X = [x_{i,j}] = \begin{pmatrix} x_{1,1} & x_{1,2} & \cdots & x_{1,d} \\ x_{2,1} & x_{2,2} & \cdots & x_{2,d} \\ \vdots & \vdots & \ddots & \vdots \\ x_{M,1} & x_{M,2} & \cdots & x_{M,d} \end{pmatrix}$$

where $X \in \mathbb{R}^{M \times d}$ is the matrix of features, M is the number of samples $=$ 14040 corresponding to 270 repetitions $k \times 52$ classes w. d is the total number of features $= 450$ corresponding to 45 attributes $\times$ 10 electrodes.

Among the features, there are two types, temporal and spectral features. For a better understanding, each one of them is explained below.

- *Temporal features:* Are the variables, which are in the time domain and quantified each T seconds of time. The features used are: Area under the curve, Mean absolute value, Root mean square value, Variance of EMG, Entropy, Simple square integral, Histogram, Willison Amplitude, Waveform length [1,9,10,12,16]
- *Spectral features:* It give us, the time-frequency representation of a signal where we can obtain a more complete description of the physical phenomenon. The most common techniques used in the extraction of spectral are Curtosis, Shanon, Fischer asymmetry coefficient, Peak frequency, Average frequency, Modified Average Frequency, Wavelet transform [5,8,10,11,16].

Movements Selection. Many movements can hinder the classification problem, so it is necessary to identify the largest number of classes, which can be classified without problems. By virtue of the above, we suggest a criterion based on the Euclidean distance (ED) and the standard deviation (SD). From the characteristics matrix its calculated the centroid **c** of the points cloud (PC) for each movement, as the mean value of the repetitions k, belonging to each yth class. Euclidean Distance of each class its calculated as the root of square differences between co-ordinates of a pair of centroids.

Euclidean distance between centroids allows evaluate how much far away are the classes, and the standard deviation says what so compact is a points cloud. To improve the performance of the classify its necessary that PC of each movement be far away and as compacts as possible. So a parameter that allows to evaluate these two features between two different classes is defined as:

$$P(y_1, y_2) = \frac{ED(\mathbf{c1}, \mathbf{c2})}{SD_1 + SD_2}, \tag{1}$$

where $ED(\mathbf{c1}, \mathbf{c2})$ is the euclidean distance between the centroids of the class 1 (y_1) and class 2 (y_2), SD_1 and SD_2 are the standard deviation of classes 1 and 2. SD must be inversely proportional to parameter in order to maximize P and improve the classification process. The movements for which the parameter P is greater are selected.

The movements that present the best separability are: contraction and extension of middle and ring fingers, wrist contraction and extension, writing tripod grasp, tip pinch grasp, lateral grasp, power disc grasp and turn a screw. Several of these movements have great activity of the flexor digitorum superficials and of the extensor digitorum superficials.

Features Selection. A subset of the original data set is taken, to obtain this subset the Relief algorithm is used. Relief calculates a feature weight for each feature which can then be applied to rank and select top scoring features. RELIEF detects the interactions between attributes to determine those that are most relevant and those that work well in groups.

To select a suitable number of characteristics to train the classifiers, a test is carried out with the KNN classifier. We evaluated the performance of the classifier, varying the number of characteristics. From this test, it can be seen in Fig. 2, that 20 characteristics are enough to obtain a good performance. This 20 features are used for the next step, the comparison of each classifiers.

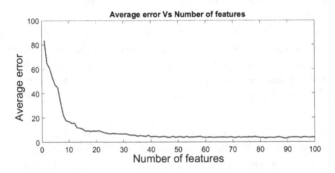

Fig. 2. Results of the selection of features, as the average error varies according to the number of features.

2.3   Classification

With the new feature matrix, the classification of these movements is carried out with the following techniques [1,6,8,17,18].

1. K-nearest neighbors (KNN): It's a method of non-parametric supervised classification, which utilizes a distance measure relative to the k-closest neighbors of a point to assign a class to a given data record. The number of the nearest neighbors is optimized with respect to the leave-one-out error on training set.
2. Artificial neural network (ANN): This heuristic classification technique emulates the behavior of a biological brain through a large number of artificial neurons that connect and they are activated by means of functions. The neurons are distributed in hidden layers, in this work a neural network is trained with a back-propagation algorithm with a hidden layer with 10 neurons. The weight initialization consists of setting all weights to be zero. Sigmoidal functions are used in the output. The dataset is used for training, validation and test.

3. Parzen-density-based classifier: This probabilistic-based classification method requires a smoothing parameter for the Gaussian distribution computation, which is optimized.

3   Experimental Setup

To carry out the different experiments of this stage, we used the toolbox of Matlab called PrTools. This toolbox has all necessary functions as classifiers and performance indicators. From the reduced feature matrix, we obtain two sets in a random way, each group is balanced in the number of samples. Classifiers are trained with 75% of the data and validated with the remaining 25%.

To ensure the repeatability of the experiment, and that the results do not depend on a specific data group, the tests are repeated 30 times with the three classifiers. In each test the percentage of performance is obtained and at the end of the 30 repetitions an average of the tests is obtained. The results of each test are reported in the next section.

4   Results and Discussion

Based on the tests carried out and the performance results recorded in Fig. 3 it is clear that the ANN present a better performance than KNN and Parzen. Nevertheless all classifiers have error percentage under 10%. The performance of ANN is 93.92%, KNN is 90.89% and PARZEN is 91.09% using 20 features.

Figure 3 also reveals a greater uniformity of the ANN than KNN and Parzen classifiers in each of the tests, giving a standard deviation of 1.12% for KNN, 0.93% for Parzen-density-based classifier and 0.35% for the neural network. This results are comparable to [1], where with back-propagation neural networks a 98.21% performance was obtained but classifying only 5 movements what limits the control options. In [17] the results of pattern recognition EMG signal using wavelet transform and Artificial Neural Network (ANN) classification has an accuracy rate of 77.5% identifying 8 movements. For this reason it is emphasized that an adequate search of EMG signal characteristics in combination with the appropriate selection of movements allows obtaining a good performance of the ANN classifier. The recognition rates were 84.9% for the KNN in [19] where five wrist movements were classified. It is considerable that this result is due to the appropriate selection of movements based on Euclidean Distance criteria, also used by the KNN classifier.

The process of selection of attributes showed that the most relevant features were: Maximum concentration of histogram, standard deviation, Willison amplitude, modified average frequency, entropy of the signal in the time domain and entropy of the first level of decomposition of the wavelet transform. Most of the relevant information is concentrated in 4 electrodes, corresponding to the flexor and extensor muscles of the forearm.

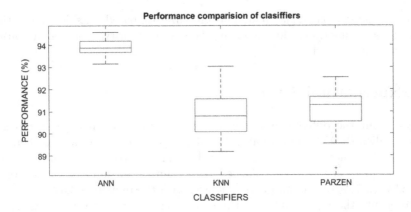

Fig. 3. Performance of the classifiers. In the following order, ANN, KNN and Parzen.

5   Conclusions and Future Work

This work presents a evaluation of different features of signal analysis, a dimension reduction method and a criterion to evaluate separability of classes. With the aim to improve movements classification with EMG signals. Experimentally we prove that the with the selected movements and the features used it is possible to implement a human - machine control interface with good performance. On the other hand a set of features that help in the movement recognition of upper limb is proposed. We identify 12 movements that with the characteristics described in Sect. 2 present a greater separability, it was also possible to identify the muscles that have the most intervention on these movements.

As a future work, we will explore the possibility to apply this knowledge in a prosthesis prototype with own signals of EMG.

Acknowledgments. This work is supported by the "Smart Data Analysis Systems - SDAS" group (http://sdas-group.com), as well as the "Grupo de Investigación en Ingeniería Eléctrica y Electrónica - GIIEE" from Universidad de Nariño. Also, the authors acknowledge to the research project supported by Agreement No. 095 November 20th, 2014 by VIPRI from Universidad de Nariño.

References

1. Phinyomark, A., Phukpattaranont, P., Limsakul, C.: A review of control methods for electric power wheelchairs based on electromyography signals with special emphasis on pattern recognition. IETE Tech. Rev. **28**(4), 316–326 (2011)
2. Aguiar, L.F., Bó, A.P.: Hand gestures recognition using electromyography for bilateral upper limb rehabilitation. In: 2017 IEEE Life Sciences Conference (LSC), pp. 63–66. IEEE (2017)
3. Rodrguez-Sotelo, J., Peluffo-Ordoez, D., Cuesta-Frau, D., Castellanos-Domnguez, G.: Unsupervised feature relevance analysis applied to improve ECG heartbeat clustering. Comput. Methods Programs Biomed. **108**(1), 250–261 (2012)

4. Atzori, M., et al.: Electromyography data for non-invasive naturally-controlled robotic hand prostheses. Sci. Data **1**, 140053 (2014)
5. Podrug, E., Subasi, A.: Surface EMG pattern recognition by using DWT feature extraction and SVM classifier. In: The 1st Conference of Medical and Biological Engineering in Bosnia and Herzegovina (CMBEBIH 2015), March 2015, pp. 13–15 (2015)
6. Vicario Vazquez, S.A., Oubram, O., Ali, B.: Intelligent recognition system of myoelectric signals of human hand movement. In: Brito-Loeza, C., Espinosa-Romero, A. (eds.) ISICS 2018. CCIS, vol. 820, pp. 97–112. Springer, Cham (2018). https://doi.org/10.1007/978-3-319-76261-6_8
7. Atzori, M., et al.: Characterization of a benchmark database for myoelectric movement classification. IEEE Trans. Neural Syst. Rehabil. Eng. **23**(1), 73–83 (2015)
8. Krishna, V.A., Thomas, P.: Classification of EMG signals using spectral features extracted from dominant motor unit action potential. Int. J. Eng. Adv. Technol. **4**(5), 196–200 (2015)
9. Negi, S., Kumar, Y., Mishra, V.: Feature extraction and classification for EMG signals using linear discriminant analysis. In: International Conference on Advances in Computing, Communication, & Automation (ICACCA) (Fall), pp. 1–6. IEEE (2016)
10. Phinyomark, A., Limsakul, C., Phukpattaranont, P.: A novel feature extraction for robust EMG pattern recognition. CoRR abs/0912.3973 (2009)
11. Ahlstrom, C., et al.: Feature extraction for systolic heart murmur classification. Ann. Biomed. Eng. **34**(11), 1666–1677 (2006)
12. Han, J.S., Song, W.K., Kim, J.S., Bang, W.C., Lee, H., Bien, Z.: New EMG pattern recognition based on soft computing techniques and its application to control of a rehabilitation robotic arm. In: Proceedings of 6th International Conference on Soft Computing (IIZUKA2000), pp. 890–897 (2000)
13. Kononenko, I.: Estimating attributes: analysis and extensions of RELIEF. In: Bergadano, F., De Raedt, L. (eds.) ECML 1994. LNCS, vol. 784, pp. 171–182. Springer, Heidelberg (1994). https://doi.org/10.1007/3-540-57868-4_57
14. Kira, K., Rendell, L.A.: A practical approach to feature selection. In: Machine Learning Proceedings 1992, pp. 249–256. Elsevier (1992)
15. Halaki, M., Ginn, K.: Normalization of EMG signals: to normalize or not to normalize and what to normalize to? (2012)
16. Romo, H., Realpe, J., Jojoa, P., Cauca, U.: Surface EMG signals analysis and its applications in hand prosthesis control. Revista Avances en Sistemas e Informática **4**(1), 127–136 (2007)
17. Arozi, M., et al.: Electromyography (EMG) signal recognition using combined discrete wavelet transform based on artificial neural network (ANN). In: International Conference of Industrial, Mechanical, Electrical, and Chemical Engineering (ICIMECE), pp. 95–99. IEEE (2016)
18. Shin, S., Tafreshi, R., Langari, R.: A performance comparison of hand motion EMG classification. In: 2014 Middle East Conference on Biomedical Engineering (MECBME), pp. 353–356. IEEE (2014)
19. Kim, K.S., Choi, H.H., Moon, C.S., Mun, C.W.: Comparison of k-nearest neighbor, quadratic discriminant and linear discriminant analysis in classification of electromyogram signals based on the wrist-motion directions. Curr. Appl. Phys. **11**(3), 740–745 (2011)

Feature Extraction of Automatic Speaker Recognition, Analysis and Evaluation in   Real Environment

Edward L. Campbell$^{(\boxtimes)}$![ORCID], Gabriel Hernández, and José Ramón Calvo

Images and Signals Group, CENATAV Research Division, DATYS Enterprise,
7th A Street # 21406, Playa, Havana, Cuba
{ecampbell,gsierra,jcalvo}@cenatav.co.cu

Abstract. An Automatic Speaker Recognition is a biometric system that allows you to identify and verify people, using voice as a discriminatory feature. The purpose of this paper is the feature extraction stage, performing an analysis of effectiveness in real environment. The features extraction has as objective to capture the associated characteristic space of the speaker, being the Mel features and its linear variant the most used methods. In real conditions, the environment over which the speech signal is processed tends not to be ideal, nor is the duration of the speech, so it's necessary to use robust techniques for assuring a lower degradation grade of system effectiveness; techniques such as Power Normalization, Hilbert Envelope and Modulation of Mean Duration are described, analyzed and evaluated.

Keywords: Automatic Speaker Recognition · Feature extraction
Robustness

1   Introduction

An Automatic Speaker Recognition (ASR), is non-invasive biometric systems, because they use the voice as a discriminatory feature, also it present a great versatility during the evaluation so this is a process that only requires that user speaks, which constitutes a natural act of human's behavior [13]. The state-of-the-art of ASR is based on the UBM/i-vector methodology, using PLDA as a measure of distance [2]; and for the features extraction, Mel features predominates, which will be dealt with later on.

The voice has basically six information levels [13], from spectral (lower level) to semantic level (upper level), and the complexity during information extraction process increases proportionally regarding level on which it's worked. This article is addressed to spectral level, because it has the shortest necessary voice segment (between 20–30 ms) for extracting useful information that characterizes the speaker [13]. Besides, a transformation from the spectrum to the cepstral domain is made for increasing features robustness. In real conditions, the voice

Y. Hernández Heredia et al. (Eds.): IWAIPR 2018, LNCS 11047, pp. 376–383, 2018.
https://doi.org/10.1007/978-3-030-01132-1_43

can be accompanied by all noise kind, as public transport sound, channel distortion, even reverberation, for this reason is important to use stable techniques in noisy conditions; Power Normalization, Hilbert Envelope and the Medium Duration Modulation are some robust methods that will be analyzed.

Regarding structure of the article, first we will analyze classical methods such as MFCC, LFCC and LPCC, and after that we will describe and evaluate robust extraction techniques, concluding with an analysis regarding effectiveness.

2 Classics Feature Extraction

Mel Frequency Cepstral Coefficients. Mel Frequency Cepstral Coefficients (MFCC) is one of most cited and used techniques in the speech processing community. It's based on the simulation of cochlear auditory capacity, with the design of an uniformly spaced filterbank in the Mel frequency scale, which when is transformed to the linear frequency scale, the spacing between filter is linear in the range of first 1000 Hz, and logarithmic for higher values (see Fig. 1) [12]. Functionally, this technique is based on a first process of windowing and overlapping, then signal power spectrum is estimated and divided in sub-bands through a Mel filterbank, after that is logarithmically compressed, and finally the Discrete Cosine Transform (DCT) is applied [4,12] for accumulating information in the first coefficients.

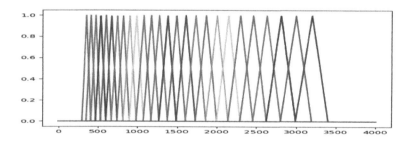

Fig. 1. Scaled filterbank on Mel frequency

Linear Frequency Cepstral Coefficients. Linear Frequency Cepstral Coefficients (LFCC) is a technique similar to MFCC, with the exception that it uses a filterbank located on a linear frequency scale (see Fig. 2), with an uniform separation between filters [18] that allows to obtain a higher signal resolution at high frequencies, because the separation between filters doesn't increase along with frequency, differently to MFCC.

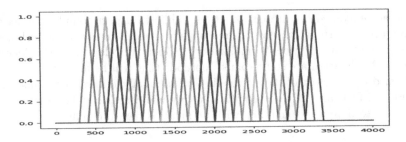

Fig. 2. Scaled filterbank on linear frecuency

Linear Prediction Cepstral Coefficients. A model very used for simulating the speech production process is the source-filter model (see Fig. 3), this is composed of a source that switches between a periodic pulse (sound signal) and a random noise generator (non-voiced signal), representing the glottal flow source [7].

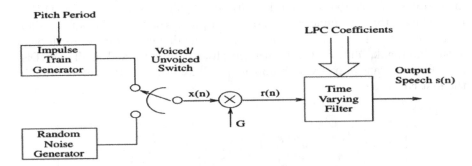

Fig. 3. Filter-source model of speech production

The frequency contribution of the phonatory device is determined from a time-varying all-pole filter, whose poles are obtained from the linear prediction coefficients (lpc) of the voice segment to be processed. These coefficients singulate vocal tract configuration of the speaker and function as a discriminative element in the recognition system [7]. They are named linear prediction because the signal current sample can be determined by the weighted sum of **p** previous samples and **p** linear prediction coefficients [9], the used samples amount fix the order and precision of the estimation. For determining the prediction coefficients, is used Levinson-Durbin autocorrelation method [9], and after that is done the transformation to cepstral domain (see Eq. 1) for increasing robustness.

$$c_i = -a_i + 1/i \sum_{j=1}^{i-1} (i-j)a_j c_{i-j}, \quad for \quad i \quad \epsilon \quad [1, M], \tag{1}$$

where c_i and a_i are respectively the cepstral coefficient and the linear prediction coefficient of order i, M is the order of the Levinson-Durbin autocorrelation method.

3   Robust Feature Extraction

A feature is robust when it has a stable effectiveness both in ideal conditions or uncontrolled environment (noise, reverberation, etc.), the second condition is the most common in the practice. Due to the uncontrolled environment over which the voice is processed, great importance has been attached to the study of features with these characteristics [1]. All techniques described below use a gammatone filterbank (see Fig. 4), and are defined as robust by speech processing community, so this filterbank presents a more stable behavior against noise compared to the triangular filterbank used in LFCC or MFCC [15]. The impulse response of a gammatone filter [16] is defined in the Eq. 2.

$$h(t) = \gamma * t^{\tau-1} * exp(-2\pi b) * cos(2\pi f_c * t + \theta), \tag{2}$$

where γ and τ are respectively the amplitude and filter order, while b and f_c are the bandwith and center frequency in Hertz.

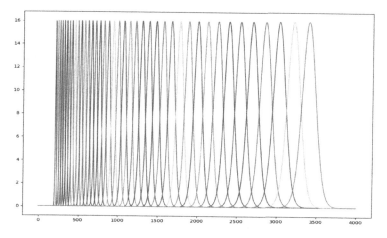

Fig. 4. Gammatone filterbank of 40 dimension

Mean Hilbert Envelope Coefficients. A gammatone filter modulates in amplitude and frequency the signal at its input [14], so is necessary to demodulate the output signal from filter for recovering the transmitted information. Mean Hilbert Envelope Coefficients (MHEC) extract this information from estimated Hilbert envelope of signal, that is, to separate AM component from the FM component [14]. The extraction process of this feature is described below [14]: pre-emphasis, windowing and overlapping, band division of each window using the gammatone filterbank, estimation of Hilbert envelope [14] in each band and to filter it through a low-pass filter with cut-off of 20 Hz, later a vector is formed per window, where each sample **i** of the vector represents the average value of the smoothed envelope samples in the band **i**, the size of the vector is determined by the number of used filters in the bank; finally, the mean vector is compressed with $1/15^{th}$ root and transformed to the cepstral domain through the Discrete Cosine Transform (DCT). The low-pass filter is applied in order to eliminate rapid changes in the signal, which are usually attributed to noise.

Medium Duration Modulation Coefficients. This feature is named Medium Duration Modulation Coefficients (MDMC) because it employs a window of 52 ms, a greater length than the 20–25 ms that are used in the traditional windowing. After the windowing and overlapping, the signal is processed with a gammatone filterbank, and the output of this is demodulated using the Teager operator (see [8] for analyzing Teager operator). The process is continued with an estimation of power per band of the demodulated signal, obtaining for each window a vector whose dimension coincides with the number of bands in which the signal was divided, to then apply root compression with a factor of 1/15. Finally, it's transformed to the cepstral domain using the DCT. The extraction process described is based on [11].

Power Normalization Cepstral Coefficients. This technique is similar to those described above, that is, the front-end processing is applied, including the use of gammatone filterbank, but no demodulation techniques are applied, a simple normalization of mean power per window is done, continuing with a root compression with a factor of 1/15 and the transformation to the cepstral domain. See [5,6] for investigating more about the design of Power Normalization Cepstral Coefficients (PNCC).

4   Experiments and Results

The used ASR in this experiment was based in UBM/i-vector methodology. The evaluation was done on the competition samples of NIST_SRE08[1] on common condition 7, which are real samples of telephonic conversations in English; the used training and test condition was short2 and short3 respectively[2]. The first evaluation was done using the original audio samples of enroll and test, which have a duration of 5 m each. The robustness against noise was checked processing the test samples with the FaNT tool [3], adding a signal-to-noise ratio (SNR) of 5 dB with crowd noise, after that, a second evaluation is done. The effectiveness on short-term signals was also checked, limiting the original enrollment and test samples to a maximum duration of 10 s. The Table 1 shows the configuration of the features used for the evaluation. The used database in the experiment is 10 years old, but this isn't an impediment for resolve the problem that appears when several articles are read and their experiments use different databases,

---

[1] The meta-data training was done with telephonic samples of NIST04 and NIST05.
[2] Visit the web site "https://www.nist.gov" for searching the evaluation plan of NIST_2008 and knowing more about these conditions.

which avoids to make a direct comparison between the suggested techniques in each article, in our case, the same database is used for evaluating classical and recent techniques, allowing the direct comparison of the main techniques in the stated-of-the-art.

Table 1. Feature configuration

Parameters	MFCC	LFCC	LPCC	MHEC	MDMC	PNCC
Pre-emphasis	0.97	0.97	0.97	0.97	0.97	0.97
Windowing (ms)	25	25	25	25	52	25
Filterbank type	Mel	Lineal	-	Gammatone	Gammatone	Gammatone
Filterbank dimension	40	26	-	40	40	40
Bandwidth (Hz)	300–3800	300–3400	-	300–3400	300–3400	300–3400
Prediction order	-	-	60	-	-	-
Compression	Log	Log	Log	Root	Root	Root
Cepstral coefficients ($+ \triangle$ and $\triangle \triangle$)	57	50	42	57	60	57
Normalization	CMVN	CMVN	CMVN	CMVN	CMVN	CMVN

The Table 2 shows Equal Error Rate (EER) obtained from the evaluation over 3 conditions.

Table 2. EER (%)

Features	Real	Noisy	Short duration	Geometric mean
MFCC	**5.695**	11.617	20.956	11.151
LFCC	5.922	12.694	22.323	11.883
LPCC	7.970	30.067	27.560	18.762
MHEC	6.337	11.617	**17.995**	10.983
MDMC	7.972	13.899	18.830	12.778
PNCC	5.922	**11.463**	18.451	**10.779**

5 Analysis and Conclusions

Regarding the LFCC and MFCC results, the best performance was obtained by MFCC, because the amount filter on low frequency is higher than LFCC, and this a spectral region with more speaker information, in the case of a male speaker, so the fundamental frequency is relatively low [17]. Besides, LPCC have the worst performance, the linear prediction didn't demonstrate have a good space for characterizing to the speaker, its vocal tract simulation is not effective neither against noise or short duration. The robust technique group had a better performance in uncontrolled environment, specialy in short duration, this is a

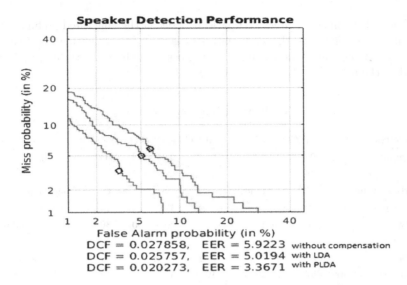

Fig. 5. EER of PNCC with methodology i-vector applying differents compensation methods

frequent condition that limit an ASR, because the available signal time for the enrollment and test usually is short. Besides, the audio background, it can have crowd noise, for example, in a meeting; in this other case, the robust features have also shown a better performance. The feature with the best general performance was PNCC, with a geometric mean of 10.779%, for this, PNCC was used in other experiment, applying the PLDA and LDA methodologys over the i-vector methodology for reducing channel and speaker variability, and whose result is present in the Fig. 5, which shows the Detection Error Trade-off (DET) and the Detection Cost Function (DCF). One objective of this paper is to compare features extraction techniques that use digital signal processing techniques, but in the future experiments, techniques based in neural networks (as bottleneck network) will be analyzed and evaluated, because these can add a new characteristic space that improve the EER [10].

References

1. Benesty, J.: Springer Handbook of Speech Processing. Springer Handbooks. Heidelberg, Springer (2008). https://doi.org/10.1007/978-3-540-49127-9
2. Hernández, G.: Métodos de representación y verificación del locutor con independencia del texto. Ph.D. thesis, Instituto Superior Politécnico José Antonio Echeverría (2014)
3. Hirsch, H.G.: F a N T - Filtering and Noise Adding Tool, March 2005
4. Yang, J., Xie, S.J. (eds.): New Trends Developments in Biometrics. InTech, November 2012

5. Kim, C., Stern, R.M.: Feature extraction for robust speech recognition using a power-law nonlinearity and power-bias subtraction. In: INTERSPEECH 2009, 10th Annual Conference of the International Speech Communication Association, Brighton, UK, 6–10 September 2009, pp. 28–31 (2009)

6. Kim, C., Stern, R.M.: Power-normalized cepstral coefficients (PNCC) for robust speech recognition. IEEE/ACM Trans. Audio, Speech Lang. Process. **24**(7), 1315–1329 (2016)

7. Kondoz, A.M.: Digital Speech, Coding for Low Bit Rate Communication Systems, 2nd edn. Wiley, London (2004)

8. Kvedalen, E.: Signal processing using the teager energy operator and other non-linear operators. Cand. Scient Thesis (2003)

9. Makhoul, J.: Linear prediction: a tutorial review (1975)

10. McLaren, M., Lei, Y., Ferrer, L.: Advances in deep neural network approaches to speaker recognition. In: 2015 IEEE International Conference on Acoustics, Speech and Signal Processing, ICASSP 2015, South Brisbane, Queensland, Australia, 19–24 April 2015, pp. 4814–4818 (2015). https://doi.org/10.1109/ICASSP.2015.7178885

11. Mitra, V., Franco, H., Graciarena, M., Vergyri, D.: Medium-duration modulation cepstral feature for robust speech recognition. In: IEEE International Conference on Acoustics, Speech and Signal Processing, ICASSP 2014, Florence, Italy, May 4–9 2014, pp. 1749–1753 (2014)

12. Singh, N., Khan, R.A., Shree, R.: MFCC and prosodic feature extraction techniques: a comparative study. Int. J. Comput. Appl. **54**, 0975–8887 (2012)

13. Ribas, D.: Reconocimiento Robusto de Locutores en Ambientes no Controlados. Ph.D. thesis, Instituto Superior Politécnico José Antonio Echeverría (2016)

14. Sadjadi, S.O., Hansen, J.H.L.: Mean hilbert envelope coefficients (MHEC) for robust speaker and language identification. Speech Commun. **72**, 138–148 (2015)

15. Shao, Y., Jin, Z., Wang, D., Srinivasan, S.: An auditory-based feature for robust speech recognition. In: Proceedings of the IEEE International Conference on Acoustics, Speech, and Signal Processing, ICASSP 2009, Taipei, Taiwan, 19–24 April 2009, pp. 4625–4628 (2009)

16. Slaney, M.: An efficient implementation of the Patterson-Holdsworth auditory filter bank. Technical report, Apple Computer, Perception Group, Advanced Technology Group (1993)

17. Traunmller, H., Eriksson, A.: The frequency range of the voice fundamental in the speech of male and female adults (1995)

18. Zhou, X., Garcia-Romero, D., Duraiswami, R., Espy-Wilson, C.Y., Shamma, S.A.: Linear versus Mel frequency cepstral coefficients for speaker recognition. In: 2011 IEEE Workshop on Automatic Speech Recognition & Understanding, ASRU 2011, Waikoloa, HI, USA, 11–15 December 2011, pp. 559–564 (2011)

Author Index

Printed in the United States
By Bookmasters